Psychology Gone Astray:

A Selection of Racist & Sexist Literature from Early Psychological Research

Charles I. Abramson & Caleb W. Lack, Editors

Psychology Gone Astray: A Selection of Racist & Sexist Literature from Early Psychological Research

Copyright © 2014 Charles I. Abramson & Caleb W. Lack

Published by *Onus Books*

Printed by Lightning Source International

Cover design: Caleb W. Lack and Travis Bond

Trade paperback ISBN: 978-0-9926000-3-7

OB 07/11

We dedicate this book to the masses of people discriminated against because of their sex, race, ethnicity, or mental status as a result of the abuses of psychological research during our early history, and hope that this book can help to both raise awareness of these issues and prevent such abuse from happening again.

Acknowledgements

This book would not have been possible without the unwavering support of our families. We would specifically like to express appreciation to our wives, Ms. Zeyna Abramson and Ms. Alison Babitzke. Special thanks are also due to Ms. Kathryn Schrantz, who retyped the manuscripts reprinted here. We also indebted to Mr. Jonathan MS Pearce, the publisher of Onus Books, who had the courage to publish this book.

If the misery of our poor be caused not by the laws of nature,
but by our institutions, great is our sin.
- Charles Darwin (1839)

CONTENTS

Introduction

There has been much material written about the role that the field of psychology played in its early days in establishing and perpetuating racism, sexism, and anti-Semitism. Some of the best known include the work of Cornwell (2003), Gould (1981), Hunt (1993), Jacoby and Glauberman, (1995), Loehlin, Lindzey, and Spuhler (1975) and Röder, Kubillus, and Burwell (1995). As academic psychologists, we were surprised of how few students, and even colleagues, know about this chapter in the history of psychology.

To document the lack of coverage of this important chapter in the history of psychology all one has to do is to walk over to your bookshelf and look at any introductory psychology text. We, for example, have looked at eight recent introductory psychology texts on whether this early literature was discussed. We focus on introductory texts because it is here where many students receive their first formal training in psychology. As mentioned, in the context of distortions in the coverage of behaviorism, students rely on introductory texts as an important source of information about the field – including its history and methodology (Abramson, 2013). Of the texts we surveyed, none of them discussed the contribution that psychology has made to the early perpetuation of racism, sexism, and anti-Semitism (Ciccarelli & White, 2014; Gray, 2011; Krause & Corts, 2012; Okami, 2014; Schacter, Gilbert, Wegner, & Nock, 2014; Wade, & Tavris, 2012; Wood, Wood, & Boyd, 2014; Zimbardo, Johnson, & McCann, 2014)

We believe that this lack of coverage is unfortunate because it misses a real opportunity to educate students on how psychology has been used as a weapon against women, African Americans, Jews, and others. These early studies are a golden opportunity to teach students how to make valid comparisons between groups, the danger of making incorrect comparisons, and the political and social consequences of poorly designed research. Understanding such studies also provide students with what might be called "living examples" in experimental design, and ethics. There is also the danger that this early history of psychology will be all but forgotten – and in our view it should not be. Thus we felt a need to create a volume containing some of these original articles.

In selecting these articles and material we were intentionally provocative. The main purpose of this volume is to help educators and students learn about, and

1

teach others, how to identify the misuse of science as applied to the study of human differences. Many of the articles in this book, and the original interpretation of the results, will be disturbing to our readers. Our intent is not to disparage the science of psychology but to help in the ongoing battle against such misuse of data and research methodology. As such, the articles selected contain both egregious examples of racist and sexist study methodology and data interpretation. In addition, some articles we have included are more balanced and reasoned in their conclusions. We also hope this book will increase awareness of race- and gender-based issues, help students and scholars learn to properly evaluate scientific articles and literature, and to provide in one source the original, complete articles that you, the reader, can examine. This is obviously preferable to relying purely on secondary sources. This book provides much easier access to the articles reprinted herein, as many of them are not readily accessible to the general public or are from older journals that are difficult to find.

This book has been designed to be used with a wide variety of courses. These include introductory psychology, experimental design, the history of psychology and science, comparative psychology, evolutionary psychology, multicultural or cross-cultural psychology, classes on the psychology of women and under-represented groups, psychology of law, social psychology, statistics courses, and research methods courses. It could also be used outside the field of psychology when studying history or sociology, especially in terms of the scientific racism movement. Another option would be as a sourcebook for the professor who is teaching such courses, who would now be able to easily access ancillary material related to racism and sexism via the articles reprinted here, the websites contained in the supplements, and the quotes presented at the end.

This book contains two original chapters followed by 22 reprinted articles, supplemented by a number of extras. The first chapter will give definitions of race across time, a brief history of the rise of scientific racism and its fall, and some examples of how such research impacted social and educational policy. The second chapter will focus on methodology and design issues when comparing different groups and includes guidelines for properly evaluating such research. Then, preceding the reprinted articles, is a list of discussion questions to aid in evaluating the merit and scientific soundness of the articles based on those principles discussed in Chapter Two. Following the articles is a number of classroom activities designed to stimulate discussion and critical thinking on some of the issues raised by the articles. While these chapters and the articles provide the core of the book, a number of useful supplements are also included. These include reading suggestions, a list of websites related to race and psychology, and famous (or shocking) quotes of scientific racism. We have also reprinted the text of a law that was enacted in 1913 in Wisconsin, to show the impact that the research discussed and reprinted in this book had on the real world.

In conclusion, we hope that this book provides a useful addition to the bookshelf of those who study and teach in the social sciences. The authors welcome all comments regarding this book, the field of racial and gender differences, and the misuse of data.

References

Abramson, C. I. (2013). Problems of teaching the behaviorist perspective in the cognitive revolution. *Behavioral Sciences, 3*, 55-71.

Ciccarelli, S. K., & White, J. N. (2014). *Psychology 4th ed.* Boston, MA: Pearson.

Cornell, J. (2003). *Hitler's scientists: Science, war, and the devil's pact.* New York, N.Y.: Penguin:

Gray, P. (2011). *Psychology 6th ed.* New York, N.Y.: Worth.

Gould, S. J. (1981). *The mismeasure of man.* New York, N.Y.: Norton.

Hunt, M. (1993). *The story of psychology.* New York, N.Y.: Doubleday.

Jacoby, R. & Glauberman, N., Eds. (1995). *The bell curve debate: History, documents, opinions.* Times Books: New York.

Krause, M. & Corts, D. (2012). *Psychological science.* Boston, MA: Pearson.

Loehlin, J. C., Lindzey, G., and Spuhler J. N. (1975). *Race differences in intelligence.* San Francisco, CA: W. H. Freeman.

Okami, P. (2014). *Psychology: Contemporary Perspectives.* New York, N.Y.: Oxford University Press.

Röder T., Kubillus, V., and Burwell, A. (1995). *Psychiatrists – The men behind Hitler.* Los Angeles, CA: Freedom Publishing.

Schacter, D. L., Gilbert, D. T., Wegner, D. M.; Nock M. K. (2014). *Psychology 3rd ed.* New York, N.Y.: Worth.

Wade, C. & Tavris, C. (2012). *Invitation to psychology 5th ed.* Boston, MA: Prentice Hall.

Wood. S. E., Wood, E. G., & Boyd, D. (2014). *Mastering the world of psychology 5th ed.* Boston, MA: Pearson.

Zimbardo, P. G., Johnson, R. L., & McCann, V. (2014). *Psychology: Core Concepts 7th ed.* Boston, MA: Pearson.

Race, Psychology, and Scientific Racism

Caleb W. Lack & Charles I. Abramson

Webster's dictionary defines the term "race" in a number of ways: a competition of speed; a swift current of water; to cause to go swiftly; any of the three primary divisions of mankind distinguished by the color of skin; any geographical, national, or tribal ethnic grouping; and several others (Guralnik, 1987). For the purposes of this chapter, the concentration will not be on the term "race" as derived from the Old Norse *ras*, meaning "a running." Rather, race as derived from the Italian *razza*, meaning "progeny or breed" will be the focus. For such a small, innocent-sounding word, few others in the English language have the ability to ignite as much discussion and controversy. Race, its exact meaning and the implications of that meaning, has been an enormously important issue in society for the past several centuries (Graves, 2001). As with many other socially important issues, science has played a significant role in how race is perceived and defined, and has influenced diverse areas, including public policy, immigration laws, and education (Gould, 1996). This chapter will first trace the evolution of the current, modern idea of race and then examine the role that psychology played in what can best be described as scientific racism—the use of science to enforce and support racist views and policies. Also under examination will be the rise and decline of scientific racism, and how it is still alive today.

Pre-Darwinian Views of Racial Differences

The idea of race as a biologically determined feature is a relatively modern construct, dating only from the late 1700s (Richards, 1997). Indeed, before the Renaissance, the very concept of what is now known as "race" was defined entirely in social and cultural terms, rather than biological (Weizmann, 2004). Many historians agree that in ancient Mediterranean civilizations, discrimination based purely on skin color did not exist. Rather, discrimination based on social classes and cultural differences was the norm in Greek (Demand, 1996), Roman (Dupont, 1994) and Persian cultures (Frye, 1993). The view of many of the most prominent Greek philosophers, including Plato and Aristotle, was that not conforming to *their*

5

standards of civilization were what made one less than the civilized person, a view applied to even those Greeks who did not live in a *polis* (Weizmann, 2004). If anything, the views expressed by prominent Greeks, including the semi-legendary physician, Hippocrates, are supportive of an environmental rather than hereditarian view of differences among peoples (see Friedmann, 1981; and Snowden, 1983 for further discussion).

With the rise of Christianity across Europe, the viewpoint that all of humankind shared a common ancestry came into prominence (Hannaford, 1996). In Christian mythology, all were originally descended from Adam and Eve, and even more recently from the sons and daughters of Noah, the only members of humanity to survive the Great Flood described in Genesis. The widespread belief was that the diversity of the world's peoples could be explained by the differences in Noah's children. The fact that one of his sons, Ham, had been cursed for seeing his father drunk and naked and that Ham's descendents were cursed with black skin and inferior talents and skills, was often used to discriminate against those with darker skins (Johnson & Bond, 1933). This monogenistic view of humanity became especially prominent during the Christian-Moorish wars in Spain during the 8th century, when a number of statutes were passed that discriminated against individuals with Jewish or Moorish "blood" (as described in Weizmann, 2004). While many of these laws were highly contested across much of Spain and in fact renounced by the highest levels of the Church, some scholars have argued for this movement as the anticipation of later definition of race based upon biology, including the use of the term "blood" to refer to the degree of "racial pureness" one possesses (e.g., mixed-blood, half-blood; Teo, 2004).

The use of the word "race" in its current connotation as national or ethnic group did not enter into the popular parlance until the late 1700s (Richards, 1997), although it had been used to describe one's ancestry since the mid-16th century (Weizmann, 2004). Even at this point in time, the term was used primarily to describe the different nationalities and different "types" of people living in the same nation (e.g., Franks and Gauls in France, Normans and Anglo-Saxons in Britain; Banton, 1998). For at least one major theorist, this intersection of "national characters" and Newtonian views of science represented a basis from which the modern ideas of race and racial differences would spring, culminating in 1748 with the publication of Baron de Montesquieu's, *The Spirit of Laws* (Hannaford, 1996). Hannaford perceives this book, with its emphasis on the differences between societies based on geographical location rather than cultural terms, and its combination with the thought behind the Neo-Platonic idea of the "Great Chain of Being," as two of the most direct antecedents to the view of race as biologically determined.

The concept of the "Great Chain of Being" was developed by Plotinus, a 3rd century Neo-Platonist, who believed that everything existing on the planet could be arranged into "an unbroken hierarchy from the lowest material level to the highest level of perfection" (Weizmann, 2004, p. 32). While Plotinus, himself, did not use this idea to rank different nationalities, instead seeing all of humankind as occupying the same high status, writers in the late 18th and early 19th centuries used this idea to rank humankind, most often with "Blacks" on the bottom and "Whites" on the top of the chain (Jordan, 1977 as detailed in Weizmann, 2004). It should be noted, however, that the majority of the influence of the "Great Chain of Being" was in a popular, not scientific, sense. Many scientists of the time, including Linnaeus and Blumenbach, rejected the idea of the "Great Chain" but still divided humanity into a number of different races in their biological systems of classification (Marks, 1995). Some scholars (e.g., Hannaford, 1996) see this biological classification of humans as having developed from the writings of Thomas Hobbes, with his "might makes right" philosophy and denial of humans as separate from nature, and John Locke, with his reframing of Aristotle's distinction between species. By rejecting Aristotelian views of a solitary, human nature, their work provided the framework for a scientific view of race and racial differences (Hannaford, 1996). From the viewpoint of someone working in the United States, the fact that Locke was influential in laying the grounding for a scientific view of racial differences is especially interesting, given his influence on the development of the early American republic (Stephens, n.d.). It should also be noted that the view in which different skin color constituted biologically disparate races was fully embraced by the majority of educated people in the Americas, including many prominent politicians, among them Benjamin Franklin and Abraham Lincoln (for their own words on the matter, see Franklin [1751] and Lincoln's debates with Douglas [1858]). These lines of thought eventually lead to the development among scientists living in America of a polygenistic view of race, in which each race is considered a biologically separate species (Gould, 1996).

It should be noted at this point that several prominent historians view the development of modern views of race in a slightly different fashion. As early as 1906, Sir Sidney Olivier was maintaining "race consciousness based on color" developed due to the rise of British colonialism, particularly the African slave trade (as quoted in Dearborn & Long, 1934). Olivier did not dispute that the social movements described above contributed to the new, biologically based view of race, but saw the rise of the slave trade in the Americas as the main, driving force (see Zinn [1995] for a more thorough overview of this argument).

Despite different views concerning the root cause, by the 19th century the view of races as hierarchical and separate had become firmly entrenched in both popular and scientific thought. The view espoused since the time of the ancient Greeks, that culture and social class influenced the development of "race" and racial differences, had become completely reversed. It was now believed that innate biological characteristics of different "races" influenced the expression of culture and society (Richards, 1996; Weizmann, 2004).

Evolutionary Theory and the Rise of Scientific Racism

While the view that humankind could be divided into superior and inferior "races" had become widely accepted in the Western world by the mid-19th century, it still lacked a super ordinate structure within which to operate. With the emergence of evolutionary thought in general and the publication of Charles Darwin's (1859), *The Origin of Species*, in particular, those who sought a reason for the supposed biological underpinnings of "racial inequality" quickly found their framework (Dennis, 1995). Darwin wrote on the biological evolution of different species of animals and did not concern himself with either the social or the cultural ramifications of human evolution in this book (although he would do so later with the publication of *The Descent of Man* [1871]). He would, however, soon see his ideas adapted for and used in the defense of racist science and policies, most notably by anthropologists, including Louis Agassiz and Samuel George Morton (Gould, 1996); Herbert Spencer, who actually developed the phrase "survival of the fittest" (Richards, 1996); and Francis Galton, Darwin's cousin and the founder of the Eugenics movement (Fancher, 2004).

The initial use of evolutionary theory for what would currently be considered racist purposes, and thus the emergence of scientific racism, was not by psychologists (because a coherent field of "psychology" did not exist at the time), but rather by physical anthropologists. The belief that overt physical differences reflected innate psychological differences drove anthropologists to measure and describe even the minutest distinctions between Europeans (who were considered the paragon of perfection even before such measurements were made) and other races (see Gould, 1996 for an excellent critique of such research). These anthropologists developed innumerable ranking systems that, according to them, scientifically demonstrated racial and sex differences. Such differences were then interpreted as representing where each race (and the sex within each race) lay on an evolutionary scale, with the results always supporting the evolutionary superiority of the Caucasian male (Richards, 1996). In addition to physical differences among the races, many scientists began to collect information on the obvious inferiority of the other races, especially the "Negro," in a multitude of aspects, all of which clearly showed those races to be evolutionarily behind those of European descent. This data included information on maturity levels, individual variance, impulsivity, emotionality, sexuality, and a host of other characteristics (Loehlin, Lindzey, & Spuhler, 1975). This idea, that members of different "races" could somehow be measured and classified on an evolutionary continuum, would come to be fully embraced by a number of early and influential psychologists, setting the stage for what would become known as Social Darwinism and psychology's role in scientific racism.

An early proponent of using Darwin's theory to examine human traits was Francis Galton (Fancher, 2004). Galton is often and rightfully remembered for the large number of contributions he made to the field of psychology, with some seeing his claim as the "founder" of psychology rivaling even Wilhelm Wundt's (Fancher, 1996). Unfortunately, an often-overlooked fact is that Galton can also be viewed as the first psychologist to endorse the ideals and methods behind scientific racism, for several reasons. First, Galton's highly influential work, *Hereditary Genius* (1892, first published in 1869), includes two chapters ("The Comparative Worth of Different Races" and "Influences that Affect the Natural Ability of Nations") that reflected his beliefs that races differed regarding their evolutionary fitness and that it was possible to rank different races. Second, Galton established the study of individual differences and, with Karl Pearson, developed the statistical methodology most often used in such studies (Richards, 1996). These beliefs and methodology would become fully realized in Galton's most infamous contribution to science: Eugenics. In the early 1880's, Galton composed this term to describe the science of human improvement through increased procreation among the upper classes of society and/or the prevention of procreation among the lower classes (Fancher, 2004). These theories would combine with later research on intelligence and mental disease to influence

9

the implementation of racist education, immigration, and sterilization policies in Europe and the Americas. Galton, however, was far from alone in influencing the development of scientific racism in psychology.

Perhaps even more so than Galton, Herbert Spencer was responsible for the introduction of scientific racism in psychological thought (Dennis, 1995). Spencer derided what he called the lesser or primitive races, attributing their incompetence in attaining proper civilization to a lack of mental energy directed towards higher mental functions (Johnson & Bond, 1933; Richards, 1996). While Spencer himself did not attempt to gather quantitative support for his theories, he actively encouraged others to measure these differences by whatever means possible. By using scientific and psychological language to explain the lack of evolutionary progress in so-called "primitives" (by which he meant anyone not of European heritage), Spencer helped set the stage for the development of "racial psychology" in the late 1890s.

Rise of Empirically "Supported" Racial Differences

While racial differences had been sought and "found" by comparing the bodies, skulls, and brains of different races since the early 19th century, the dawn of the 1890's saw the rise of a new type of measurement: psychological measurement. (This new approach to measurement is not to suggest that the seeking of physical differences was abandoned. Rather, it continued until the mid-20th century by a number of scientists [Gould, 1996]). In 1895, what is generally considered the first empirical psychological paper on racial differences was published: "Reaction Time with Reference to Race" (Bach, 1895). The hypothesis of this paper, that the reaction time of people "lower" on the evolutionary ladder would have faster reaction times because they spent less time engaged in "higher" mental functions, was directly based on Spencer's theories, whom Bach cited in his introduction. Through a pitifully small sample size of whites, "Africans," and Indians (only 33 total subjects) and a poorly constructed methodology, Bach concluded that Indians had the fastest reaction times, followed by "Africans," and then whites. Although he originally hypothesized that "Africans" would have the fastest reaction time because they were the most primitive of the races, Bach quickly adjusted his theory so that their natural reactions were considered to be slowed by being in slavery for so long (Bach, 1895).

Only two years passed before the next paper on racial differences was published. This paper compared the memory skills of whites and blacks and found that blacks performed better, overall (Stetson, 1897). Luckily, however, the author appeared not at all disturbed by this finding, instead explaining his findings by declaring that the blacks had an "acknowledged deficiency in reasoning power" (Stetson, 1897, p. 289) and labeling memory as a primitive skill. Obviously, the more primitive race (read: blacks) should certainly perform better, but they did so only by a slight margin. One has to wonder if such an explanation would have been put forth had the white students performed better. In a review of similar research on sex differences, Woolley (1914, p. 305) remarks on how girls have frequently outperformed boys and yet "no one has drawn the conclusion that girls have greater native ability than boys. One is tempted to indulge in idle speculation as to whether this admirable restraint from hasty generalization would have been equally marked had the sex findings been reversed!" She then goes on to cite the various, highly creative ways in which findings that do not support white male supremacy are reinterpreted to minimize female abilities, just as was happening in the research on racial differences (Woolley, 1914).

Several authors see the ease with which many researchers in the area of racial differences spun their results as contributing to a "no-win" situation for all races other than whites (e.g., Gould, 1996; Richards, 1996). To quote from a review of racial differences research published prior to 1910:

> The student will find numerous references to psychological traits, but these statements are too frequently the gratuitous by-products of "investigations" which began with the avowed conviction that mind, and differences in mental constitution, proceeded straightforth from a physical foundation. Discussion of racial differences often began with self-confident statements regarding the "well-known" psychological differences, and used the anatomical and physiological data unearthed as a frame upon which to restretch the originally assumed mental differences. (Johnson & Bond, 1933, p. 337).

11

Such *a priori* assumptions as regarded racial differences were widespread, although some scientists worked against these notions, with little success (see, for example, Dewey, 1902; Thomas 1907). But that research prior to 1910 would soon become dwarfed in comparison, as the rise of Race Psychology in America and its influence on public policy would trigger a landslide of research examining every possible difference one could imagine between the races, including intelligence, behavior, memory ability, and academic skills (Daniel, 1932).

Rise and Fall of Race Psychology in America

Race Psychology (or "Empirical Racism," as Richards [1996] describes it) began with several underlying themes. First was to guide educational policy in segregated schools, as it was believed that different races needed different curriculums and methods of education, as befitted their natural differences in ability and intelligence (Richards, 2004). While such research initially focused on the issue of "Negro" education, examination and proposed reform of American Indian schools soon followed (e.g., Hunter & Sommermier, 1922). Second was to guide immigration laws, a project closely related to attempts to improve (or at least stop the decline) of the American national character by following the tenets of Eugenics (Gould, 1996). The third theme was the increase in the scientific validity of Race Psychology by finding the "norms and the measures of variabilities around these norms" (Garth, 1921, p. 359). These tenets would guide the majority of research into racial differences from 1910 onward. Rather than perform a comprehensive overview of all the literature that can be considered part of the Race Psychology movement, which would require an examination of well over 300 articles (Richards, 1996), the impact on social policies and popular thought will instead be examined.

The earliest Race Psychology research focused on what was commonly called the "Negro Question." This primarily focused on the differences between white and black children and the educational implications thereof (Richards, 2004). The recent American importation of intelligence tests at this time provided the means to measure mental differences in what was considered an unbiased, scientifically based fashion (for an examination of how racially biased these tests truly were, see Gould, 1996). Given the heavy cultural loading of many of the items and the lack of proper methodology, it is unsurprising that the black students were continually outperformed by the white students on these intelligence tests. What is surprising is that few if any of the authors of such research find it prudent to mention the cultural bias against blacks present on such tests (Price, 1934). Instead, the core belief of Race Psychology that differences on tests and measures are due to underlying racial differences is continually espoused and seen to be reflected by the findings, in spite of what today seem to be obvious environmental differences (e.g., in the amount of money received by white versus black schools).

The findings of Race Psychology's research on the "Negro Question" can be boiled down to two main points: "Negroes" are inferior to whites due to innate racial differences and segregation of schools is the best policy, since black students would fail and white students would fail to thrive in desegregated schools (Richards, 1996). During this period, several of the other arguments that would become routine also developed, including what is typically known as the "mulatto hypothesis:" a higher degree of white blood is correlated with higher intelligence and other mental abilities (Loehlin, Lindzey, & Spuhler, 1975). While the policy implications of these results supported arguments for the continued disparity between white and black education systems, the next wave of research would have an even greater impact on American social policy.

Perhaps the most influential examination of "intelligence" among different racial groups and nationalities was the work done by Robert M. Yerkes in testing Army draftees into World War I with the infamous Army Alpha and Army Beta tests (Richards, 1996). The results of the testing and the conclusions drawn from those results proved to have an enormous impact on how intelligence in general, and the intelligence of immigrants and blacks in particular, was viewed. The most popular report on the matter was by a student of Yerkes, C.C. Brigham. His *A Study of American Intelligence* (1923) was much briefer than Yerkes' (1921) report on the findings (210 rather than 900 pages) and, as a result, was more easily digested and regurgitated by the public. The results were shocking. Apparently, white Americans had an average mental age of 13 years, just above what was considered to be "moron" status. The results were even grimmer for blacks and immigrants, who averaged about 11 and 10 mental years of age, respectively. While the methodology, testing procedures, and statistics used to arrive at these conclusions were all horribly flawed, they nonetheless had a tremendous social impact (Gould, 1996).

The impact of the Army tests was immediate. Psychology had gained a new respect as a true science, especially the subfield of mental testing (Richards, 1996).

The results were more than could have been wished for by those seeking the continuation of segregation against blacks, 89% of whom were "morons" according to the results. The findings were also used to further support the arguments of those who believed that race-mixing was detrimental and should not be allowed (e.g., Davenport & Steggerda, 1929). But the issue where the most impact was seen was on the immigration debate. Since the late 1880's, an unheard of number of immigrants had been pouring into the United States on both the East and West Coasts. While the majority of the West Coast immigrants were Chinese, no one European country contributed the majority of the new arrivals on the West Coast. Instead, a mix of Jewish, Russian, Italians, Greeks, Irish, and German natives poured through the gateway city of New York, mostly to an unfriendly reception (Zinn, 1995).

Concern over the fitness of such immigrants (highly prompted by eugenically minded scientists; Richards, 2004), led to the examination of differences between whites and the various immigrant groups. Much like research into the "Negro Question," early researchers ignored or downplayed environmental influences on testing results while fully supporting their *a priori* assumptions concerning the inferiority of a variety of immigrants (e.g. Goddard, 1913, 1917). Until the results of the Army tests had been released, however, there were no truly large-scale research projects examining the "intelligence" of immigrants. However, with these results, movements to restrict immigration gained scientific backing for their arguments, which carried a large amount of weight with lawmakers (Richards, 2004). Along with a host of other social factors, the results of the Army tests assisted in Congress passing the Immigration Restriction Act of 1924, which capped the number of new immigrants allowed into the United States per year. Then President Coolidge made the following remark as he signed the bill into law: "America must be kept American" (as quoted in Gould, 1996, p. 262).

The research on Race Psychology in America peaked during the mid-1920s and was seriously in decline by 1930, although other countries increased their output during the 1930s and staved off its decline for another few years (Richards, 2004). Several reasons are apparent for such a shift in thought (Barkan, 1992). First, several prominent psychological researchers disavowed their previous research as racist and wrongly interpreted, including T.R. Garth (1931), considered by many to be the most prolific Race Psychologist, and Brigham (1930) himself. Second, a huge shift in how anthropology viewed race, led most prominently by Franz Boas (1931), occurred at

14

the same time. Boas and others maintained that any racial differences were purely a result of social factors and forces, not innate biological differences (Farber, 2003). Lastly, the newly emerging field of population genetics, especially the work of Theodosisus Dobzhansky (1941), began to shift towards seeing race as describing subdivisions of species with the ability to interbreed and produce healthy offspring. It was argued, therefore, that focusing on one particular aspect of phenotype, such as skin color, to group races was an arbitrary means of classification with no more inherent meaning than classifying races based on hair or eye color (Farber, 2003).

Unfortunately, however, the damage had already been done. Legal segregation in school systems would continue until 1954 and the landmark *Brown v. Board of Education* decision by the Supreme Court, while illegal segregation and inequality in educational opportunities persist to the present day. Based on pre-1924 immigration levels, some 6 million people from areas of Southern and Eastern Europe devastated by World War II, including many Jews, were denied entrance into the United States because of the Immigration Restriction Act (Gould, 1996). While both of these movements had multiple social factors that made them acceptable to the majority culture, science in general and psychology in particular played no small part in the initiation and maintenance of both.

Although Race Psychology proper died down in the immediate years proceeding World War II, the battle over racial differences, particularly with regard to intelligence, would continue. In particular, the publication of several extremely controversial books and papers, including Arthur Jensen's (1969) "How Much Can We Boost I.Q. and Scholastic Achievement?". Herrnstein and Murray's (1994) *The Bell Curve*, and J. Phillippe Rushton's research (e.g., Rushton & Ankney, 1996), all of which espoused highly hereditarian views, served to further polarize academicians and scientists. Debate in more public circles also continues, with documentaries and books espousing arguments for and against the reality of race and racial differences (e.g., PBS's *Race: The Power of an Illusion* [2003] and Sarich & Miele's [2004] *Race: The Reality of Human Differences*). While the debate over racial differences and their causes is not settled (and will likely not be any time in the near future), it is important to recognize the contexts in which the modern, American view of race developed and the mistakes that science as a whole, including psychology as a field, has made in the past in order to avoid popular misconceptions of what race is and thus avoid previous mistakes and misgivings.

References

Bache, R.M. (1895). Reaction time with reference to race. *Psychological Review, 2*, 474-486.

Banton, M. (1998). *Racial Theories (2nd ed.).* Cambridge, UK: Cambridge University Press.

Barkan, E. (1992). *The Retreat of Scientific Racism. Changing Concepts of Race in Britain and the United States between the World Wars.* Cambridge, UK: Cambridge University Press.

Boas, F. (1931). Race and progress. *Science, 6*, 1-8.

Brigham, C.C. (1923). *A Study of American Intelligence.* Princeton, NJ: Princeton University Press.

Brigham, C.C. (1930). Intelligence tests of immigrant groups. *Psychological Review, 37*, 158-165.

Daniel, R.P. (1932). Basic considerations for valid interpretations of experimental studies pertaining to racial differences. *The Journal of Educational Psychology, 23*, 15-27

Darwin, C. (1859). *On the Origin of Species by means of natural selection, or the preservation of favoured races in the struggle for life.* Retrieved from http://darwin-online.org.uk/converted/pdf/ 1859_Origin_F373.pdf

Darwin, C. (1871). *Descent of Man.* Retrieved from http://darwin-online.org.uk/converted/pdf/1871_Descent_F939.1.pdf

Davenport, C.B., & Steggerda, M. (1929). *Race crossing in Jamaica.* Carnegie Institution of Washington Publication, 395, 471-502.

Dearborn, W.F., & Long, H.H. (1934). The physical and mental abilities of the American Negro: A critical summary. *Journal of Negro Education, 3*, 530-547.

Demand, N. (1996). *A History of Ancient Greece.* Boston, MA: McGraw-Hill.

Dennis, R. M. (1995). Social Darwinism, scientific racism, and the metaphysics of race. *Journal of Negro Education, 64*, 243-252.

Dewey, J. (1902). Interpretation of the savage mind. *Psychological Review, 9*, 217-230.

Dobzhansky, T. (1941). The race concept in biology. *Scientific Monthly, 52*, 161-165.

Dupont, F. (1994). *Daily Life in Ancient Rome.* Malden, MA: Blackwell Publishers.

Fancher, R.E. (1996). The measurement of mind: Francis Galton and the psychology of individual differences. In R.E. Fancher, *Pioneers of Psychology (3rd ed.).* New York, NY: Norton.

16

Fancher, R.E. (2004). The concept of race in the life and thought of Francis Galton. In A.S. Wilson (Ed.), *Defining Difference: Race and Racism in the History of Psychology*. Washington, DC: American Psychological Association.

Farber, P. (2003). Race-mixing and science in the United States. *Endeavour, 27*, 166-170.

Franklin, B. (1751). *Observations concerning the Increase of Mankind, Peopling of Countries, etc.* Retrieved from http://www.historycarper.com/resources/twobf2/increase.htm

Friedman, J.B. (1981). *The Monstrous Races in Medieval Art and Thought*. Cambridge, MA: Harvard University Press.

Frye, R.N. (1993). *The Heritage of Persia*. Cleveland, OH: World Publishing Company.

Galton, F. (1892). *Hereditary Genius: An Inquiry into Its Laws and Consequences (2nd ed.)*. Retrieved from http://www.mugu.com/galton/books/hereditary-genius/ on December 5, 2013.

Garth, T.R. (1921). The results of some tests on full and mixed blood Indians. *The Journal of Applied Psychology, 5*, 359-372.

Garth, T.R. (1931). *Race Psychology*. New York, NY: Whittlesey.

Goddard, H.H. (1913). The Binet tests in relation to immigration. *Journal of Psycho-Asthenics, 18*, 105-107.

Goddard, H.H. (1917). Mental level of a group of immigrants. *Psychological Bulletin, 14*, 69-70.

Gould, S.J. (1996). *The Mismeasure of Man, revised and expanded*. New York, NY: W.W. Norton.

Graves, J.L. (2001). *The Emperor's New Clothes: Biological Theories of Race at the Millennium*. New Brunswick, NJ: Rutgers University Press.

Guralnik, D.B., Ed. (1987). *Webster's New World Dictionary of the American Language*. New York, NY: Warner Books.

Hannaford, I. (1996). *Race: The History of an Idea in the West*. Baltimore, MD: Johns Hopkins University Press.

Herrnstein, R.J., & Murray, C. (1994). *The Bell Curve: Intelligence and Class Structure in American Life*. New York: Free Press

Hunter, W.S., & Sommermier, E. (1922). The relation of degree of Indian blood to score on the Otis Intelligence Test. *Journal of Comparative Psychology, 2*, 257-277.

Jensen, A. (1969). How much can we boost I.Q. and scholastic achievement. *Harvard Educational Review, 39,* 1-123.

Johnson, C.S., & Bond, H.M. (1933). The investigation of racial differences prior to 1910. *Journal of Negro Education, 3,* 328-339.

Jordan, W.D. (1977). *White over Black: American Attitudes toward the Negro, 1550-1812.* New York, NY: Norton.

Lincoln, A. (1858). *The Lincoln-Douglas debates of 1858.* Retrieved from http://www.nps.gov/liho/debates.htm on December 4, 2013.

Loehlin, J.C., Lindzey, G., & Sphuler, J.N. (1975). *Race Differences in Intelligence.* San Francisco, CA: W.H. Freeman and Company.

Marks, J. (1995). *Human Biodiversity: Genes, Race, and History.* New York, NY: Aldine de Gruyter.

Price, J. (1934). Negro-White differences in general intelligence. *Journal of Negro Education, 3,* 424-452.

Richards, G. (1997). *'Race,' Racism and Psychology: Towards a Reflexive History.* New York, NY: Routledge.

Rushton, J.P., & Ankney, C.D. (1996). Brain size and cognitive ability: Correlations with age, sex, social class, and race. *Psychonomic Bulletin and Review, 3* (1), 21-36.

Sarich, V., & Miele, F. (2004). *Race: The Reality of Human Differences.* Westview Press: Boulder, CO.

Snowden, F.M., Jr. (1983). *Before Color Prejudice: The Ancient View of Blacks.* Cambridge, MA: Harvard University Press.

Stephens, G. (no date). John *Locke: His American and Carolinian legacy.* Retrieved from http://johnlocke.org/about/ who_is_john_locke_essay.html on May 28, 2013.

Stetson, G.R. (1897). Some memory tests of blacks and whites. *Psychological Review, 4*(3), 285-289.

Teo, T. (2004). The historical problematization of "mixed race" in psychological and human-scientific discourses. In A.S. Winston (Ed.), *Defining difference: Race and racism in the history of psychology,* pp. 79-108. Washington, DC: American Psychological Association.

Thomas, W.I. (1907). The mind of woman and the lower races. *American Journal of Sociology, 12,* 593-611.

Weizmann, F. (2004). Type and essence: Prologue to the history of psychology and race. In A.S. Wilson (Ed.), *Defining Difference: Race and Racism in the History of Psychology*, pp. 21-48. Washington, DC: American Psychological Association.

Yerkes, R.M. (ed.) (1921). Psychological examining in the United States Army. *Memoirs of the National Academy of Sciences, 15*.

Zinn, H. (1995). *A People's History of the United States, 1492-Present (Revised and Updated Edition)*. New York, NY: HarperPerennial.

Methodological Issues in Comparative Research

Caleb W. Lack & Charles I. Abramson

What is it that makes a field of study a science? Many would argue that the use of the scientific method to generate and answer hypotheses is, if not the only requirement, one of the major conditions. The use of the scientific method in psychology to study human behavior is one of the primary reasons why psychology is considered a science. The ability to critically analyze methodology is crucial to determining how much credence a study deserves. As pointed out in the preceding chapter, poor methodology and questionable conclusions plagued many early studies comparing the abilities of different races and genders. The purpose of this chapter is to give the reader the necessary information to be able to properly evaluate the methodology used in a psychological experiment, particularly those involving comparisons between groups of people. Five areas of critique will be briefly examined: purpose of the study, variables being studied, design of the study, results of the study, and other factors that may influence the methodology.

The first thing to consider when critiquing a study is its purpose. The research question or hypothesis should be clearly stated. The reasoning behind the hypothesis should also be made explicit, including previous research that led the researcher to put forth his or her hypothesis rather than other plausible alternatives. In the absence of previous research, the theory and assumptions behind the hypothesis should be given in great detail. If the researcher has made a compelling case for his or her hypothesis, then the next area of interest can be critiqued.

Although it would seem to be an area where a researcher would lavish detail and attention, issues related to the variables under examination are nonetheless deserving of careful analysis by any consumer of research. Both the independent and dependent variables should be easily identified. Each variable under study should be defined and described in detail. For example, if a researcher plans to study racial differences, he or she should describe the exact criteria by which people were assigned to different racial groups, including any previous research that has used the same criteria and why such assignment would be considered appropriate. The way in which the dependent variable is measured should also be given in enough detail so that no ambiguity is present. Examples of this could be detailing the instruments used to record reaction time or the type of test used to measure intelligence (as well as the working definition of intelligence used in the study).

Related to the definition and labeling of the variables under study are the presence or absence of any controls. First, determine if any controls were used in the study. If so, does the researcher make a strong case for what they are and the reasoning behind using those variables instead of others? If the researcher does not control for any extraneous factors, should he or she have done so? When examining a study to determine if any controls would have been needed, several issues should be kept in mind. First, consider if the groups under comparison were exposed to roughly equivalent economic or educational experiences. If the two groups were raised in radically different environments and exposed to very disparate educational and/or enrichment opportunities, that fact would need to be either controlled for in some fashion or mentioned by the researcher in the discussion of results. As another example, if the two groups have different levels of familiarity with the types of tasks they are asked to perform during the course of an experiment, the results would undoubtedly need to be considered in a different light. Finally, controlling for the potential cultural bias or relation to social status in any measures or instruments used to compare groups of people must also be taken into account. This is most likely to occur in measures of intelligence, which are often highly dependent upon the type of learning and skills obtained by a majority culture.

After a thorough critique of the above points, one can move into the actual design and methodology of the research project. The first thing to examine is the researcher's description of the design of the study, which should be detailed enough to allow the reader to replicate the study with no difficulty. This should answer the five "W" questions: who, what, when, where, and how. The answer to "who" should include descriptive information on the demographic variables of the subjects, such as age, education level, ethnicity, economic status, and so forth. Also, take note of whether the groups under comparison are of equal sample size, as well as any statistical corrections (or lack thereof) if the sample sizes are not equal. It should also include who the researcher is that conducted the experiment, his or her credentials, and possible personal biases. Knowing about who the researcher is can help to understand any personal or vested interest they may have in interpreting a study's results in a particular fashion. Finally, knowing who funded the research can also provide insight into any possible interpretations of the data.

The "what" answer needs to include descriptions of both any instructions the subjects were given and the exact procedure that was used to answer the research question, with a focus on ensuring that the design of the study was sufficient to allow the comparison of the groups under examination. The description of the test or testing instrument needs to have information on the normative sample (if any exist), focusing on the appropriateness of using the test or instrument with the populations being studied, as well as its validity and reliability for measuring the proposed construct. In comparisons of groups of differing linguistic backgrounds, this may become an issue of test translation and if the test has been adapted from the original language or if it had been literally translated into the new language. If the same test is not being used with both groups, does the researcher include a reason for doing so? And, if different tests are being compared, statistical corrections (such as conversions to z-scores) should be taken to increase the validity of any interpretations of the data. The final piece of the "what" question relates to the hypotheses of the study. Does the researcher make clear what results would either support or fail to support the hypotheses?

Answering "when" is important if a study is attempting to compare groups who were not tested at the same time. For example, if the researcher was comparing two groups of children on a measure of intelligence, they would need to be examined at the same time on the academic calendar. Testing one group in fall and one in spring would most likely results in higher scores for those tested in spring, since many intelligence tests actually measure previous learning experiences. Similar to "when" is the question of "where." Groups being compared should be tested in similar environmental conditions, since differences in one's environment (e.g., room temperature, light amount, amount of distracters or noise) can impact the performance on any number of different tasks. The researcher should make the reader aware of any testing or experimental situations which may have impacted the performance of either group being compared.

Finally, the question of "how" primarily relates to the sampling procedure. The method that the researcher used to obtain his or her subjects should be examined carefully. In comparing groups, were steps taken to gather samples that differed only on the factor in question (i.e., race or sex)? If the groups greatly differed on multiple social economic factors, such as education level or income, the researcher should at least acknowledge these differences in discussing the results, if not attempting to control for them.

After determining the strengths and weaknesses of a study's methodology, one should move to the results and discussion sections. Often, these are the most heavily read sections of an article, but can also be the sections most fraught with problems and personal biases. One of the major issues with results sections is the use (and misuse) of statistics. Especially today, when increasingly powerful and obscure statistical analyses are easily conducted by anyone with the proper software, readers must be mindful of which statistical tools are most useful to answer study hypotheses and which may be being misused.

The first question one should ask when examining a results section is if the experimental data is being presented in a statistically accurate manner. Ways to determine this are many. For example, are the researchers reporting the probable variation on each measure used in the study, or picking and choosing? If reporting, are they making both the central tendency (mean, median, mode) and the extent of the group's variability known? In other words, are you being made aware of the full range of scores, rather just a mean and standard deviation? This is needed due to potential skewing of the data that can occur with small samples that have large outliers, or clusters of outliers that are not representative of the sample as a whole.

Next, readers must ask if the proper statistical procedures are being used to compare the groups. There are numerous free online guides available (see the end of this chapter for some examples) to help determine what type of tests should be used in various situations. Even for relatively novice researchers, these guides can help one determine if the tests chosen by the researchers match up with what is most commonly used for that type of data and questions. If there appears to be a mismatch between data, questions, and tests, readers should be cautious about the results, unless a solid explanation is offered by the researchers.

Related to choosing the proper tests is being able to verify the statistical tests used to obtain the given results. In other words, is enough information about the data given to permit verification of the statistics used and the results obtained? Or are some of the needed data (standard deviations, for example) missing from the results section? If it is, then it is quite hard to confirm results of analyses, which could lead one to question why this information was left out.

Once analyses have been scrutinized, the next step in a careful reading of a paper is to examine how the researcher is interpreting their results in the discussion section. In other words, does the data match the interpretation? Are the statements the experimenter making about what the statistical analyses mean matching up with your reading of the analyses, or is the researcher going beyond the data to support his or her *a priori* ideas? Some factors that are important to consider when examining the discussion section and the conclusions an experimenter draws from a study's results.

For example, a careful reader will need to consider that a paper may not be completely unbiased. Ask yourself, what are the author's political and religious affiliations? How might they have influenced the design and interpretation of the experiment? If the study was funded, who was the funding source? What were their religious and political affiliations or agendas? Although the scientific method helps to eliminate potential biases, very little research is truly completely uninfluenced by external desires and drives, so it is crucial that readers be aware of potential conflicts of interest.

What was the public impact of the study (if it is a historical study), or what is the potential public impact of a new study? How did it impact either social policy or future research? Are there likely to be changes in how people perceive certain groups as a result of this study? If so, are those changes consistent with potential religious or political agendas supporting the research financially? How have other researchers reacted to the study, as well? Are there any major denouncements by prominent researchers or declarations of support?

One should also consider their personal thoughts about the paper. What was your personal reaction to the study and the author's interpretation of the results? Did you agree or disagree with it? Why or why not? What could be done to improve the study's methodology or results to address your concerns? What type of study would you design to follow-up these results, either to clarify uncertainties or test for other important influences on any found differences?

In sum, being able to do a critical analysis of an empirical study and the results is a crucial tool of any competent consumer of research. By asking questions similar to those detailed in this chapter, one can gain a richer, fuller understanding of whether or not a particular study is sound or unsound, victim to bias or free from them. This in turn allows for more confidence in the results being accurate, or allows one to instead dismiss the results as being unfounded or problematic. Not all research is created equal, especially research that examines controversial issues such as racial or gender differences. This guide can help you separate out the good from the bad, the ugly, and the pseudoscientific.

Examples of statistical flow-charts:

- Choosing an Appropriate Hypothesis Test – located at http://www.diss-stat.com/choosing.pdf
- Choosing a Stats Test – located at http://www.gardenersown.co.uk/about/mark/choosestats.html
- Flow Chart for Selecting Commonly Used Statistical Tests – located at http://abacus.bates.edu/~ganderso/biology/resources/stats_flow_chart_v2003.pdf

Preface to the Reprinted Works

With the reader now familiar both with some of the historical background on scientific racism and sexism as well as the methodological issues that must be attended to when doing comparative research, we turn our eyes back across time0. Immediately following this section are reprints of 22 articles spanning the period from 1895 to 1930. These articles all deal, in one way or another, with attempts to find or explain differences between groups of people, including racial/ethnic groups and the sexes. They run the gamut from experimental studies to letters to the editor, from research reviews to theoretical papers. Together, they were chosen to showcase the wide variety of thought and quality of work being done at this early point in psychology's history, both positive and negative. It is expected that our readers will find some of the work and the conclusions, to say nothing of the language used in them, offensive.

But, rather than just reading them and becoming offended and dismissing them as the crude work of sexist or racist people, we the editors offer you a challenge. Take this opportunity to sharpen your observation and research skills, as well as your critical thinking ability, rather than just passively absorbing the material. Presented below are two ways to do so. First is by answering at least one of the below thought-questions after reading each reprint. Doing so will help you to truly engage with the material and further understand the implications of the work for modern psychology.

1. What changes would you have made in the experimental design of this study?
2. How could the results have been interpreted differently based on the data?
3. Describe the differences and similarities in the political climate between when this study was conducted and today. How would they have influenced the interpretation of the results?
4. Given today's guidelines for research involving humans, would this study have been approved by an Institutional Review Board? Why or why not? What changes would have to be made if it would not be approved today?
5. What is the importance of examining gender and race based differences in contemporary society? Is it important to conduct such research today? Would you personally be interested in conducting such research? Why or why not?
6. If you are not, pretend you are a member of one of the minority groups examined in the study. Would reading the results of this study influence your

thoughts on entering a career in a scientific field? Would it impact your view of science in general in a negative or positive fashion?

7. Using the guidelines presented in Chapter Two, redesign this experiment to better answer the question under consideration.

8. What skills or training should a researcher possess to be able to properly conduct the type of experiment in this study? Did the author have these skills? How would this have impacted the study?

9. Having read these studies, has your view of psychology as a science changed? Do you think studies today are conducted in similar fashion? Find examples of recent research that confirms or denies your views.

10. Do you believe it is possible for a scientist or researcher to distance him or herself from the social and political environment of the time? Why or why not? Should political affiliations and sources of funding be noted when presenting research? How would knowing such things color your interpretation of the author's results? For example, would a study funded by a governmental agency such as NIMH that showed racial differences be looked upon differently than a similar study funded by an organization such as the Klu Klux Klan or the NAACP?

11. Think on how scientific results and research in avenues such as magazines, newspapers, or television have influenced your perception of gender and race based differences. Does reading the original articles impact you differently from being presented with only brief snippets of information from media sources? In what way?

12. After reading some of the original research on race differences, what is your view of programs such as Affirmative Action? Did it change after reading this research? Do you think such programs should continue to be implemented?

13. What stereotypes do you hold about any of the groups being compared in this study? Did the results and interpretation of this study reinforce or disconfirm any of those stereotypes? How could the results of this study be used to move forward a racist or sexist agenda?

For an even more in-depth engagement with the material, or for those using this book in a classroom or reading it as a group, the below activities are also offered. They have been designed to raise awareness and increase the salience of issues raised by the studies reprinted in this book. While the discussion questions above can be answered individually, these activities will generally require multiple people to participate in and be exposed to a wide variety of opinions and thoughts on gender and race differences (but could be adapted to an individual study).

1. Design a simple reaction time study comparing gender or race-based differences. What problems did you encounter? What were the results? How do you interpret those results?

2. Complete an Institutional Review Board form (a typical form is available for download at https://compliance.vpr.okstate.edu/IRB/forms.aspx) for one of the studies reprinted in this book. Invite a member from your local university's Office of Research Compliance (which you can find easily via searching their website for "Institutional Review Board") or a veteran social science researcher to go over the form and discuss issues related to ethical research with the group.

3. Have a debate around one of the following issues after having read the chapters and some of the reprinted articles.

    a. Are there inherent gender or race differences among humans?

    b. What is race? Does it exist or is it a social construct? Is it a valid concept anymore based on our current understanding of genetics?

    c. What is intelligence? Can it be measured? If so, how?

4. Have each member of the group research one of the authors whose work is reprinted in this book. Then have each person present a brief biography of him or her to the entire group. How does further knowledge of the life behind the name change (or not) your perception of the author and the article?

5. Find out if any of the articles reprinted here are still being cited in current literature by using search engines such as Google Scholar or Web of Science. In what way and in what area of research are they being cited? How often are they being cited and how has that changed across time?

6. Have each group member each find a sexist or racist website that provides some type of scientific evidence to support its views. Then discuss what type of research the website's builders used to support their views and the scientific merit of that research.

7. Take a trip to the local university library and find several of the journals that the articles here are reprinted from. What other types of research was being published by those journals? Critique one or two of the other research articles

29

in that journal using the criteria from Chapter Two. Are the journals still active today? What type of research does the journal currently publish?

8. Pick two or three of the studies reprinted in this book and conduct a power analysis on the sample sizes of each using the Power & Sample Size Calculator (available online at http://www.statisticalsolutions.net/pss_calc.php). Discuss whether the number of subjects in each study was large enough to reliably detect whether any differences were actually present.

9. Stage a debate between one person portraying Lewis M. Terman, the father of mass-marketed "intelligence" tests, and another portraying Walter Lippmann, an influential journalist who was against "intelligence" testing. Use Lippmann's original writings (available at http://historymatters.gmu.edu/d/5172/) and Terman's replies (available at http://historymatters.gmu.edu/d/4960/) to aid in speaking with each person's "voice" during the debate.

10. Obtain a copy of C.C. Brigham's (1923) *A Study of American Intelligence* (either via a local library or online at https://archive.org/details/ studyofamericani00briguoft) and critique it using the guidelines presented in Chapter Two. How does his methodology and use of statistics hold up using those guidelines? Discuss if and how any of the results should have been presented differently, and how the study could have been improved methodologically.

It is our hope that, by reading the following reprints and engaging with them actively via the above questions and activities, readers will gain more than by simply reading. With that being said, we now present the following articles, arranged in chronological order (an exception is being made for the Hollingworth articles, as we think that reading these two summaries together makes for a richer experience). Please note that we have attempted to retain the original formatting as much as possible, but that due to size differences between journals and this books, some tables and charts may be slightly out of sync with the original articles.

1. Bache, R.M. (1895). Reaction time with reference to race. *Psychological Review*, *2*(5), 475-486.

2. Cattell, J.M. (1903). A statistical study of eminent men. *Popular Science Monthly*, *62*, 359-378.

3. Wells, F.L. (1909). Sex differences in the tapping test: An interpretation. *The American Journal of Psychology, 20*(3), 353-363

4. Rentoul, R.R. (1910-11). Sterilising the insane. *ER, 2*, 74-76.

5. Kenealy, A. (1911). A study in degeneracy. *Eugenics Review, 3*(1), 37-45.

6. Burt, C. (1912). The inheritance of mental characters. *Eugenics Review, 4*(2), 168–200.

7. Hansen, S. (1913). The inferior quality of the first-born children. Eugenics Review, *5*(3), 252–259.

8. Cobb, J.A. (1914). The alleged inferiority of the first-born, *Eugenics Review, 5*(4), 357-359.

9. McDougall, W. (1914). Psychology in the services of eugenics. *Eugenics Review, 5*(4), 295–308.

10. Bruner, F.G. (1914). Racial differences. *Psychological Bulletin, 11*(10), 384-386.

11. Simon, T. (1915). The measurement of intelligence. *Eugenics Review, 6*(4): 291–307.

12. Woolley, H.T. (1914). The psychology of sex. *Psychological Bulletin, 11*, 353-379

13. Hollingworth, L.S. (1916). Sex differences in mental traits. *Psychological Bulletin, 13*(10), 377-384.

14. Hollingworth, L.S. (1918). Comparison of the sexes in mental traits. *Psychological Bulletin, 15*(12), 427-432.

15. Gates, A.I. (1917). Experiments on the relative efficiency of men and women in memory and reasoning. *Psychological Review, 24*(2), 139-146.

16. Grier, N.M. (1918). Comparative mentality of Jews and Gentiles. *The Pedagogical Seminary, 25*(4), 432-433.

17. Garth, T.R. (1921). The results of some tests on full and mixed blood Indians. Journal of Applied Psychology, *5*(4), 359-372.

18. Goldberg, J.A. (1922). Incidence of insanity among Jews. *Mental Hygiene, 6*, 598-603.

19. Brierley, S.S. (1923). A note on sex differences, from the psycho-analytic point of view. *British Journal of Medical Psychology, 3*(4), 288-308.

20. Garth. T.R. (1923). A comparison of the intelligence of Mexican and mixed and full blood Indian children. *Psychological Review, 30*(5), 388-401.

21. Goodenough, F.L. (1926). Racial differences in the intelligence of school children. *Journal of Experimental Psychology, 9*(5), 388-397.

31

22. Lamb, E.O. (1930). Racial differences in bi-manual dexterity of Latin and American children. *Child Development*, *1*(3), 204-231.

Bache, R.M. (1895). Reaction time with reference to race.
Psychological Review, 2(5), 475-486.

REACTION TIME WITH REFERENCE TO RACE

By R. MEADE BACHE

The fact of the coordinated existence to common observation of the apparently completed, final man, obscures in the minds of the multitude the rationale of his muscular movements. It is generally believed that in health, every one of those movements, either in waking or sleeping, is derived from an act of either self-conscious or semi-self-conscious will. But physiology proves that some movements are simply reflex, as when, for instance, the hand may be said to draw itself away from a burn, and that others, although secondarily reflex, are still purely automatic, as when a child, having learned to walk, can walk thereafter without other self-consciousness than that necessary to start the machinery of walking; and of course every one knows that the vital movements, such as the beating of the heart and self-consciousness and will. Deep down in the physical constitution of man, graduated to his present condition through successively higher and higher types, with corresponding advance in structure and function, lies plain evidence of the derivation of certain contradistinguished movements, namely, automatic as contrasted with volitional movements. As the skull itself was, as discovered by Goethe, derived from upper vertebrae, it needs no demonstration to prove that, in the preceding period, there was no brain; and as all animals now provided with crania must then, nevertheless, have lived and moved and had their being, it also stands to reason that will, which has its organic seat in the brain, could have had no existence in that preceding period.

What, then, in one era of that primordial time, representing millions upon millions of years ago, constituted animal life? What indeed in some of the present forms of life, as in the case of the simplest, the amoeba, entitles them, as little protoplasmic masses, to be regarded as possessing animal life? Assimilation of food in a way analogous to digestion, and with a difference from vegetable life,—through a law almost universal even in the misty borderland between the lowest forms of animal and vegetable life,— the imbibition of nutriments in higher chemical combination than vegetable life can use it. So, also, in some of the past history of incipient man, he, too, was a creature destitute of capacity for that designed taking of food and direction of energy, destitute of any capacity for movement except that which was purely reflex, not purposive. It follows, as proved by biology, anatomy, and physiology, working hand in hand, that man having been evolved from successive forms which, at the beginning and long afterwards, were reflex in their movements, must continue, in harmony with his present environment, to be so endowed. Development depends upon natural selection and functional uses, and these are in turn dependent upon environment, and man's environment has not so changed as to enable him to dispense with reflex, and secondary-reflex, combined in automatic movements.

The foundation of man's earthly existence is and was what Huxley terms 'the physical basis of life,' protoplasm; and now, in the highest estate which he has reached, metabolism of that basis, the chemical building up to higher forms and the breaking down to lower forms of protoplasm, represents the varying intensity with which he lives. So varied in its conditions and consequent manifestations is this physical basis of life that Dr. Michael Foster writes in the article 'Physiology,' in the Encyclopaedia Britannica, "the protoplasm of one muscle must differ from that of another muscle in the same kind of animal, and that protoplasm of Smith's biceps must differ from that of Jones's." Biologists and physiologists do not deny to protoplasm, even in its simplest forms, the quality of consciousness. If they did, it would be impossible to draw the line where consciousness begins in one form of life and where it ends in another. In a certain broad, intelligible sense, it may be said generally, that where we see life of even the lowest form assimilating food of a certain chemical constitution, there is animal existence and consciousness. There are exceptions in plant life, but they are few. But the consciousness referred to is not the kind that is covered by the term 'self-consciousness,' or by another term that is used to mark the distinction—'awareness.' By way of illustration of the difference, it may be said that the eye may be open and picture of surrounding objects necessarily on the retina, but yet the mind may take no cognizance of the picture: the picture must be seen, but it may not be perceived. So also, in the lower protoplasmic life, there is consciousness for the requirements of mere being, but not 'awareness' of being and its manifestations.

As, at the remote period indicated, in which millions upon millions of years are involved, man having no skull, and therefore no capacity of 'awareness,' his functions were then only reflex. Graduated beyond that point, he yet, in correspondence with his acquired vertebrate formation, become possessed of nervous structure serving the needs of his advancing form of life. If the being from which he was derived had no skull, it had neither cerebrum, cerebellum, pons, nor medulla oblongata, all of which are contained within the skull. He must at one time have had only a spinal cord, the present structure of which makes it a nerve centre as well as a conductor of nervous impressions. Therefore, in the being which was to become man, the spinal cord, which now represents the nervous agency of voluntary movements and tactile impressions must, as it was not dominated by will through the presence of brain, have been the seat of mere vital impressions and reflex action unaccompanied by perception. An animal, the amphioxus, the lowest of the vertebrates, still extant, has no head, but merely a vertebral column. The condition of man differs essentially now from that of his past. In addition to the spinal cord's being now more highly differentiated, it may also now be dominated by the will, through the organ of the brain, and it generally is, even in a measure during the incoordination of the nervous system during sleep, for the sense of existence and of personal identity is never lost even in dreams.

Endowed as man now additionally is, he consists of two physical beings, one of which, automatic, may or may not at times be dominated by the other, the intellectual, gifted with perception, intention, and will. He is, moreover, so organized now, and must so remain as long as the requirements of his present environment endure, as to bring it about that the dominant brain can give general, instead of particular, instructions to its automatic slave, which the latter will faithfully carry out to the extent of its physical ability. The automatic man is the educated slave of the brain, as proved by the fact that the art of walking, as well as all other complex actions, had to be acquired through the expenditure of a certain amount of instruction, attention, effort, and time. Walking is a complex muscular performance in which the man wills that his body shall walk, and leaves to his automatic part the execution of the task. Having been once acquired, the ability has become and remains purely automatic, and whatever may be said of walking applies with equal force to any other complex muscular movement of man. One should not suppose that when an athlete is striking the punching bag of a gymnasium with the utmost rapidity of which he is training capable, that each blow emanates from a special act of will. If that were so, each blow would show the 'reaction time' of the man; that is, the interval between perception and action. But this is obviously not so, for the number of blows, dividing the time in which they are struck, proves that intermediate perception between every two is eliminated. When, for instance, Corbett, the boxer, stands in profile and strikes the bag as rapidly as possible, the play of his forearms resolves itself into a blur, in which their outlines are scarcely visible. In striking the punching bag, perception for each action represented by a blow is discarded. The will determines that the blows shall be delivered, that they shall be delivered with a certain rapidity, and it continues throughout the operation to supervise their delivery, but it cannot supervise each, any more than it can determine their speed, which necessarily depends upon the automatic excellence of the instrument with which it is dealing. The will, which means simply the mind resolved into action, has, in the case under consideration, nothing to do with the matter but to start, to preside over the action, to modify, and to stop it.

The preceding statements of fact bring us face to face with an important conclusion to be drawn which entirely differs from popular conception of the subject. Herbert Spencer somewhere calls attention to the contrast between the savage and the civilized man, in the circumstance that the former is so much more than the latter a creature of secondary reflex movements, and he illustrates this by remarking that, if a savage hurts his foot against a stone, the likeliest immediate response on his part is to kick the stone; an action indicating a development far inferior to that of a civilized, not to say an intellectual man. Now, the popular notion is, that the higher the intelligence of a man, the more immediately responsive his movements must be to stimulus. But we have already seen reason to believe that, all educated movements being automatic, it is the lower, and not the higher man, who should be more responsive to stimuli of the sort which are related to secondary reflex action, that men, in proportion to their intellectuality, should tend less and less to quickness of response in the automatic sphere, that the reflective man should be the slower being. That this is so I have for a long while believed, and I find to my mind a sufficient reason for its so being in the fact that the automatic preceded the intellectual condition of man, and that, with the decline of his primal rude life, secondary reflex movements should have become in lesser and lesser degree a necessity for his self-preservation. He should have discarded, I thought, in proportion to his intellectual advance, whatever was becoming less and less useful to him in his changed environment. In all evolution is modified of discarded whatever there is of lessening or no requirement for life under new conditions.

The popular notion that the more highly organized a human being is, the quicker ought to be the response to stimuli, is true only of the sphere of higher thought, not at all of that of auditory, visual, or tactile impressions, which invite secondary reflex action. As here stated, response to such stimuli, not depending upon the more highly organized, but upon the less highly organized portion of the nervous system, the most ordinary intelligence should suffice for its exercise; and in proportion to intellectual advancement, there should be, through the law of compensation, a waning in the efficiency of the automatism of the individual. It has been contended, as an unanswerable argument, by a crucial test, that other things being apparently equal, high intelligence in one man as compared with another would result in the favorable issue to him of pugilistic contest in which he might be engaged in such contests. The answer, therefore, is that, other things being equal, relatively greater intelligence should give its possessor the victory, but only on the condition that the intelligence is superior, but not high, for it does not require high intelligence to conduct a pugilistic contest; while, on the other hand, inasmuch as the intelligence requisite for the conduct of a pugilistic contest is at best low, if one of the combatants, otherwise apparently equal, be an intellectual man, that is, has intelligence far beyond the purpose, and the other has nothing but intelligence sufficient, the former would be handicapped by his lesser relative automatic excellence, lost perforce of his intellectuality. His intellectuality having been gained at the expense of his automatic capacity, he would be defeated by the man whose lower, but sufficient, the former would be handicapped by his lesser relative automatic excellence, lost perforce of his intellectuality. His intellectuality having been gained at the expense of his automatic capacity, he would be defeated by the man whose lower, but sufficient, intelligence had subtracted less from his primitive constitution. The law of compensation is binding, and declares that growth in one direction of correlated structure and function involves diminution in another, and here we have a case of distinctly correlated structure and function. In a word, the automatic superiority of the less intellectual man being greater as such than that of the other, and his intelligence quite equal to the purpose of pugilism, he would win in a pugilistic contest. If it were otherwise, then the theory here brought forward, as supported by observation, and be experiment remaining to be finally presented, would fall to the ground.

Pride of race obscures the view of the white with reference to the relative automatic quickness of the negro. That the negro is, in the truest sense, a race inferior to that of the white can be proved by many facts, and among these by the quickness of his automatic movements as compared with those of the white. Many men, however, resent any claim for him of superiority, even in the low sphere of automatic movements, notwithstanding that there are several negroes and mulattoes at the present day in the ring whose excellence is scarcely approached, some of whom have often cheerfully encountered opponents of much greater size and weight for the privilege of being able to prove their skill. When additionally it is considered that the negro has in pugilism the advantage over the white in length of arm and thickness of skull, it ought easily to be seen that, with equal opportunity, were prejudice not so strongly against him, he would be regarded as the boxer *par excellence* of the world. It would be vain to say that Corbett is as quick as, or quicker than, any negro boxer. He may be quicker than any present negro boxer, but even that is doubtful. It is, however, contrary to all scientific practice to generalize from the case of a single or even of a few individuals by way of establishing a law. It is relative race characteristics of which there is now question, as previously there has been question of the relation between different individuals of the same race. Anyone who will dispassionately observe any group of skylarking whites, and compared them with a group of negroes under the same circumstances, would be forced to admit that the latter are quicker in their movement; that the negro is, in brief, more of an automaton than the white man is. When bluff John L. Sullivan declared of the colored boxer, Jackson, that he would not fight him because of his race, he probably builded better than he knew when using the word superiority in the sense not related at all to a pugilistic contest.

Having, from observation, for a long while believed the fact to be as here stated, with reference to the relative automatic excellence of individuals of lower races as compared with those of higher ones, and having additionally ascribed the fact, if it be a fact, to the cause mentioned, I finally determined to submit the matter to the test of experiment. With magneto-electric apparatus, now so common and easily adapted to various investigations of the sort, Professor Lightner Witmer, of the University of Pennsylvania, has at my suggestion made a number of experiments for determining the reaction time of Whites, Indians, and Africans, with the results as given below. The reaction time of women, as settled by the same indisputable method, was long since determined as less than that of men, and this result, it will be observed, is in strict accordance with the fact that the brain development of men, as compared with that of women, is greater, even when taking into account the relatively greater weight of normal individuals of the male sex as compared with that of normal individuals of the opposite one.

Although I do not, in contradiction of my own statement, mean to imply from the few experiments here presented, that they should be regarded as conclusive of the views here expressed, yet I present them for what they are numerically worth, with the intention to increase their number, and in the hope that, from the fact of their presentation, other persons will be led to follow the same line of investigation.

CAUCASIAN RACE

Different Persons	Age.	Auditory. Mean of 10 Observation.	Mean Variation.	Visual. Mean of 10 Observation.	Mean Variation.	Electric Shock Mean of 10 Observations	Mean Variation.
1	22	135	7.0	152	10.0	141	4.0
2	24	130	7.0	140	8.0	128	11.0
3	16	141	13.0	174	10.0	137	9.0
4	14	132	8.0	159	10.0	138	3.0
5	15	182	20.0	214	6.0	142	14.0
6	19	147	19.0	164	11.0	119	13.0
7	18	139	12.0	155	22.0	150	11.0
8	19	170	15.0	191	12.0	229	27.0*
9	29	123	6.0	164	9.0	121	7.0
10	15	234	17.0	201	12.0	229	15.0*
11	24	119	7.8	118	3.0	103	6.7
12	15	111	12.1	145	3.9	133	6.8
Final Means:	19	146.92	12.0	164.75	9.7	136.33	10.6

*In all the tables the figures represent thousandths sec. Compare times in this line by all three tests. They are abnormally slow.

INDIAN RACE

Different Persons	Age.	Auditory. Mean of 10 Observations.	Mean Variation.	Visual. Mean of 10 Observations.	Mean Variation.	Electric Shock Mean of 10 Observations.	Mean Variation.
1	18	165	5.7	168	8.5	152	3.5
2	21	115	5.5	121	3.9	100	3.4
3	14	128	5.4	148	6.2	118	2.5
4	23	144	6.1	127	3.1	122	3.6
5	14	70	6.2	119	4.8	94	5.3*
6	16	104	11.0	139	9.9	121	5.4
7	16	109	10.1	151	6.3	123	2.4
8	17	107	10.6	120	6.2	90	3.9
9	17	120	13.0	141	6.9	120	8.2
10	18	117	12.4	141	7.7	110	5.8
11	19	100	5.3	118	3.7	114	4.6
Final Means:	17 ½	116.27	7.7	135.73	6.1	114.55	4.4

*Pure blood Indian. Abnormally quick.

AFRICAN RACE

Different Persons	Age.	Auditory.		Visual.		Electric Shock	
		Mean of 10 Observations.	Mean Variation.	Mean of 10 Observations.	Mean Variation.	Mean of 10 Observations.	Mean Variation.
1	16	114	7.2	157	8.4	107	10.3
2	19	113	10.4	148	14.2	103	5.4
3	19	127	7.7	131	4.6	100	3.6
4	20	125	5.7	138	6.9	120	6.0
5	19	164	24.7	173	7.0	137	13.9
6	22	164	13.4	187	10.7	178	8.7
7	26	121	13.8	118	11.8	103	5.0
8	34	148	4.0	159	5.9	141	7.7
9	38	109	4.8	105	11.2	118	6.5
10	16	120	6.0	162	8.0	112	5.0
11	25	126	5.0	144	7.0	128	8.0
Final Means:	23	130.00	9.3	152.91	8.7	122.91	7.3

The first thing that strikes one, upon examination of the tables, is the relative slowness of the Whites, as compared with the Indians and the Africans. This is in accordance with the theory. But what is not in accordance with it, is that the reaction time of the Indians is shown by the tables to be less than that of the Africans, and the African is not so high in race as is the American Indian. It is possible, however, that the eventual explanation of this, when enough observations shall have been secured to demonstrate a law, will be that the Indian belongs to a race which for centuries cultivated quickness of movement as a necessity of his existence. Besides, the so-called Africans on the list have a larger intermixture of white blood in their veins than have the Indians on the corresponding list. It would seem, however, that the largest factor, as a disturbing element, is derived from the circumstance that the African, of the class here referred to, of whatever infusion of white blood in his veins, inherits the physiological effects from generations of slavery. It must be, if we can ascribe to the Indian, through the influence of heredity, an extraordinary low reaction time, that we should admit, through heredity, the effect of converse conditions to which the African has been subjected. Whoever has seen slaves hoeing, in their listless fashion, in a cotton-field, or engaged in other forms of labor, must feel well assured that the mental attitude thereby betrayed could not fail in the course of generations to modify physical function.

In sum, the conclusion must be, so far as the tables may elucidate the subject, that the African is quicker than the White, despite his hereditary history, and the Indian is quicker than both, perforce of his hereditary history.

I wish to call attention to a strange detail, to the case of No. 5, on the list of Indians. That case happened to be one of a full-blooded Indian, and as is seen, his reaction time is marvelously low. If 70 had appeared alone as the result of the auditory test, it would be justifiable to discard the observation, but the auditory, visual, and tactile tests all correspond, in due relation to each other, and therefore it is impossible to regard this as any other than an exceptional case of quickness even amongst Indians. It is interesting to contrast this with the case of No. 10, amongst the Whites, with reaction time about three times slower than the reaction time of the Indian No. 5. Here again we perceive, as in the case of Indian No. 5, that the times, as determined by the auditory, visual, and tactile tests correspond perfectly, and that we must regard this as a case of abnormal slowness of reaction time even among Whites.

In the list of Whites there are twelve individuals, and in the list of Indians, eleven, but only ten in the list of Africans. But, then, it must be considered, that in each of the first two lists mentioned is included an abnormal case,—one of slowness and one of quickness. It would take more than one or two additional cases to produce an entirely satisfactory mean. To obtain perfectly satisfactory final means it will be necessary, of course, to make many more observations, and these I hope eventually to secure.

The views which I have expressed I had entertained, from observation, for very many years, long before I suspected the scientific bearing which they have. I never found any one, however, to whom I communicated them who seemed to recognize their probable truth, and it was at the beginning, and for a long period afterwards, impossible to prove the correctness of my position until the creation of electrical physiological apparatus enabled any one to put to a crucial test any such theory as is here presented. When at last the apparatus was invented, and the convenience came to me in the facility afforded by Dr. Witmer, I availed myself of the opportunity. The article which I here present was written several months ago, while the experiments at the University were proceeding. I had intended to publish it at once, and let the experiments follow, but upon reflection, I concluded to postpone its publication until it was in my power to give something that would at least point in the direction of the truth in my hypothesis, for otherwise, it might be received with entire incredulity. Now that I am able to present matter, which certainly does point, if it does no more

41

than point, in the direction indicated, I do not hesitate any longer to publish what I have held back.

It only remains to add, for the benefit of the general reader, that the record, as represented in the tables, is made in thousandths of a second, as registered by the electromagnetic physiological apparatus. In the auditory test, the subject, upon hearing the prescribed short sound, releases a telegraphic key upon which his finger is resting. The difference of time between the sound as it takes place and the release of the key is recorded by the apparatus. In the visual tests, a long pendulum is suspended away from the perpendicular in a room adjoining that in which the subject sits. The subject releases the telegraphic key at the moment when he sees a flash of light given by the pendulum-bob passing a small opening in the room where he is placed. The difference of time between the actual passage of the bob and the time when the telegraphic key is released is recorded by the apparatus. In the tactile test, a slight electric shock is given to the wrist of the subject. The difference of time between the shock and the removal of the hand from the telegraphic key is recorded by the apparatus.

Cattell, J.M. (1903). A statistical study of eminent men. *Popular Science Monthly, 62,* 359-378.

A STATISTICAL STUDY OF EMINENT MEN

By PROFESSOR J. MCKEEN CATTELL,
Columbia University

The accounts of great men in biographies and histories belong to literature rather than to science. Modern science is either genetic or quantitative. It seeks to discover those uniformities which we call causes and to use that method of description which we call measurement. It is now time that great men should be studied as part of social evolution and by the methods of exact and statistical science.

History is only the last chapter of organic evolution, and both where similar causes are at work and where new factors have arisen, the parallel between social and organic evolution is instructive. While the Darwinian principle of natural selection as an explanation of the origin of species has an aspect which makes it almost as naive as the doctrine of special creations, it has given an extraordinary stimulus to modern thought. Natural selection is no cause of the origin of species or of anything else but the environment is the condition of the survival of species and of individuals. Evolution has progressed through the occurrence of variations sanctioned by the environment. We are, it is true, not only ignorant of the causes of variations, but even of their nature. We do not know whether one species has been derived from another by gradual variation in many individuals or by sudden jumps in a few. We do not know whether the type prescribes the individual or whether the individual prescribes the type. Yet in spite of our ignorance not only of the causes but even of the nature of organic evolution the distinctions formulated by the naturalist are fruitful when applied to social evolution.

It is evident that there are two leading factors in producing a man and making him what he is—one the endowment given at birth, the other the environment into which he comes. The main lines are certainly laid down by heredity—a man is born a man and not an ape. A savage brought up in cultivated society will not only retain his dark skin, but is likely to have also the incoherent mind of his race. On the other hand, environment has at least an absolute veto. Had the infant Newton been cast among

43

Hottentots he could have announced no laws of motion. But were those differences—small from the point of view of organism, great from the point of view of function—which distinguished Dante from his Florentine fellow townsmen innate or due to the circumstances of his life? Here the biological parallel may be serviceable. Are those variations which produce new species caused by the environment? Can life be regarded as the resultant of physical forces? Many zoologists and physiologists answer in the affirmative, but in large measure in spite of, physical forces—these tend to the dissipation of energy, they are the causes of death rather than of life. So in like manner it seems that the environment would tend to reduce the great man to its level rather than to lift him above it—Dante wrote in spite of his surroundings, not on account of them. Still the environment counts for much. If the seed of the white pine is dropped among New England rocks it will grow into a small bush, if planed in the rich soil of the south it will become a great tree. We have the 'Divine Comedy' because Dante had 'the steep stairs and bitter bread' in place of Beatrice.

As the environment tends to reduce all things to its level, so heredity tends to maintain the type. Whence then the great man who brings something new into the world? Carlyle had the same heredity and the same initial environment as his brothers. Why should he write of heroes and become one, while they remained peasants? Why, we may ask the theory of organic evolution, should certain individuals of a species possess variations tending to greater complexity, which lay down the lines of evolution? Perhaps all we can say is that the question 'why' is more in place in the nursery than in the laboratory. Why heredity should maintain the type is as obscure as why new types should arise. If the world were a chaos, no questions would be asked, as it is a cosmos it must have a certain definite order. But if when we ask 'why' we really mean 'how,' then we have the plain way of science before us. We can investigate the stability and variability of the type, we can study the effects of the environment on the individual. We know perhaps in a general way that any great war will find the material at hand for the making of a Grant and a Lee, and, on the other hand, that a Shelley may be what he is in spite of heredity and environment. More exact knowledge can only come from an inductive study of facts.

As in organic evolution the effects of variations are less obscure than their causes, so in social evolution we can trace more easily the influence of great men than we can account for their origin. As we ascend the scale of animal life and human development the role of social tradition becomes increasingly potent. A new trait in a single individual among lower animals, even though it may be both useful and stable, can have but an infinitesimal effect in altering the species. In man a new advance made by a single individual becomes quickly the property of all. Let fire be discovered and we have a trait that endows every one. Let the printing press be invented and each can speak with a thousand tongues. Let Dante see the ideal of romantic love and every boy and girl in Christendom has his life altered thereby. What we now are—as men— depends chiefly on social tradition; withhold it for a generation and we should revert to savagery and further. It is also true that social tradition sets the course of organic development. Individuals who are unfit for their social environment can not survive in it; those who possess variations, however slight, making adjustment to social conditions and social ideals more easy are more likely to survive and to transmit their traits. If we depended only on social tradition, progress would be limited by the extreme range of individual adaptations. But by the preservation of stable variations in the line of social evolution, we secure a new type from which new forward variations are more likely.

Whether great men really lay down the line of social evolution or only anticipate and hasten its necessary course is an unsolved question. Are great men, as Carlyle maintains, divinely inspired leaders, or are they, as Spencer tells us, necessary products of given physical and social conditions? If Dante had not set the ideal of romantic love, would it not have come from other sources? Did Darwin do more than express what was 'in the air' and hasten by a dozen years the necessary course of science? We can only answer such questions by an actual study of facts. When we regard the noteworthy men that have appeared in the world, it is evident that they have but little in common. 'Some are born great, some achieve greatness, and some have greatness thrust upon them.' We have men of genius, great men and men merely eminent. Thus many a genius has been a 'mute inglorious Milton' lacking the character or the circumstance for the accomplishment of his task. Washington was scarcely a genius, but was a truly great man. Napoleon III was neither a genius nor a great men but was eminent to an unusual degree. But if we simple take those men who have most attracted the eyes and ears of the world, who have most set its tongues and printing presses in motion, we have a definite group. Beginning with this we can analyse and classify; we can study these individuals, their causes and their effects; we can regard them as types of a given age and race; we can use them to measure interests and tendencies.

For these purposes our first need is a definite list of the most eminent men, sufficiently large for statistical study.* The method I followed to discover the 1,000 men who are preeminent was this: I took six biographical dictionaries or encyclopedias*—two English, two French, one German, and one American and found the two thousand men (approximately) in each who were allowed the longest articles. I then selected the men who appeared in this lists of at least three of the dictionaries, and from these (some 1,600) selected the thousand who were allowed the greatest average space, the value of the separate dictionaries being reduced to a common standard. Thus was obtained not only the thousand men esteemed the most eminent, but also the order in which they stand.

This list represents the point of view of these dictionaries, and would be somewhat different had other works been selected. Mathematical science can indeed assign a probable error to each name on the list, and tell us how likely it is that the man should be there, and within what limits his place on the list is likely to be correct. But the greater men of the thousand would remain whatever the authorities collated; and although the personal names of the lesser men might vary, this would affect but little the statistics sought. The preparation of this list required more work than may be supposed, but it has an objective impartiality and value, which it would not have if the names had been selected by an easier method.

According to this list the ten most eminent men are Napoleon, Shakespeare, Mahommed, Voltaire, Bacon, Aristotle, Goethe, Caesar, Luther, Plato. There is no doubt that Napoleon is the most eminent man who has lived. Yet it should give us pause to think that this Titan of anarchy stands first in the thoughts of most men. It is curious that these ten preeminent men are so widely separated in race and age—two Greeks, two Frenchmen, two Germans, two Englishmen, one Roman and one Arab: two in the fifth century and one in the first century before Christ, one the sixth, one

---

* The statistics of this paper were presented to the American Psychological Association in December, 1894, and an abstract was published in *The Psychological Review* for March, 1895. It was read in its present form as a lecture before the Philosophical Club of Yale University in 1897.

* 'Lippincott's Biographical Dictionary,' 'The Encyclopedia Britannica,' Rose's 'Biographical Dictionary,' 'Le dictionnaire de biographie generale,' Beaujeau's 'Dictionnaire biographique' and Brockhaus's 'Conversationaslexicon.' There is no biographical dictionary in German nor any encyclopedia as satisfactory as the Bratannies, neither do such works exist in Italian, Dutch or Scandinavian, otherwise it would have been desirable to have used them.

in the fifteenth, two in the sixteenth and three in the eighteenth century. The ten names last on the list are Otho, Sertorius, Macpherson, Claudian, Domitian, Begeaud, Charles I of Naples, Fauriel, Enfantin and Babeuf. These are scarcely great men, yet they fairly represent the lower limits of the thousand who are most eminent. Each hundred in the list shows a nice gradation in eminence. There are indeed many cases where each of us would shift a man up or down, but further examination will show that the opinion in such cases in usually individual, not having the objective validity of this series. I give for reference the thousand preeminent men of the world in the order of eminence, divided into groups of one hundred.

Napoleon, Shakespeare, Mohammed, Volatire, Bacon, Aristotle, Goethe, Julius Caesar, Luther, Plato, Napoleon III, Burke, Homer, Newton, Cicero, Milton, Alexander the Great, Pitt, Washington, Augustus, Wellington, Raphael, Descarte, Columbus, Confucius, Penn, Scott, Michelangelo, Socrates, Byron, Cromwell, Gautama, Kant, Leibnitz, Lock, Demosthenes, *Mary Stuart*, Calvin, Johnson, Robespierre, Frederick the Great, Aurelius, Hegel, Petracrch, Horace, Charles V. (Germany), Mirabeau, Erasmus, Virgil, Hume, Guizot, Gibbon, Pascal, Bossuet, Hobbes, Swift, Thiers, Louis XIV, Wordsworth, Louis XVI, Nelson, Henry VIII, Addison, Thuedides, Fox, Racine, Schiller, Henry IV. (France), W. Herschel, Tasso, Jefferson, Ptolemy Claudius, Augustine, Pope, Machiavelli, Swedenborg, Philip II, Leonardo da Vinci, George II, Julian, Pythagoras, Macaulay, Rubens, Burns, Mozart, Humboldt, Comte, Cousin, Cuvier, Justinian, Eripides, Camoens.

Talleyrand, Fenelon, Carlyle, Pius IX., Pitt, More, Hannibal, Spinoza, Chateaubriand, Abelard, Grant, Charles I (England), Darwin, Mazarin, Bolingbroke, *Elizabeth* (England), Ovid, *Joan d'Arc*, Livy, Corneille, Rabelais, Huss, a'Becket, d'Alembert, Grotius, Peter I., Polo, Linneus, Raleigh, Palmerston, Lamartine, Jos. Bonaparte, Tennyson, Plutarch, Charlemagne, Aristophanes, Melanchthon, St. Ambrose, Richelieu, James I. Hunter, Hugo, Disraeli, Dryden, Origen, Titian, Boccaccio, Alberoni, Lessing, Fichte, Condillac, Dickens, Wallenstein, Schelling, Durer, Charles XII., Kepler, Trajan, Knox, Constantine, La Fontaine, Van Dyck, Cervantes, *Steel*, Eippocrates, Louis XVIII, Clive, Rembrandt, Diderot, Cahucer, Montaigne, Napier, *Sand*, Marmont, Tiberius, Peel, Francis I (France), Nicholas I, William I, J. S. Mill, Sophocles, J. Adams, Webster, Athanasius, Bently, Savonarola, Marlborough, J. Cook, Seneca, Zwingle, Cavour, Buffon, Goldsmith, Brougham, Alexander VI, Gerson, Alexander I (Russia), Louis XV, R. Bacon, Pericles.

47

Herodotus, Hadrian, Davy, Frederick II (Germany), *Catherine II*, Conde, B. Jonson, Antony, Lucretius, Pompey, James II (England), Canning, Strafford, Mencius, La Fayette, A. Hamilton, Alfred the Great, Gassendi, Cortez, Beethoven, L. Bonaparte, Sevigne, Xenophen, Wycliffe, Alfieri, Charles X (France), Harvey, Marius, Juvenal, Firdousee, Gutenberg, Lope de Vega Carpio, La Place, Garibaldi, Necker, Froissart, Arias, Aeschylus, Etienne, Epicurus, Mithridates, Isocrates, Jerome, A. Jackson, Canova, Atterburty, Bulwer, Gay-Lussac, Wilhelm I (Prussia), Neibuhr, Fielding, George IV, Haller, Schleiermacher, J. Watt, St. Bernard, William III, Joinville, Arago, Fouche, Handel, Spenser, Lagrange, Herder, Velasquez, Bunsen, Alcibiades, De Foe, Hastngs, Colbert, Metternich, Richard I, Tertullian, Lamennias, Leo X, Cobden, Gustavus Adolphus, Wieland, Berkeley, Law, *Maintenon*, Cranmer, Coleridge, Chrysostom, Beza, Murat, Mazzini, Condorcet, Polybrius, Ariosto, Chatterton, Pliny (Elder), Turgot, Tacitus, Malebranche, John of England, Danton, Chalmers, Germanicus, Haydn.

St. Basil, William of Orange, Longfellow, Philip IV, Sully, Huygens, Louis XI, Montesquieu, Eugene, Charles II (England), Bernadotte, A. Severus, Klopstock, Innocent III, Zorcaster, Attila, G. Monk, A. Smith, Ney, Victor Emmanuel, Prescott, Pindar, Beranger, Gregory VII, Beaumarchais, Rossini, Bentham, Drake, Moreau, Faraday, Boetius, T. Moore, S. Clarke, Channing, Alexander II (Russia), *Maria Theresa*, Wagner, Priestley, *Josephine*, Thackeray, Copernicus, Blucher, Soult, Maximilian, Carnot, Philo, Averrocs, Calderon, Bolivar, Sulla, Ali-weli-zade, Le Sage, Heine, Boyle, Loyola, *Marie Antoinette*, Wesley, Poussin, Winckelnann, Turenne, R. B. B. Sheridan, Weber, W. Hamilton, Avicenna, Shaftesbury, Bright, Catullus, Boerhaave, C. Grey, Leopold I (Germany), W. Irving, Henry IV (Germany), Tamerlane, Massena, Retz, B. Constant, Reuchlin, Sainte-Beuve, Baxter, K. W. Humboldt, Jnner, Liebig, Philip II (Germany), Aquinas, Dumouriez, Murillo, Lucian, Agassi, Mehemet Ali, Wolsey, Solon, Jansen, Lavoisier, R. Walpole, Hogarth, Derby, Bichat, Sherman, Frederick W. III (Prussia), St. Simon.

Wilkes, Phidias, Philip Augusts, Mendelssohn, Boniface VIII, Cobbett, Bailey, Emerson, Joseph II (Germany), Russell, Vanban, Ferdinand V (Spain), Bayle, Archimedes, *Christina*, Scipio, Thou, T. Fairfax, Metastasio, Louis IX, L'Hopital, Marat, Guicciardini, Berzelius, Akbar, Sarpe, Varro, Armenius, Vergniaud, Bayard, Gregory I (Pope), Louis XIII, Beaton, Wilberforce, Tieck, Andrews, Lycurgus, O'Connell, Burnet, Reynolds, Seward, J. Franklin, Galen, A. Dumas, Alaric,

Campanella, Arnauld, Balzac, Plautus, a'Kempis, Richelieu, Pius VI, Terence, Charles VII (France), Renan, Pizarro, Henry II (England), Martial, Theodosius, R. Blake, J. J. Sealiger, Cardan, Cowper, Musset, Pius II, Villars, Helvetius, Belisarius, Candolle, W. Temple, Palestrina, Robertson, Strauss, Kotzebue, Bach, Madison, Hesiod, George I (England), Dupin, F. A. Wolf, St. Hillarie, Farragut, J. Q. Adams, Cato (Elder), Gluck, Grote, Cyrus, Bunyran, J. L. Grimm, L. Bonaparte, Antonius, Pius, Chesterfield, Pius VII, Leopardi, L. de Medici, Richard II, Gouvion St. Cyr, Gregory Naz, Warburton, Strabo.

Euclid, Desmoulins, *Genlis*, Clarendon, De Witt, Essex, Brahe, Eusebius, Mahmud II, Ferdinand VII (Spain), Frederick I (Germany), Euler, G. Howard, Reid, Gambetta, Ledru-Rollin, Lulli, Michaelis, Mahmud, Southey, Monge, Lucullus, Oersted, Hutten, Selden, Henry VI, Hawthorne, Villemain, Gall, Goldoni, Beaumont, Aguessesu, Beaubarnais, J. F. cooper, Catilins, Clement, J. B. Rousseau, Castlereagh, Fontanelle, Casaubon, Caellini, Charles VI (France), L. R. St. Simon, Lavater, Jacobi, Herod, *Margaret of Anjou*, Philip VI (France), Richter, Voss, Mackintosh, Lao-TAze, Paracelsus, Persius, Tehmistocles, J. C. Wolf, Ampere, George II (England), Huskisson, Aeschines, Albuquerque, Bruyere, Dalhousie, Suwaroff, Hampden, Coligni, Photius, Cudworth, Alva, Pufendorf, Rumford, Anderson, de Malherbe, *Mary*, J. B. Jourdan, Louis XII, Theodoric, Barrere, Titus, Ranke, Aurelian, *Gaskell*, T. Paine, Herbart, Lee, Phocion, *Mme. Roland*, Henry III (France), St. Pierre, Ingres, Warwick, Garrison, Erskine, Halley, Cato (younger), Gustavus I, Vasco da Gama, Maupertuis, Guyon, Courier.

Albertus Magnus, Boehme, E. T. W. Hoffmann, T. E. Hook, Marot, Henry I (England), Massillon, Quintilian, Monmouth, Maecenes, Philip V, Michelet, Luxembourg, Tintoretto, Vespucci, Saladin, G. Buchannan, Henry V (England), Butler, Anselm, Rochefouceauld, Charles the Bold, Manutius, Gustavus III, Cornelius, John of Austria, Delille, Adanson, Cherubini, Champollion, *Boleyn*, Ronsard, Meyerbeer, Ramus, Steele, Servetus, Orleans d'P., Gray, Josephus, Royer-Collard, F. C. M. Fourier, St. Francis, H. Clay, Gioberti, Desaix de Voygoux, Grattan, Monteccuculi, Sacy, Bruno, Paley, Jerome Bonaparte, Barras, Maury, De la Vigne, Ali (Ibn abi talib), Cavaignac, Cromwell, Charles d'Orleans, Sterne, Malesherbes, Middleton, Vico, Berthollet, *Janc Grey*, A. Sidney, Salmasius, Pliny (younger), MacDonald, Sallust, Saxo, Marmontel, Clarendom, Sylvester II, J. Taylor, Lamarck, Holbein, Henry VIII, Volta, Rosa, Whiston, Hatiy, Cyprian, A. Chenier, Dicoletian, *Pompadour*, J. Herschel,

Kaulbach, Poggio, Holberg, Miller, Henry IV (England), Oehlenschlager, Boden, Manes.

Sappho, Sarto, Anaxagoras, *Isabella of Castile*, A. W. Schlegel, Justin, Godoy, Epaminondas, P. Henry, Fulton, Dumont d'Urville, Garrick, Andrieu, Ginguene, Regnard, Du Gueselin, Wellesley, H. Vernet, *George Eliot*, Fuller, Heraclitus, Newman, Struensee, Thorwaldsen, *Cleopatra*, Zeno, Pouskin, E. Coke, Augereau, *Bronte*, Jerome of Prag., Aurungzebe, Vespasian, Philopoeman, VAnc, Jouffroy, Bonnet, Giotto, Agrippa, Alcuin, Gregory of Nyssa, Proudhon, Politian, Arndt, Freret, R. hall, Charles IX (France), *Anne*, Smollett, Demetrius Polior, Democritus, Gay, Cabanis, J. Flaxman, Gallatin, Fouquet, Cujas Guido Reni, C. S. Gracchus, Jeffreys, Gardiner, Oxenstierna, Kleber, Scipio, Mabillon, Lacepede, Stewart, Lyell, Rameau, Cassini, Lalande, Sumner, Parker, Plotinus, Cagliari, Lacordaire, *Marguerity d'Angoulene*, Kosciusko, P. H. Sheridan, Tocqueville, Hipparchus, Henry III (England), Whitegift, Rudolph I, de Volney, Jugurtha, Prior, Menage, Oken, Murray, Bellarmino, Churchill, Laffitte, Henry II (France), W. Jones, J. Owen, Cecil, Darius I, Charles Edward Stuart, Donizetti.

Hammer-Purgstall, J. L. David, Propertius, Boileau, Leighton, Correggio, Grouchy, Francke, Lysias, Lannes, Bonner, Pichegru, Brigena, Casanova, C. de Medici, Nadir (Shah), Whitefield, J. P. J. d'Orleans, Lucan, Teniers, Richard III, Apelles, Meckiewitz, Ximines, Sobieski, E. Irving, Stein, Hoche, Louvois, Saadi, *Montague*, Alfonso X., Scribe, Oudinot, Livingston, E. Herbert, K. W. F. Schlegel, Mariana, Rienzi, Sixtus V, Hahneman, Celsus, von Gentz, Deak, Pym, Gustavus IV, Monroe Gauss, Keats, C. Bell, Godwin, De la Croix, Charles VI (Germany), Edward IV, Ennius, Epictetus, Ferdinand II, Harold II, Zeno, Ficsole, Pestalozzi, Dundonald, Tippoo Sahib, Clovis, Huet, Maistre, Cagliostro, Ray, Malthus, Atticus, Barrow, Somers, Arkwright, Wren, Quinet, Nodier, Krlidener, Bede, Claude of Lorraine, Theocritus, L. Stanislaus, Hooker, P. Sidney, Muller, Maimonides, Odoacer, Henault, *Theresa*, Barthez, Espartero, Decazes, *Martineau*, T. Brown, Fermat, Agathocles, Empedocles, Charles V, Banks, Zinzendorf, Thierry.

T. S. Gracchus, Delambre, Caligula, Edward III (England), Richardson, Porphyry, Nicole, Waller, Balboa, Solyman, *Catherine de Medici*, La Harpe, Pole, Tharpes, *Marie de Medici*, Procopius, Lactanius, Borgia, Berengarius de Tours, Tallien, Camden, Armstrong, Jeffrey, Capo, Sismondi, R. Owen, Apuleius, St. Just, Spontini, W. Laud, Irenaeus, Lacretelle, J. B. Lulli, Paul I (Russia), Stilicho, Arbuthnot,

Dampier, Auber, Gregoire, Dolet, La Chaise, Francis II (Germany), Dolomieu, Aesop, F. M. Grimm, Dupuytren, M. J. Brutus, Feuerbach, Barnaveldt, Farel, Akenside, Prince Albert, Bouillon, Hanser, Frederick Wilhelm II (Prussia), Gerando, W. Wallace, Chamfort, Agrippa, Garat, Audubon, A. Doria, Harcreerce, Cowley, Heyne, Martinez, Petronius, *Hortense*, Mohammed II, Mai, Sue, J. Barry, Marivaux, Sebastian, Rotrou, W. Russell, Suchet, Paoli, Bopp, Romilly, Montalambert, John XXII, Rohan, Iamblicus, Bernhard, Simonides, Baggesen, Raspsil, Thomson, Louis I, Otho, Sertorius, Macpherson, Claudianus, Domitian, Bugeaud, Charles I (Naples), Fauriel, Enfantin, Babeuf.

The preparation of this list was incidental to the main purpose of my research, and I do not wish to lay undue stress upon it. Still it is of interest to find that we can compare and even measure a thing as intangible as the eminence of great men. We should not need to refer to such a list to decide whether Homer or Virgil is the more eminent; but it may satisfy that curiosity which is the beginning of science to know that there are to the best of our present knowledge twelve men more eminent than Homer and fifty-six men more eminent than Virgil. Further by reckoning the probable errors it is found that the chances are even that Homer's place on the list is between 10 and 26 and Virgil's is between 42 and 98.

But while our general knowledge apart from any such list as this may suffice to compare Homer with Virgil as accurately as is needful, this does not hold for men whose work is not readily comparable. Is Raphael, Descartes or Columbus the more eminent? As a matter of fact they stand respectively 22d, 23d, and 24th on the list and are equally eminent. I do not see how this result could have been reached from any general knowledge we may have of the work and fame of these men. Or again, Newton follows Homer and Hume follows Virgil on the list, consequently Newton is as much more eminent than Hume as Homer is than Virgil.

Things can be arranged in order more easily than they can be measured. We know that one sound is louder than another, though we may be unable to say whether it is more or less than twice as loud. We can arrange without much difficulty the examination papers of our students in the order of excellence, though unable to decide that one paper is twice as good as another. But the theory of probability makes even the measurement of the eminence of great men possible.

If all the men of the races and ages with which we are concerned were arranged in order, we might divide them into quarters. Supposing there to be one hundred million individuals in all from whom these men might have arisen, taking the adult male population of the countries and periods producing nearly all of them, we should have the end the 25 million least deserving of credit, including the defective and delinquent classes. Then we should have two groups each containing 25 million, one falling below and one rising above the average. These are the ordinary men who depart from the median by an amount less than the probable error. Then at the upper end we have the group of 25 million individuals who through some special trait or through a combination of traits rise above the others. At the extreme end of this group are the thousand preeminent men of our list.

What a man is and does is the result of innumerable influences, chiefly small and independent, some pulling him down and some lifting him up. In so far as this is the case, the men will be grouped together and depart from each other in a certain definite fashion. The matter can most readily be illustrated by taking a single trait such as height. If these men were placed in a row arranged according to height, the tops of their heads would form a curve of which an exaggerated form is given. In a general way the middle man would be of the average height, say 5 ft. 8 in., and a great part of all the men would be of nearly this height, one quarter being not more than 1 ½ inches shorter and one quarter not more than 1 ½ inches taller. The line of the heads would be nearly horizontal, but would gradually slope more and more, until at one end we should have the comparatively few dwarfs and at the other the few giants. These relations can be illustrated by the bell-shaped curve, whose properties are well known.

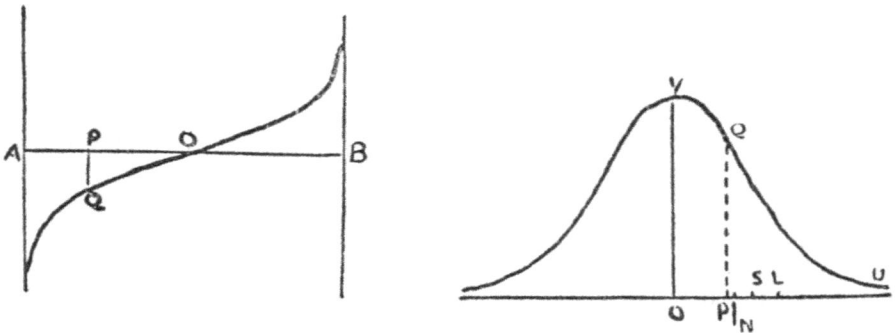

OGIVE AND THE BELL SHAPED CURVES SHOWING THE
DISTRIBUTION OF TRAITS

Five feet eight inches is the average height of men, and the number of men of that height (within say 1/10 in.) is proportional to the line OY. The number of men say

1 1/2 inches (within 1/10 in.) larger than the average by an amount equal to the probable error or 1 1/2 in. is proportional to the line *PQ*, and the number of men within these limits, one quarter of all the men, is proportional to the are *OTQP* which is one quarter the area of the curve. The number of men 6 ft. 2 in. in height—who depart from the mean by 6 in., or four times the probable error—would be *OU*, only 1/50 as many as are 5 ft. 9 1/2 in. in height, and but three in a thousand of all men would be taller than 6 ft. 2 in.

Now applying this to the collective traits giving efficiency, we have one half of all men coming within the limit *OP* which may be taken as a unit of measure. The total number of men surpassing the average by four times the amount of the average departure would be about 300,000. Most of us may hope to fall within this group. The thousand preeminent men filling the extreme area of the curve would begin at a point six times the average departure, and the relative excellence of the greater men on the list can also be expressed numerically.

Turning now to the distribution of these eminent men in time and race we may review statistics not wholly devoid of interest. The number of great men born in each half century since the beginning of history is shown in the accompanying curve. In still more remote ages there were leaders of men, gods, prophets and heroes, whose names are forgotten or obscured, and at the beginning we have four names, representing rather work than persons—Zoroaster, Homer, Hesiod, Lycurgas—followed by the rise of Greek civilization and culture—the most notable event in the world's history. Here we have a race as superior to us as we are to the negroes—a great race, for whose origin we can no more account than we can explain the birth of Shakespeare at Stratford-on-Avon. The curve shows the progress of the Greek race as represented by its great men—leaders then and now in war, in statesmanship, in philosophy, in literature, in art—and its more sudden decline in the third and second centuries before Christ. But the supremacy relinquished by the Greeks was grasped by the iron hand of the Romans, who in the centuries just before Christ rise rapidly and then fall. The relation of Greek to Roman civilization is shown in a separate figure.

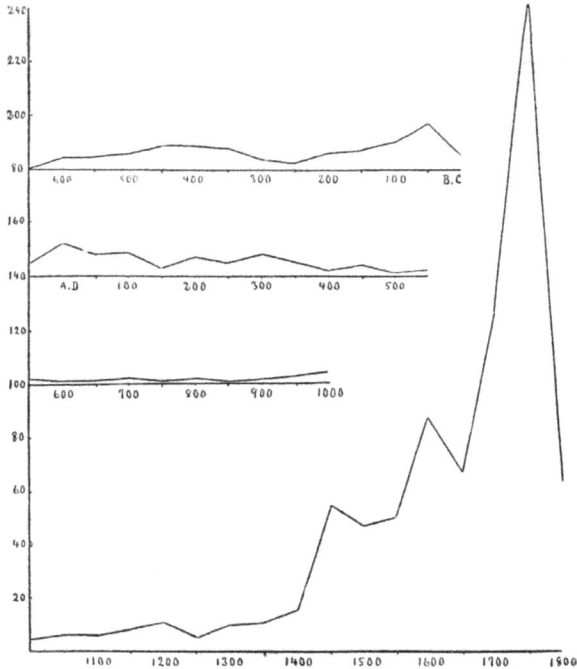

THE CURVE REPRESENTS THE DISTRIBUTION OF THE THOUSAND
MOST EMINENT MEN OF HISTORY FROM 600 B.C. TO THE FIRST
HALF OF THE NINETEENTH CENTURY.

The numbers are given on the left side, the ordinates of height of the curve above the base line representing the number of eminent men born in each half century. Thus there were five preeminent men born between 600 and 550 B.C. and 241 in the second half of the eighteenth century. As men attain eminence about fifty years later than they are born the periods of productivity are one place further to the right.

These curves—which of course give only a graphic representation of quantitative relations whose general character we all know—indicate that heredity, including under the term both stability and variability of the stock, is more potent than social tradition or physical environment. We have these races forming by their own inherent genius a social environment far beyond anything the world had ever witnessed, but when this was at its maximum it had not power to counteract the weakening influence of race admixture and exhaustion of the stock. The physical environment also remained the same, and those who would account for Greek and Roman culture by the favorable position of the two Mediterranean peninsulas—their climate, soil, coast line and the like—should tell us why these could not maintain what they had formed. Why should the Greeks then have resisted the countless hordes of Persia, while recently on the same ground they fled before a few thousand Turks? Physical environment and social tradition may be conditions of development, but they are not its efficient causes.

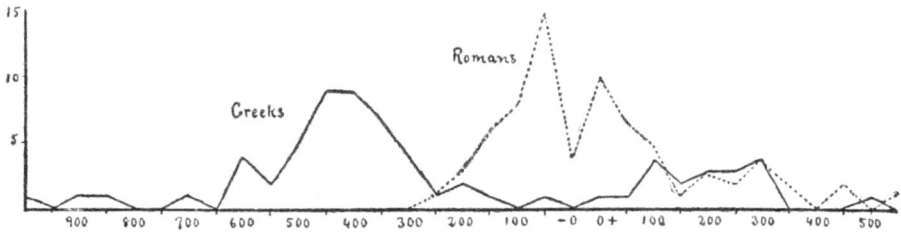

THE CURVES SHOW THE DISTRIBUTION OF EMINENT MEN IN THE GRECO-ROMAN PERIOD.

Following the extraordinary development of the two nations of classical antiquity we have a decline, not sudden, for Rome still produced soldiers and writers, the Christian Church had its leaders and theologians, and the Greeks witness their Indian summer in Alexandria. But the light fails toward the fifth century—never, however, to be quenched, for there were always one or two to pass on the torch until the fire was rekindled in newer races. In Britain, in Germany and in France there developed centers of civilization. The mixed races of Italy gave birth to an art and a literature rivaling that of Greece. The Roman Catholic Church fairly established its authority by the great men in produced. It was a strange time, all Europe was in turmoil, but university were established and the arts of peace flourished in the midst of wars.

The curve shows a rise from the tenth century increasing in rapidity as it proceeds. As the list includes only men no longer living, and as many of those born during the first half of the nineteenth century were still living and had not even attained eminence when the books of reference on which the list is based were compiled, the absolute numbers of those born since 1800 have no value, but they serve for comparison.

The increase in eminent men as we approach our own day may be partly a matter of perspective. Still the numbers should normally increase with larger population

55

and multiplication of opportunity and interests. It is unfortunately very difficult to compare the number of great men with the total population from which they arose. Were a curve of this sort drawn, however, it would be very different from that here exhibited. The rise in modern times would be much less; and the Greek and Roman periods would surpass that of the end of the eighteenth century.

In our curve there are three noticeable breaks. Perhaps nothing could serve better than such a curve to impress on the minds of school children, or even on our own, the eddies in the stream. It must be remembered that the curves give the numbers of men born in each half century, while the period in which they flourished is about fifty years later. Thus in the fourteenth century there was a pause followed by a gradual improvement and an extraordinary fruition at the end of the fifteenth century. Painting is represented in Italy by Raphael, Angelo, Leonardo, Titian, Correggio, and Sarto, in Germany by Holbein and Durer. Savonarola failed, while Luther led a reformation. Columbus discovered a new world and Copernicus discovered innumerable worlds. There was then a pause in progress, until a century later England and France took the lead. Spenser was quickly followed by Shakespeare, who did not stand alone among English dramatists. A little later Moliere, Racine and Corneille represented the drama in a group of eminent French men of letters. Descartes and Bacon revived philosophy and science; while Italy, failing in art, produced Galileo.

The latter part of the seventeenth century was a sterile period, followed by a revival culminating in the French revolution. Here, as in other periods, it is difficult to decide how far men were made eminent by circumstance and how far great men were leaders in new movements. The social upheaval in France gave eminence to political and military leaders who otherwise would have remained in obscurity, and given a Napoleon his complement is a Wellington. The progress of science may in part be an answer to the demands of increasing population. But philosophy and art also witnessed a renaissance. In Germany we have Kant, Goethe and the development of music, in England, poets speaking a new language. Here great men seem not so much the creatures as the creators of their environment.

As we come nearer to our own times it becomes increasingly difficult to measure tendencies by the methods we are using. The positions of men on the list are subject to larger probable and constant errors. Byron may be a household word on the continent and Shelley unknown, while the best criticism may place Shelley above Byron. Our list places Mendelssohn above Bach and ignores Schumann altogether—while the last thirty years have altered not only critical opinion, but also popular taste.

If we regard now more especially the racial distribution of our great men, we get results conveniently exhibited in the accompanying figure. The heights of the rectangles are proportional to the number of great men produced by several nations. France leads, followed pretty closely by Great Britain. Then there is a considerable fall to Germany and Italy. Rome and Greece are nearly alike. America has produced one more eminent man than Spain (not on the chart) which is followed by Switzerland, Holland, and Sweden. We then reach the nations headed by Russia, which have produced fewer than 10 preeminent men. The shaded rectangles show the distribution of the 500 men who are the most eminent and the heavily shaded rectangles the hundred who are the greatest of all. Here the relations are somewhat altered. Great Britain surpasses France, and Greece has produced more exceptionally great men than Germany.[*]

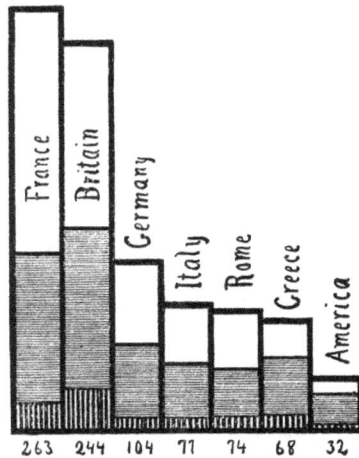

THE RECTANGLES ARE PROPORTIONAL TO THE NUMBERS OF THE MOST EMINENT MEN PRODUCED BY DIFFERENT NATIONS.

The shaded parts represent the more eminent five hundred, and the heavily shaded parts the hundred most eminent of all.

We have already noticed the curves showing separately the Greek and Roman periods. Similar curves for the leading modern nations are given in the chart. The Italian

---

[*] These relations are somewhat dependent on the authorities collated; their validity may be assigned by the calculation of probable errors, but there may be a constant error due to the fact that the collation of names depends chiefly on French and Anglo-Saxon standards.

renaissance is followed by its decadence with a partial revival in recent times. Germany for one short period in the fifteenth century rivaled France and England, but in the two following centuries lagged far behind, to rise with great rapidity in the eighteenth century. France and Great Britain, as we have seen, have produced nearly the same number of great men, and their curves during the centuries cross and recross. The British curve is somewhat more regular than the French, exhibiting perhaps certain racial characteristics. As has been already stated, the French revolution brought into prominence many men not truly great, and the position then attained by France is not held in the nineteenth century. In so far as the curves for the nineteenth century are valid, the promise for America is large. We should during the twentieth century produce more notable men than any other nation. It is ill for us, having the largest population and the richest resources, if we do not keep this promise.

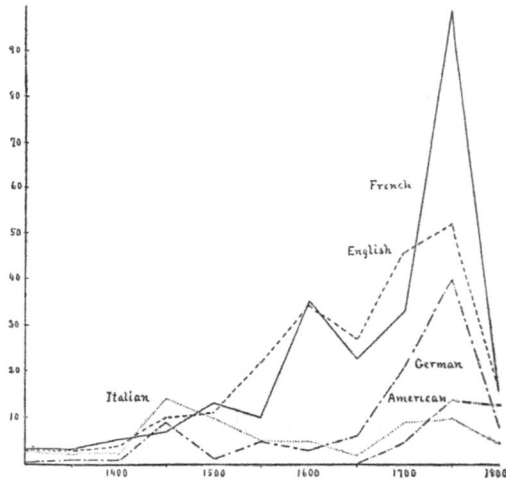

THE CURVES SHOW THE PRODUCTION OF GREAT MEN AT
DIFFERENT PERIODS BY SEVERAL OF THE LEADING NATIONS.

Our racial divisions are given to us ready made. The subject becomes more difficult when we try to class eminent men in accordance with their traits. We can, however, perhaps use the tripartite subdivision current in psychology. There we are apt to treat separately cognitions, feelings and volitions. This classification proves useful when applied to the traits of great men. Some excel because they have strong wills, are quick and sure in action. These become leaders in war and in political affairs. Others have strong feelings—artists, poets, men of letters. Others surpass in pure thought—philosophers, scholars, men of science. Distinguishing then men of action, men of feeling, and men of thought, we secure the curves shown on the accompanying chart. It is seen that more men are eminent for action than for either thought or feeling, though if the latter two classes are combined it is found that the quiet work of the student has after all produced more eminent men than war and politics. Each class shows an increase as we approach our own time and the secular variations affect them together, though it is noticeable that men of thought have been much more constant in their appearance and bid fair to surpass the others in the twentieth century.

In passing I may state that modern psychology does not admit that we can divide mental processes into such as are cognitions, such as are feelings and such as are volitions, any more than we can divide physical bodies into such as have size, such as have color and such as have weight, but must rather regard these as aspects of all mental processes. So with our great men—if a man excels in action he probably is not deficient in feeling and judgment—on the contrary these are probably strong. My statistics show, contrary perhaps to the current opinion, that a man who excels in one direction is likely also to excel in others. An artist is much more likely to be a poet than is an ordinary man and is, though in a less degree, more likely to be a soldier or a man of science.

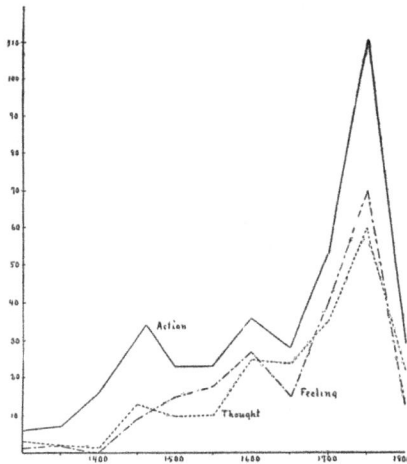

THE CURVES SHOW THE RELATIVE NUMBERS OF MEN OF ACTION, MEN OF THOUGHT, AND MEN OF FEELING AT DIFFERENT PERIODS.

59

Curves showing further subdivisions are also given. From the upper chart it is clear that there have been more eminent statesmen than soldiers, especially since the beginning of the eighteenth century. Soldiers are also surpassed in numbers by men of science and our curves foretell the gradual cessation of wars. Churchmen and theologians are of decreasing importance in human affairs. It is interesting to note that the sterility at the end of the seventeenth century and the subsequent revival hold for nearly every separate department. Fiction and belles-lettres make the only exception, their growth in the seventeenth and eighteenth centuries continued in the nineteenth century, and the number of prose writers, novelists, essayist and the like, who attained eminence in the past century, surpasses that in any other department. Any librarian can confirm this by telling what books are most read. Poetry and art seem to be failing. Next to politics and belles-lettres, science occupies the most important place.

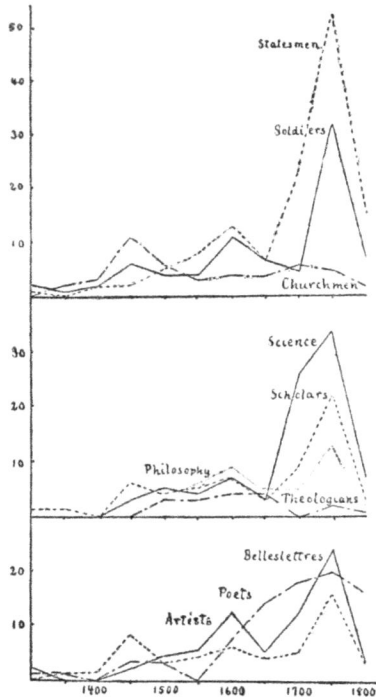

THE CURVES SHOW THE DISTRIBUTION OF MEN OF ACTION, MEN OF THOUGHT AND MEN OF FEELING, SEPARATED INTO GROUPS FOR DIFFERENT LINES OF ACTIVITY.

The first five hundred were separated from the five hundred less eminent men, but they were found to be nearly equally divided in the different classes, except that there are more very great poets and fewer very great men of letters.

The accompanying chart shows the contributions of different nations to different departments. It is evident that France has excelled in war, in belles-lettres and in science—England in politics, in poetry and in philosophy—Italy in art. Germany has produced ten and Italy six of the eighteen great musician. Of the fourteen great explorers England has produced five and Spain four.

There are two somewhat anomalous classes of eminent men which I have not as yet mentioned. Hereditary sovereigns and those made eminent purely by circumstance. The hereditary sovereigns included are of course only the more eminent, 102 in all, but they can not be compared with the other classes. Only eight have been included under the class of those eminent by circumstance, of whom Casper Hauser is typical—but several others, especially the wives of kings, might be placed there.

I have spoken throughout of eminent men as we lack in English words including both men and women, but as a matter of fact women do not have an important place on the list. They have in all 32 representatives in the thousand. Of these eleven are hereditary sovereigns and eight are eminent through misfortunes, beauty or other circumstances. Belles-lettres and fiction—the only department in which woman has accomplished much—give ten names (of which three are in the first 500) as compared with 72 men. Sappho and Joan d'Arc are the only other women on the list. It is noticeable that with the exception of Sappho—a name associated with certain fine fragments—women have not excelled in poetry or art. Yet these are the departments least dependent on environment and at the same time those in which the environment has been perhaps as favorable for women as for men. Women depart less from the normal than man—a fact that usually holds for the female throughout the animal series; in many closely related species only the males can be readily distinguished. The distribution of women is represented by a narrower bell-shaped curve.[*]

---

[*] Since the above was written Professor Karl Pearson has questioned the lesser variability of woman. The matter can only be decided by facts; these statistics certainly show greater variability for the male.

61

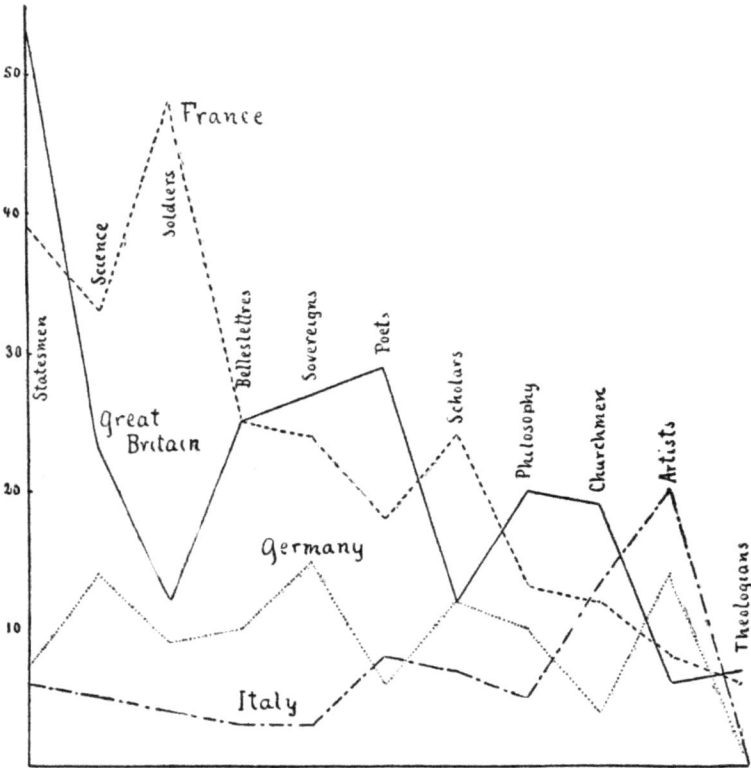

THE CURVES SHOW THE RELATIVE CONTRIBUTION OF
DIFFERENT NATIONS TO DIFFERENT LINES OF ACTIVITY.

This paper is only preliminary to the real object of my research. We have many books and articles on great men, their genius, their heredity, their insanity, their precocity, their versatility and the like, but, whether these are collections of anecdotes such as Professor Lombroso's or scientific investigations such as Dr. Galton's, they are lacking in exact and quantitative deductions. Admitting that genius is hereditary, or, what is more doubtful, that it is likely to be associated with insanity, we have only the 'yes' or 'no' as our answer. But this is only the beginning of science. Science asks how much? We can only answer when we have an objective series of observations, sufficient to eliminate chance error, such as this list of a thousand preeminent men.

When we have such a series we can use what psychological insight we possess to classify our material. We can seek to distinguish genius from talent, and, having given these terms a more exact signification, can secure quantitative data regarding their relative frequency under varying conditions. We can determine how the man of unusual endowment in its various manifestations differs from his fellow men, both in those traits which distinguish him from them and in those traits which he shares with them. With traits that can be measured such as length of life, height, etc., we can readily compare the several classes of eminent men with other classes in the community. In the case of other traits, insanity for example, we must first determine its prevalence, according to a proper definition, in the various classes of eminent men and can then give a definite statement as to its relative frequency among them and a comparison with other classes. Other more intangible traits I am also endeavoring to measure. Qualities such as originality or kindliness are graded on a scale of eight, mistakes are eliminated by the numbers and we secure fairly reliable averages. The different classes of eminent men can then be compared *inter se*, and with other classes of the community, when the data for these are at hand. Then we have the distinctions on which I have already dwelt. We can only determine the causes of great men and their effects by a careful study of a number sufficiently large to eliminate accidental causes and errors in our estimate; but having done this, our results can be expressed in the definite measures of exact science.

In conclusion attention may be called to the practical importance of such determinations. Science must precede the applications of science. The father must discover the laws of the pendulum before the son can apply them to the clock. A Faraday and a Henry must investigate the phenomena of electricity before we can have the electric motor. It is evident that applications of psychology and sociology are not as yet numerous or important. But may not this be chiefly because the scientific principles are wanting? Education and government are carried on by the rule of thumb, not because this is the best way, but because we lack the knowledge to prescribe a better way. The struggle for existence, careless of the individual, proceeds with reckless waste of life, and it is only the fit that survives, and not what we regard as the best. The Chinese civilization of the age of Confucius was more stable than that of classical Greece. The progress to our present civilization may have depended largely on the comparatively few men who have guided it, and the civilization we hope to have may depend on a few men. Can we not with the knowledge we have and with the knowledge we should acquire do more to produce such men, to select them, to train them and to use them?

63

We can not perhaps apply the methods of horticulture to society, nor carry Plato's Republic into effect. But great men tend to be proportional in numbers to the total populations producing them and to the average of the stock. If we can improve the stock by eliminating the unfit or by favoring the endowed—if we give to those who have and take away from those who have not even that which they have—we can greatly accelerate and direct the course of evolution. If the total population, especially of the well endowed, is larger, we increase the number of great men. We should make sure that all are given such preliminary education and opportunity that none fail through lack of these. Lastly great men and also the well endowed should be so placed that their abilities are not spent on trivial or selfish ends.

We may have still stocks that are immature—the Slavs, the Czechs and the Scandinavians—and there is a possibility of vitality in the negroes. But we have finally broken the links between us and the lower animals. When our stock is exhausted when there are no longer variations towards what we regard as advance, then for thousands of years the human race may be dependent on the social tradition now set. We are perhaps beginning to fail in art and in poetry, but for a century or more science and its applications will probably be at their maximum. What is accomplished during this short period must be either the foundation for a new stock or the endowment policy for a long old age.

Wells, F.L. (1909). Sex differences in the tapping test: An interpretation. *The American Journal of Psychology, 20*(3), 353-363

SEX DIFFERENCES IN THE TAPPING TEST: AN INTERPRETATION

By FREDERIC LYMAN WELLS, Ph.D., Assistant in Pathological Psychology in the McLean Hospital, Waverley, Mass.

While it is doubtful if we ought to attach to the speed of repeated voluntary movements the fundamental significance accorded to it by some of its earlier investigators, certain sex differences have appeared in the writer's experience with the test that would seem to justify a brief presentation. The subjects whose results form the basis of the present discussion are ten men and ten women, with two exceptions nurses in the McLean Hospital, and of corresponding age and environmental level. It would be very difficult under other conditions than the present to equal these groups of subjects in homogeneity, co-operativeness, and unaccustomedness to the conditions of psychological experiment. For this reason, a significance may perhaps be attached to the present results which the limited number of subjects might otherwise largely vitiate.

The experiment with the ten men have already been described in detail,[1] and those with the ten women are essentially similar. Two experiments are performed with each subject, each consisting of five 30" series of tapping with each hand, the right hand preceding in the first experiment and the left hand receding in the second experiment. From the results of these experiments as performed, we derive various functions, the principal ones with which we are here concerned being as follows: The relation to each other, in respect to gross rate, of five successive 30" series of tapping with the same hand, the series being separated by rest intervals of 2'30".

The gross fatigue effect, as given in the "index of fatigure", (f) which index is derived by dividing the average number of taps in the last five 5" intervals (25" of tapping) by the number in the first 5" interval. The fatigue curve, or curve of the decrease in the number of taps executed during the six successive 5" intervals of a 30" series.

---

[1] *American Journal of Psychology*, XIX, 1908, pp. 437 ff.

The relation of the right hand to the left hand, as given in the "index of right-handedness" which is the average number of taps executed in five successive 30" series by the left hand, divided by the corresponding average for the right. The higher this index, the better the left hand in proportion to the right; above 1.00 the left is absolutely superior to the right. The mean variation of successive experiments in the same individual, *i.e.*, the constancy of his results to each other.

We shall first examine those aspects of the results concerned with differences in the average of performance, and later those functions which deal with the relative variability of the sexes about the averages.

The previous researches which afford material for the study of sex differences in the tapping rate are concerned mainly with children and adolescents. While they do not maintain absolute correspondence, their general indication is that the boys are faster than the girls, and that the sex difference increases with age, so that we should expect to find here a consistent superiority of the men over the women.

The actual results are best presented in the form of curves, which give the total number of taps executed in each of five successive 30" series of tapping. The continuous lines represent the tapping rates of the men, the dotted lines those of the women; the right and left hands, and first and second experiments being as indicated on the curves themselves. Thus in the first series of the first experiment with the right hand, the men execute 192.3 taps, the women 199.4; in the fifth (and last) series of the second experiment with the left hand, the men have 175.1 taps, the women 170. The curves give the fluctuations in rate from series to series. (Plate I.)

Briefly, the women surpass the men in the performance of the right hand in the first experiment. Elsewhere they are inferior, and they are much more inferior in the second experiment than in the first. The women are more favored in the first experiment, by virtue of its being the first, than the men, and they lose more in the second experiment, as such, than the man. The first experiment represented the first contact of any of the subjects with the test. There is thus of course a primary *Neuigkeilsantrieb* which is absent in the second experiment. This scarcely affects the men at all; indeed, their second experiment is as a whole somewhat better than the first. On the other hand, the women are in the second experiment markedly inferior to their first performance, in the absence of this *Neuigkeilsantrieb*.

There is a corresponding sex difference in the fluctuation in rate of the successive series, as illustrated in the curves. Just as the first experiment has a special

Neuigkeilsantrieb, so is there a secondary *Anfangsantrieb* in the first series of each record of either hand. If the curves are examined, it will be seen that this first series is, relatively to the rest of the curve, very much higher in the women than in the men; *i.e.*, the women also indicate more strongly the presence of this secondary *Anfangsantrieb*. The indication of *Schlussantrieb* at the conclusion of each experiment (the last series with the left hand in the first experiment, and that with the right hand in the second) is also more marked in the women.

PLATE I

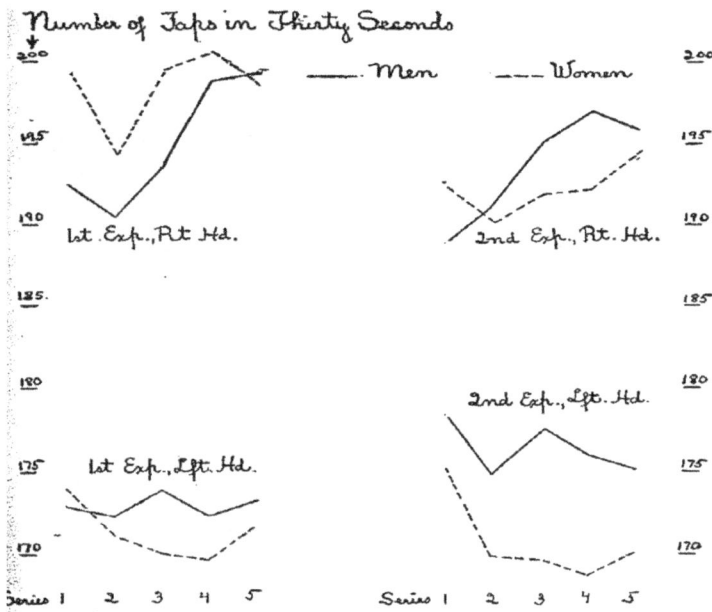

As regards susceptibility to fatigue, previous studies, while differing somewhat from the present in manner of calculation, leave a slight balance of probability in favor of the men as the less susceptible to fatigue. As given in terms of the *f*, the present experiments average as follows:

Comparative *f*'s of the two groups.

	R1	R2	L1	L2
Men	.90	.91	.88	.90
Women	.90	.91	.87	.89

(In the tables, R1, R2, L1, L2 will be employed to indicate the first and second experiments with the right and left hands respectively.)

That is, the last 25" tapping averages from 87% to 91% as fast as the first 5". There is no immediate sex difference worth mentioning, especially when we find that the mean variations average about .03. Such infinitesimal differences as exist are in favor of greater fatigue immunity for the men. It is noticeable that in both men and women the left hand is more susceptible to fatigue than the right, and the first experiment more so than the second, this latter presumably a manifestation of less *Antrieb* in the second experiment.

The writer has previously mentioned that in the tapping test the fatigue phenomenon seemed remarkably independent of the fatigue sensation accompanying the work. This generalization was based on experiment with men only, and the results with the women do not bear it out so well.[2] Each of the women was asked whether sensations of fatigue were present, and if so, in which hand they were more prominent; it being then noted whether greater fatigue sensations on one side corresponded with greater fatigue phenomena on that side. The results were as follows.

Sensations of Fatigue	*Phenomena of Fatigue*
None	No significant difference
Equal	Equal
Only in left	More in left
More in left	More in left
More in left	No significant difference
More in left	No significant difference
More in left	More in left
More "tension" in right	More in left
More in right	Equal
Probably more in right	More in left

---

[2] The experiments with the men antedate those with the women by about a year.

We obtain a positive relation in five cases, four are equivocal, and one is negative. This correspondence, while by no means good, is rather better than seems to obtain among the men, though the inquiries with them were not so systematic. If there is a sex difference here, *i.e.*, in that the women's introspective account of fatigue sensation shows a better correspondence with the actual fatigue phenomena than that of men, its most reasonable interpretation would seem to be that the women's performance is more influenced by fatigue sensation. It should be mentioned that subsequent features in the results on fatigability bear out this interpretation.

PLATE II

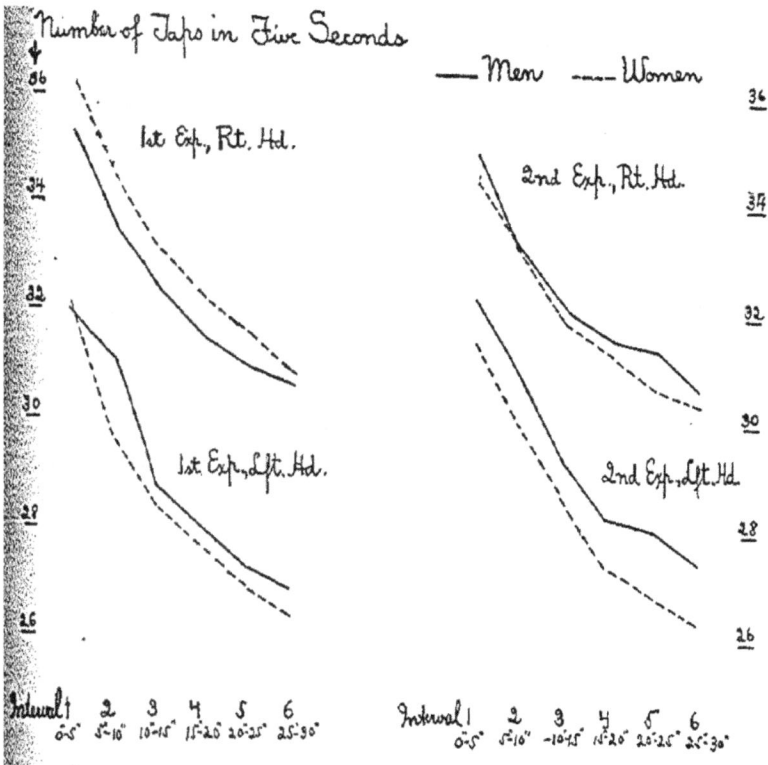

The accompanying cut shows the fatigue curves of the right and left hands in each experiment, the curves of the two groups of subjects being superposed. As previously, the continuous lines are the records of the men, the dotted lines those of the women. The curves are of the ordinary shape and show no characteristic sex difference in form. The relative inferiority of the women in the second experiment, already mentioned, is again evident. Another sex difference may be mentioned here, namely that the women are more inferior to the men with the left hand than with the right, *i.e.*, the right and left hands are farther apart in the women than the men. In the gross, this difference is best expressed in the index of righthandedness, which averages as follows in the two experiments.

	1st Experiment	2nd Experiment
Men	.89	.91
Women	.87	.89

In both groups the index is higher in the second experiment than in the first; *i.e.*, the preceding hand is more favored as such. The writer has previously mentioned this as a normal property of the test; but it is more probably related to *Anfangsantrieb* than to any generalized fatigue effect upon the following hand. It is seen also that the index is throughout lower in the women, the difference being just at the limits of probable error. This shows again that for this function there is more bilateral asymmetry, the right and left hands are farther apart, in the women than in the men.

Up to the present we have been dealing with averages only, reserving the mean variations for separate discussion, since these have a special bearing upon the question of sex differences. It seems to be very generally accepted that at least in most aspects, individual differences tend to be greater in men than in women, and it may be worthwhile to examine the data from this point of view. Only the mean variations need to be presented, since it would be hardly possible to consider the more minute features of the problem of variability from a basis of ten cases of each group.

In initial rate, *i.e.*, the rate for the first 5", as well as in gross rate, *i.e.*, rate for the whole series of 30", the mean variations of the different groups are as follows.

	R_1		R_2		L_1		L_2	
	5"	30"	5"	30"	5"	30"	5"	30"
Men	3.3	14.0	3.9	14.3	3.0	17.6	3.5	15.9
Women	2.8	14.3	2.1	13.8	2.3	13.2	2.8	14.6

The women are practically throughout less variable than the men. In the m. v. of the gross rate (30") this difference is not so well marked, and for a reason that is worth analysis. Attention has already been called to the fact that there was in the men a marked tendency for fatigue to decrease the individual differences. This tendency is also present in the women, but very much less so than in the men; indeed, at the end of the 30" the variability of the two sexes is practically equal. Under fatigue, the individual differences of the women become relatively greater than those of the men.

As it previously appeared that there was no characteristic sex difference in the average of the f's, so were we fail to find it in their variability. The mean variations of the f's are practically the same in men and women throughout. As may however be inferred from what has just receded, this equality is purely superficial; the f itself shows no sex difference, but both of its factors (the first and the remaining five intervals) do. Inasmuch as the women are to a certain extent less variable in the initial interval, if they continued to be equally so throughout the rest of the fatigue curve, the m. v. of the f's would show equally the smaller variability of the women; but inasmuch as we find the variability of the f's equal, or nearly so, it follows that the fatigue curves of the women have under fatigue gradually increased in variability relatively to those of the men.

Absolutely, the fatigue curves of the women (whose average is given in the cuts on p. 357) resemble each other in from somewhat the more closely, as is indicated in the fact that in the women the mean variations of the successive 5" intervals are consistently smaller than those of the men. It is in this, an important aspect of the results, that smaller variability of the women is the most unequivocally illustrated. The average m. v.'s of the six successive intervals in the two experiments for the men and women are as follows:

	R_1	R_2	L_1	L_2
Men	2.4	3.0	2.4	2.7
Women	2.1	1.9	2.3	2.4

In view of what has been said, however, it is more than probable that at the end of 60" of tapping the variability of the women would exceed that of the men.

It was noted previously that the right and left hands are farther apart in the women than in men. It is also observable that the difference between the right and left hands is more variable in the women than in the men, the figures being as follows.

71

	1st Experiment	2nd Experiment
Men	.035	.033
Women	.047	.041

The relationship of the two hands in these experiments is affected mainly by the matter of precedence of either hand in the test. We saw that this factor affected the tapping rates of the women somewhat more than those of the men, and we see here that it also affects them more variably than those of the men.

As an aspect of the same general result, it may be noted that the day to day variability in gross rate was in the women strikingly greater than in the men. Taking the mean variation of the two experiments performed for each hand in each subject, we obtain for the two experiments the following results in the men and the women.

	Right	Left
Men	1.6	3.5
Women	3.4	3.9

That is, the first and second experiments differed much more from each other in the women than in the men. (*Cf.* p. 354).

Considered individually, one could attach no special significance to these data as isolated facts; and it is much more reasonable to regard them as secondary to other characters of sex difference having a more fundamental value. The results are best discussed in their relation to two such characters, which may be cited according to Havelock Ellis, as the less variability of women, and the greater affectability of women. The latter is perhaps the most fundamental sex difference that exists on the psychical side, and indeed, were it not so apparent to everyday observation in general, it could be asserted positively for the group of subjects immediately concerned. This being the case, we must expect that the affective factor in every feature of the experimental conditions will influence the performance of the women to a significantly greater extent than it will those of the men. And in review of the points of sex difference previously mentioned, it seems that, as the sex difference appear most markedly in those features of the experiments in which the affective element is the most prominent, so are these differences most reasonably interpreted as the expression of this fundamental sex difference in affectability. It is, of course, possible to construct other hypotheses which will cover the various points of difference observed; but it is a precarious logical system which interprets with a variety of assumptions a series of observations referable to a known fact.

To this we must add, that besides being more affectable, the women were much more variable in their affectability than the men. This was clearly observable in the differences of experimental attitude. The women went at the test in much less of a routine manner; they more frequently evidenced desire to examine and understand the apparatus, and were more likely to express concern as to the object and outcome of the tests, and regarding future experiments. The men showed a more uniform behavior in these respects than did the women, and their attitude toward the test was in general a more "objective" one. Among the women a varying amount of persuasion was occasionally demanded; but it was always apparent that the subjects were really co-operative, and that the seeming inadequacy was wholly the product of an exaggerated affective reaction to the unaccustomed conditions of the experiment.

There are operative in these experiments four special affective influences: the precedence of the hands in the experiment, the sensations of fatigue, the use of the preferred or unpreferred hand, and the relative novelty of the test. The sex differences are marked principally according to the amount which these factors influence the special aspect of the results under consideration.

To particularize, the women are much more susceptible to the influences of *Antrieb* than are the men. The *Anfangsantrieb* of the inception of the experiments was illustrated in the record of the preceding right hand in the first experiment and perhaps even more strikingly so in the second experiment with the preceding left hand. As between the successive 30" series, the influence of a secondary *Anfangsantrieb* is apparent in that the first series in the men. The apparent failure of the women to bear up so well under fatigue sensations indicates a heightened responsiveness to an affect of the opposite character.

If the greater difference between the right and left hands in the women is significant, an analogous interpretation is possible in that we perhaps try harder in doing what we expect to do better. The subjects naturally expect to do better with the right hand, and so try harder with it the women, on an average, harder than the men. In a more affectable group, the hands might thus appear, in general, farther apart.

There are certain features of the test which we should hardly expect to be influenced by these differences in affectability, and which in fact do not seem to be so. The individual differences in tapping rate are slightly greater in the men than in the women, and the form of the fatigue curve is also more constant in the men, though it tends to become less so. Here we seem to have a sex difference referable rather to the generally lesser variability of women, already mentioned as a fundamental sex difference. In the remaining results, however, we find this general tendency toward lesser variability in women in conflict with the special factor of the greater affective variability of the women, and we shall find that in these cases, this latter factor is sufficiently potent to more than offset the other, so that the final figures show from almost every viewpoint, a lesser variability of the men.

Mention has been made of the fact that under fatigue the individual differences of the women do not show the same tendency to decrease as those of the men. As we previously judged the women to be more responsive to sensations of fatigue than the men, we now find them to vary more in their responsiveness to them than the men, the former being an aspect of the women's greater affectability, the latter of their greater affective variability. And as we found the right and left hands to be farther apart in women than in men, so now we find the index of righthandedness to be more variable in women than in men; the greater difference a product of greater affectability, the greater variability of the difference a product of the greater affective variability.

The greatest affective difference that is objectively given in these tests is perhaps that between the first and second experiments; certainly the sex difference is very well marked here, the women being relatively much better in the first experiment than in the second. The women respond readily to the *Neuigkeilsantrieb* of the first experiment, and miss more strongly the interest of novelty in the second; a more even experimental attitude is indicated in the men.

To briefly recapitulate, no immediate sex difference was indicated in the absolute rate of tapping, in the gross amount of fatigue loss during the 30" period, or in the form of the curve of this fatigue loss. More detailed examination of the results, however, indicated sex difference as follows:

The women relatively surpass the men in those periods of work most likely to be subject to special *Antriebe*.

The introspective accounts of the fatigue sensations given by the women agree better with the objective fatigue phenomena than those of the men seem to do; hence the women are probably more influenced by fatigue sensation than the men.

The right and left hands are farther apart in women than in men.

In initial rate (5") the women are considerable less variable, in the gross rate (30") slightly less variable than the men.

In the 30" work period employed, the shape of the work curve is considerable less variable in the women than in the men, but the women show a tendency to relatively increasing variability under fatigue. (*Cf.* 2.)

The relationship of the right and left hands is more variable in the women than in the men.

The first and second experiments differ more from each other in the women than in the men.

The above sex differences are found mainly in those features of the experiment which especially involve the affective factor in the subject's attitude; and they are manifestations of the greater responsiveness of the women to this affective element. When this factor is not especially involved, the individual differences of the women tend to be less than those of the men; but when it is involved they are greater, illustrating not only the presence of greater affect among the women, but also the greater variability of this affect. Thus the differences found are not fundamental sex differences, but are secondary to certain differences in temperament; and in a group of subjects in which these temperamental differences were by any chance reversed, we should expect to see the experimental differences also reversed.

It is very possible that a practiced experiment can interpret these temperamental differences in the subjective attitude from observations of the general behavior under experimental conditions more reliably than through the crude introspection of a naïve subject. And though introspective accounts of the subjective attitude often seems to add little enough to the significance of the experiment, we might still be exposed to grave error in concluding from this that the subjective attitude does not still influence the results of such observations to a marked degree. In the foregoing, it has been endeavored to indicate the extent to which certain rather elementary motor functions might be influenced by what is perhaps the most important single factor in the subjective attitude, its susceptibility to affective influences.

Rentoul, R.R. (1910-11). Sterilising the insane. *ER*, *2*, 74-76.

DISCUSSION

STERILISING THE INSANE

For some time past I have advocated the sterilisation of the insane; my voice has been like a voice in the wilderness. On January 1st, 1909, there were, in England and Wales, no fewer than 128,787 officially certified insane: with an increase of 2,703 in the year. But there are a great many at large who are not "officially" reported. In 1859 there were only 36,762 certified insane.

The insane rate since then has increased by 250 per cent., while the population has increased by 81 per cent., and evidently—judging by our "do nothing" policy—we are quite content to go on marrying and breeding more and more degenerates; and to expend yearly millions of pounds sterling upon these—an expenditure which gives us no results.

In 1903 I proposed (among other points) that we should make it illegal for anyone to join in marriage, idiots, imbeciles, feeble-minded, epileptics, habitual criminals, and vagrants. I also suggest that these poor products of our civilisation and Christianity should be so surgically operated upon—sterilised—that they would neither become fathers nor mothers.

It may be that new proposals in an *old* country are always the product of an ill-balanced mind, or to be labelled heretical. But on February 10th, 1907, the legislature of the State of Indiana passed the following Act:

"An Act entitled an Act to prevent procreation of confirmed criminals, idiots, imbeciles and rapists—providing that superintendents or boards of managers of institutions where such persons are confined shall have the authority, and are empowered to appoint a committee of experts, consisting of two physicians, to examine into the mental condition of such inmates.

"Whereas heredity plays an important part in the transmission of crime, idiocy, and imbecility, therefore, be it enacted by the General Assembly of the State of Indiana, that on and after the passage of this Act, it shall be compulsory for each and every institution in the State entrusted with the care of confirmed criminals, idiots, rapists,

77

and imbeciles to appoint upon its staff, in addition to the regular institution physician, two skilled surgeons of recognised ability, whose duty it shall be, in conjunction with the chief physician of the institution, to examine the mental and physical condition of such inmates as are recommended by the institutional physician and board of managers.

"If in the judgment of this committee procreation is inadvisable and there is no probability of improvement of the mental condition of the inmate, it shall be lawful for the surgeons to perform such operation for the prevention of procreation as shall be decided safest and most effective. But this operation shall not be performed except in cases that have been pronounced unimprovable."

Again on August 12th, 1909, the State Legislature of Connecticut enacted:

"An Act concerning operations for the Prevention of Procreation. — Be it enacted by the Senate and House of Representatives in General Assemble convened:

"Section 1. — The directors of the State prison and the superintendents of State hospitals for the insane at Middletown and Norwich are hereby authorised and directed to appoint for each of the said institutions, respectively, two skilled surgeons, who, in conjunction with the physician or surgeon in charge at each of said institutions, shall examine such persons as are reported to them by the warden, superintendent, or the physician or surgeon in charge, to be persons by whom procreation would be inadvisable.

"Such board shall examine the physical and mental condition of each persons, and their record and family history so far as the same can be ascertained, and if in the judgment of the majority of said board, procreation by an such person would produce children with an inherited tendency to crime, insanity, feeble-mindedness, idiocy, or imbecility, and there is no probability that the condition of any such person so examined will improve to such an extent as to render procreation by such person advisable, or, if the physical or mental condition of any such person will be substantially improved thereby, then the said board shall appoint one of its members to perform the operation of vasectomy or oophorectomy, as the case may be, upon such person. Such operation shall be performed in a safe and humane manner, and the board making such examination, and the surgeon performing such operation, shall receive from the State such compensation, for services rendered, as the warden of the State prison or the superintendent of either of such hospitals shall deem reasonable.

"Section 2.—Except as authorised by this Act, every person who shall perform, encourage, assist in or otherwise promote the performed of either of the operations described in Section 1 of this Act, for the purpose of destroying the power to procreate the human species: or any person who shall knowingly permit either of such operations to be performed upon such person—unless the same be a medical necessity—shall be fined not more than one thousand dollars, or imprisoned in the State prison not more than five years, or both."

There need be no objection to such an operation as is here suggested. It is very simple, practically painless, makes no difference at all to the bodily functions, and has no ill-effects of any kind. It prevents nothing but the power to procreate. It is the outcome of modern scientific knowledge, and must not be confounded with older and much more drastic methods.

In this country the cry is often — "Let me alone"; "Don't worry me"; "Wrongs will right themselves"; or, "I needn't worry; things will last my time." Such a mixed policy of hypocrisy and slavish desire to tread the beaten track will not work for good.

We howl about the increase of paupers. Yet we allow the pauper to leave the workhouse to get married. We howl about the increase of criminals. Yet we allow criminals to marry and to beget more criminals. And we howl about the increase of insanity and the feeble-minded. Yet we allow these to marry and to beget offspring fully qualified to perpetuate the weakmindedness of their progenitors. Surely a noble and worthy national policy!

Some time ago I called attention to the fact that five feeble-minded women had given birth to fifteen feeble-minded infants. Later still, Dr. Potts stated that in one workhouse 16 feeble-minded women had given birth to 116 idiot children. Dr. Branthwaite in his annual report (for 1905) on Inebriate Homes, states that 92 habitual inebriate women had had 850 babies.

What can these children become? More inebriates; more degenerates; because of women admitted 200 were found to be suffering from mental defect.

If we can, by sterilizing a large number of mental degenerates, people classified as habitual criminals, and vagrants, lessen the total of this world's suffering; lessen the number of children so cursed and weighted down by parental defects that they can never become useful citizens; and if we can lessen the unwise sum of money now expended upon the upkeep of our motley civilisation—using it for better purposes—

then let us give up the useless policy of breeding and cultivating a species of British subjects who will not only be a heavy millstone round our necks, but will go on breeding more degenerates to require more asylums and far greater expenditure.

I may add, that the State Legislatures of Pennsylvania and Oregon have passed Bills authorising Sterilisation, but, so far, the Governors of these states have not yet agreed to sign them. These Bills will be again presented, and if passed by a majority of each House, the Governor's Veto will be passed over, and so they will become law.

R. R. RENTOUL, M. D.

Kenealy, A. (1911). A study in degeneracy. *Eugenics Review, 3*(1), 37-45.

A STUDY IN DEGENERACY

By ARABELLA KENEALY, L.R.C.P.

There is an infant of my acquaintance who, I think, must make the angels weep. Moreover, he is a serious stumbling-block in the path of the eugenist.

His limbs are large and firm, his fists are hard and mottled. His skin is of a clear and glowing pink, his blue eyes are round and shining. He has never for a day of his nine months of existence suffered from an ailment or distress. Finally, as might have been expected, he has won a prize at a Baby Show. Looking as he does a picture of happy and incomparable health, he is the admiration and the envy of mothers of infants apparently less well physically equipped.

And his incomparable health it is which is a stumbling-block in the path of Eugenics.

For both of his parents are sickly, ill-grown and perpetually ailing.

"How now about heredity?" scoffs the unbeliever. "Here, surely, is a living contradiction of its tenets. Here, surely, is proof positive that Nature is perfectly capable of looking out for the next generation, no matter what its parentage. For is not the child of this unhealthy couple as healthy a child as we know?"

The phenomenon is worthy of attention, although to the biologist the explanation should not be far to seek. This Prize-Baby of the incomparable health is a Degenerate. The popular conception of a degenerate is, of course, a hunchback, a cripple, an imbecile, a criminal, one blind, deaf, or otherwise defective, or afflicted with some or another disease with a name to it. And yet an absolute and typical degenerate may be, like this baby, none of these things, but may, on the contrary, be possessed of every limb, organ, faculty and sense normal to humanity. But—and here lies the key to the position—all his faculties and structures are of a grade so low, so inferior to the average as to constitute a lapse from the normal type.

Degeneracy expresses itself in an infinite variety of forms. The lack of that constitutional power essential to the due human equipment in every department of capacity, physical and mental, which characterises a normal human being, may show in complete absence of one or more organs of faculties, or spreading itself, as it were, evenly over the whole organisation, it may show in a general inferiority of structure, of function, and of mental calibre. The individual then lacks no limb, organ, or sense, but all the limbs, organ, and senses he possesses are, biologically, of a grade below the normal. He may be perfectly healthy, well balanced and efficient upon this lower grade of being, precisely as a negro or a Kaffir may be healthy, well balanced and efficient upon the plane which is his normal in the evolutionary scale. But a grade of tissue and of mental or moral calibre which is perfectly normal to a negro of a Kaffir is abnormal and constitutes degeneracy in a member of a higher race.

A degenerate, in short, may be defective and patently abnormal, or he may be a mere reversion to a former and inferior type.

In the latter case, the resources of the organism being stinted (owing to parental constitutional impoverishment), the stint, in the place of expressing itself in some specific defect or diseases, entails a dropping of the whole organization to a lower gear. The individual thus reverts to a former and inferior type, one which was perhaps normal to an antecedent evolutionary epoch in the stock from which he has sprung, but is abnormal, or degenerate, in that stock to-day.

So with this infant of my acquaintance. To one in the secret of it, a glance at his bald, base head, at his pink and smiling animal face, reveals at the same time the fact of his degeneracy and the source of his lusty vitalism.

His skull from poll to brow presents an easy and discreditable descent. Little of moral or of intellectual capacity has he, while the strictly physiological regions of his brain, those presiding over the functions of mere organic life, are largely developed. One conjectures that during his ante-natal growth, owing to a stint of maternal nutritive supply, the nascent organism found no wherewithal to equip itself duly in the higher departments, and accordingly reverted in mass to a type lower in human caliber than the stock upon which it was grafted, or that the "graft," owing to parental impoverishment, was inherently degenerate.

For whereas both parents are mentally and morally up to the normal standard, but below it in physical vitality, their child is of a type which is obviously below the normal mental and moral standard, but is above it in lusty vitality.

Possibly it is less in the degree of constitutional power possessed by an individual than in the fashion in which this power is distributed among the faculties, that true degeneracy lies.

"My (financial) expenditure is Me," says Emerson. The man of crude tastes may possess means equal in those of the man of culture, the difference between them is shown in the essential values of the objects upon which each expends his means. So, too, with evolutionary development. The man of higher organization is he whose vital resources are duly invested in his nobler qualities. But the children of a noble family, should their parents fall into financial straits, must necessarily come down in the world, exchanging their fine ancestral home for a middle-class villa, so, also, the children of fine evolutionary stock, should their parents fall into constitutional bankruptcy, must perforce, in the place of inheriting the parental habitation, go lower in the scale of life.

It would seem that the main difference between Disease and Degeneracy—and there is all the difference in the world, so far as the Race is concerned—is that in Disease we have an organism endowed still with healthy aspirations, struggling against its own inherent disabilities or against the disabilities of its environment, doing its best in the teeth of adverse factors to sustain its evolutionary level, to recuperate ailing and devitalized tracts of cells, or when these have lapsed beyond the power of redemption, as in cancer, tuberculosis, suppuration and so forth, to evict them from its economy; while in Degeneracy healthy aspirations no longer exist, the struggle for the survival of the higher in the organism against the lower in the organism having ceased, and the cells having conformed in mass to a lower grade of being.

This, then, is what has happened to the degenerate infant I am describing. He is not diseased, he is not defective, nor is he sickly. On the contrary, he is a complete human infant with ever limb, organ, and faculty duly and harmoniously developed and properly functioning, and he is, moreover, charged with abundant nervous forces wherewith to energise his capabilities.

In this latter particular he serves for a striking contrast to his circle of baby contemporaries. For these, like the majority of modern, artificially-fed, anemic, neurotic infants, with whom digestion spells dyspepsia, growth implies ache and weariness and development entails disability, are perpetually suffering from some or another distress. And yet these suffering infants are, from an evolutionary standpoint, superior to him in absolute human health notwithstanding that they are afflicted with physiological ills. For *their* suffering is the expression of the evolutionary aspirations of cells which are striving to maintain a high level of living, while *his* physiological contentment is the inertia of cells which have conformed to a lower type.

Pain is the prayer of nerves for healthy blood. Pain and distress are the voices of aspirations after vital elements indispensable to high health. When we suppress (as much of present-day medical treatment aims at doing) the voices of such aspirations toward higher health, we merely so blunt the conscience of cells to their essential higher needs that they cease to demand the fulfillment of these, and in consequence deteriorate. Anodynes stop the cry of pain, as opium will still the cry of hunger, but anodynes can no more supply the elements for which the tissues are crying than opium can nourish the body.

The whole secret of Health and of Evolutionary Development, lies in the healthy aspirations of the tissue-cells.

Once in the remote ages of the pre-historic Past there was a single cell we know now as the amoeba, in which lay hid the latent aspiration to become a man. That aspiration is now accomplished fact. And the single-celled amoeba, "the protoplasmic father of man" by virtue of the aspiration in it (derived we know not whence) so triumphed over all the antagonistic forces and conditions of its environment, adding ever and ever in its potential capacities, realizing ever more and more of its potential ideals, that it has now become the complex many-celled being, modern man.

So to-day man sustains or continues his evolutionary development by virtue of the aspirations of his many cells, every one of which contains in latency the incalculable forms still intervening between us and the perfect human type.

The moment, however, that the cells, in mass or in part, in the place of aspiring to yet higher ideals or of sustaining those already achieved, conform, without protest of pain or of disability, to a lower grade of being, Devolution has begun. In that moment, man, having evolved from, has taken the first step in reverting to, the single-celled amoeba.

My "healthy" infant, his cells ceasing to aspire, and conforming without protest to the lower grade to which they have relapses, has turned back his face to the darkness whence his kind have come. And he has ceased to suffer because he has ceased to aspire. His suffering circle of contemporaries suffer, however, because they are still striving. Their disabilities and pains are the expression of a biological divine discontent amid their myriad cells struggling for higher existence, struggling against al the disabilities of impoverished constitutional resources, of the ignorance of nurses, of the neglect of mothers, who proffer them the stone of artificial feeding in the place of the living bread of mother-milk, struggling, suffering, and yet fighting bravely to sustain the evolutionary level of their poor little nobly-fashioned heads, of the soul-light in their eyes, of the human beauty in their faces, of their finely modeled limbs—in a word, of the higher humanity in so far as that has been realised in them. And it is their very struggle for the survival of the higher in them which taxes their powers and entails disabilities.

To employ that which might seem to be a contradiction in terms, their health is the source of their disease. They are like well-born persons hard put to it to keep up a fine ancestral dwelling. To maintain its structure in good conditions expends the greater portion of their available resources. They would be far less straitened were they to cease from striving to keep the whole building in good repair, and lapsing from their standards, were to abandon the higher chambers of their dwelling and to content themselves with occupying only lower floors—as has happened to my degenerate infant.

A duty lies, I venture to think, with the eugenist—to draw finer distinctions regarding healthy than have hitherto been drawn to recognise that the first function of health is so to maintain the standard of the tissues that they shall not lapse from the type achieved by the particular stock from which they have sprung, even though this standard is maintained at a the cost of some debility and suffering. Such debility and suffering are to be regretted, and Eugenics must seek to secure for everybody's parentage which will not only entail organisation true to standards, but will also transmit enough of vitality to maintain these standards without tax of suffering.

I have been frequently impressed by seeing that among children brought to hospital, the noblest and highest types die off almost without a struggle, while the ill-formed and degenerate clutch on greedily to the very last shreds of life, and battle through. I have asked myself—Is health not health? Is Nature mocking us, that these unfit survive while the fit succumb? For the very unfittest and the very fittest alike die; the very unfittest because they seem to have nothing more than a frail and casual holding, as it were, within the poorest tenement-physiques; the very fittest because the tax upon their resources made by maintaining their more worthy dwelling-places, leaves them no powers wherewith to meet the strain of illness.

And between these two are the great mass of the Average, of which in the main the best types are handicapped by disability or die (for the reason given), while the inferior, struggling less bravely to maintain standards or letting these lapse altogether, win through the least effort. Before I had found what I think may be light upon the subject, it was a source of perpetual pain and perplexity to me to see the most beautiful, the sweetest-natured, and the most finely-fashioned children suffer or die, while the ugly, the misshapen and the ill-conditioned suffer far less and when ill fight with an uncanny eagerness—and success—for life. Until I realised that ill weeds grow apace because choicer growths demand fostering conditions for their survival and development, it had seemed to me almost that Nature was possessed by an unholy craze to eradicate the fairer flowers from her human garden.

The higher the organism the more sensitive it is to adverse factors of its environment, and the more complex and insistent its needs. For this reason the very finest types of children, as the very worst—and particularly the children of the poor—succumb or live handicapped by some or another disability, the higher organisation being, in our day of impoverished vitality, over-taxed by the struggle to sustain the standards of its type against adverse circumstances,—while the worst are endowed with so little vitality as readily to be extinguished.

The general view is that parents whose children are what is known as "healthy"—which in our superficial way of regarding things, means merely that their physiological processes are normally performed and that they show no symptoms of disease—have acquitted themselves satisfactorily so far as the Race is concerned. In point of fact, however, such parents may have done the worst possible injury to the Race by having allowed the type to deteriorate in their offspring. If the evolutionary development of the Race is to be sustained and is to continue, children must not only be born "healthy," but they must be born also of good type.

The degenerate infant who is serving me for text, upon whom his parents pride themselves and whom his circle inordinately admires, is, poor babe! base and crude of type. In him, the racial stock has suffered such a deterioration that many generations of mating with higher stock will be necessary to raise it to the level of average humanity.

There is no graver menace to a race than is furnished by such sturdy degenerates. For not only do they in their own persons and in that of their offspring debase the type, but exhibiting no symptoms of disease, they are not commonly recongised as degenerates, and accordingly prove stumbling-blocks in the way of the Eugenic propaganda. The eugenist, realising that in order to continue evolutionary development every generation must be an infinitesimal advance upon the last, should not allow himself to accept the definitions of "health," nor the glowing descriptions of "fine infants," which satisfy the short-sighted observer and confound our creed.

The "healthy baby" born of diseased or indifferent stock so frequently flaunted before us as a living refutation of our faiths, should be recognised as a mere revision to an anterior and lower type—a degenerate, in short.

Here lies the explanation of that which seems to be an anomaly when the refined and highly-organised but neurotic and over-taxed mothers of our cultured classes produce, as they do frequently, offspring of the crude, rough-hewn, and unintelligent peasant type. Such women, deficient in mother-power, are able to supply only impoverished resources wherewith their offspring building their developing bodies. The embryo, thus stinted, relapses in all, or in tracts merely, of his tissue, to a cruder phase of the stock from which he is springing, lapses from the higher organisation evolved by generations of fostering conditions and environment, and reverts to the boor, so letting slip perhaps ten generations of achieved development—development which is thus lost to the Race.

A valuable object-lesson is supplied, indeed, by a type of women common to-day, all nerves and restless activity, her spare frame a figure of famine modishly draped, highly civilised, because possessing so little of nature, highly educated and fastidious, while her children are, on the contrary, crude, clownish, and uncomely.

Seeing her with them one derives an impression that she is taking her gardener's family for a holiday. They are her very own, however, and she will frequently, quite innocent of biological implications, boast of their rough-hewn frames and their robust "health," and congratulate herself upon the fact that they have inherited none of their mother's neurotic or other constitutional disabilities. For here is a fragile neurotic, a tangle of jangled nerves, whose threadbare constitution is perpetually breaking into holes, nevertheless mothering sturdy, phlegmatic offspring, whose natural avocation in life would seem to be—the plough.

The biologist sees no anomaly however. The thing is an expression merely of a recognised natural law. The parental resources being—in the mother at all events—in a state of bankruptcy, the developing embryo could find no wherewithal to equip itself according to the evolutionary traditions of its stock, and in consequence reverted to the type of some ancestral wielder of the spade.

Mothers, bankrupt of constitution, when they produce, on the contrary children delicate and ailing but of higher type, pervert the maternal function far less gravely than is done with their offspring are crude and strong. For such delicate and ailing children may by care and attention be so recruited as to become fairly efficient members of the Race, while at the same time preserving the valuable traits of more highly-developed humanity; whereas the sturdy degenerate stock will require perhaps ten generations of eugenic development to reclaim it from its evolutionary lapse.

Burt, C. (1912). The inheritance of mental characters. *Eugenics Review, 4*(2), 168–200.

THE INHERITANCE OF MENTAL CHARACTERS

By CYRIL BURT, M.A., Lecturer in Experimental Psychology in the University of Liverpool

Among those who study man, there is a growing body of opinion which assigns to mental facts a significance far more profound than to physical. "Psychic forces," runs an oft-quoted maxim of a contemporary sociologist; "are the true causes of all social phenomena." It is, therefore, of importance to enquire what in turn are the true causes of psychic forces. Are the agencies which determine the capacities of a man or nation predominantly those which arise from the environment and act upon the individual after birth? Or are they rather rooted in tendencies hereditary in the family or the race, which determine irrevocably the dominant lines along which its members shall develop, long before they are born? This is a question which has often been argued in the case of physical characters; it is a question which, thanks to the psychological complications of every social science and of every social problem, requires discussion yet more imperatively in the case of intellectual, emotional, and moral characters, in a word, for qualities of mind.[1]

As to physical characters there can be now no controversy. In body, man is subject to heredity like every other animal; and, it seems, he is subject to it in precisely the same considerable degree.

In the case of many bodily features, the degree to which heredity influences man has been measured with numerical exactitude. This is done by means of the method of correlation. Where a plurality of partial causes co-operate in contributing to a given effect, it is convenient to measure the influence of each by a single fraction. This is known as the co-efficient of correlation. It expresses the tendency to some form of

---

[1] There are but few books dealing specifically with the subject of mental inheritance. Perhaps the most comprehensive is that of Ribet, *L'Heredite psychologique* (9· ed., 1910. Eng. trans., 1875). Written, however, before work upon inheritance in general had demonstrated the need for technical, quantitative, and experimental methods, its standpoint is observational and analytic and its style popular.

concomitant variation (such as resemblance) between two variables (such as the stature of fathers and the stature of their sons). It may have all possible values ranging from +1 (representing complete correspondence) through 0 (indicating total absence of correspondence), to -1 (representing complete inverse correspondence. Stature provides a convenient illustration. If every son were of the same height as his father the co-efficient of correlation would be unity, this is 1.00. If a son resembled his father in height no more than any other person taken at random, the co-efficient would be 0, or zero. If every soon were as short as his father was tall, the co-efficient would be -1.00. On actually measuring the stature of some 4,886 pairs of sons and fathers, the degree of resemblance between them has been calculated to be .50 or 1/2; this means that, on the average, the sons deviate from the mean height of the population by about half as much as the father. In health, in colour and curliness of hair, in colour of eyes, in length and breadth of head, the degree of resemblance between parent and offspring, or between one brother and another, is among men much about the same; numerically it varies from .42 to .62. Among animals, the co-efficients of correlation for inheritance vary from .44 (ratio of right antenna to frontal breadth in the green fly to .52 (coat colour in horse); that is, again, approximately 1/2. It follows that physical inheritance is of the same order of intensity in man as in the lower animals.[2]

Mental inheritance, however, is still a matter for disagreement. Its very existence is constantly disputed and occasionally denied. A well-known writer on heredity has argued as follows: "Suppose a child of refined and educated English parents were reared from birth by African cannibals; then in body, when grown, he would resemble his progenitors more than his captors. But does anyone believe the same of his mind?" He would be pale in complexion and fair of hair; but he would talk cannibal talk, think cannibal thoughts, eat cannibal meat, just as if he were cannibal born. In body European, he would be African in mind; his skin would be white, but his soul black. The very essence of mind, it is urged, is the power to learn by experience. Man is, before all others, the educable animal. Hence, while his body may be shaped by inheritance operating before birth, his mind must be built up by experience after birth. It is, add many, inconceivable that one individual soul can hand on in carnal reproduction its characteristics to another soul. Mental inheritance is, therefore,

---

[2] Karl Pearson, 'On the Laws of Inheritance in Man' (II.), *Biometrika*, Vol. III. (1904), p. 157.

renounced. "The evidence is overwhelming that mental and moral qualities are not inherited in the same sense as physical qualities."[3]

In weighing arguments such as these, an important distinction must be observed at the outset. We must discriminate between those properties of the mind which we may loosely term its capacities, and those which we may term its contents. The contents of the mind, its memories and its habits, its thoughts and its ideals, these are not inherited; they are without doubt acquired during the lifetime of the individual. But the capacity to acquire, and the inclination towards certain acquisitions, these may be present from the beginning. Were no other mental characteristic hereditary, educability, *ex hypothesei*, is. Consequently, differences in educability may be hereditary too. My son might learn far less from his African captors than yours, were both to fall into such hands; though the differences would seem negligible, when compared with what both might have learnt had they not been deprived of the benefits of civilisation. Hence, while gross or absolute achievements are obviously affected by gross environmental differences, within the same environment the relative achievements may differ in a way which allows of no other explanation than inheritance.

For the rest, psychology need no longer rely on *a priori* speculation. It turns to scientific research. Evidence is available in researches carried out upon the mental characteristics both of individuals and of peoples.

I. MENTAL CHARACTERS OF INDIVIDUALS

A. The Fact of Mental Inheritance

The first question that confronts us is the question of fact: *are* mental characteristics inherited? In studying individuals three main lines of investigation have been pursued: the collection of family records, the calculation of statistical values, and the application of experimental tests.

1. PEDIGREES

Family records have been collected chiefly for the more extreme cases of mental capacity,—for mental ability and genius, and for insanity and mental defect.

---

[3] Archdall Reid, *Sociological Papers*, Vol. III., pp. 92-3, cf. *id.*, *The Laws of Heredity*, p. 420.

First in time, and foremost in celebrity, is the collection published by Sir Francis Galton.[4] Galton obtained pedigrees of nearly a thousand eminent men,—judges, generals, statesmen, scientists, poets, painters and divines. Each was sufficiently eminent intellectually to rank as one man in four thousand. He then examined the careers of their relatives. Among these he discovered 89 eminent fathers, 114 eminent brothers, and 129 eminent sons,—in all over 300 immediate relatives of the same degree of eminence as themselves. In addition there were 200 equally eminent men of the next degree of kin. The chance of a son of an eminent man showing eminent ability himself appeared to be about five hundred times as great as that of the son of a man taken at random.

The evidence lends some colour to the assumption that specific kinds of ability are inherited as well as high degrees of ability generally. The families of the Wesleys and the Bachs produced an amazing number of talented musicians. Mendelssohn and Meyerbeer are the only musicians in Galton's list whose eminent relatives achieved success in careers other than that of music. Among politicians the only analogous exception is Benjamin Disraeli, whose father was not a politician, but (as indeed was Benjamin) a man of letters. Among the scientists specialisation of inheritance is even more marked. The family of Galton himself and the allied families of Darwin and Wedgwood have produced no less than sixteen men of high scientific attainments, of whom nine were Fellows of the Royal Society.

The influences at work in the several cases Galton analyses in detail. He concludes: "Men who are gifted with high abilities easily rise through all the obstacles caused by inferiority of social rank...Men who are largely aided by social advantages are unable to achieve eminence, unless they are endowed with high natural gifts." There are, nevertheless, many who admit the facts, but reject the conclusion. They still insist that such genealogies may merely illustrate the value of the mental atmosphere of a cultured home or the power of social influence and opportunity.

Let us, therefore, turn to the opposite end of the scale of mental excellence.

Of all cases of mental inheritance the most fully established and most generally recognised is the inheritance of feeble-mindedness. Feeble-mindedness commonly dates from birth. Reference to the mental state of the parents and grandparents often discovers defect transmitted through three, four, or even five generations. Perhaps the most convincing mass of evidence is that incidentally accumulated by the Royal

---

[4] *Hereditary Genius* (1869, 2ª ed., 1892)

Commission appointed at the commencement of the century to enquire into the provision made for the feeble-minded. The majority of the witnesses called before it attached supreme importance in the causation of mental defect in children to a history of mental defect in the parents or near relatives; and the general opinion was that, "apart from very rare accidental injuries, there is no such thing as manufactures feeble-mindedness."

In the majority of cases, inherited mental defect is not so radical as to resist all attempts at subsequent training or control. In a proper environment and under adequate supervision, the feeble-minded are neither completely useless to the community, nor entirely unable to contribute to the cost of their own livelihood. In the colony at Sandlebridge, a colony started under Miss Dendy nine years ago by the Lancashire and Cheshire Society for the Permanent Care of the Feeble-minded, the children can knit and make baskets; the women are taught laundry work; and the men work on the farm. Both themselves, and neighbouring schools and institutions, they supply with milk, fruit, vegetables, or other commodities. In 1910 the profit from the land thus farmed was over £500.

The efficacy of training raises the question of the transmissibility of acquired characters in acute form. Where the feeble-minded have been educated and marry, will their children inherit the specific results of their parents' education or will they inherit the original defect? To this question we must return when we have reviewed the evidence of mental heredity in general.

Insanity presents a more difficult problem. It is never present at birth; and in the relatives the neuropathic tendency may manifest itself in multiform ways,—as temperamental melancholy, drunkenness, pauperism, vagrancy, hysteria, epilepsy, criminality, or mere eccentricity,—without appearing as certifiable insanity. Dr. Mott has studied the family records, the individual history, or the post-mortem observations of several thousands of lunatics in comparison with patients mentally sound; and has published many illustrative pedigrees.[5] His conclusion is the following:—

---

[5] F. W. Mott, 'The Inborn Factors of Nervous and Mental Disease,' *Brain*, Vol. XXXIV., pts. ii, and iii. (November, 1911). *Id.*, 'Heredity and Insanity.' EUGENICS REVIEW, Vol. II., No. 4 (January, 1911). *Loc. cit.*, p. 279. The writer expressly leaves out of account cases admitted for (1) general paralysis of the insane which is an acquired disease due to the late effects of an infection by a specific organism; (2) organic brain disease from old age, arterial disease, softening and tumour formations, and (3) true alcoholic insanity with dementia (p. 251).

Hereditary predisposition is the most important factor in the production of insanity. Causes such as alcoholism, infective diseases, auto-intoxication physical injury, especially head injuries and shocks, emotional shock, sexual excesses, and unnatural practices, are too often wrongly assigned as the sole cause of nervous and mental disease to the neglect of the inborn. There are individuals born of sound stocks, that no acquired conditions,—drink, poisons engendered within, head injuries, emotional shock, distress and even profound misery and destitution combined,—can render insane. There are others, and these are generally from a neuropathic stock, whose mental conditions may be disturbed by any one of these conditions, or very frequently without any apparent cause except the conditions appertaining to the sexual functions in adolescence, the puerperium and the climacteric.[6]

In certain forms there are strong tendencies to inheritance of the same type of insanity. 'Similar inheritance' has been found in periodic (manic-depressive) insanity, in delusional insanity, and apparently (among brothers and sisters) insanity of adolescence (dementia praecox), and chronic mania or melancholia. The general rule, however, is for a different type to appear.

The evidence from family records is thus even more cogent in the case of imbecility and insanity than in the case of genius and talent.[7] All these, however, are mental characteristics of an exceptional kind; and exceptions do not necessarily prove the rule. We pass, therefore, from the extremes to the mediocre; from the genealogy of the genius and the pedigree of the defective, to the statistical study of the ordinary man.

2. STATISTICS

In tracing the family history of genius or insanity, it is commonly assumed that each individual is either definitely a genius or not; that each individual either definitely has neuropathic tendencies or has not. Normal individuals, however, can seldom be

---

[6] *Brain, loc. cit.,* p. 84.

[7] *The Treasury of Human Inheritance,* which the Eugenics Laboratory has recently commenced to publish, includes authentic pedigrees of the descent of mental characters, pathological and valuable. Thus Parts I. and II. contain pedigrees of deaf-mutism, of legal and administrative ability, and of legal and literary ability; Part III. contains pedigrees of insanity, and of commercial ability and liberal thought.

separated in this fashion into sharply demarcated classes. Their mental characters seem rather to vary continuously. They are thus amenable to measurement in terms of a continuous scale. In such cases it is preferable, at any rate in initial researches, to proceed from investigations in the mass rather than from individual instances. This is the principle adopted by the statistical or biometric study of heredity.

Of all statistical studies of mental inheritance the most elaborate is that published by Professor Karl Pearson.[8] The data chosen for examination were the psychical qualities, characterising school children from the same families, and estimated by their school teachers. The material took upwards of five years to collect. Schedules were prepared; and on these the teachers were asked to classify the several pairs of brothers and sisters, according to a prearranged scheme, as 'self-assertive' or 'shy'; 'quick intelligent,' 'intelligent,' 'slow intelligent,' 'slow,' 'slow dull,' 'very dull'; and so on. The characters chosen were traits accessible to observation in daily life. Vivacity, temper, popularity, conscientiousness, self-consciousness, self-assertiveness, and general ability,—these were the psychical qualities assessed. Between 3,000 and 4,000 schedules were returned from some 200 schools. To the data thus obtained were applied the statistical methods elaborated for the biometric study of the inheritance of physical characters in man, in animals, and in plants. For the mental characters of the children the co-efficients of correlation range from .43 to .64, averaging .52. Now these figures are almost exactly the same as those obtained in the same way from the same children for physical characters; those average .53, ranging from .43 to .62. In either case the resemblance between members of the same families is roughly 1/2. "We are forced," concludes Professor Karl Pearson, "to the general conclusion that psychical characters in man are inherited within broad lines in the same manner and with the same intensity as physical."   These results are corroborated by results obtained from studying the mental resemblance, not of brothers and sisters, but of parents and offspring. Thus, the degree of parental resemblance in intelligence or ability, as estimated in family records, appears as .58 (Pearson); as estimated by Oxford class lists, as .49 (Schuster).

Somewhat similar figures are yielded by the researches of investigators in other countries. In New York, for instance, the spelling abilities of some 600 children were recorded, and the performances measured in statistical terms by the individual's deviation from the group average for children of his age and sex. The coefficient of

---

[8] Karl Pearson, 'On the Laws of Inheritance in Man; II., On the Inheritance of the Mental and Moral Characters in Man.' *Biometrika* (1904), Vol. IV., pt. ii., p. 131.

correlation between children of the same family was found to be .50.[9] Subsequent studies of spelling have shown that similarities of previous training at home or school have little influence. Hence, the resemblance must be due to inheritance. Another American investigatory has measured the resemblances in intellect and morality of nearly seven hundred historical personages, members of royal families of Europe. Between fathers and offspring the coefficients of correlation are .30 in the case of both intellectual and moral capacities.[10]

More recently two Dutch investigators sent out to all the doctors in Holland schedules containing questions concerning psychical characters observable in ordinary life.[11] Each recipient was requested to select one family concerning which he happened to have exact knowledge and in which the children were by preference all grown up, and to answer each question for each member of the family. The list contained ninety questions. They dealt with feelings, inclinations, occupations, intellectual qualities, and miscellaneous and secondary characteristics of the most varied kind. The following are samples:

Is the person concerned resolute or undecided?

Is the person concerned in politics a radical, a liberal, a conservative, or indifferent?

Is the person concerned entirely credible, or inclined to exaggerate or embellish statements, or is he a liar?

The numerical results have been subjected to further statistical treatment and have been converted into terms of the more usual statistical constants.[12]

The final result is as follows:

"The mean co-efficients of resemblance between fathers and sons, and between mothers and daughters...come in each case to very nearly one-third,—the value originally proposed for the parental inheritance co-efficient by Mr. Galton." The

---

[9] E. L. Earle, 'The Inheritance of the Ability to Learn to Spell.' *Columbia Contributions to Philosophy, Psychology and Education*, Vol. XI., No. 2.

[10] F. A. Woods, *Mental and Moral Heredity in Royalty*, 1906.

[11] Heymans and Wiersma, Beitrage zur spezielien Psycholgie anf Grund einer Massenuntersuchung, *Zeitschrift fur Psychologie*, Bd. XLII. (1905, 1907). pp. 1-127 and pp. 258-301.

[12] Schuster and Elderton, 'The Inheritance of Psychical Characters,' *Biometrika*, Vol. V. (1905-7), pp. 460-469.

resemblances between parents and offspring of the opposite sex are smaller, *viz.*, about one-fifth to one-fourth. The original investigators believe that the resemblance is due mainly to heredity, since in traits subject to training and home influence resemblance is scarcely at all larger than in traits but little subject to them.

The smaller size of the last two sets of coefficients may readily be explained. In these cases the capacities estimated were more complex, and therefore somewhat more accessible to the differentiating influence of a different life-history. The persons possessing them were older. And their characteristics were less immediately under the observations of those making the estimates. Making allowance for the vast differences between the methods adopted and the points chosen in collected the data, there is an astonishing agreement between the statistical results yielded by different investigations.

In the case of mental characters it is of especial interest and importance to compare the influence of heredity with that of environment. This further problem has also been attacked statistically.[13] The nature of the home environment has been estimated by ascertaining the physical, economic and moral state of the parents, their employment and their tendency to drink, the number of persons per room, the cleanliness and state of clothing of the child. The correlation of these environmental circumstances with the child's mental capacities, chiefly his intelligence and keenness of vision, have been calculated. The coefficients published vary from -.16 to +.24. The negative sign indicates that an environmental condition apparently unfavourable appears associated with favourable development of the child. I find that the average of the coefficients concerned with mental capacities alone works out at +.02. In contrasting figures measuring the relative influence of nature and nurture upon capacity generally, including both body and mind, Professor Karl Pearson conclude: "The influence of environment is not one-fifth that of heredity; and quite possibly not one-tenth of it."[14] Omitting the figures given by him for purely physical and bodily characteristics leaves the averages comparatively unchanged. Hence, the foregoing conclusion may be applied to the relative influence of environment and heredity upon mental characters alone.

---

[13] David Heron, *The Influence of Unfavourable Home Environment...on the Intelligence of School Children,* and other publications of the Eugenics Laboratory, London.

[14] Karl Pearson, *Nature of Nurture,* p. 27.

Many psychologists have criticised the validity of the figures yielded by the foregoing statistical researches.[15] They urge the following points. The accuracy of the statistical methods employed in evaluating the data cannot compensate for inaccuracies necessarily entailed in collecting them. It may even impart a spurious sense of exactitude. No material is afforded by the majority of the investigations for estimating and eliminating the errors made by the teachers, the doctors, or the biographers who engaged in the collection. Such errors may be either systematic or random, either regular or irregular. The influence of random errors in estimating the individuals' characters may have been considerable. Many of the questions and tables provide only two classes (*e.g.*, emotional, unemotional; popular, unpopular). In but few cases (*e.g.*, political opinions, children's intelligence) does the scale supplied possess as many as four grades or even three. Insertion in the wrong class must, therefore, have had serious consequences wherever it diminished the real resemblances. The consequences of such errors have been measured by more recent investigators. It has been estimated that, were allowance made for these, the coefficients affected would be increased to exorbitant values; correlations of .5 (ability) would swell to correlations of .8; correlations of .7 (children's athletics) would be increased to nearly unity. Such figures could not be true. It would mean that the brothers and sisters measured were as alike as the Corsican brothers or Galton's 'identical twins.'

The underlying correlations, therefore, must have been from the outset falsely enlarged. Correlations are commonly enlarged by systematic errors concealed in the observations upon which they are based. Against such a suspicion the data in question are by no means secure. Informed, as they were, of the issue at stake, the observers may have unconsciously inserted into their testimony the very conclusions it was proposed to deduce from their reports. In the case of children's athletic power, much of the resemblance is admitted in the original memoir to be "wholly spurious"; schools with an athletic reputation and an athletic cult, it would seem, tended regularly to return all brothers as alike athletic; other schools tended to report them as non-athletic. Similar differences in personal standards and ideals may have similarly magnified the resultant coefficients in the case of other characteristics. Where one person collected data for but one family this danger becomes most serious. A doctor with a high ideal of industry

---

[15] C. Spearman. 'The Proof and Measurement of Association between Two Things,' *American Journal of Psychology*, Vol. XV., 1904, pp. 72-101. Thorndike, *Educational Psychology* (1910), pp. 81-4.

would tend to rate a family that worked indifferently hard, as lazy; while an easy-tempered doctor might report a somewhat less energetic family as industrious.

Some of the errors, therefore, probably magnified that resemblances; some probably minimised them. We cannot assume that the opposite tendencies were equal. Hence, little emphasis can be laid upon the size of the resultant coefficients or their similarity. Beyond the facts that the coefficients for mental characters, where the environmental influence is problematic, resemble in magnitude the coefficients for physical characters (such as eye colour), where environment could obviously had no influence; that where certain environmental influences have been gauged, they do not appreciably affect certain other mental capacities—beyond these facts, there is no cogent evidence to show that heredity is really responsible for the correlations found. Two sisters may resemble one another in conscientiousness, not because they inherit it from their parents, but because their parents have given them both the same moral training; two brothers may resemble one another in bad temper, not because they inherit it from bad-tempered parents, but because their parents have been so good-natured as to spoil them both.

The foregoing researches relied for their data upon subjective impressions. These impressions were derived by untrained observers in ordinary daily intercourse, and formulated in popular terminology, with no standardisation of the rating other than the observers' own ideals. The same objections will be discoverable in all such investigations. The concrete qualities thus accessible—emotionality, popularity, thrift and the rest,—are two superficial and too complex. They cannot provide a single scale of uniform gradations. They cannot convey the same idea to the different observers. They cannot be governed by the same set of causes in the different persons observed.

For the study of inheritance, therefore, we must turn to simpler mental functions,—functions which can be scientifically defined, functions which can be objectively measured, functions which can be affected by but few factors. These can be isolated and measured only by means of experimental tests.

3. EXPERIMENTS

Of recent years apparatus has been devised to test simple mental capacities independently of subjective impressions. By means of a chronoscope, it is possible to measure, in terms of thousandths of a second, the quickness of a person's response to various stimuli; and the response may be arranged to include mental processes of all degrees of complexity. By means of a galvanometer, it is possible to measure, in millionths of an ampere, the change of electrical resistance in the body of a person undergoing emotional excitation; and, when other conditions are kept constant, the change proves a reliable index of the degree of emotion felt. For testing the acuity of the senses, the efficiency of the memory, the power of concentration, or the scope of attention, other instruments have been contrived. Applied to students in the laboratory, these yield valuable results. For work upon school children, elaborate instruments are best discarded. They are, as a rule, too alarming, too costly, and too cumbersome. Simpler experiments have, therefore, been invented. But the principles involved are essentially the same.

The earlier attempts to measure mental ability by means of laboratory tests appeared to give extremely discrepant results. The introduction into experimental psychology of statistical devices showed that the apparent discrepancies were due rather to inadequate methods of evaluating the results than to deficiencies of the experimental tests themselves.[16] Subsequent investigations have demonstrated both advantages and the defects of such tests. Their chief advantage is that they differentiate both the kinds and the degrees of innate capacities with much greater rapidity, accuracy, and minuteness than personal impressions or examination results. Their defect is that they involve special investigations and specially trained investigators; hence data can be accumulated only from small groups of individuals.

Both advantages and defects are illustrated in the following investigation.[17]

A series of experimental tests were applied to thirty children of a higher Elementary School, thirteen children of a Preparatory School at Oxford, and a boy congenitally feeble-minded.

The children were all between the same age limits. Twelve tests were employed. They dealt with typical mental functions of varying degrees of complexity: discrimination in lower and higher senses; movement, simple and controlled; memory; learning' scope of apprehension; and maintenance of attention. The tests chosen do not involve to an appreciable degree acquired skill or knowledge. They consist of simple mental tasks for the most part unlike anything the children have ever previously

---

[16] C. Spearnan, 'General Intelligence Objectively Measured and Defined,' *American Journal of Psychology*, Vol. XV., No. 2, (April, 1904), p. 222.

[17] Cyril Burt, 'The Experimental Investigation of General Intelligence,' *British Journal of Psychology* (December, 1909), Vol. III., Parts 1 and 2.

practised. Experiment shows that they are comparatively unaffected by practice at different tasks, or, within obvious limits, by age. There is reason, therefore, to believe that the differences revealed are mainly innate.

By repeating the tests and calculating the correlations between the several series, measures of their reliability or self-consistency may be obtained. The better tests give reliability coefficients of over .8 or even .9. Independent estimates based upon general impressions or examination results are commonly found to range from .5 to .7. Further investigation has shown that the better tests are but little affected by irrelevant conditions, such as the sex or social status of the children tested or the training of the experimenter testing them.[18]

The performances of the several groups gave harmonious results. All the tests except two gave significant positive correlations with careful empirical estimates of intelligence. In the two exceptions (touch and weight discrimination) the correlations were either negative or negligible. In these, however, the feeble-minded body excelled, though at the other tests his performances were, as a rule, the worst of all. Five tests gave correlations with intelligence of over .5. Amalgamated they gave intelligence coefficients of .85 and .91. The coefficients were far higher than those yielded by the school examinations, which, as their high correlations with the memory tests indicated, measure chiefly the power to memorise. -

The children tested at the Prepatory School were nearly all sons of men of eminence in the intellectual world—university professors, college lecturers and tutors, Fellows of the Royal Society, and bishops. The children at the Elementary School were mainly sons of small tradesmen. Calculations showed that, with two exceptions, the average performances of the Prepatory boys were all superior to those of the Elementary boys; in most cases superior even to those of the cleverest group of the Elementary boys. The two exceptions are the tests for the two lower senses—touch and weight. These two are precisely the tests, and the only tests, which yielded negative correlations with intelligence. Hence, it appears that wherever a process is correlated with intelligence, there children of superior parentage resemble their parents in being themselves superior.

We have already seen that proficiency at such tests does not depend upon opportunity or training, but upon some quality innate. The resemblance in degree of

---

[18] Cyril Burt, 'Experimental Tests of Higher Mental Processes and their Relation to General Intelligence,' *Journal of Experimental Pedagogy* (November, 1911), Vol. I., No. 2, p. 93.

intelligence between the boys and their parents must, therefore, be due to inheritance. We thus have an experimental demonstration that intelligence is hereditary.

At Liverpool, tests involving more elaborate apparatus, such as the chronoscope and galvanometer, have been applied to students and older children of the same families, and to parents and their adult offspring. The results hitherto obtained are far too few to be conclusive. So far as they go, they appear in the main to corroborate the results obtained by statisticians. The correlation coefficients measuring fraternal and paternal inheritance vary about .3. Of the mental functions tests, the lower and simpler processes appear to be more dependent upon heredity than the higher and more complex, the emotional more than the intellectual, and the intellectual more than the moral. If these conclusions be confirmed, they will form a sinister comment upon our present system of education. The present system seems far more concerned with training the simple mechanical processes, such as memory, than the higher processes, such as reasoning; and with training the intellectual processes rather than the moral. It thus aspires to train the very processes which seem least amenable to training.

One other experimental research deserves especial mention.

By means of simple tests Professor Thorndike measured the resemblance of fifty pairs of twins. The test employed were: — writing the opposites of a set of words, marking A's on a page of printed capital letters, marking words containing certain combinations of letters, marking mis-spelled words, and finally tests of addition and multiplication. Children of the same parents, not twins but about the same age, were also measured, but only in the first two tests. For them the coefficient correlation fell between .30 and .40. The twins, however, show a resemblance which is twice as great as this. For them the coefficients of correlation range from .71 to .90, averaging .78. Of the mental processes, those most subject to training (addition and multiplication) appear, it is true, to yield a correlation slightly higher than those least subject to training; but the differences between them are too slight to be of significance. If due to environment the resemblances should increase with age, so long as the children remained at the same school and lived at their own home. The experimental results, however, show that the older they are, that is, the further they are from birth, the smaller are the correlations: for twins 9 to 11 years of age the coefficients average .83, for those 12 to 14 years of age they average only .70. Hence the resemblance is originally due to birth, and is diminished progressively by the post-natal influence of environment.

The specialization of inheritance was strikingly exhibited in the resemblances of twins. It was found that twins might be indistinguishable from each other in their powers of mechanical association, and yet prove extremely dissimilar in their powers of sense-perception. So with other traits. Specific capacities can thus be inherited in total independence of one another.

The influence of environment has also been directly illuminated by experimental research. So far as mental capacities are concerned, training in one mental performance affects other mental performances, even those commonly regarded as due to the operation of the same faculty, to an astonishingly small extent. Training in memorising prose, poetry or tables does not appreciably affect power to memorise letters, dates or nonsense syllables, much less improve the faculty of memory, measured by recognised experimental tests, as a whole.[19] Apparent improvement is due, not to development of mental contents, — specific memories, specific habits, specific interests, available ideas of method or of aim.

It appears, therefore, that the effects of post-natal training are unexpectedly circumscribed, and never transferred to functions other than the limited functions specifically trained.

CONCLUSION

We have now reviewed the chief researches carried out along three convergent lines of investigation. By itself no one of them is free from objections. Taken together, however, their main results are in close agreement. This agreement is more impressive, because the several lines of investigation have hitherto been followed in complete independence of one another, one school often severely criticising the methods adopted by the others.

Among individuals, mental capacities are inherited. Of this the evidence is conclusive. General mental efficiency (that is, 'intelligence' or 'ability,') and its absence are undoubtedly inherited both in extreme and in moderate degrees. Special mental capacities are probably inherited also, the several qualities being transmitted in relative independence of one another. The intensity of mental inheritance appears closely to resemble that of physical inheritance both in man and in other animals; and, so far as mental capacity rather than mental content is concerned, far to outweigh the intensity of environmental influences.

---

[19] W. G. Sleight, 'Memory and Formal Training,' *British Journal of Psychology*, Vol. IV., pts. 3 and 4 (December, 1911)—the most recent and thorough of all investigations upon this problem.

The fact of mental inheritance, therefore, can no longer be contested, and its importance can scarcely be over-estimated.

B. *The Principles of Mental Inheritance*

So far it is with the fact of mental heredity that I have dealt; I now propose to glance at its principles. So far we have seen only *that* mental qualities are inherited; we may now turn to see *how* they are inherited. The central problem may be stated thus: Does mental inheritance follow the same laws as physical inheritance, or does it follow laws of its own?

In relation to the inheritance of physical characters, the ruling principles, at all events in orthodox biology of the present day, are those associated with the names of Weismann and of Mendel.

1. WEISSMANNISM

The doctrine advanced by Weissmann is this: Natural selection of spontaneous congenital variations is adequate to explain all the facts of evolution. In consequence, the inheritance of post-natal characters, acquired by individuals during their lifetime, is an inconceivable, unnecessary, and illegitimate assumption. As regards physical inheritance, this doctrine is now generally accepted.[20]

Now there is no doubt that it is in the field of mental progress that Weissmannism encounters its greatest difficulties. Consider any instinct; for instance, that of feigning death; or, among certain flat-fish, that of swimming on the side. The latter involves at least four coincident and co-operative adaptations: a reflex tendency to swim on the side, a displacement of the eyes to guide the movements, an alteration of the protective colouring of both surfaces of the body, and numerous changes in the structure of the body and fins. It is so easy to explain these as first acquired by the efforts of an unusually intelligence animal, then fixed as a habit, and finally inherited.

---

[20] It is fair to recognise that the biological question is by no means finally closed; and that experiment may yet furnish evidence against an absolute acceptance of Weissmann's principles. But if inheritance of acquired modifications remains a theoretical possibility, nevertheless, to have evaded demonstration hitherto, its effects must be infinitesimal and for practical purposes negligible. This, I think, is now non-controversial.

It is so difficult to believe that they originated by the accumulation of little alterations of structures, bit by bit, till the whole was complete. For, it would seem, each bit is useless without the rest; indeed the half is not only less valuable than the whole, it is actually more dangerous than none at all. An animal who made a half-hearted feint of death would be eaten up far more certainly than if he had been content, like the rest of his species, to run away. Nor can we postulate a sudden and complete variation: to attribute the origin of the side-swimming flat-fish to a single vast 'mutation' would be absurd. Such arguments as these have led certain writers to assume that mental acquisitions may be handed on, even if bodily acquisitions are not. They have postulated a sort of Racial Memory and even a sort of Racial Soul. Were such a postulate proven, it would relegate psychological inheritance to a shadowy limbo of its own; it would upset the only intelligible explanation of heredity,—the theory of a continuous germ-plasm; it would completely shatter the application of Eugenic principles to all qualities of the mind.

There is, however, an alternative possibility. It is a possibility which explains all serious difficulties, which in some cases is an undoubted fat and which makes no such demand upon our power of imagining the mysterious and the vague. This is the principle known as Organic Selection. Overlooked by biologists, it was discovered simultaneously by two psychologists: Lloyd Morgan in England and J. M. Baldwin in America. It postulates the inheritance only of small variations, occurring in all directions and successively accumulated; but it points out that a variation which occurs in the direction of the future complex instinct is, in an intelligent animal, by no means necessarily useless. For, while imperfect, it can meanwhile be eked out by intelligence, by acquired habits and conscious guidance; it will in turn co-operate with intelligence; and the two together will save the animal's life, where one alone will not. Thus sheltered, the incomplete variation will now be handed on to offspring; the complete intelligent action will not. But sooner or later, another portion of the completed adaptation will occur spontaneously and fortuitously among the subsequent congenital variations. This again will be protected, handed on, and so survive. Thus by the co-operation of mind, natural selection can evolve the most complex properties of mind, without these properties being inherited except when inborn and not merely acquired.

With the enunciation of this principle the gravest objections against extending the doctrine of Weissmannism to cover also the facts of mental evolution and inheritance disappear. The psychological world has been ransacked for further instances irreducible to natural selection; but without success. Language has been suggested as a crucial case. The members of each nation have spoken their respective mother tongues for centuries. Yet, beyond a common tendency to articulation attributable with ease to pure natural selection, there is no sign of the characteristic habit thus repeatedly acquired being transmitted to the young by inheritance. Till recently, one experimental result remained difficult to explain away. This concerned the nervous system—the place where, as we have seen, transmission would be of greatest value. Brow-Sequard found that, among guinea pigs, the offspring of animals whose sciatic nerve had been cut exhibited what appeared to be a form of epilepsy, and other neurotic tendencies, similar to those induced in the parents by the operation. Recent research, however, has shown that the nature of the symptoms and their causation were entirely misconceived. Some of the most striking of all apparent instances of 'lapsed intelligence,'—the working instincts of certain moths and beetles, which lay their eggs but once, or die before the results of their activities are achieved—these are at most certainly due to the natural selections of blind variations. Being sterile, the working bees have no offspring, to which to transmit the skill their intelligence might be supposed to have taught them. The moths and the beetles have no opportunity of learning the requisite actions, or of observing their effects, even assuming that they had the intelligence to await, to watch and to comprehend them. These processes, therefore, can never have been individually acquired. Hence, there is no reason to assume that, when individually acquired, such processed are ever inherited.[21]

In the case of man, the most conclusive evidence against the inheritances of acquired mental characteristics is afforded by the history of civilisation. Never have forces acted upon the mind with such persistence and in such numbers as during the historic period: never have habits, memories and ideas been acquired and re-acquired upon so vast a scale. Yet, there is a striking consensus of opinion to the effect that, in the main, the human race has, in its innate qualities, remained practically stationary. In inborn mental constitution the civilised inhabitant of Paris or London of to-day is, if anything, inferior rather than superior to his prehistoric ancestors. The evidence from the size and conformation of their skulls, from the tools and weapons they invented and manufactured, from the rude sculptures and paintings upon their implements and caves suggests that in native ability the primitive peoples inhabiting Europe before the dawn of history were not a whit behind their descendants. Civilisation, therefore, has

---

[21] Graham Brown, An Alleged Specific Instance of the Transmission of Acquired Characters. *Proc. Roy. Soc.* (1912), B., Vol. 84.

been an advance in mental content, stored in the environment and re-acquired with each succeeding generation, rather than an improvement in hereditary capacities or an inheritance of the improvements acquired. All that is mentally inherited is the original constitution common to the race and the congenital variations that from time to time spontaneously occur.

This is the inference of the most competent authorities.

"If," says Lloyd Morgan, "mental evolution in man be manifested rather in the progressive advance of human achievement than in the progressive increment of human faculty; if the developmental process has been transferred from the individuals to their environment,...if there be thus no conclusive evidence that faculty is improving, but rather the opposite; it all this be so, then it would seem that the ground is out away from under the feet of those who regard mental evolution in man as due to inherited increments of individually acquired faculty. It would seem probable that with the waning influence of natural selection, there has been a diminution also of human faculty. Hence, there is little or no evidence of the hereditary transmission of increments of faculty due to continued and persistent use."[22]

By the human mind, therefore, as by the animal organism, acquired characters are never inherited.

2. MENDELISM

The laws associated with the name of Abbe Mendel are of even greater interest than the doctrine of Weissmann. Unlike the statistical laws studied by the biometricians, the Mendelian laws are most clearly established in the case of discontinuous traits; traits which can be sharply separated into classes, and studied in their distribution among the individual members of particular families. There appears, however, some ground for the hypothesis that all physical traits which are truly hereditary as such are discontinuous: that every organisms is biologically a patch-work or mosaic of unit-characters each of which is dealt with separately in inheritance. Perhaps the most interesting case of Mendelian principles in man is the inheritance. Perhaps the most interesting case of Mendelian principles in man is the inheritance of

---

[22] Lloyd Morgan, *Habit and Instinct* (1896), pp. 345-346.

eye-colour.[23] If a husband possessing pigmented irises, that is, so-called brown eyes, being himself of an unixed brown-eyed stock, marry a wife whose irises are non-pigmented, and whose eyes, therefore, are pure blue, the hybrid offspring tend all to have brown eyes. The presence of the pigment is perpotent; brown eyes are, as it is termed, 'dominant.' If, now, we mate a hybrid (and, therefore, brown-eyed) son with a hybrid (and, therefore, brown-eyed) daughter, half of their offspring will be hybrids like themselves, brown-eyed, but of a mixed stock. But the blue eyes have not finally disappeared. They were only latent in the hybrid son; or, as it is termed, 'recessive.' Of the rest of the grandchildren, one half will be blue-eyed, and will always breed true; it mated with blue eyes, they will never reproduce brown. The other half will brown-eyed, and will also breed true; if mated with unmixed, not hybrid, brown eyes, they will never reproduce blue. Thus the presence of brown pigment in the iris is a unit-character; it never really blends on crossing; and its presence or absence may persist through an indefinite number of generations, or be entirely eliminated in three. Its presence is inherited only through those who possess it; whereas its absence may appear to skip a generation.

There is some evidence that hair-colour is transmitted on analogous, though perhaps, more complicated lines.[24] These two characters are of peculiar importance, because as we shall presently see, they are characteristic of the so-called Teutonic race;

---

[23] Hurst, 'On the Inheritance of Eye-Colour in Man,' *Proc. Roy. Soc.* (B) Vol. LXXX., 1908. Davenport, 'Heredity of Eye-Colour in Man,' *Science* (1907), Vol. XXVI., p. 589.

[24] Hurst, 'Mendelian Heredity in Man,' EUGENICS REVIEW, Vol. IV., No. 1 (April, 1912). Davenport, 'Heredity of Hair-Colour in Man,' *American Naturalist* (April, 1909). Vol. XLIII., p. 193. Salaman (*Journal of Genetics*, Vol. I., p. 273; EUGENICS REVIEW, Vol. III., No. 4), adduces evidence of analogous behaviour in the facial characteristics of races in marriages between Jews and Gentiles. He believes that 'the Jewish facial type, whether it be considered to rest on a gross anatomical basis, or regarded as the reflection in the facial musculature of a peculiar psychical state, is subject to the Mendelian law of Heredity.' This is of special interest to the temperaments; and, in cases of inter-marriage, the temperament appears commonly to be transmitted in correlation with the physiognomy. These extensions of Mendelism, however, have not escaped severe criticism. A recent writer in *Biometrika* (1912, Vol. VIII., pts. 3 and 4), even contends: 'It is not too much to say that the endeavour to make man a complex of sharply-defined unit-characters has failed, and failed completely. Even the researches of Hurst, which were received with an almost lyrical enthusiasm by the adherents of Mendelism, are not above suspicion.'

and in England, of the three main European racial types, the Teutonic is by far the most easy to recognise, both in bodily habit and in mental temperament. Other simple cases, such as congenital cataract and brachydactyly, leave no doubt that Mendelian formulae apply to man so far as physical characters are concerned.

In mental heredity the applicability of Mendelian formulae would be of peculiar importance. Psychical characters are peculiarly complex. Sterilise the criminal, it is said; and you may be sterilising useful independence as well as disastrous immorality. Sterilise the insane; and you may be sterilising, not only dangerous eccentricity, but the priceless originality of some allied genius. How, too, can you draw sharp lines between the normal and the abnormally good or bad? Do they not merge into one another by insensible gradations? Upon Mendelian principles the answer would be clear. Though, like eye-colour, apparently continuous, and found in every shade, grade, and blend; yet, again like eye-colour, such characters may really depend upon discrete units, fundamental to them, which are inherited alternatively, and may, by appropriate matrimonial unions, be segregated, eliminated, or preserved.

Are there, then, any signs of Mendelian inheritance in mental characters?

They are found most conclusively in the case of congenital colour-blindness, night-blindness, and (less certainly) in deaf-mutism. These are specific defects of the two most important senses, hearing and sight. Mendelian principles seem to hold good in two instincts in fowls; probably, of feeble-mindedness; and more certainly, in at least one type of insanity (Huntingdon's chorea) and at least one type of ability (musical talent).

Perhaps the most suggestive possibilities are to be sought, not on the intellectual or cognitive side of mental life, but on the emotional or conative. Some years ago, in the course of a series of simple psychological experiments, Professor Binet noticed a marked opposition between the temperaments of his two daughters.[25] One child, Armande, appeared to be unpractical, imaginative reflective; and, in her reflections and imaginations, sentimental and original. The other, Marguerite, was the reverse. He was even able to measure this difference in quantitative form. On the basis of his results, he distinguished two antithetical mental types,—an objective type, and a

---

[25] *L'Etude experimentals de l'Intelligence* (1903). Also, *Les Idees modernes sur les Enfants* (1910), p. 252 sq., 'Remarques sur quelques types intellectuals,' esp. pp. 262-276. A brief description of some of the experiments and their results will be found in Myers, *Introduction to Experimental Psychology*, Chapter VII.

subjective type. His differentiation was severely criticised; two cases were declared to be far too few to support such a generalisation.

The same and similar tests have been recently repeated upon a large number of Liverpool school-children for other purposes. The same dichotomy has unexpectedly recurred. In particular, two children, whom we may call Margaret and Mary, yielded numerical differences almost exactly parallel to those exhibited by Marguerite and Aramnde. Like Marguerite, Margaret is practical and objective. Mary is reflective, subjective, and sentimental, like Armande. Margaret is hard-headed, Mary is soft-hearted. Now, these two children present as striking a contrast in physique and physiognomy as in temperament. Margaret is tall, fair, blue-eyed; in face long, but angular; narrow, but not very narrow, in head. Mary is short, dark, brown-eyed; oval in face and very narrow in head. Margaret belongs to a North Europeans or 'Teutonic' type; Mary resembles the South European or 'Mediterranean' type. Margaret recalls the conventional portrait of the 'Saxon'; Mary, that of the 'Celt.' Both parents are dark, short, and 'Celtic.' Upon enquiry it proved that while three grandparents were dark and came from the West of Ireland, one was tall and fair and hailed from Yorkshire.

M. Binet had not described the physical characteristics of his two daughters. In answer to a letter he replied, not long before his death, that the characteristics of his daughters had persisted comparatively unchanged and were therefore presumably innate; further, that in head-form and colour of hair and eyes they presented analogous differences to my own pair. 'Marguerite,' he writes, 'est en effet plus blonde, les yeux plus bleus, et le crane plus large que Armande.' He was not, however, disposed to connect the physical sign with constrat in mentality by a necessary law.

Several similar cases have since been observed. The small number as yet accumulated leaves the evidence suggestive, rather than conclusive. There are, too, distinct cases of disharmonism:—'Celtic' temperaments correlated with Teutonic physique, like the brown eyes that are sometimes found with fair hair, or the broad faces that are more rarely found upon narrow heads. Such as it is, however, the evidence indicates strongly that the two temperaments follow, with more or less complication, Mendelian laws.

Finally, it is commonly believed that antithetical temperaments are possessed by the two sexes. This may or may not be true. Experiment shows that certain mental differences, constant though small, obtain.[26] As we pass from higher capacities, such as systematic thought, to lower capacities, such as movement and sensory discrimination, as we turn from intellectual processes on the one hand to instincts and emotions on the other, the sex-differences appear to become more pronounced. The most striking is the relative freedom of women from colour-blindness as contrasted with its frequency among men. Now the phenomenon of sex-limitation inheritance seems explicable only upon Mendelian lines,—upon the principles, that is, of dominance and segregation. Wherever it appears in mental characteristics, therefore, it argues that these mental characteristics are themselves according to Mendelian modes.

So far as our meagre evidence goes, the same principle that govern physical inheritance appear to govern mental inheritance too. The peculiar limitations in the evidence even point to a reason why the same principles govern both alike. The innate mental differences between one individual and another, between one racial type and another, and between one sex and another, suggest by their very nature and distribution, that they are correlated with innate physical differences; they appear secondary to, and dependent upon, differences of sense-organ, differences of muscle, differences of internal organs and viscera, differences of internal secretions and glands, and finally, differences in the architecture and chemistry of 'brain and nerve,' that is, of the central nervous system itself. The inferences, and even the premises, are as yet but matter for tentative and unverified speculation. Nevertheless, in view of all these intimations, it remains, I think, a legitimate working hypothesis to suppose that the vehicle of mental inheritance is, at bottom, material; that so far as hereditary differences and hereditary likenesses are concerned, soul depends on body, matter conditions mind.[27]

---

[26] *Cf.* Cyril Burt and Robert Moore 'The Mental Differences between the Sexes.' *Journal of Experimental Pedagogy*, Vol. I., No. 4 (June, 1912), and ensuing numbers.

[27] In describing mental inheritance as 'material,' I do not mean to imply that it is merely mechanistic. But, if it is non-mechanistic, it is so only in so far as it shares this characteristic with all forms of inheritance, physical included. The quasi-vitalistic interpretaions of heredity and evolution, which have been so brilliantly enunciated by Driesch and Bergson, and which are now finding favour with so many biologists, are non-mechanistic; the psychologist may even conceive them as immaterial and animistic; but, I believe, to most biologists, they represent principles which, though non-mechanistic, are not anti-materialistic. Upon the part played by mind in evolution, it is necessary only to refer to Mr. McDougall's volume, *Body and Mind*.

II. MENTAL CHARACTERS OF RACES

Hitherto we have enquired into the facts and principles of mental inheritance as they emerge in the study of the mental characters of individuals. We now pass to the mental characters of peoples. Those who have discussed the influence of remote ancestry, or race, have commonly ignored the exacter knowledge recently obtained as to the influence of immediate ancestry, or family. Hence, the issue here becomes more problematic. Examined, however, in the light of facts and principles learnt in the field of individual psychology, the existence and nature of racial inheritance becomes comparatively clear. Evidence may be sought in two directions: from experimental investigations among savage peoples, and from statistical investigations among civilised.

1. *Savage Races*

It has commonly been believed that in the distance-senses, smell, hearing and vision, uncivilized races are vastly superior to civilised; and, in intelligence, vastly inferior. These beliefs are based upon the observations of travellers, and these in turn upon casual impressions. Such sources yield no information as to how far the differences described are innate. For this we must turn to the results of scientific measurements.

In 1898 trained experimental psychologists joined an English expedition to the Torres Straits to investigate for the first time by means of an adequate laboratory equipment a primitive people under their ordinary conditions of life.[28] Subsequently at the St. Louis Exhibition in 1904, Professor Woodworth tested a number of different races.[29] The results of these and similar investigations are in striking contrast with common belief. Among primitive races, visual acuity is but little superior to that of Europeans; their marvellous powers of sight are found to depend upon powers of inference and interpretation, that is, upon interests, habits, or knowledge acquired. Their discrimination by ear is discovered to be slightly inferior to that of Scotch peasants; considerably inferior to that of English town children, especially those of the intellectual classes. Among Papuans, Dyaks and Todas, touch discrimination is superior

---

[28] *Reports of the Cambridge Anthropological Expedition to Torres Straits* (1903), II., part ii., p. 189, sq., *cf.* also Myers, *Introduction to Experimental Psychology*, pp. 91-102.

[29] Woodworth, 'Racial Differences in Mental Traits,' *Science, N.S.*, Vol. **XXXI**. (1910), pp. 171-186.

to that of children from the country or from the slums; and far superior to that of cultured persons, such as University graduates and undergraduates. Thus the differences in the senses, the oldest mental traits, are constant and small. In higher intellectual processes the difference seems to be a little larger, but still unexpectedly small. The only sign of considerable inferiority was found among Negritoes from the Philippines, and Pygmies from the Congo. At one test, intended to measure intelligence, the Pygmies hardly did as well as the "feeble-minded" and "higher grade imbeciles" in the American asylums. These races are believed to have degenerated. It is unfortunate that no emotional tests have yet been applied; as here the racial differences are probably larger than in any other region of the mind.[30]

Professor Woodworth thus sums up the general results. "We are probably justified in inferring that the sensory and motor processes and the elementary brain activities, though differing in degree from one individual to another, are about the same from one race to another."[31]

The differences then in innate mental capacities between civilised and uncivilised races, though apparently characteristic, appear astonishingly slight. This confirms our conjectures as to the mind of primitive peoples existing before the dawn of history. In either comparison, the superiority of the modern civilised man is due not to hereditary powers and capacities, but to mental contents and achievements, transmitted and accumulated, not by inheritance, but by tradition.

2. *European Races*

Let us now compare the civilised peoples, not with the uncivilised, but among themselves. Considerable mental differences appear superficially to characterise the inhabitants of different European countries, and of different areas within those countries. Their nature is a matter of popular knowledge. The peoples of South Europe, such as those of Italy and Spain, are commonly described as speculative and deductive in thought, and vivacious, impulsive, fickle, choleric, alternately melancholy and gay, in action and in feeling. The peoples of the North, such as the English, the

---

[30] The doctrine that the chief peculiarities of the primitive mind are to be sought in its emotional side, not in its intellectual side, is perhaps the novel feature of Mr. Franz Boas' recent work, *The Mind of Primitive Man* (New York, 1911).

[31] *Science, l.c.* (I should like to have the word 'about' italicised).

North German, and the Scandinavians, are commonly allege to be, in thought, empirical and inductive; and in feeling and in action, reserved, sanguine, bold, enterprising, independent. The former are depicted as light-headed and hot-blooded; the latter as hard-headed and cold-blooded. The peoples of Central Europe, such as those of South Germany and Russia, are commonly described as phlegmatic, conservation, catholic, stable, submissive, unprogressive, heavy and slow. Even within the British Isles there are well-attested mental differences among the various local types. We are accustomed to contrast the Irish and the Welsh with the English and the Scotch. To the stranger,[32] the former appear to be as lively and as loquacious as the latter are reserved and taciturn; as imaginative and as emotional as the others are truthful and just. Easily elated and as quickly collapsing, "inconstant, mobile, musical," "always ready to react against the despotism of fact," possessing "a quick genius checkmated for the want of strenuousness or else patience," the disposition of the Welsh and Irish has formed a theme for comment for centuries.[33] With them contrast the Yorkshireman.

"In few parts of Britain does there exist a more clearly marked moral type than in Yorkshire...The character is essentially Teutonic, including the shrewdness, the truthfulness without candour, the perseverance, the energy and industry of the Lowland Scotch, but little of their frugality or of the theological instinct common to the Welsh and Scotch, or the more brilliant qualities which sometimes light up the Scotch character. The sound judgment, the spirit of fair play, the love of comfort, order and cleanliness, and the fondness for heavy feeding are shared with the Saxon Englisman, but are still more strongly marked, as is also the bluff independence...The mind, like the body, is generally very vigorous and energetic; and extremely well adapted to commercial and industrial pursuits, as well as must be admitted,—probably one reason why Yorkshire, until modern times, was generally behindhand in politics and religion.[34]

These differences are said to reappear in the geniuses springing from families indigenous to the various localities. Thus, of the 120 most eminent British men of science twenty-one are Scotch and only one Irish; of the forty-two most eminent actors none are Scotch and six Irish. The Anglo-Danish geniuses have been mathematicians (*e.g.*,

---

[32] *E.g.*, the American Anthropologist, Ripley, *The Races of Europe*, p. 333.

[33] The quotations are from Giraldus do Barry (twelfth century), Honri Martin, *Les Races Anciennes d'Irlandes* (1878), and Matthew Arnold, respectively.

[34] Beddoe, *The Races of Britain* (1885), p. 252.

Newton, numerous Cambridge men) or geologists (Darwin); the East Anglian, natural historians (Francis Bacon, Gilbert, Ray), or surgeons; the Southern, scientists, physiologists (Harvey, Stephen, Hales, Huxley), and physicists (Adams, Thomas Young).[35]

Are these regional differences in intellect, temperament and character due to heredity and race, or to environment and tradition? On the one hand, we have seen that even between European and non-Europeans races, and between pre-historic and civilised races, the innate mental differences are amazingly small; on the other hand, as attested both by type of skill and by type of culture and custom, these small differences have often persisted unaltered in certain areas through all the vicissitudes of history, or have followed the movements of the several peoples as they migrated into other grounds.

The chief criteria for the classification of European races are certain physical features. These are, more particularly, three: the shape of the head and face, the colour of the hair and eyes, and stature. Of but little value independently, taken together, and checked by less regular cues such as physiognomy, language and history, they appear comparatively reliable. Three fundamental racial groups are commonly distinguished. Descendants of palaeolithic man are dubious and rare; ignoring these, (1) the oldest extant European race appears to be the short, dark, narrow-headed, oval faced peoples, found in greatest frequency in South Italy and Spain. Its members resemble in many respects the men of Neolithic culture, the men who developed the culture of the age of polished stone, and left their implements, their short skeletons, and their long skulls interred in long burros or mounds. In the British Isles, it appears to form the chief element in the so-called 'Celtic,' or rather Celtic-speaking populations. This is variously known as the Iberian, South European or Mediterranean race. (2) A shortish, darkish, pre-eminently broad-headed, round-faced face is found around the Alps, in Central France, and Little Russia; and is sometimes identified with the peoples that brought the Celtic language and a bronze civilisation, perhaps from Mongolian Asia, into Western Europe; taught them apparently to the older inhabitants; then themselves died out or migrated again eastwards, leaving their ancestors' round skulls buried in round burrows. These are variously known as the Celtic, Celtic-Slavic, Apline, or Armenoid races. Finally, (3) a fair-haired, blue-eyed race, tall, and rather long in head and face, appeared in historic times from the regions around the Baltic.

---

[35] Havelock Ellis, *A Study of British Genius* (1904).

As Saxons, Danes, Norse, Franks, Lombards, Burgundians, Goths, Ostrogoths, and Visigoths, they overran all Europe, thrusting the older races into the remote uplands and isolated peninsulas. Their purest representatives are to be found in Scandinavia. They form the Nordic or Teutonic race. Tuetonic, Alpine, Mediterranean,—North European, Central European, South European,—this threefold classification we may perhaps accept.[36]

Among the racial groups thus distinguished by physique, the anthropologists of the nineteenth century discovered also certain hereditary peculiarities of temperament or mind. To sum them up in a single term, popular or technical is undoubtedly fallacious. Briefly, and therefore loosely, we may epitomise them thus. The North European race and the South European race they seem to have conceived as active or, as we might now say, 'conative,' races. The Central European race as passive or non-conative. The activities of the South European were conceived as imaginative or emotional in tendency, or in a word, affective. Those of the North European as intellectual and practical, in a word, cognitive. It will be seen that these suppositions account with some plausibility for the local differences in temperament noted above.

The racial school of sociologists, the hereditarians, derived much of their data from French sources. In France, each of the three fundamental types is fully represented. Statistical surveys of the population according to stature, colour and form of head are in agreement. They point to a strong Teutonic element in the North, spreading from the basin of the Seine further north into Flanders, and southwards towards Bordeaux; a strong Mediterranean element along the Southern coast, spreading up the Rhone to meet a Teutonic stream at Lyons; and four isolated Alpine groups, in the Vosges mountains, the Savoy Alps, the Auvergue Plateau, and the peninsula of Brittany. Further surveys have been utilised to throw light on the intellectual, moral and artistic, domestic, social and political tendencies of these areas. It appears that the Teutonic and the Mediterranean departments yield the largest proportional number of noted men of letters, and obtain the greatest number of awards made by the Salon at Paris; in Alpine departments these distinctions are rare. The several Alpine districts,

---

[36] This is not the place to estimate the validity of the criteria proposed, the measurements made, the calculations based upon them, or the attempts to combine physical characters into racial types. It is sufficient to warn the reader that every step in the procedure has been severely criticised.

however, are peculiarly free from divorce and suicide, which becomes intense in the Teutonic areas. Except in Brittany, and disregarding cities, the Alpine inhabitants tend to occupy separate dwellings,—homes of their own; the Tuetonic inhabitants prefer tenements and boarding houses. In the elections of deputies the Alpine areas return chiefly conservatives; the Teutons and Mediterraneans radicals. These differences harmonise well with the hereditary differences assumed; and the general coincidence of geographical distribution of the mental characters with those of the physical is most alluring.

Analogous coincidences have been traced in other countries,—such as Germany and Italy. Many, indeed, contend that they do not harmonise with those discovered in France; yet an impartial analysis finds but few contradictions.[37]

Of recent years a new school of anthropo-geography has arisen. Like Mill and Buckle in an older generation, these writers are thorough-going environmentalists. The psychological characters of human societies they attribute to their material environment, geographically and economically regarded, almost as exclusively as the hereditarians attributed them to race.[38]

Thus, the mental features of Teutonic and Mediterranean France, enumerated above, they deduce from the fact that these peoples happen to have settles in fertile and populous, river basins and coasts; those of the Alpine populations they ascribe to the infertility and isolation of the mountain areas in which they are confined.

Now it is impossible to deny all efficacy to environment, natural and social alike. It is impossible to deny that, where civilisation has suspended natural selection, peculiarities of social environment still contribute to a large extent to determine the mental character, and especially the mental contents, of the individuals who compose a nation or community. It is impossible to deny that, before civilisation conquered nature, the natural environment must have determined the capacities of the surviving races by eliminating those that were mentally unfit to live in it under primitive conditions. Thus, a nomadic people would be evolved upon the steppes; and inactive, sedentary people upon fertile plains; a daring, roving independent people among maritime fiords. The

---

[37] For further discussion, see Ripley, *The Races of Europe*, Chapter XIX. 'Social Problems, Environment *versus* Race.

[38] Perhaps the best elaboration of the principles of this school in English is to be found in Miss Semples' *Influences of Geographic Environment, on the basis of Ratzel's system of Antropo-geography* (1911).

difficulty which confronts the exclusive environmentalist is this: when the races thus evolved migrate to new regions, they do not completely or immediately acquire characteristics suited to their new mode of life, but may for centuries preserve the old. Nor are the elements preserved merely the ancient beliefs and institutions handed on by tradition. The persistence of a tradition alone would imply the persistence of the temperament to which it was congenial. The Alpines of Celto-Slavs from the mountains preserve the temperament of a mountain race in the plains of Brittany and White Russia. Irish and Jewish emigrants are notoriously true to their racial character all the world over. The Teutons of Cumberland, in an infertile, sparsely populated area, are as suicidal as the most densely populated parts of the 'black country,' while the survivors of the old British populations left unmolested by the Teutonic invasions from the South and East in and around Hertfordshire, are as immune to suicide as Wales, or Cornwall, North Scotland or Ireland, in spite of their proximity to London.[39]

To meet this difficulty the environmentalists make two flagrant biological assumptions, which they seldom think to question. They assume, first of all, that, after the environment has operated upon a community through a number of generations in succession, the characters, thus cumulatively re-impressed upon it must become for the time hereditary. Secondly, they assume that, when migrating populations meet and mingle, their peculiar characteristics blend and neutralise one another, thus at length producing a homogeneous and characterless race once more, upon which environment can act afresh.

These assumptions, however, are in violent antagonism with the principles of Weissmann and Mendel. There is, we have seen, every reasons to believe that acquired mental characteristics are not inherited; and that innate mental characters do not necessarily blend, and but may segregate and persistently reappear in their original purity. Nor is there any reason to believe that since the dawn of history, among the civilised peoples either of the present or the past, environment has operated by way of

---

[39] Morselli, *Suicde* (Int. Sci. Ser., 1881), Maps, *ad. fin.*, Tabs. 1 and 4. The persistence of these racial tendencies, irrespective of changes in economic, social, or material conditions, is at length finding recognition among leading economists and social writers. *Cf.*, for instance, Marshall on 'The Character of Englishmen,' *Principles of Economics* (1898), pp. 34-5; or the Webbs, on racial differences in the 'Instinctive Standard of Life,' *Industrial Democracy* (1902), esp. footnote, pp. 697-8.

natural, economic, or social selection to alter fundamentally the innate racial characters as originally evolved.

Finally, it is important to remember one further point. If the conditions incidental to life in a populous district affect the mental characteristics of a people, it is the mental characteristics of the people that have made them prefer the populous district. Statistical investigations have established this. The population of towns grows steadily darker in complexion, shorter in stature, and narrower in head. The population of the countryside remains broad-headed. The darkness might be ascribed to 'dominance'; the shortness to poverty; the head-shape itself has sometimes been found to change among immigrants in one or two generations. But even the environmentalists have chosen the more obvious explanation. "We are forced to the conclusion," says Ripley, "that there is some mental characteristics of the long-headed types, either their energy, ambition, or hardiness, which makes them peculiarly prone to migrate from the country to the city; or else, a peculiar disinclination on the part of the broad-headed race thus to betake itself to towns."[40]

The plausibility of the environmentalist is thus left reposing upon a single, slender point,—its superior intelligibility. It is easy to picture the mode of operation of the environment. It is hard, as yet, to imagine the mechanism of heredity. This is a seductive basis for a theory; but for a theory otherwise unsupported, it is inadequate. It is a motive, not a reason, for belief. Not intelligibility, but verifiability, is the test of truth. Wherever we have hitherto been able to verify and measure the influence upon mental capacity of heredity and environment, namely, in every method used for studying the characters of individuals, there we have found heredity operating, operating indeed mysteriously, yet operating surely and powerfully; there we have found the operation of environment elusive, transient, and negligible. Accordingly, when we turn to races, we have no right to repudiate a principle indicated *prima facie* by the evidence before us, established as a *vera causa* by evidence elsewhere, inevitable in the long run even when the alternative hypothesis has been exploited to the uttermost.

Environment, therefore, may explain the differences in different societies of the traditional mental contents. Heredity remains indispensable to explain the differences in mental capacities. These differences are the more fundamental.

---

[40] *The Races of Europe*, p. 548.

We recognise, then, the presence of hereditary mental differences even among the races of civilised Europe. Like the differences between civilised and uncivilised, these differences must again be small. But a slight bias may produce large deflection. Eluding the experimentalist, either because in degree they are so small, or because in kind they are emotional rather than sensory or motor, these differences may well have sufficed, in the national selection from those mental contents which form the common stock of civilisation, to determine a choice of institutions, customs, and beliefs congenial rather than uncongenial to the native temperament of each community. Each community, by its minute hereditary proclivities, thus accumulates a vast tradition, markedly characteristic, eventually unique, but not itself hereditary. Indulge now in a flight of fancy. Imagine that all the babies born in France had at one time been exchanged at birth for those born in England; that ultimately England had become secretly peopled with inhabitants of purely French extraction; and France with inhabitants purely English. Suppose further that the occasion chosen was the generation preceding some crisis in the natural history,—the Protestant Reformation or the French Revolution. Would the most ardent advocate of the omnipotence of the environment dare to maintain that the nation would nevertheless have continued its original career, or that its subsequent history would not have to be rewritten?[41] Mental inheritance, then, not only moulds the character of individuals; it rules the destiny of nations.

CONCLUSION

We have now reviewed the chief evidence for the inheritance of mental characteristics both in the individual and in the race. We have noticed the principles which such inheritance obeys. In the case of the individual, we found the influence of heredity large and indisputable; in the case of the race, small and controverted. In neither case can it be suggested that the facts are so ill-attested as to be unworthy of practical consideration, or so insignificant as not to merit further scientific research. In both cases the principles indicated, and the methods available, are analogous to those which have proved so pregnant in recent investigations of heredity in other spheres. Yet scarcely a fact, and not a single principle, is placed beyond the need for corroboration; and, thanks to the intimate bearing of psychology on social welfare, such corroboration is in urgent request. There assuredly could be no problem upon which

---

[41] The suggestion is, I believe, Mr. McDougall's.

historians and geographer, traveller and administrator, biologist and experimentalist, statistician and psychologist, could so fruitfully concentrate their wisdom as the problem of heredity and its influence upon the mind.

Hansen, S. (1913). The inferior quality of the first-born children.
Eugenics Review, 5(3), 252–259.

THE INFERIOR QUALITY OF THE FIRST-BORN CHILDREN.

By SOREN HANSEN.[1]

The great decline in the birth-rate in most civilized countries has brought into prominence the question of the inferior quality of the earlier children and given it an interest, which extends far beyond the family circle. At the present time about 75,000 children are born in Denmark each year and of these probably a hundred or so are weak-minded. Whether among these there are 16 or 25 first-born is naturally of no importance save to the persons concerned and their relatives, but *if it is a general rule* that the earlier children are of essentially inferior quality in comparison with their brothers and sisters, then the racial quality of the nation as a whole may be reduced when the birth-rate falls, simply because the first-born constitute an increasing proportion of the nation. In Berlin, for example, the proportion of first-born has increased from 22 per cent. in 1885 to 33 per cent. in 1906, and in France the proportion is almost 50 per cent., while in Denmark they only amount as yet to one-fourth of the total number of children.

That the earliest born children are of inferior quality to the succeeding *at birth* is an indisputable and long-known fact of experience. They weigh less, they are more frequently still-born, and of those that come into the world alive a much larger proportion die in the first year, but the belief has prevailed hitherto that the difference gradually vanishes in the later years, and certainly in the first attempts to prove its persistence in the more advanced year-groups were not convincing. It had not been remarked that the problem is much more complicated than seemed probable at first sight, and sufficient attention was not paid to all the many collateral circumstances that affect investigations of this kind. Whilst much of the criticism advanced has been quite superficial, some of the objections have led to a deeper probing of the question and have brought the study of this equally strange and important phenomenon on to more rational lines.

---

[1] Translated from the Danish by H. M. Kyle.

In the following pages a condensed summary will be given of the evidence, that the earlier born children, not only at birth, but even at a much later period in life, are inferior in quality to the later children. Every one will be able to judge, whether the evidence is satisfactory, as no special mathematical or other scientific acquirements are necessary for its understanding.

For this purpose pulmonary tuberculosis has been chosen. This disease is acquired in general at a very early age, whilst the organism has still but feeble powers of resistance, but does not usually reach its full development until the individual is considerable older. It is further so common that no great difficulty is experience in obtained a sufficiently large material for statistical importance.

On going through the journals of the consumptive section of the Oresund Hospital in Copenhagen information has been obtained regarding the serial position in the family of 3,522 tubercular patients. Arranging these in table like the accompanying we at once obtain a general picture of the size of the families concerned and the serial position of the patients in each. We see—in the column farthest to the right—that there were 988 first-born, 713 second-born, 568 third, and so on. As there were 178 marriages with one child, 301 with two children, and on the whole a large number of marriages with few children, it is not surprising that there are many of the first-born, but if we wish to know whether there are more or fewer than there should be if the birth number has no influence, we must examine how many there would be, if the patients were distributed over the birth numbers (first-born, second-born, etc.) in the same proportions as the total number of sound and diseased children.

If we assume that the 3,522 tubercular patients represent just as many marriages, it is evident that there must have been 3,522 first-born in these marriages, and if we deduct the 178 marriages with only a single child from this number we obtain the number of the second-born children or 3,344. Deducting from this the number of marriages with only two children we obtain the number of third-born, or 3,043 and so on. Lastly, adding together all these numbers we ascertain the total number of children in all the marriages, thus 20,600, and of these, 3,522, as mentioned, or almost a sixth part were tubercular. Taking now this proportion of one-sixth (more exactly 0.171) as the normal relation of diseased to sound children, no matter what the birth-number is, we find that there should be among the diseased 602 first-born, 572 second-born, 520 third-born, and so on, whereas there are in reality 988, 713, 568, and so on.

NUMBER OF CHILDREN IN THE MARRIAGES.

Birth-number	1	2	3	4	5	6	7	8	9	10	11	12	13	14	15	16	17	18	19	20+	Total
1	178	155	170	128	107	74	52	45	26	19	10	9	6	3	-	5	-	-	1	-	988
2	-	146	134	106	100	77	44	45	22	12	9	11	5	1	-	1	-	-	-	-	713
3	-	-	120	109	85	68	56	51	32	19	11	4	1	5	2	1	1	2	-	1	568
4	-	-	-	115	63	81	60	33	31	18	9	7	8	1	1	-	-	-	-	-	427
5	-	-	-	-	75	54	35	38	19	23	10	7	3	3	2	1	-	1	-	-	271
6	-	-	-	-	-	81	43	29	11	12	10	8	3	1	-	-	-	-	-	-	198
7	-	-	-	-	-	-	44	36	13	7	5	6	-	-	1	-	-	-	-	1	113
8	-	-	-	-	-	-	-	49	12	5	6	3	2	2	1	-	-	-	-	1	81
9	-	-	-	-	-	-	-	-	25	6	4	6	2	1	-	2	-	-	-	-	46
10	-	-	-	-	-	-	-	-	-	28	8	2	1	3	2	3	1	-	-	-	48
11	-	-	-	-	-	-	-	-	-	-	6	9	3	1	2	1	1	-	-	-	23
12	-	-	-	-	-	-	-	-	-	-	-	14	5	2	-	2	1	-	-	1	25
13	-	-	-	-	-	-	-	-	-	-	-	-	2	5	-	1	-	-	-	-	8
14	-	-	-	-	-	-	-	-	-	-	-	-	-	2	-	-	-	1	-	-	3
15	-	-	-	-	-	-	-	-	-	-	-	-	-	-	2	1	1	-	-	-	4
16	-	-	-	-	-	-	-	-	-	-	-	-	-	-	-	3	2	-	-	-	5
17	-	-	-	-	-	-	-	-	-	-	-	-	-	-	-	-	-	-	-	-	-
18	-	-	-	-	-	-	-	-	-	-	-	-	-	-	-	-	-	-	-	1	1
Total	178	301	424	458	430	435	334	326	191	149	88	86	41	30	13	21	7	4	1	5	3,522

This simple calculation shows, that among the 3,522 tubercular patients, there were 386, or about 64 per cent., more first-born than there should be, if the birth-number is of no consequence. Nevertheless, we cannot take this result as definitive until we have carefully determined, whether the method is correct. It has to be noted, first of all, that we are only dealing with children of the marriages which have produced consumptive patients. The possibility is not excluded, that for some reason or another too many first-born have come under observation, and that the surplus noted does not agree with the actual condition. Thus, there seems something wrong, when we notice that all the children in the marriages with but one child, and almost half the children of the marriages with two children, were tubercular, since this is not the case among the population in general. We can get rid of this objection in a very simple manner by excluding entirely all the marriages with but one child, or with few children, or even more simply by taking account only of the marriages with a certain number of children for example, five, and we then find that of the 430 tubercular patients issuing from such marriages 107 were first-born, whereas there should only be one-fifth or 86. Moreover, we can also investigate whether the families represented in the hospital contain more or fewer first-born than in the total population of Copenhagen, and the result of this investigation is quite decisive.

According to the census taken in Copenhagen on February 1st, 1901, there were 17,819 marriages with children, and in these there were altogether 69,940 children. Of these 17,819 or 255 per thousand were first-born, whereas in the families represented in the Oresund Hospital there were 20,600 children, and 3,522, or 171 per thousand, first-born.

This difference arises from the fact that the tubercular patients were on the whole grown-up, thus born in marriages of so old a date that child-bearing had ceased, which was not the case with all the marriages of the census.

On closer examination it appears that in marriages of less than five years' duration there were 613 per thousand first-born, in marriages of from 5 years to 10 years' duration 337 per thousand, and so on.

If we exclude these marriages and only take account of those of 25 years' duration and more we find that in these there were 173 per thousand first-born, or almost precisely the same proportion as in the families represented in the hospital. Among the latter, as already mentioned, there are 171 per thousand, or almost a sixth part of all the children, whereas the number of first-born tubercular patients amounted to almost a fourth of the total number. A direct comparison of the number of first-born in all marriages, without regard for their duration, with that among the tubercular patients, with an average age of about 30 years, is not permissible.

It might seem probable that the considerable surplus of first-born tubercular patients arose from the fact that they were older than those born later and thus had been longer exposed to the risk of infection. To inquire into this condition information regarding the age of the patients has been obtained in the case of a somewhat smaller material from Boserup Sanatorium. This embraces 2,113 tubercular patients, and shows that the average age of all the men was 29.6, of all the women 27.4 years. This was quite independent of the birth-number. If we divide this material into two groups for each sex, such that the first group contains the first three birth-numbers, the second all the later children, we find that the earlier born men are even a little younger than the later born, namely 29.5 against 29.8 years old, whilst there is no difference for the women. This result is in good agreement with what has long been known regarding the vitality of the first year or the first two years their chances of life are not less but rather a little better than those of the later born, not because they are in any way stronger, but because the mortality increases with the size of the family and the increasing difficulties of obtaining sufficient care and nourishment. This well-known condition leads to a result that at an age of about 30 years there are almost as many first-born in the world as later born. According to some investigations there are even a little more, though the difference is not so great, that it can explain the large number of first-born tubercular patients. It is greatest in countries where the birth-rate is low and where special care is taken of the few children born, especially when the desire is to have not more than a few. In France, for example, we may estimate that at the age of 30 years there are almost 790 out of 1,000 first-born children alive against about 725 out of 1,000 fifth-born.

We have not any similar investigations for Denmark, but if we start from the French data we may estimate that in the above-mentioned 430 families with five children there would be 90 tubercular patients, if the birth-number were of no importance, whereas there are 107. Thus, even under this very wide presupposition there is an appreciable surplus; but, as a matter of fact, there is no reason to believe that in Denmark there really are more first-born than later children living at thirty years of age; consequently, we should not expect 90, but as shown above 86 first-born among the 430 tubercular patients born in the marriages with five children.

It has been necessary to refer to this point in some detail, since it might, partly at least, have explained the greater frequency of tuberculosis among the first-born, if

127

the birth-rate in Denmark were as low as that in France. In investigations of this kind it is necessary to think of every conceivable source of error, and under this heading we have just the great difference in the composition of the population in the different countries. To compare the frequency of the first-born in a Copenhagen sanatorium with the conditions in a country district in Denmark would be just as erroneous as to compare the conditions in an English sanatorium with those in New South Wales. Further, the material must emanate from within such a short period of time, that no essential changes have occurred during the interval in the birth-rate, and at every point we must always deal with the actual conditions. Lastly, we have to make certain that the material is as trustworthy and accurate as possible, and in this respect the information from sanatoria is much superior to that of insurance societies, where we have always to discount the fact that the insured are not interested in remember cases of tuberculosis among their brothers and sisters. But when we have duly considered all these difficulties we may safely conclude that the result is as correct as statistical investigations can be.

Fromm the investigations discussed here it may be taken as certain that pulmonary tuberculosis is considerably more frequent among the earlier children than among the later, and it may be considered, from all we know about the initial causes of this disease, that this is due to the feebler resisting power to tubercular infection of the earlier by comparison with the later children. This again probably arises from imperfect nutrition during pregnancy, since the channels of circulation in the genital organs of the mother are not yet so well developed as to be able to provide the embryo with sufficient nourishment. Our information on this point is certainly meagre, but in any case it is a probable explanation, which is in good agreement with well-known fact, that abortions are very frequent among newly-married women. The first child born at full term, excluding those conceived before marriage, is born on an average at least sixteen months after marriage in the case of younger mothers and much later for older. That such a total or partial undernourishment of the embryo is able to affect disadvantageously the quality of the first-born child in many ways seems evident, and there is thus nothing improbable in the fact that it is frequently troubled by defects, which reduce its vitality to such an extent that it dies before or shortly after birth. In many cases, however, these defects are of such a nature that the child can live with them and even attain a considerable age. The question is, therefore, whether the difference is of such frequent occurrence that it can be detected statistically, as in the case of pulmonary tuberculosis. The available investigations indicate that this is really the case, but with regard to imbecility, epilepsy, and similar defects, the evidence is not yet absolutely convincing.

If we ask, finally, whether the inferior quality of the earlier children is actually so low that it may influence the racial quality in general, when the number of the first-born increases in proportion as the birth-rate decreases, we must certainly answer in the positive, yet the danger has been greatly overestimated. The racial quality is dependent on so many other conditions, that it is only to a certain extent influenced by the greater or smaller number of the first-born children, and with regard to infantile mortality especially there is sufficient evidence that it is considerably less in families with few children than in families with many. But even in this connection we must guard against general conclusions. Whereas the conditions in France have reached a considerable amount of stability, because the birth-rate there has been low for many years already, it is not excluded that in England and the other English-speaking countries the racial quality may really have been reduced as a direct consequence of the falling birth-rate. Since the fertility of marriages decreases much more rapidly among the well-to-do than in the lower levels of the population, it is quite possible that, hand in hand with the social displacement accompanying this, there will be a decline in the mental and physical level, which may be fateful for the nation unless attention is called to the danger. In other countries also the declining birth-rate is a social phenomenon, which deserves attention. The experience of France indicates that the movement can hardly be stopped, but the consequences may be guarded against by special care of the children that come into the world, and especially of the first-born, for the reason that they are less well equipped by nature for the struggle for existence.

Cobb, J.A. (1914). The alleged inferiority of the first-born, *Eugenics Review*, 5(4), 357-359.

THE ALLEGED INFERIORITY OF THE FIRST-BORN

In the October number of the EUGENICS REVIEW there is a paper by Mr. Soren Hansen adducing evidence that amongst the tuberculous patients in Copenhagen hospital there were 61 per cent. more first-born than might be expected if liability to consumption were independent of order in the family. This evidence is corroborated by M. Lucien March, who, in the same volume, quotes further similar evidence from Professor Pearson as regards tuberculosis, and also gives diagrams showing an excessive number of first-born amongst criminals, lunatics, and sufferers from extreme myopia.

It has been suggested in explanation of these results that prenatal conditions are less favourable in the case of the first-born. But if this unfavourable environment has such an enormous influence of the subsequent life of the child, then the principle of the predominance of nature over environment, which is at the basis of the eugenic movement, will have to be reconsidered. I do not, however, believe that there is sufficient evidence of the inferiority of the first-born, and will proceed to criticise Mr. Hansesn's paper. Before doing so I should say that I believe my criticisms to be equally valid against other writers who have arrived at conclusions similar to his.

I suggest that there are three sources or error in Mr. Hansen's paper. The first is in his method of calculating the probable number of first-born.

Mr. Hansen deals with 3,522 patients. These persons had 17,078 brothers and sisters. The total number of persons in the 3,522 infected families was therefore 20.600, of whom 3,522 were patients. How many first-born should one expect to find amongst these 3,522 patients? Mr. Hansen argues thus about one-sixth of all the members of the infected families were patients, and there were 3,522 first-born in all the families. Therefore we should expect to find about one-sixth of 3,522, or 602 first-born patients. Now in making this calculation he takes no account of the fact that there must be one patient in each family. He simply takes 3,522 persons at random from amongst the 20,600 members of the infected families and asks how many first-born there are amongst these 3,522 persons. He should have taken one person at random from each of the 3,522 families. The difference between the two methods can be shown by a simple example. Suppose that there are two families one consisting of one member only, the other of 20 members. If (following Hansen's method) two persons are taken at random from the two families combined, the probable number of first-born will be $\frac{2 \times 2}{21} = .19$; while, if (following my method) one is taken from each family the probable number of first-born will be one from the family of one and $\frac{1}{20}$ from the family of 20, the total being 1.05.

To calculate the probable number of first-born from Hansen's table, on page 254, we take 178, the number of patients with no brothers or sisters who are all first-born, one-half of the fraternities with two members, one-third of those with three and so on, then the sum $178 + \frac{301}{2} + \frac{424}{3}$, etc., which equals 891 is the expected number of first-born. This compares with Hansen's expectation of 602. The actual number is 988, 11% more than my number and 64% more than Hansen's.

The method of calculation which is adopted by Dr. Hansen was used by Professor Pearson in "A First Study of The Statistics of Pulmonary Tuberculosis," and by Dr. Heron in "A First Study of the Statistics of Insanity," and also apparently by Professor Pearson when constructing a diagram referring to criminals, which is quoted in the October number of this REVIEW.

There is a second source of error which is deserving of notice. It has hitherto been assumed that if a person of a given age is selected at random from amongst fraternities of a given size than all positions in that fraternity are equally likely. But this is not the case. If the number of births has been increasing he is more likely to be one of the older members of his fraternity, and if the number has been decreasing he is more likely to be a younger member. For while the number of births is increasing there are more children born every year who belong to the first half of their fraternities than who belong to the second half.

Take any man A. who was born in 1870 and suppose that we know that he has or has had a brother B., who is five years older or five years younger than himself, which year 1875 or 1865 is the more probable as the year of B.'s birth? Obviously, if there were more males born in 1875 than in 1865 B. is more likely to have been born in 1875. A. then it is more likely to be B.'s elder brother than his younger. The excess of first-born due to this variation of yearly births is not very easy to calculate. But I think one can safely assert that it is by no means negligible.

A third possible source of error is inaccuracy of the data. The information as to size of family and order of birth seems to have been obtained from the patients themselves, some of whom may have been stupid or careless, and it must have been very difficult to check the accuracy of their information. This suspicion of inaccuracy has been strengthened by an examination of Mr. Hansen's table, which shows a remarkable bias towards even numbers both as regards the size of the families and the patient's position in them. The numbers of the patients who described themselves as tenth in a family of 10 and twelfth in a family of 12 also seem strangely high.

Now it is a curious fact that inaccuracy would be liable to cause an apparent excess of first-born. For the mistake most likely to be made would be the omission of those brothers or sisters of the patient who died before the patient was a year old. Such omissions might considerably raise the proportion of those described as first-born, and although the calculated expectation of the proportion of first-born would also be raised, it would not be raised to the same extent. To give an example.

Suppose there are twelve fraternities, each consisting of two brothers, and that in each fraternity one brother dies within a year of his birth and the other brother survives and becomes a patient. In half the cases it is the elder brother who survives. He describes himself as first-born in a family of two. In the other six cases the younger brother survives. As he has not recollection of his elder brother who died before he was born he describes himself as an only child. So we have twelve persons, six of whom are described as belonging to fraternities of one and six as belong to fraternities of two. We should expect according to the ordinary calculation to find nine first-born amongst these twelve persons, while, in fact, we find all twelve described as first-born. The omission of elder brothers was died young has therefore raised the apparent number of first-born to 33% above the expected number.

A similar result can be shown in the case of larger fraternities. It therefore seems possible that the apparent excess of first-born may be partly due to this factor.

J. A. COBB.

McDougall, W. (1914). Psychology in the services of eugenics.
Eugenics Review, 5(4), 295–308.

PSYCHOLOGY IN THE SERVICE OF EUGENICS.[1]

By W. MCDOUGALL, M.B., F.R.S.,
Reader in Mental Philosophy in the University of Oxford

We are becoming accustomed to speak of the science of eugenics; yet, from the standpoint of the philosopher who would classify the sciences in a comprehensive and logical scheme, eugenics would hardly be granted a place among the pure sciences. It is, or aspires to be, an art rather than a science. But, like medicine, engineering, and education, it is an art which is concerned with and which must consist in the application of knowledge established by the pure sciences; that is to say, it is what we commonly call an applied science; and it has the same claim to the title of science as these other applied sciences, medicine, engineering and education. Like these, it must be based upon and must apply the knowledge built up, not by any one science, but by a whole group of sciences.

What gives such arts as medicine and engineering the right to be recognised as sciences, is that they are not content simply to take and apply whatever knowledge may be put at their disposal by the pure sciences; but rather they define their own special problems, problems which in many cases the pure sciences would hardly have discovered or attacked; and, adopting and adapting the methods of research worked out by the pure sciences, they apply them to throw light upon their own special problems. In this way each of the great applied sciences calls to its service a body of worker who apply specialised methods of research—and upon whom it relies, more and more as it develops, for the detailed special knowledge that is required for the guidance of its practice.

In these respects the parallel between eugenics and these other applied sciences is exact. But in one important respect the position of eugenics is peculiar. Each of these other applied sciences grew up in the service of an art that had long been practised without any scientific basis. Men bound up their wounds and prescribed herbs, they built bridges and houses, and they trained their children, for thousands of years, before

---

[1] Read before the Eugenics Education Society, Nov. 6·, 1913.

anyone attempted to systematise any body of knowledge for the guidance of such practices. Now, the peculiarity of the position of eugenics is that it cannot originate as these other applied sciences did, namely, in sporadic scattered endeavours to obtain a little light for the guidance of an art already existing and long practised. Eugenics is in the peculiarly difficult position, that it must become an applied science before it can be applied. For the design of improving the human breed is the product of the last step of evolution, it results from the human race attaining to self-consciousness; or, at least, it can only become an effective purpose in proportion as the human race attains to a collective self-consciousness and becomes capable of collective volition. In less technical language, eugenics can only work towards its end by establishing its ideal in the mind of the community as an aim approved and accepted by public opinion. Therefore eugenics has to make secure its scientific foundations before it can begin to make application of them. It behooves us therefore to examine with the greatest care the relations of eugenics to its parent sciences, in order that the scientific basis may be laid as securely and as rapidly as possible.

It is generally recognised that eugenics has to find one of its principal supports in biology; but it is not so generally recognised that it must rely even more directly upon psychology, conceived as the empirical study of the mind. Hitherto eugenists, in so far as they have recognised in any degree this necessity, have done so in a very partial manner only, treating psychology as merely an aspect or minor department of biology. But whatever may be the philosophically correct conception of the relation of psychology to the rest of the biological sciences, the practical and actual relation is one of relative independence; i.e., psychology is taking shape as an observational and experimental science which pursues its own problems by its own methods. And it is therefore of the first importance that the applied science of eugenics should take pains to establish intimate relations with psychology, and that it should apply its results and adopt and adapt its methods of research for application to its own problems.

For it will, I suppose, be generally agreed that eugenics is even more deeply concerned for the preservation and, if possible, the improvement of mental sanity and vigour and the level of intellectual and moral efficiency in the human stock, than for its bodily perfection. So long as our bodies were healthy and hard, we could tolerate with equanimity some actual decline of the average standard of stature and bulk and muscular power. And it is especially the mental qualities of the race (mental being taken in the widest sense to include all that we call intellectual, moral, and spiritual qualities) that seem to be threatened by the conditions of high civilisation. It is the paradox and tragedy of high civlisation that, in the present and in all previous ages, its tendency has been to destroy or eliminate just those mental superiorities by which it has been built up and which are essential for its maintenance and further progress.

That eugenics has been a little slow in openly proclaiming psychology as its nearest relative among the sciences was due largely to the fact that psychology is, as compared with most of the other biological sciences, still in a very early stage of its development; and especially this is true of that branch of psychology which can be of most service to eugenics. Throughout the modern period psychology has been studied mainly from the point of view of philosophical and biological speculation, and has been chiefly concerned with the task of discovering the general laws of mind and mental process, just as physical science is concerned to discover the most general laws of matter and of physical processes. And the results achieved by psychology of this kind are not of direct service to eugenics.

But there is another way of approaching the study of the mind which, as we have been recently reminded by Professor Max Dessoir in his "Outlines of the History of Psychology," was actively pursued by the philosophers both of classical antiquity and of the middle ages; namely, the study of the peculiarities of mental endowment of individuals. It is this branch of psychological study (Professor Dessoir proposed to call it psychogenesis) from which eugenics has most to hope. For the knowledge which is required as the scientific basis of eugenics is, above all, a knowledge of the heredity of mental qualities; and this can only be obtained by the study of the peculiarities of endowment of related individuals.

It is true that something may be done and has been done by statistical methods which rely only upon such knowledge of individuals as may be inferred from their achievements in life, without attempting any psychological analysis of their mental endowment. The great fount of eugenics, Francis Galton, threw open this line of research and did epoch-making work along this line, as we all recognize. And others have followed it up and have obtained interesting results (Schuster, Karl Pearson).

But statistical work of this kind would seem incapable of bringing the exact knowledge of mental heredity required by eugenics, so long as it relies only upon popular psychology, and investigates only such vaguely defined and complex qualities as talent, or genius, or popularity, or good temper, or capacity for success in the various professions. That is to say, students of mental heredity must make use of the principles, the results, and the methods of systematic psychology, must apply them to their own special problems; and more especially they must concern themselves with psychognosis.

137

Now this branch of psychology, after a long period of neglect, is once more being actively pursued. In Germany its principal exponent is Dr. William Stern, who has written a valuable systematic treatise upon it, under the name of "Differential Psychology." But it is also called "Individual Psychology," and that, I think, is the most appropriate English name for this study. Francis Galton himself clearly saw this necessity for the detailed study of the qualities of individuals; and in those researches, reported in his classical work, "Inquiries into human faculty," in which he applied exact measurement to a number of comparatively simple mental powers, he really initiated the modern revival of individual psychology, by introducing the experimental method of observation into this field. At the time when Galton undertook these researches, the experimental methods of psychology were just beginning to attract attention and to be actively developed in Germany, and Galton's work did much to promote their development. Nevertheless, the experimental methods continued to be evolved principally for the sake of and in the service of the general problems of psychology, rather than of individual psychology.

Galton's method of mental tests fell into some disfavour with the professed psychologists; and some of the leaders of the present day revival of individual psychology show themselves ignorant or forgetful of Galton's pioneer work in this field, work of the very first importance; for it is to the application of the experimental methods in the form of mental tests that we must chiefly look for progress of our knowledge of mental heredity. Only such methods can overcome the difficulties that are encountered, when we pursue the statistical study of mental heredity on a basis of popular psychology only. These difficulties must be familiar to all who have discussed the bearing upon eugenics of such work as Galton's study of "Genius." The critic always discounts the value of such evidence by raising the objection that the sons of men of talent or genius start with special outer advantages, so that their success in life is no proof that they have inherited exceptional abilities; or he attributes similarities of the careers of relatives, whether in form of successes or failures, to similarities of social and general environment. And, though we may not feel that such objections are well founded, there seems to be no way of overcoming such difficulties, other than the way of experimental observation or mental tests.

Let me pass now to my proper topic, and attempt to show you very briefly some of the ways in which the experimental method can (we may hope) bring up more exact knowledge of the kind we need as the basis for eugenics.

We may distinguish three principal directions of such experimental work that are supplementary to one another, but which may be and are being pursued more or less independently of one another.

The experimental method of mental tests may be applied to the problem of the analysis of the complex mental powers that we make use of in ordinary life into elementary or relatively simple powers. If such relatively elementary powers can be defined and measured they will not improbably be found to be in many cases unit factors in heredity, and themselves inheritable not only as regards presence or absence in the make up of any individual, but also as regards the degree of strength in which they are transmitted from generation to generation. Such an analysis and the determination of the heritability of such unit factors is the ideal to be aimed at; needless to say, we are at present very far from the accomplishment of it. But it is much that we can conceive a method for attacking the problem experimentally.

Let me illustrate by indicating one step that seems already to have been made in this direction. We commonly speak of this man or that as being more or less intelligent; and in so doing we mean to imply that his conduct generally, or in most of the relations of life, bears the marks of what we mean by intelligence; and if we try further to define intelligence it seems to mean a readiness and ease of adaptation of conduct to a variety of circumstances. It is probably this that was aimed at by Professor Karl Pearson in his well-known research in which he classified his subject as quick, moderately quick, slow, very slow.

Now some psychologists have believed that there is no such entity as general intelligences, or no one inheritable factor which is a main condition of what we call intelligence—reaching this conclusion by deduction from general principles. But since our general principles in this region are still of very questionable validity, this procedure is very unsatisfactory. We ought to have perfectly open minds towards such a question; and to seek to decide it by carefully gathering the empirical evidence.

This was the line taken by Professor Spearman. He asked himself—Is there any truth in this popular notion of general intelligence? and he conceived a method of putting the matter to the test of experiment.

Suppose we apply to a large number of individuals (say 50 or more) several (say six or more) mental tests, each demanding a mental operation of a different kind, though not of a very highly specialised kind; and we express the degrees of proficiency displayed by the individuals in respect of each test by proficiency in any of these tasks, no doubt, depends in each case upon a number of mental factors: some of which may

139

or may not be identical in some or all of the several tasks. If proficiency in the several tasks does not at all depend upon mental factors common to some or all of the tasks, we shall probably find no appreciable correspondence or similarity of order between any two or more of the lists expressing order of merit of the 50 individuals. But, if proficiency in any two or more of the tasks depends in any large degree upon a common mental factor, i.e., upon some function involved in each of the two or more tasks, then we may expect to find some degree of similarity of order in the corresponding lists of order of merit. And conversely, if we find such correspondence or agreement between two or more lists, i.e., if those names which appear high in the one list are high also in the other list; then we may infer with some degree of probability that this correspondence is due to the operation of some one factor or function in the execution of both tasks. And the closer this correspondence the more confidently may we make this inferences, e.g., if the correspondence between any two lists were exact, if the order of merit were exactly the same in any two lists, then we could infer with high probability that proficiency in the two tasks depended in a very large, in a predominant, degree upon a factor or factors equally involved in the execution of both of them. This kind of correspondence is called in technical language correlation or positive correlation.

Applying this principle, Dr. Spearman found that the orders of merit achieved by a series of individuals in a number of simple mental tests did show a considerable degree of correspondence or positive correlation.[2] And he found further that these orders showed also significant degrees of positive correlation with the order of merit in respect of "general intelligence" assigned to the same individuals by persons intimately acquainted with all of them. These results seem then to justify the popular conception of "general intelligence" as a factor or psycho-physical function that is common to and plays a considerable part in a number of different complex mental operations. Similar and, in some respects, more convincing results have been obtained by Messrs. Burt and Flugel in a research in which they applied Professor Spearman's method, using a different sets of tests, and with certain other modifications of procedure which were thought to be improvements.[3]

These results, then, bear out in some measure the assumption of a great function involved in a wide range of mental operations, which provisionally we may

---

[2] "General Intelligence objectively determined and Measured," Amer. Journ. Of Psychology, Vol. XV.

[3] "Experimental Tests of General Intelligence," British Journal of Psychology, Vol. III.

call "general intelligence." And, if further research should confirm this tentative conclusion, we must regard it as one of the greatest importance for eugenics; for we should have discovered a measurable factor which is involved in, and is an important factor or condition of proficiency in, many mental operations; a factor which is possessed in very different degrees by different individuals.

The next step would be to enquire—Is the strength or intensity of this factor, "general intelligence," innately determined?—(and there is every probability that it is)— and further, Is it hereditary, and if so in what degree? And it seems very probable that by the application of similar methods these questions also can be answered.

I have cited these investigations in order to illustrate what I mean by the analysis of the mental powers and the discovery of relatively elementary mental functions. It is probable that, by the extended application of this method, we may discover and measure other such elementary functions. And the strictly logical order of investigation would be first to exhaust the possibilities of such analysis—to establish and define all the elementary functions that can be thus detected; and afterwards to measure the degree of their heritability, and to measure their strength in individuals and in the social classes.

But the sciences seldom or never follow the strictly logical order in their development; nor is it desirable that investigators should hold themselves bound to attempt to follow that order. And so we find that the other two main lines of psychological experiment in the service of eugenics are already being pursued.

II. One of these, the second of our three lines, is to apply mental tests directly to the task of detecting, and, so far as possible, measuring any differences of mental endowment that may obtain between the various classes and strata of the population; primarily in any one community such as our own nation or one university.

You are aware that there has long been an acute conflict of opinion on the question of differences of innate mental endowment of the social classes. One party dogmatically denies the existence of any such differences. The other party (basing itself on the consideration that the upper strata of society have in the long run been formed and continually regulated by the operation of the social ladder, which leads persons and stocks of good abilities upward and those of inferior abilities downward in the social scale) assume, often with a similar confidence and dogmatism, that the upper social strata are in the main natively superior in mental endowment to the lower. Hitherto we have no data for the formation of an opinion other than vague general impression, and the presumption in favour of the second view afforded by the consideration of the social ladder.

The citation of instances of sons and laboring men who have risen to positions of honour and wealth cannot decide the question in the negative; nor can the demonstration of the large proportion of distinguished men who come from the relatively small well-to-do classes establish the positive answer. For in these cases we cannot discount the influence of the differing opportunities, and of social environment and education.

The application of mental tests to considerable numbers of individuals drawn from the different social strata seems to offer the only possibility of obtaining a definite answer. Of the importance of this problem I need say nothing. That it is widely recognised is sufficiently shown by the many publications, which, in recent years, have drawn attention to the difference of rates of reproduction of the social classes, and in most cases have regarded the facts as of very grave significance. But, as is well known, all these many well-meant warnings make but little impression on the public mind; just because the assumption on which they are founded, namely, that of some positive correlation between social level and superiority of mental endowment, has not been demonstrated, and is repugnant to the feelings of the great majority of the public.

In order to apply mental tests to throw light on this question we must devise a series of tests, proficiency in which shall be as nearly as possible independent of special education; i.e., they must test capacities which are developed by such modes of mental activity as all social classes are equally called upon to exercise and have equal opportunities of exercising; e.g., it is impossible to make use of the results of school and college examinations for this purpose, because these results are so largely determined by educational opportunities of widely different kinds.

Again, the tests selected must be adapted to throw light on as many aspects as possible of our mental endowment; provisionally, while we are still ignorant of the primary or elementary hereditary factors of mind, we must attempt to measure such ill-defined characters, as "general intelligence," "mechanical memory," "logical memory," "power of concentration," "power of sustaining a mental effort" "capacity for distributing the attention," "quickness and accuracy of judgment," "readiness in seizing logical relations." And we must hope to improve our tests and our combination of them for this purpose in the light of the experience we gain in the course of such investigation.

Thirdly, we should apply our tests to young subjects, i.e., to children at the earliest age at which they become trustworthy subjects for such experiment; because the younger we take our subjects, the more will native endowment predominate over the influence of special training and experience in determining degrees of proficiency. And, fortunately, school children from the age of about 11 or 12 years are in other respects excellent and convenient subjects for such investigation.

I may point to an interesting suggestion of an answer to the question we are considering afforded by the work on school children, down at Oxford by Messrs. Burt and Flugel, to which I have already referred; and I may say that we are following up this clue with good hope of obtaining interesting results. But, of course, such work demands the expenditure of much time and energy by many investigators, before we can hope for convincing demonstration of the truths required as a basis for eugenic precepts.

The third principal line of application of psychological experiment in the service of eugenics is the direct attack upon the problem of mental heredity. This is the necessary supplement of the other two lines of work already noticed. It must proceed by applying mental tests to large number of near relatives, of the same and of different generations; and so determine how far such relatives show greater similarity of degrees of proficiency in the various tasks than persons not related by blood.

And in choosing our tests with this end in view we must primarily seize upon all peculiarities or qualities in respect of which individuals who wide differences that cannot be attributed to differences of training and environment, putting aside the question of their value.

I may mention that, as is already known to many members of this society, Dr. Schuster has equipped a laboratory on the premises of the society and proposes to direct the work of it more particularly to this problem, to this direct attack upon the problems of mental heredity; and I believe that Professor Brown, at King's College, has put on foot a similar or allied enquiry into mental variability.

We may, I think, anticipate that these three lines of work will now go steadily forward; that they will converge more and more, that they will mutually aid one another, and that within a few years time they will achieve results which will be generally recognised as having given us that firm foundation of fact which is the urgent need of eugenics at the present time.

The work will require much patience, energy, and ingenuity; but if it offers a fair prospect of attaining the knowledge we need, and which can be obtained in no other way, members of this society will not regard any such expenditure of effort as excessive.

In conclusion, I would say a word or two about a question of even larger scope than national eugenics. Galton, in his later days at least, was inclined to regard eugenics as properly concerned only with the life of the highly civilized nations. But can we as citizens of the British Empire continue to observe this limitation? Is it not obvious that practical statesmanship is already confronted with problems, the decision of which should be largely determined by eugenic considerations and by answers to questions which lie within the province of eugenics, broadly conceived as concerned for the future welfare of the whole human race.

Eventually, eugenics must face this larger problem. And then it will require positive knowledge of the mental endowments of the various subraces of mankind; and especially it will require to know as exactly as possible the mental endowments of the progeny produced by the crossing of these subraces. For already we see widely manifested the tendency for large masses of population to transfer themselves from one country and from one continent to another. Especially in north and south America, and in many of our colonies, do we see the juxtaposition within the same areas and political communities of individuals drawn from many different subraces.

And, whenever such juxtaposition occurs, the crossing of these varieties of the human species will eventually occur on a larger or smaller scale. Even so determinedly exclusive a people as the Jews have, as is well known, interchanged much of their blood with other peoples. In fact, we seem to be approaching a period of universal miscegenation. Is this tendency, fraught with immense possibilities for good and evil, to be allowed to go on in an utterly blind manner? Or is mankind, conscious of itself as a whole, to take intelligent thought for its own future and to attempt to regulate in some manner and degree these processes of racial mixture. It is clear that the civilised governments are already exerting great powers of interference, that their powers of regulation are almost limitless, and that problems of this kind will confront them with increasing urgency. Are, then, their decisions to be made utterly without regard to eugenic considerations? Surely such considerations should have an altogether predominant weight in deciding such questions. For it is, I think, clear that healthy political organisms cannot grow up where the population consists of two or more racial stocks that remain persistently averse to intermarriage, and therefore racially distinct. We see this illustrated sufficiently in the United States of America and in South Africa and elsewhere. And it seems highly probable that some blends of the human subraces are eugenically admirable and others disastrous. In order to illustrate the position by a case in which the question is already acute, I refer to the United States of America. There the old population is chiefly descended from the subraces of North Europe. But during the last decade there has been a tremendous stream of immigration from South and South-East Europe, and already the cry is hear that this stream should be checked, that it threatens the future of the States. In Canada and Australia, too, similar problems already confront practical statesmanship. Are these great areas to be reserved for the European or North European stock? or should yellow and brown and black be freely admitted; eventually to form by blending new subraces?

These are great questions on which, as it seems to me, eugenics must strive to express its opinion and make its point of view felt. But it can only do so on a basis of exact knowledge of mental endowment and mental heredity. And the acquisition of such knowledge is the task of psychology. Much has already been said or written on these questions of racial psychology; but very little is established; and it is difficult to see how progress with them is to be made, if we do not apply the methods of experimental and relatively exact observation now being worked out by psychology.

I have not attempted to lay before you a statement of results achieved by psychology in the service of eugenics, because hitherto those results are few and slight. I have rather attempted to indicate a program of work that lies before us, and the nature of some of the methods by aid of which we may hope to make progress with it; for it is of the first importance for the progress of that work that the members of this society, which embodies and focuses enlightened opinion on these topics, should take an intelligent interest in this programme and give it their sympathy and support.

Bruner, F.G. (1914). Racial differences. *Psychological Bulletin,*
11(10), 384-386.

RACIAL DIFFERENCES

By FRANK G. BRUNER
Chicago, Ill.

The perplexing questions arising out of the Negro problem in the South have given rise to some interesting, though not always convincing, discussion of the psychological differences between negroes and whites. Discussions which are not fairly anchored in experimental data are apt to be of little value and indeed often rest on erroneous presuppositions. Of such character is a paper by Bardin (2), who, ignoring such authorities as Boas, Haddon, Rivers and others, begins with the postulate that the negro and white races differ in physiological and mental organization to the same extent as they do in certain obvious anatomical features. He thence argues that difference in culture are fundamental and ineradicable. Of somewhat similar character is the paper by Jordan (3), who however professes to speak from personal acquaintance with the negro population in various parts of the South. His experience is that the more nearly white are the mixed bloods, as judged from skin color, the more do they approach the whites in mental and social alertness.

Experimental tests were made by Baldwin (1) on 37 white and 30 colored delinquent girls, ranging in age from 13 to 21 years, inmates of a Pennsylvania reformatory. Learning capacity was tested by a substitution test, with the average result that the negro girls did only 62.4 per cent. as much work as the whites in a given time, and made 245.3 per cent. more errors. The negro girls were "much slower to warm up to the occasion," and the first to drop back and lose interest. They were difficult to arouse and could not be forced or stimulated except, temporarily, through flattery. Their work was more irregular than that of the white girls, and dependent apparently on moods. While working at the tests they seemed only partially occupied with the task in hand, for at the same time they were making random movements, mumbling, grumbling, humming, and saying original and funny things. The fact that the tests failed to enlist the interest of the negroes to the same degree as the whites makes it difficult to judge of the real capacity for learning of the two groups.

The Binet-Simon tests were applied by Miss Strong (6) to 120 negro and 250 white children in the schools of Columbia, S. C. Unfortunately for our purpose, racial differences were purely an incidental consideration with the author and are not worked out adequately; but the following results are suggestive: 60.8 per cent. of the colored, as compared with 25.2 per cent. of the white children, rated below age in mental development; at age there were 30 per cent. of the negro and 42.9 per cent. of white children; and above age 9.2 per cent. of the negro and 26 per cent. of white children. The tables show another interesting point on which the author makes no comment. At the ages of six, seven and eight just about twice as many negro children as white rate below age, whereas for the ages of ten, eleven and twelve the superiority of the whites over the negroes is but slight. This suggests that the rate of maturing may be more rapid with the negro children, so as to make them older, mentally, at the age of twelve than white children of the same age.

Mayo (4) contributes a valuable study of the learning capacity of whites and negroes living under similar social and economic conditions and subjected to identical tuition and media of instruction, by comparing the school marks received by negro and white pupils of the New York City High Schools. The 150 negroes available for study were compared with an equal number of white pupils, selected at random from the same classes attended by the negroes. The median mark of the white pupils in all subjects taken together was 66; of the colored pupils, 62; and 29 per cent. of the colored reach the median mark for the whites. The average deviation is 7 for the white pupils and 6.5 for the colored. The per cent. of colored pupils reaching the median mark for whites in each group of school subjects is as follows: in modern languages, 33; in mathematics, 32; in history, 31; in science, 29; in Greek and Latin, 27; in English, 24; in the commercial branches, 22. These results tend to dispel the common conception of the negro as relatively good in English and especially inferior in subjects requiring abstract though, such as science and mathematics. The poor showing of the negroes in English cannot be explained by home environment, since the white pupils who are here compared with the negroes come, many of them, from the homes of recent immigrants, in which little English is spoken. On the whole, the negroes seem to be distinctly below the whites, though the overlap is sufficient to make it easily possible to teach the two races in the same classes.

The common opinion that primitive peoples have existed in all stages of mental development, reaching down to a condition slightly above that of the ape, is challenged by Spiller (5), who cites authorities to show that even the native Australians display a surprising degree of intellectual power. From the testimony of missionaries and teachers who have lived among primitive peoples, he reaches the unwarranted conclusion that all the peoples of the Earth are virtually equal to Europeans in mental and moral capacity. As a matter of fact, personal experience with a primitive people in their customary surroundings affords a very unsafe basis for estimating their mentality. A test of the power of meeting unfamiliar situations is necessary.

A very suggestive scheme for the study of any social group is offered by Thomas (7), who reports that he has applied it to the study of the Negro and of some European peasants. He assumes that the main factor responsible for the differences in mental and social attainment found among different peoples is expressible in terms of interest, stimulation, imitation, opportunity, occupational differentiation due to traditional or geographical limitations, and mental attitude in general. With Boas and others he believes that the general organization of mind is much the same in all races of mankind, and that the relative intelligence and advancement of a social group are dependent on the objects to which they give attention.

REFERENCES

BALDWIN, B. T. The Learning of Delinquent Adolescent Girls as Shown by a Substitution Test. J. of Educ. Psychol., 1913, 4, 317-33.

BARDIN, J. The Psychological Factor in the Southern Race Problem. Pop. Sci. Mo., 1913, 83, 368-374.

JORDAN, H. E. The Biological Status and Social Worth of the Mulatto. Pop. Sci. Mo., 1912, 82, 573-582.

MAYO, M. J. The Mental Capacity of the American Negro. Archives of Psychol., 1913, No. 28. Pp. 70. Also Columbia Contrib. to Philos. and Psychol., Vol. XXII, No. 2.

SPILLER, G. The Mentality of the Australian Aborigines. Sociol. Rev., Oct., 1913, 1-6.

STRONG, A. M. Three Hundred Fifty White and Colored Children Measured by the Binet-Simon Measuring Scale of Intelligence. Ped. Sem., 1913, 20, 485-512.

THOMAS, W. I. Race Psychology, Standpoint and Questionnaire. Amer. J. of Sociol., 1912, 17, 725-775.

Simon, T. (1915). The measurement of intelligence. *Eugenics Review*, 6(4): 291–307.

THE MEASUREMENT OF INTELLIGENCE[1]

By DR. T. SIMON

Translated from the French by Dr. W. C. SULLIVAN

In the ordinary course how do we gauge anyone's intelligence? We receive a first impression of the individual's general demanour, of the aspect of his physiognomy, of the vivacity of his look, of the mobility of his features. We take in all these elements at a glance. We feel them as a single general impression. Then, when we wish to find a more solid basis for our opinion, we are no longer content with this external view; we seek to reach what lies behind the façade; and to do this, we get into conversation. To make a person talk is the best way that has yet been found for ascertaining what he has in his mind. In conversation, the sound of our interlocutor's voice, the flexibility of its intonation, the fineness of its shades, are all elements that tend to confirm or weaken the opinion that we may first have formed. And then the degree of attention that he gives us, for we are always sure that our remarks are worth listening to; this quickness to grasp our meaning, saving us from any need to present, under simpler forms, the idea we wish to convey or to illustrate it by concrete examples; his replies, which anticipate what we were going to say, or which sum up a complex question in a few vivid words—by such various details as these we are able in the course of conversation, to estimate the intelligence of the speaker.

But it is obvious how entirely subjective such a mode of procedure must be, to what an extent it is based on fugitive impressions. As a matter of fact, what usually happens in that we form in this way at the start a very positive and decided opinion; we say, this is a man of average intelligence, or this is a man of superior intelligence, and then, at the first objection that is raised, we modify our judgment, and as we pursue our examination further, we discover proofs of stupidity in the man whom we judged

---

[1] Delivered at a meeting of the Eugenics Education Society held by kind permission of the Royal Society, at Burlington House, April 18·, 1914.

highly intelligent because he seemed to agree with all our opinions, or we find indications of quickness of wit in one whom we had set down as hopelessly evil.

Nor is this the only defect of the ordinary method: the opinion based on it is strictly personal to the individual who formulates it; it requires in him that aptitude which we characterise as the art of understanding men, and which consists doubtless in knowing how to give its proper value to each of the several elements which we have touched on. Further, if we can estimate the intelligence of an adult after this fashion—because we have a schematic conception of what an adult is and how he ought to acquit himself in an ordinary conversation—we have nothing of the sort in the case of a child, we have no fixed points to guide us in judging of intelligence during that period of continual evolution.

Without, therefore, questioning in the least the value of a clinical examination, one principal merit of which is its admirable flexibility, it has been impossible not to feel the need of substituting a purer method for the ordinary method which we have just criticised. From the theoretical point of view, the question had long been urgent. It was becoming no less so from a practical point of view in France at the time when Binet specially directed his activity to its solution, for in 1906 the Ministry of Public Instruction had just appointed a commission to inquire into the measure proper to be taken in the education of abnormal children—of those children who are designated in England by the term "feeble-minded"—and as a first step it was necessary to be able to recognise them.

It was to such preoccupations as these that the metric scale of intelligence owed its origin. Consonant with that origin, it is applicable above all, and almost exclusively to children and to defectives, but it embodies at the same time a general principle of method which admits of further development in measuring intelligence.

A glance at the accompanying table will show you the brief enumeration of the test which we use, 62 in number, these test being for the most part arranged in groups of 5, each group under the rubric of a given age.

> 3 months. — Follow with eyes the movement of an object.
>
> 9 months. — (i.) Attend to sounds; (ii.) grasp an object on contact; (iii.) grasp an object on seeing it.
>
> 1 year. — Recognise food.
>
> 18 months. — Say "mama" spontaneously.
>
> 2 years. — (i.) Walk; (ii.) obey one simple direction.

3 years. — (i.) Point out nose, eye, moth; (ii.) repeat two digits; (iii.) enumerate the objects in an engraving; (iv.) point out the longer of two lines.

4 years. — (i.) Tell whether a little boy or a little girl; (ii) name key, knife, penny; (iii.) repeat three numerals; (iv.) point out the longer of two lines.

5 years — (i.) Find which is the heavier of the two boxes; (ii.) copy a square; (iii.) repeat a phrase with ten syllables; (iv.) count four pennies; (v.) reconstruct a card cut out diagonally into two pieces.

6 years. — (i.) Distinguish morning and evening; (ii.) define common objects-fork, chair, table, horse, mother—by use; (iii.) copy a rhomb; (iv.) count 13 pennies; (v.) compare a number of drawings of faces from an aesthetic point of view.

7 years. — (i.) Point out right hand and left ear; (ii.) describe an engraving; (iii.) do three simple errands; (iv.) give sum of three pennies and three halfpennies; (v.) name four colours—red, blue, green, yellow.

8 years. — (i.) Make mental comparison between fly and butterfly, wood and glass, paper and cardboard; (ii.) count from 20 to 0; (iii.) point out feature missing in incomplete figures; (iv.) give the date; (v.) repeat five numerals.

9 years. — (i.) Take 2d. out of a shilling and give the change; (ii.) define common objects (see above) otherwise than by use; (iii.) recognise all the current coins; (iv.) name the months; (v.) answer five easy questions.

10 years. — (i.) Arrange six boxes (3, 6, 9, 12, 15, and 18 grammes) according to weight; (ii.) copy two simple geometrical designs from memory; (iii.) criticize absurd statements; (iv.) answer five difficult questions; (v.) bring three given words into two phrases.

12 years. — (i.) Resist a suggestion; (ii.) bring three given words into one sentence; (iii.) say more than 60 words in three minutes; (iv.) define abstract words; (v.) re-arrange a simple sentence, the words of which have been put out of their order.

15 years. — (i.) Repeat seven numerals; (ii.) find three rhymes for a given word; (iii.) repeat a sentence of 26 syllables; (iv.) interpret an engraving; (v.) explain an unfinished account of a common episode.

Adults. — (i.) Paper-cutting test; (ii.) mental construction of figure formed by transposing pieces of bisected rectangle; (iii.) distinguish between abstract words of similar sound or similar meaning; (iv.) indicate three differences between a king and the president of a republic; (v.) give précis of a selected passage of prose.

Each of the tests is in the form of question or of a simple little operation varying in difficulty. They require practically no apparatus, or at all events so little and of so simple a sort that anyone can make its most complicated elements in a few moments, and when prepared it is as easy to carry about as a stethoscope. Further, all the tests are so quickly got through that probably the longest of them is that which consists in asking the subject to repeat as many words as he can in three minutes, and the determination of the subjects mental age does not take more than 20 minutes, and may be arrived at in an even shorter time.

(Three tests — putting together divided card, the paper cutting test, and description of pictures — were then demonstrated by the lecturer.)

So much by way of example, but the essential point, and that on which I wish especially to insist, because it is the very principle of the method and its original feature, is the seriation of our tests. There is a hierarchy in this arrangement. And it is not a hierarchy established by *a priori* considerations. It is based on facts. Here is the way it was arrived at. We proceeded by several stages. The first stage consisted in trying a number of the tests. Taking a series of weak minded subjects, chosen more or less at random, we picked out amongst them the most pronounced cases, those where there could be no doubt as to the defect of intelligence and it was with these subjects—idiots, imbeciles, and low grade morons—that we tried such tests, for example, as offering an object and observing in what way it was grasped, or showing a picture and asking a description of it. It turned out that tests which, in our opinion, should have presented no difficulty were missed, while others, which seemed to use to be equivalent, were successfully got over. Gradually all that fell into order; and we accepted as the tests solved by those subjects whom we recognised clinically as the most defective; while we ranked as difficult, as requiring more intelligence, more intellectual resources, the tests which were performed only by the subjects of manifestly higher development. During this first phase, accordingly, our tests were grouped in terms of intelligence and in conformity with clinical indications. Second stage: it is an idea which must suggest itself to any observer of states of intellectual non-development that they may be compared to the different phases of childhood. You will find, for instance, in Esquirol such expressions as this; after he has described a case of imbecility, he will add: "this young imbecile resembles in every respect an infant of 5 years of age." This, however, in the pages of the alienists is only a mere phrase, a comparison which is little more than literacy. We, on the contrary, had got hold of a series of exact tests on which to base our estimate of an arrest of intelligence; our recollection of our first results and some additional experiments showed us, between the replies of our asylum patients and the replies of children, strange analogies amounting often to an absolute identity. It was the obvious course to ascertain whether the grades which we had found in feebleness of mind really corresponded to grades of age in normal children. Our first investigations were rather timid, for we limited ourselves to the ages of 3, 6, and 9 years. They were sufficient, however, to prove to use that the seriations of tests which we had based on differences of intelligence held good when we applied these tests to children of different ages. We were accordingly led to formulate the following postulate—*intelligence is a function of the child's age*; and we then entered into a third period in which we applied ourselves to following the development of an infant mentality year by year. We multiplied the number of tests. We tried them methodically in the schools on children of 6, 7, 8, and 9 years, and so on. And in this way, by long afternoons of observation, by patient labour, often irksome because monotonous, but always fruitful, we reached the seriation which we now utilise.

Here, then, is the meaning of the groups by age which you see in our table. It means that, if, for instance, we take a number of children of 5 years old in a Paris elementary school and make them copy a square, count four objects and so on, these children will perform these operations successfully and they will also do all the tests allotted to the ages below 5 years, while, on the other hand, they will be incapable of dealing with the tests in the higher groups; *e.g.*, they are quite well able to count four pennies but they cannot count 13.

And now you will understand why I said a moment ago that what was essential in the method is the seriation of the tests. It is because that seriation gives us at once the value of the subject's responses to the tests. Suppose—and I am quoting to you an actual instance—that we are examining a worthy man of some 50 years of age, and that, in the usual course, we ask him his name and he gives it correctly, and we then ask him his age, and he answers in all good faith, "I'm 12 years old." Of course, we know at

155

once that we are dealing with a defective. But, thanks to our scale, we know something more; we can have a strong presumption that his intellectual level is between 3 years and 6 ears, for 3 years is the age when the surname is correctly given, and 6 years is the age when a child knows how old he is.

In the case of all our first tests, for ages from 3 to 12 years, our investigations were made in infant and elementary schools. Two other parts of our scale remain; one, having to do with the lower degrees, from 3 months to 2 years; the other, on the contrary, with the upper region of the scale, that is to say, with the tests for 15 years of age and for adults. With regard to the lower degrees, they have only been studied by us in crèches, and the results are therefore subject to qualification, and may not apply to children brought up under other conditions. As for the test which we give as corresponding to the adult intelligence, they have been arrived at from experiments made on members of associations of former pupils of the elementary schools. All we have to note specially about the results we have obtained with these subjects is, then, that they refer to ages subsequent to school years.

This, then, is our method, and it is after the manner I have described that is has been devised. It is above all a result and an epitome of observed facts. If we have assigned certain tests to the age of 9 years it is because we have found that they are successfully passed by children of that age, while they were not passed by children of 8 years, and so on.

II.

Now, what is it exactly that we measure?

(1) We measure intelligence as a whole; and this is what I mean; if we could study closely each of these tests, one after the other, we should find first that they all require attention and good will, and also a certain amount of comprehension, but in different degrees; it does not need much sustained effort to perceive the difference between two weights of 3 and 15 grammes; it demands closer application to arrange five weights in order when of the respective values of 3, 6, 9, 12 and 15 grammes; for the subject to point his nose is certainly easier than to take 2d. from a shilling and give the change. On the other hand, the passing of certain tests—repeating digits or phrases—depends above all on immediate memory; other tests, such as the naming of colours or enumerating the months, seem to depend on positive knowledge; while success in others again is the result of the subject's power of judgment, as, for instance, in detecting an absurdity. Or it may be the inventive capacity that we bring into play,

as when we require the subject to get three words into a phrase; or it may be the power of visual representation, as in the paper-cutting test. Or else it is all these faculties, more or less, that are utilised, for we must recognise that their isolation is artificial and a figment of theory, and that in reality every mental operation, even if it be but the simples sensation, requires the activity of the mind as a whole.

The lowest tests on the scale are tests of muscular coordination in response to sensory stimuli. Then there are tests requiring the use of words, and others, such as copying a square or a rhomb, which give proof of motor skill, and so on. We do not analyse; we grasp intelligence by its total result, without attempting to separate its constituents; and we measure it, in some sort quantitatively, pretty much as we say, when we speak of electricity, "this is a current of 100 volts."

To analyse what is attributable in the results to attention, what to memory, and so forth; to determine the part of his several faculties in accounting for the degree of a child's intellectual development—that would be a totally different task, the object of a different investigation, and of an investigation, doubtless, of no less importance, but hardly, I think, one that we are yet near being able to undertake with profit.

(2) The second point we have to deal with concerns the chief objection urged against us on grounds of theory. As we judge by results, it is at once said, "You do not measure intelligence, you measure acquired capacity (*l'acquis*); you measure a state of intellectual development, an intellectual level, if you will, but that is not the intelligence. You have, it is true, eliminated from your tests exercises of reading and writing, you may make one of your examinations without noticing whether the child you are examining knows how to read; you have not fallen into the obvious error of asking the date of Napoleon's death or the names of the chief towns of Asia, because the absence of these notions is clearly a proof only of ignorance; you have been careful to avoid also questions dealing with local matters, such as tariff regulations or the name of the reigning sovereign, for the capacity to answer such questions is due to curiosity, and to a curiosity that certain peasants lack, who, nevertheless, within the narrow circle of their immediate interests show no want of intelligence. Yes, you have taken all these precautions, but for all that your efforts remain vain. You measure results; and in these results the action of circumstances always intervenes; you put problems, but their solution always depends on what the family environment has taught the children. Here is the proof that this objection is sound: if you try your tests in a different social milieu, on a better class of the population, if, as M. Decroly and Mlle. Degand have done, you examine children of wealthy parents, these children will appear more intelligent,

157

judged by your scale, they are in advance of their age, they show themselves more developed than the children of working-class parents. And after all, when we use tests such as the enumeration of the months, or taking change out of shilling, are we not really estimating the effects of special sorts of training?"

The objection is a formidable one, and I think that I have presented it without diminishing its force. It is so plausible that we have ourselves sometimes been disturbed by it. First of all, let us recognise that it is quite true that we measure results only and that the degrees of intellectual development which we gauge are the resultants of multiple factors. When we use our scale I the psychological examination of a child, we are doing, from the psychic point of view, something analogous to what we do, from an organic point of view, when we use a tape measure. When we read off with our tape a measure of height, the figure results in part from a personal factor, a force of growth with which the individual came into existence, and in part from influences of environment, for the conditions of nutrition, temperature and the like to which he has been subjected. The measuring tape does not distinguish these elements. Stature is the resultant of these different forces, and it varies, like intellectual development, in different social milieu. Nevertheless, stature is an important measure, which we should not like to dispense with in estimating the physical state and the vigour of a child. Similarly, when our scale indicates to us the stage that a child has reached, when with its help we measure what his intellectual faculties enable him to do, this development which we measure is the result, on the one hand of a personal element, an innate cerebral constitution which enables our nervous system to make certain acquisitions and to profit by them, and on the other hand it depends on the influence of the environment, on the stimuli that we receive from our surroundings. All that is true. But none the less would it be incorrect to say that what we measure is imply this action of the milieu, for that actions would be of no effect without an intelligence to work on; we measure the whole as an indissoluble totality, as, in fact, the personal element and the environmental factors do in all likelihood present themselves in reality; for we may conceive the intelligence, not as something complete, not as a power endowed at that start with its full force, but as a function which is in process of perfecting itself, incessantly modified and as it were re-made by excitations from without. During the whole period of childhood the intelligence is in the making.

And further, it is, in fact, the intelligence that we measure, if the conditions of the environment where we measure its development are sufficiently uniform in character. Suppose that twenty years ago we planted two acorns in the same ground.

To-day we measure the trees into which they have grown, and we find their trunks of the same thickness; we say then these young oaks are of the same vigour. If, on the contrary, one of them had a stem of but half the diameter of the other, we should call it weakly, thus inferring from our observation the degree of its vital force, a factor in itself inaccessible. Our whole problem is of the same order, and we may formulate it thus: have we the right to infer from the degree of intellectual development which we find in a child, the value of that somewhat metaphysical entity which we designate by the term intelligence? This is not a question of theory but of fact, and it is for the facts to answer it.

Let us, then, take the witness of the facts. When we published our first researches and our results in 1908 and 1911, they had as their basis only a relatively limited number of observations, extending to some hundreds of children, and children who might seem to have been selected under rather special conditions, inasmuch as they were all pupils in elementary schools in Paris. When we proposed to estimate the intellectual development and the intelligence of other children by reference to this standard, it was possible to ask whether our measures were not of very relative significance. It was a measurement, no doubt, but a measurement by a standard whose value was open to question. Since then our method of measurement has been applied in England, in America, in Belgium and Holland, and in other countries. More than 5,000 children have been tried by our tests. And in a general way the results have been confirmatory, especially as regards the ages from 4 to 10 years. So that we are authorized to-day to maintain that the intellectual development which our scale shows is really representative of the average child of the white race. In other words, this international confirmation shows us that our tests imply a fairly general environment, that they are valid in the ordinary conditions under which any child in these countries has to grow up, and that they do not presuppose any special cultural influence. And if this be so, when we find differences of development between two children, it is clearly to differences of intelligence that we must attribute them. At all events this holds good of certain differences. For, on the other hand, if we examine measurements taken in certain special circumstances, such as those referred to above, measurements, for instance, of the children of wealthy parents, we find that these children show an advance of one or at most of two years. This, then, is what represents the influence of environment. So that when, in measuring the intellectual level of a child, we find a departure from the average shown by our scale, if that variation falls within the limits we have just indicated, we may inquire whether there are special conditions capable of causing it; but if these conditions are not present or if the variation is too considerable, we may infer, with a variation in the upward directions, the existences of an exceptional vigour of intelligence, while with a variation in the downward directions we shall be inclined even more positively to conclude that the intelligence is defective. Thus we arrive logically at the practical rule that we regard as backward in intelligence any child whose intellectual development is found to be two years below that of his age as shown on our scale.

With regard to the two ends of the scale—infants and adults—our certitude in adopting a schematic average of intelligence is much less. In the case of the infants, we obtained our material, as I have already pointed out, from an unfavourable environment: the children sent to crèches cannot represent an average social condition, and that, not only on account of the detrimental influences to which the children have been exposed, but also because these children, by reason of bad heredity, are probably innately inferior. This portion of our scale may, therefore, need revision. We might guess this on *a priori* grounds, and the experiments which have been made, here and there, confirm this view; the tests are too easy; in other words what we have assigned to two or even to three years ought to be put back to lower ages.

On the contrary, if our tests for 12 and 15 years and for adults are, in general, too difficult. This depends on the fact, mentioned above, that this part of our scale was framed from trials made with what might be regarded as selected material. It would be necessary to work with random samples of subjects of these ages. This is a research still to be made, and it will not be an easy one, for after school life the individuals are scattered, and they are no longer willing to lend themselves to such inquiries; adults do not like to have their intelligence measured too closely. Besides, at that period the intelligence is developed, so that we no longer have the help of differences of age to estimate the value of the differences we detect. And lastly, professional activities tend to produce a possible excessive specialisation of intellectual work, and that fact renders comparisons difficult. Nevertheless, this is doubtless only a question of adaptation. And we believe that by pursuing research by the method which we have sued, by devising for these ages new and more appropriate tests, we shall gradually overcome these obstacles, so that we shall be able to measure an adult's intelligence with the same precision as we now measure the intelligence of a child.

III.

We are, then, in a position to compare the intelligence of a given subject with that of an ideal average child. Of what use can that comparison be to us? Let us first consider its application to the examination of abnormal children. Following on the appointment of the commission to which I have referred, a certain number of classes were organised in Paris for children who could not keep up with the ordinary teaching. But what children were to be admitted into these classes? How was the selection to be made? Of course, it is easy to find children whose educational progress is behind that of their comrades. Say a child of this sort comes before us, he is 10 years old and we find him in the lowest class of the elementary school, in school work he is barely on a level with the ordinary child of 6 or 7. What is the cause of this backwardness? Perhaps it is to be attributed to irregular attendance? And in fact we do find that illness has prevented the child from sticking to his studies. But is this cause sufficient to explain the degree of backwardness? May there not also be a question of want of attention, lack of effort, idleness? Or is it due to want of brains? The examination of his cranium, the detection of his bumps or of his stigmata-these means do not allow us to solve this problem. Now try this child with our tests, he is 10 years old; we being, therefore, with the tests of that age, and he fails in them. We pass on to the tests of 9 years, and he is again unsuccessful. He only does some of the tests of 8 years, and all the tests below that age. In short, though he is 10 years old, he has barely the intellectual development of a child of 7 ⍟ years. Our opinion is now fixed, he may be lazy, but besides that his intelligence is certainly more feeble than that of a normal child. It is that of 7 ⍟ years, and the child's age allows us to hope that it may still develop. These are favourable conditions for trying to teach him under special discipline. We enter him accordingly for a special school. Had we found his level that of 3 years only, we should not have accepted him; we should have regarded him as beyond the reach of this educational method. But on the other hand, it might have happened that this child, reported from his school as backward in his studies and as mentally abnormal, is found on our examination to possess the intelligence of his age. In that case we should have to do with a simple "slacker," and we should require to have recourse to other methods than those of a special school. As its first service, then, our method is going to help us for the very object for which it was devised, namely as an instrument for selecting subjects for the special schools. It will enable us to form homogeneous classes. And above all, it will enable us—and I know no other method that can do this—to exclude from these schools subjects who are sent to them for insufficient reasons.

Now let us go to our asylums. There we find congenitally defective patients whose poverty of intelligence is such that they cannot shift for themselves if they are out in the world. Attempts have been made to distinguish several degrees amongst these subjects, but it has always been by means of notions of degree so vague that it is almost impossible for the different authors who have written on the question to understand one another or to know whether they are describing similar cases. We are told, for instance, that in imbeciles the judgment is less acute, or the attention les sustained, or the vocabulary more limited than in the feeble-minded, while on the other hand all these faculties are more developed than in idiots; but as to describing how we are to estimate this keenness of judgment, this fixity of attention, this extent of vocabulary—that always seems to be postponed. But apply to these subjects our method, and we have at once the necessary data for a definite, if conventional, division of these several categories. Here are the definitions which we have been led to propose: —

We mean by the term "idiot" an individual whose intellectual development is that of 2 years or under.

We mean by the term "imbecile" an individual whose intellectual development corresponds to that of a child between the ages of 3 and 7 years.

And finally, by the term "feeble-minded" (*debile*) we mean an individual whose intellectual level, while superior to that of a child of 7 years, is nevertheless below the average development of an adult. This latter degree of development, as I have said, is still inadequately determined. Provisionally it might be proposed to fix at 9 years the upper level of mental debility. We shall see the reasons for this selection in a moment.

Now why should we take these points, at 2, 7 and 9 years, to form the divisions in a classification of mental defectives? The reason is that to each of these degrees there corresponds an important stage in mental life; the idiot, like the child under 2 years, may in a sense understand some words, but he cannot use any; it is as though language requires for its evolution an intelligence of more than 2 years. The imbecile has the power of speech, whatever imperfections he may show in its use, but written language is beyond his reach; and it is not till 7 years of age that the child, after very much the same way in all civilised countries, begins to assimilate reading and writing sufficiently to make a rudimentary use of them.

And it is not only by these deficiencies, by this incapacity first to communicate with his fellows by speech and then to transmit to them his thoughts by writing, that our idiots and imbeciles may be characterised: to each of these degrees of defect there

162

corresponds also a difference in the possibility of social utilisation. Every being who does not reach an intellectual development of more than 2 years remains, so far as regards his powers for looking after himself, in the same condition as a child of that age; he may be able to grasp an object, to obey a simple gesture such as a motion to sit down, but he will ordinarily be unable to feed himself. On the other hand, imbeciles of the mental level of 2 to 4 years know how to make their way about in the house where they live; they are capable of learning to wash their hands, they can make an effort to dress themselves, they are able to pull a barrow or carry a weight; imbeciles from 4 to 7 years in intelligence can learn to sweep, to make a bed, to black boots; and feeble-minded subjects, above 7 years in intelligence, can be taught to sew and can be made useful in laundry and garden work. Coming to the upper limit of intelligence in mental debility, we have reason to think that a development equivalent to the normal average at 9 years of age is the minimum below which the individual is incapable of getting along without tutelage in the conditions of modern life. A certain number of facts suggest this view and are mutually confirmatory. Nine years is the intellectual level found in the lowest class of domestic servants, in those who are just on the border of a possible existence in economic independence; it is, on the other hand, the highest level met with in general paralytics who come under asylum care on account of their dementia; so long as a general paralytic, setting aside any question of active delirious symptoms, has not fallen below the intellectual level of 9 years, he can keep at liberty; once he has reached that level, he ceases to be able to live in society. And lastly, when we examine in our asylums cases of congenital defect, brought under care for the sole reason that their intelligence would not admit of their adapting themselves sufficiently to the complex conditions of life, we find that amongst the most highly developed the level of intelligence does not exceed that of normal children of 9 years of age.

It goes without saying that in these questions of social life, intelligence is not the only factor, character has also its part. None the less, it is the case that in the care and control of the defective, in judging as to their institutional treatment, the exact measurement of their intelligence is at present our surest guide.

To give a last example of the application of our method, this time in the domain of forensic medicine. A moment ago I referred to the case of a child brought under our notice for backwardness in his school work, now let us take another who is a source of trouble on account of his instability; he has even committed thefts and acts of violence, and such ominous terms as instinctive perversion and mental debility are being used to describe his state; I have myself written this diagnosis of mental debility in similar cases. Later on, armed with our method, I have re-examined these children, and I have found that, as a matter of fact, a large number of them had quite the intelligence of their age. It was not, then, a weakness of intelligence that was the explanation of their bad conduct, and you will grasp at once the importance of being set right as to this point, since on its knowledge will depend the direction of our reformatory efforts.

And the same thing holds true in a general manner for all criminal conduct, influences of environment, disorders of character, defects of judgment—how are we to disentangle the responsible factor? By patient investigations, with the help of our method, Dr. Sullivan has shown that the number of the feeble-minded amongst female criminals is much smaller than was thought. And when, on the other hand, there really does exist a condition of mental debility in an offender, how much more forcible will be your medico-legal report on the case when it is based on an examination susceptible of independent control, and is not merely the expression of a personal view open to denial and discussion.

Such are the services that may be rendered at present by an accurate measurement of intelligence. There are others that we can foresee. It is not merely in the case of abnormal children that a study of the intellectual development should allow of a fit adaptation of the educational programme. The whole of pedagogy must profit by a minute determination of the stages of progress. And so again, it is not only with the degrees of idiocy and imbecility that we should find corresponding differences in social aptitudes; it seems probable that one might also establish a hierarchy of occupations according to the quantity of intelligence which each one requires in the individual who practices it, and it would perhaps be better to begin by such a study as a guide in directing adolescents in the choice of a career instead of losing our way at the start in the effort to ascertain the presence of special aptitudes.

Again, one would like to know at what epoch in intelligence finishes its growth; one would like to know whether this growth occurs by regular progression or whether it may not advance by discontinuous ascent with critical ages and periods of special importance; one would like to know to what extent a precocious development may be the precursor of a real superiority in later life, or whether it is not merely the mark of an over-quick maturity. All these points, will, no doubt, be cleared up gradually; they require examination of many children, and that the same children be followed in their development year by year. It is to be feared that the amount of research that these problems must necessitate will delay their solution for a long time still. But remote as that solution may be, and despite the imperfections of the instrument that we bring to assist in reaching it, we may at all events set down to the credit of our method that already it has given precision to the data of the problems, and we may in advance pay homage for the results that we hope from it, to the memory of that great psychologist and indefatigable worker—Alfred Binet.

Woolley, H.T. (1914). The psychology of sex. *Psychological Bulletin,*
11, 353-379

THE PSYCHOLOGY OF SEX

By HELEN THOMPSON WOOLLEY
Cincinnati, Ohio

During the four years since my last review of the literature of the psychology of sex (PSYCHOL. BULL., October, 1910) the number of experimental investigations in the field has increased to such an extent that whereas it was difficult at that time to find anything to review, it is now impossible to review all I could find. The number of books and essays devoted to general discussions of the subject has also increased and their quality has improved very markedly. The emphasis placed on sex by the Freudian school and the interest in sex education, to say nothing of the whole feminist and woman's suffrage movement, have swelled the dimensions of the literature aside from experimental contributions to such an extent that no brief review could pretend to deal with it. Confronted by such a dilemma I have chosen the course of attempting a summary in the field of experimental psychology as complete as time and library facilities would allow, and a very brief mention of what seem to me the most important contributions to the other phases of the subject.[1]

I. EXPERIMENTAL AND STATISTICAL STUDIES

There have been two extended series of tests applied for the purpose of measuring sex differences, one by Burt and Moore (19), in England, summarized by Jones (46), and one by Cohn and Dieffenbacher (22) in Germany. A third one by Pyle (69) in the United States, less comprehensive in scope, but representing a larger number of individuals, has sex as one basis of formulation. Other experimental papers either deal with only a few phases of the sex problem, or are formulated primarily from some

---

[1] I am indebted to Mr. Charles A. Reed, librarian of the University of Cincinnati, for special library privileges and for assistance in borrowing books and periodicals from libraries at a distance, without which it would have been impossible to prepare this review in Cincinnati.

other point of view. I will make the summary by topics, referring to the parts of the special investigations under the various headings.

(a) *Heredity.* The present status of the theory of sex inheritance is very clearly and concisely summed up by Morgan (59). So far as a layman can see, there is little if anything in the theory which applies to the psychological problem. The ancient idea that the female is essentially an undeveloped male seems to be finally disproved by the fact that it requires more determiners-usually one more chromosome, or a larger sex chromosome-to produce a female than a male. When the additional sex chromosome was first discovered the assumption was that it determined maleness, doubtless because of the idea that the male was a more highly developed type. If there were any sense at all in such a formulation—which there probably is not—it would now have to be reversed. It seems certain that sex is determined at the moment of fertilization, and its determination is quite independent of environmental factors. Morgan believes that both the primary and the secondary characters of sex follow the laws of Mendelian inheritance, though not all biologists agree with him (Meijere, 55).

Secondary sexual characters are in some instances—chiefly in insects—determined independently of the sex glands. In the higher animals they are to a great extent dependent on the action of the sex glands, so much so that successful transplantation of the sex glands in the guinea pig arrives with it a development of the secondary sexual characters of the opposite sex, even to the extent of producing secretion of milk in the milk glands of the male. The mechanism by which this is brought about is that of hormones given off to the body fluids by the sex glands.

The part played by sexual selection in evolution Morgan considers very small. There is little evidence that it takes place at all in animals. Even when consciously practised it is incapable of originating modifications of species, or producing steady change in any direction. It merely serves to develop in pure strain traits which have become mixed. Modifications of species always arise as mutations, for the appearance of which no explanation can at present be offered.

Mutations when they arise may be inherited as sex-linked traits of the type of color-blindness, which are found predominating in one sex, though in certain combinations they may be inherited by the other. Both Morgan and Tandler and Gross (77), point out that it is impossible to find any single secondary character which belongs exclusively to either sex throughout the animal kingdom. For instance, superior size and brilliant plumage in some species belong to the female, while even the instinct for incubating eggs is assigned in some species to the male. Tandler and Gross interpret all secondary sexual characters as modifications of characters belonging to the species as such. They believe that the reason the sexes resemble one another after castration is merely that under those circumstances both sexes tend to revert to the original species type, an assumption which makes it unnecessary to assume the presence in each sex of the determiners of the other sex. The theory of heredity, then, seems incapable of throwing light on the question as to what systems of the body carry sex-linked factors. Conceivably any of them, including the nervous system, might. It merely describes the machinery by means of which any mutation which arises may be inherited as a sex-linked trait.

(b) *Physical Development*. Under this head I shall report a few papers which are of interest from a psychological point of view. Beik (9), instead of measuring children in absolute amounts, as most previous observers have done, measured a series of 6 1/2-year old children in terms of the proportion to adult standards for each sex. On this basis, he found girls more advanced than boys in height, weight, dentition, brain weight, and probably in the development of the skeleton. Measured in absolute terms boys are ahead in most of these respects. Hertz, in the report of the Danish Anthropological Society (26) gives a series of measurements kept for the last 27 years which show that during that time girls have gained considerably in height and weight, while boys have been at a standstill. Burgerstein (17) in reporting European statistics, states that girls show a much greater susceptibility to disease than boys.

(c) *Motor Ability*. Beik (9) found that at 6 ⑨ years, girls, measured in terms of proportion to adult attainment, were ahead of boys in motor control, in simple reaction time and in rate of tapping, boys and men—as in previous tests—have shown themselves superior (Burt and Moore 19). In card dealing, Burt and Moore found the boys quicker, while Calfee (20) found girls quicker. In card sorting and in alphabet sorting, girls were found decidedly superior by Calfee and by Burt and Moore. Culler (25) also found women faster on first fials of card sorting, though his group was small (17 of each sex) and he was not primarily interested in that point. In mirror drawing Calfee found the girls—college freshmen—faster than the boys throughout six successive trials. This agrees with previous work. Burt and Moore found the boys superior, but they do not consider their own test very reliable because of a change of method.

Mead (54) gives a small but reliable set of statistics supporting the popular opinion that girls learn to walk and talk earlier than boys. Starch (72) measured the handwriting of the entire school system of Madison, Wisconsin, and found the girls superior to the boys in speed, legibility, and form. The sex difference was greatest in

169

form. Burt and Moore found the same difference with regard to speed. Cohn and Dieffenbacher (22) found that girls read faster than boys, a result also obtained by Burt and Moore in reading and in counting for speed.

Ballard (7) found a relation between left-handedness and stammering, both of which are more prevalent among males. He tries to show that while the greater frequency of left-handedness is characteristic of the male sex, the greater frequency of stammering among boys is an artificial condition brought about by attempting to force left-handed individuals to write with the right hand. Statistics show that stammering is far more frequent among the left-handed who have been forced to write with the right hand than among those who were allowed to write with the left hand. He offers no explanation of how the result is brought about.

The tentative generalizations which may be drawn from this series of facts are (1) that girls develop faster than boys from infancy; (2) that boys re superior to girls in rapidity of movement under conditions in which the direction of attention remains fixed, as in reaction time and tapping; and (3) that girls are superior to boys in rapidity of motion in types of activity in which the direction of attention is constantly shifting-activities which involve rapid adaptations such as card sorting, mirror drawing, reading and writing.

(d) *Sensation and Perception*—(1) *Skin and Muscle Sense.* Bobertag (11) found that boys of 8, 9, and IO years are more accurate in the Binet-Simon test for discrimination of weights than girls. Burt and Moore (19) confirm this result for both children and adults. They also found the space threshold of females, child and adult, very much finer than that of males. These sex differences are in accord with previous investigations. (2) *Hearing.* Hentschel (38), who tested 250 children of each sex in Germany, found that boys discriminate pitch better than girls both when a musical interval is employed, and when much smaller differences of vibration rate are made the basis of comparison. The boys are from 2 to 7 per cent. ahead in the several series. Burt and Moore, like previous investigators, found females a little better in pitch discrimination than males. (3) *Vision.* Burt and Moore found females superior in fineness of color discrimination. Monroe (58) in giving the Binet-Simon tests to 300 boys and 300 girls of from three to six years) found that the girls excel the boys in color perception and in color naming. Burt and Moore found the boys superior in judging visual space. These results also agree with previous work. (4) *Perception.* The group of tests which belong most distinctly under this head are tests of the cancellation type, which involve both perception and motor reaction. In these tests females of all ages are uniformly better than males (Haggerty and Kempf (36), Woodworth and Wells (86), Pyle (68, 69)). The possible generalizations in this field are (1) females have a finer spatial threshold on the skin, better color vision, and more rapid motor responses to changing perceptions than males; and (2) males are superior to females in the discrimination of weights and visual areas. The results with regard to pitch discrimination are contradictory.

(e) *Memory.* There have been two sorts of experiments which may be included under this head, the rote memory experiments and those in" Aussage" or report. Under the first head there have been tests by Aall (1) using objects, by Burt and Moore (19) material not stated, by Myers (64) using words and letters in testing incidental memory, by Vertes (79) using words, by Cohn and Dieffenbacher (22) using digits, by Pyle (69) using words, and by Winch (85) using consonants. All of these workers found females superior except Cohn and Dieffenbacher, and Pyle, who found no difference of sex. These results are in accord with most previous investigations.

The experiments in the psychology of report have been carried on chiefly in Germany, Holland and Norway, and are published in German. The term *Bericht* refers to the spontaneous account given by the subject of the picture, story, or series of events presented to him, while *Verhor* refers to the results of an examination which he subsequently undergoes on the subject matter. These words I shall translate *report* and *examination*. The trustworthiness (*Treue*) is estimated by finding the proportion of correct statements to the total number of statements made, both correct and false. Spontaneity is measured by finding the proportion of correct statements in the report to the total number of correct statements in both report and examination. Some of the questions used in the examination are distinctly suggestive, which gives an opportunity to measure suggestibility. Finally it is possible to classify the kind of items reported by each sex, for qualitative differences of memory.

With regard to the extent of memory displayed by the sexes in these experiments, the results are somewhat contradictory. In view of the small number of individuals represented in many of the series (from 15, or even less of each sex, to 30) contradictions are not surprising. Aall reports two tests, one with adults (3) and one with school children (1). In both cases he followed the plan of asking for a second reproduction of the story without warning. In some groups a mental attitude of expecting an immediate reproduction had been induced, while in others the expectation

171

was that the reproduction would be deferred. In all variations of the experiments he found the extent of immediate memory greater in the female. With adults the same difference held for the second reproduction, but the school boys were better in the second reproduction than the girls. Aall is inclined to lay great stress on the latter result. The same type of test was tried by Lem (49) with school children with exactly the reverse result. His boys displayed a greater extent of memory in the immediate reproduction than the girls, while in subsequent ones, asked for without warning, the girls caught up with and at last a bit surpassed the boys. Breukink (15) and Schramm (71) both compared groups of university students. Breukink used pictures and Schramm a story. Breukink found the extent of memory a bit greater in men, while Schramm found it greater in women. Cohn and Dieffenbacher (22), and Pyle (69), whose test of logical memory belongs here, both found school girls superior to boys at all ages. With regard to trustworthiness, Breukink, Schramm, and if I understand him correctly, Aall, found women superior, Lem found boys superior, and Cohn and Dieffenbacher found no difference of sex. The latter authors report that girls have a decidedly greater degree of spontaneity.

Aall lays great stress on the qualitative differences in the reports as distinctive of sex. These analyses have been carried to too great length to be reported here. The chief point of agreement among them is that females report visual elements and particularly colors more frequently than men. Several of them also find that males report space relations more accurately than females, a fact corroborated by Myers (64) in his study of incidental memory.

Memory of dreams can be considered a special case of the psychology of report. In an Italian kindergarten in which the children take a nap every day, they were questioned immediately on waking with regard to what they had dreamed. Doglia and Banchieri (27) made records for 100 children at three years of age. The girls remembered more dreams and remembered them more fully than the boys. Two year later Banchieri (8) reexamined a large portion of the same group, and found that the same sex difference persisted.

To sum up then, females are superior to males in memory at all ages. The difference is clear and very uniform with regard to rote memory. In experiments in report sometimes one sex and sometimes the other has shown itself quantitatively superior, but on the whole the advantage is with the females.

(f) *The Effect of Drill.* Closely allied to memory are the investigations on the effect of drill. Brown (16) and F. M. Phillips (67) both tests elementary school children with respect to the efficacy of drill work in arithmetic. Brown found no difference in this respect between the sexes, while Phillips found that the boys gained more than the girls. Wells has two papers which touch on the subject, but in both instances the sex groups are too small to be significant. In one (83) he found a progressive improvement of endurance with practice which was greater in women than in men. In the other (82) he found no difference in the gains made by practising addition and number checking. Yoakum and Calfee (88) report that their freshmen boys gained more in practising mirror drawing than the girls, though they did not catch up with them. Culler (25) observed that the men of his comparable group (only 7 of each sex) gained with practice in card sorting enough faster than the women to surpass them, particularly after an interference due to a rearrangement of the system of sorting. These investigations have been very different in type, and most of them represent small groups, so that generalizations are not safe, but there have been more of them which report a faster rate of improvement with drill in boys than in girls. It is interesting to notice that these tests have been carried out with processes in which females are at the start faster.

(g) *Association.* Huber (45) carried out, with soldiers in training, the same series of free associations that Reinbold had previously tried with the girls of an advanced school. Though he states that differences of sex exist, the specific differences which he finds, such as greater uniformity in the associations of the girls, and more predicate, adjective and definition reactions on the part of the soldiers, he explains as due not to sex, but to the amount of education in the two groups. Free association tests consisting in recording the number of words which could be written in a given length of time are reported by Burt and Moore (19) as showing boys faster, and by Pyle (69) and Lobsien (51) as showing girls faster. The latter found the difference marked from 9 to 11 years, but insignificant in older children. Since girls write faster than boys, such a test cannot throw much light on the rapidity of the thought process. Free associations in which the reaction time for each word has been measured, have been very uniformly found faster in men than in women. Haggerty and Kempf (36) and Wells (81) confirmed this result. Controlled association of the type represented by fundamentals in arithmetic (addition, etc.) is usually faster n females. Burt and Moore found boys faster, but Courtis (24) with his enormous series of New York school children, and Haggerty and Kempf with university students found girls and women faster. In controlled association of the opposite type girls are also apt to be superior (Burt and Moore, Pyle, Bonser, (15)), though in this case correctness of idea is a larger factor in estimating results than time of association. Haggerty and Kempf, considering speed alone, found men faster.

The Ebbinghaus completion test has been used as a measure of sex difference by Cohn and Dieffenbacher (22), Burt and Moore, and Bonser. Burt and Moore, who call the test "completion of argument" because of the nature of the text used, found no sex difference, Pyle found the girls faster at all ages, while in the number of associations suggested by an ink blot (called a test in imagination) boys were superior.

The generalization which is suggested by these results is that males are faster in free associations, while females are faster in practised systems of associations.

Both Wells and Haggerty and Kempf discuss the reasons for the more rapid free associations of men. Both papers take the view that the lengthened time of the women is due to a greater tendency to interference and suppression of ideas. This means, as Wells points out, that the associations of women are really controlled associations—controlled by the self for various reasons—to a greater extent than those of men. He thinks it possible that this result may be due merely to the fact that men have tested women, and that a woman testing men might obtain reverse results. Haggerty and Kempf are inclined to think that his tendency to be "on guard" against embarrassment is characteristic of the female sex. Apparently the Freudian school would find this interpretation in harmony with their theory of hysteria, which they explain exclusively on the basis of the suppression and substitution of sex impulses and ideas, and which is so much more prevalent among women.

With regard to types of reproduction within the associative process, Wells (81) and Lobsien (51) give results. The only decided difference of sex observed by Wells was the greater frequency of predicate associations in women, and of coordinate associations in men, a difference which had been previously noted. Among children Lobsien found the vast majority of associations belonging to the type in which no connection was evident. He calls them "springende" reproductions. The next largest class was the coordinates, while verbal and predicate associations were very few. The sex differences were small. Taking the entire group from 7 to 15 years, he found a few more "springende" associations for girls, and a few more of each of the other three types for boys. He also, the finds coordinate associations a bit more frequent for girls. However differences of method make a comparison of results of doubtful value.

(h) *Attention.* Cohn and Dieffenbacher (22) measured attention in terms of the distraction involved in simultaneous reading and writing, in which the girls suffered less from distraction than the boys. Burt and Moore (19) used two tests, one a test of the scope of attention called the spot pattern test, a tachistoscopic test in which a pattern composed of spots is reproduced, and one called irregular dotting which consists in tapping as rapidly as possible when each tap must hit one of an irregular series of dots. In both tests they found the boys superior, though in the second one the girls were better if the time interval was short. Heymans (39) lays stress on the narrower range of consciousness of the female, which he thinks can be deduced from her greater emotionality, and which is corroborated by the greater prevalence of hysteria in women. These two tests of the scope of attention give contradictory results.

(i) *Judgment and Reasoning*. Breukink (15) tested judgments of time and space in men and women, and found men more accurate with regard to time, but no sex difference with regard to space. In judging space from memory, Myers (64) found males more accurate. Cohn and Dieffenbacher (22) thought the boys showed better judgment in their series of tests in several respects. They judged better the additional time required to learn the long series of digits than did the girls, though they came out with no better result in the end. He found that the boys had more questioned judgments in their tests of report, and that they were more trustworthy than the girls on the most essential points of the picture, though not in the report as a whole. In the logical arrangement of themes of the two sexes they found no difference. Burt and Moore (19) found boys better than girls in solving mechanical puzzles, but observed no difference in the sexes in respect to reasoning power tested by a group of tests consisting of the completion of an argument, the completion of analogies, constructing sentences, opposites, and the correction of syllogisms. Bonser (14) who made a particularly careful and many-sided investigation of a large group of children in the fourth, fifth, and sixth grades, found the boys a little ahead in the median for the series, seven tests in all. In detail there were more marked differences. The boys were ahead in reasoning out problems, in selecting correct reasons for statements, and a bit so in a completion tests. The girls were ahead in opposites, in selecting correct definitions, and particularly in the interpretation of literature. With regard to age, he found the boys ahead up to twelve years, and the girls ahead above twelve years.

The other tests which I have been able to find deal with reasoning as displayed in the solution of problems in arithmetic. F. M. Phillips (67) using the Stone tests, and Courtis (24) using his own tests found the boys better than the girls in tests of correct reasoning. Fox and Thorndike (31) report that in their group of high school pupils, girls surpassed boys in arithmetical ability, but they believe that the girls in that community were a more selected set than the boys.

On the whole, then, males have stood better than females in tests of judgment and reasoning.

(j) *General Intelligence*. Under this head there have been (1) several investigations o school marks in the United States and Europe, and statistics with regard to the number of advanced and retarded children in school systems, (2) Binet-Simon tests, (3) groups of selected tests, and (4) some single tests can be more conveniently classified here than elsewhere.

(1) The instability of school marks as a measure of ability has been strikingly brought out by Starch and Elliot, who sent an examination paper to 180 head mathematics teacher to be marked, and received grades all the way from 25 to 90! However, taken in the mass they doubtless have some significance. Baldwin (5) studied school marks in the fourth and fifths grades of a city school. He found that the girls maintained a higher standard of scholarship than the boys. In accord with this was the fact that there were more repeaters among the boys and more girls who skipped grades. Miles (57) made a study of the marks in both elementary school and high school for a group of 106 children for whom he had continuous records. The girls were consistently ahead in every grade, and in every subject except arithmetic, where there was no sex difference. Klinkenberg (47) studied school marks in a school system in Holland which was partly coeducational and partly segregated. Boys were ahead in mathematics, physical sciences, history, and geography, subjects, he remarks, in which an analytic process of though is uppermost. Girls were ahead in literary studies and languages. He states that girls do not stand examinations as well as boys, but do better in class work then on would expect from their examinations. Girls were further behind boys in geometry than in algebra, which is due, he says, to their well-known disinclination to constructive thought. Cohn (see Bobertag, 13), in the "Dritter deutscher Kongress fur Jugendbildung und Jugendkunde" gave a report on school marks in a coeducational school in Baden. Taken as a whole, he found no sex difference, but in grouping the subjects he also found no sex difference, but in grouping the subjects he also found boys better in science and mathematics, and girls in the language group. Forsyth (30) reports that the mean college grade of women in the University of Illinois is a little higher than that of the men. Heymans (39) collected statistics on this point from the universities of Holland, and found that the women rank higher than the men. The fact is so well established in this country that it has given rise to the witticism that university professors who used to object to admitting women to their classes on the ground that it would lower the standards of scholarship, now abject because the women do so much better class work that the men become discouraged and refuse to compete in the game.

The number of advanced and retarded children in large school systems in the United States have been tabulated by Bevard (10) in Washington, D. C, by Hill (41) in New Orleans, by B. A. Phillips (66) in Philadelphia, and by Lurton (52) for fifty-five towns in Minnesota. In every instance there were more retarded boys than girls, and more accelerated girls than boys.

(2) The Binet-Simon tests have been made the basis of sex comparison in the United States by Goddard (35), A. C. Strong (75), and Monroe (58), and in Europe by Bobertag (11) and Wiersma (84). Monroe dealt only with children from three to six years of age. He tested 300 of each sex, and found no sex difference on the whole, though there wer small differences in the various years. Goddard's results represent the largest number of children tested by the Binet-Simon scale under one director, 2,000 children. His table shows no clear difference of sex. Reduced to percents on the basis of the proportion of each sex who are two years or more retarded, or two years or more advanced—a procedure which he did not himself carry out—it appears that there is no sex difference in retardation (boys 18.4 per cent., girls 18.6 per cent.), but the girls have a slightly greater proportion of accelerated individuals (boys 3.7 per cent., girls 4.8 per cent.). Strong in tests of 225 white children found on the same basis a similar state of affairs, though the differences were larger—retarded, boys 9.6 per cent., girls 10.7 per cent.; accelerated, boys 3.2 per cent., girls 6.9 per cent. The European results rest on much smaller numbers. Wiersma, who tested 68 boys and 73 girls, found the girls ahead on the whole, while the boys had larger groups both of retarded and of accelerated individuals. Bobertag alone found boys superior to girls. His results are stated in terms of years and fractions of years for each sex at each age. The boys were superior at each age by amounts varying from 0.06 to 0.20 of a year. Bobertag is quite too scientific to regard this result as conclusive, since it rests on about fifteen of each sex at each age, but he remarks that if it is substantiated it would be in accord with other experimental findings. That it does not agree with the general trend of Binet-Simon tests so far is evident. It is quite possible, however, that results in the coeducational school systems of Holland and the United States may prove to be different from those in the segregated schools of Germany.

(3) Cohn and Dieffenbacher (22), Burt and Moore (19), and Pyle (69) carried out series of tests on comparable groups of the two sexes. The subjects of Cohn and Dieffenbacher varied in age from 7 to 19 years. They were selected as representatives of the better and the poorer sections of their school classes. There were about 100 of them in all. Burt and Moore tested about 140 children of 12 ⚘ to 13 ⚘ years, and about

100 university students. These two series agree in finding no sex differences as a whole. Specific differences which they report have been mentioned under the appropriate headings. Pyle, testing school children in this country, found the girls superior, but his tests were not as varied in type as the other series.

(4) Two investigations, those of Libby and his coworkers (50) and that of Franken (32), were made by means of questions on general information. Franken, though he had a considerable number of subjects, had only small comparable sex groups. The younger girls were superior to the boys, but there were no differences among the older children. Libby and his associates tested grade children from the fourth to the eighth grade, and first year high school students. They report boys superior in all age groups. The girls were more cautious in their replies, and not so likely to guess if they did not know. Ash (4) tried giving school children the choice of two kinds of tasks, one of which required original observations, and the other compilations from books. He found no sex difference on the whole, but the boys were most numerous in the group who selected all their tasks from one type, while the girls were more likely to divide the choice. With regard to mental fatigue, which should, I suppose, be regarded as an element in general intelligence, Offner (65) reports that no sex difference has been observed.

On the whole, then girls have stood better than boys in measures of general intelligence. So far as I know, no one has drawn the conclusion that girls have greater native ability than boys. One is tempted to indulge in idle speculation as to whether this admirable restraint from hasty generalization would have been equally marked had the sex finding been reversed! The usual explanation of the result offered is that girls are more docile and industrious than boys. The greater industry of girls has been turned to account by Lipmann in a novel argument for the inherent superiority of the boys. In his summary of the evidence on variability (see Bobertag, 13) he states that there are a larger number of series of measures in which the boys proved to be the more variable sex in the sense that there were more boys in the extreme quartiles of the range of values, and more girls in the two middle quarters. He argues that the greater industry of the girls would be capable of raising them from the lowest quartile to a higher one, but would not suffice to overcome their lesser native ability to the extent of raising them from a lower to the highest quartile. To limit the effects of industry so much as to make it inoperative through a whole quarter of the range of a measure seems a bit extreme.

The writers who explain the results just quoted on the ground of the greater industry of girls are also those who emphasize their greater emotionality and rapid changes of mood. They seem to find no contradiction in the fact that the sex which is most dominated by emotions and moods is also the one which has the greatest capacity for plugging away at a task whether it is interesting or not. Another explanation quite as reasonable as that of the greater industry of girls might be sought in the fact that girls develop somewhat faster than boys. In the case of university students it may be, as Thorndike points out, that the sexes are selected on a different basis.

(k) *Affective Processes, Tastes and Ideals.* The only direct experimental investigation of affective processes is that of Burt and Moore (19) in which they measured the psychogalvanic reflex in adults under stimulation of various sorts, and found the deflection in response to emotional disturbances greater in women than in men. It would be interesting to find out whether the same different obtains when a woman instead of a man does the testing of the two groups. Under those conditions the plethysmograph and respirator—which to be sure are not very safe measures—gave opposite results in my own tests. Burt and Moore believe that an analysis of the content of association reactions revealed a difference of sex in emotionality at an early age, and that the difference increases with years.

Heymans (39) attacked the question of the relative emotionality of the sexes by the questionnaire method. A large number of intelligent people in Holland filled out the blanks, and a tabulation of results showed that a larger number of women than men were classed as emotional. Moreover the traits that were assigned predominantly to women were also those assigned to emotional men. (For a discussion of the scientific value of this method see Thorndike, 78).

There have been a few bits of experimental evidence bearing on other phases of affective life than degree of affectability. E. K. Strong (76) found that women have more and greater dislikes than men and are better able to classify them. H. L. Hollingsworth (42) suggest the generalization, which he says needs further confirmation, that men resemble one another more clearly in their preferences, while women are more alike in their aversions. Kuper (48) confirmed for children Strong's statement that women have more dislikes than men. Her method was to ask 200 children, evenly divided as to sex and varying in age from 6 1/2 to 16 1/2 years, to arrange three series of pictures in the order of preference. All three series represented the same nine subjects. It is interesting to notice how nearly alike the order was for the two sexes. For girls it was religion, patriotism, children, pathos, animals, sentiment, landscape, heroism, and action. The only change in the order for boys was that the positions of children and of heroism and action together were reversed, bringing children last and heroism and action third and fourth in the boys' lists.

Ballard (96) classified preferences in the themes of free drawings made by London school children. The themes of boys in order of preference were ships, miscellaneous drawings, plant life, house, human beings, vehicles, animals, weapons, and landscapes, while for girls the order was plant life, houses, miscellaneous drawings, human beings, animals, ships, vehicles, weapons, and landscapes. Here again the order is very similar. The chief difference is that boys show a much greater liking for ships and girls for plant life. Stockton (74) tried to measure preference by means of the choice of one of a pair of words. He found far more resemblance than difference. Both boys and girls choose time words a bit more frequently than space words, words for food rather than words for dress, and adjectives rather than verbs. For words of activity boys showed a small preference, while girls choose words of passivity a little more frequently. He found that preference based on the idea of the word increased with age, and more markedly so in the case of boys than in that of girls, but neither sex based the choice on meaning to as great an extent as upon mere position.

There have been three investigations which consisted in asking each of a large number of children to state what person, whether acquaintance, historical character, or character of fiction he would most like to resemble. Brandall, reported by Gilbertson (34) worked with Swedish children, Hill (40) with American children, and Hoesch-Ernst (see Bobertag, 13) also with American children. They all agree that girls choose personal acquaintances oftener than boys, and that boys choose more public and historical characters. Brandall and Hills found that girls choose ideals from the opposite sex many times as often as boys. In the Swedish study boys choose characters from fiction more frequently than girls, while in this country the reverse was true. Brandall recorded also the reasons assigned by the children for their choices. He found that girls name moral, intellectual and artistic qualities more frequently than boys, while boys name material advantages, honor, and social position more frequently.

Anderson (3) gives the result of a questionnaire on the kind and amount of reading done by school children. She found no difference of sex with regard to amount, though girls read more books and boys more magazine articles. The girls used libraries more than boys. The preferences for kinds of literature were for boys, (1) stories of adventure, (2) detective stories, (3) and (4) war and love stories; for girls (1) love stories, (2) stories of adventure, (3) detective stories, and (4) travel and biography. Anderson also found that girls displayed a greater range in their reading, received more advice about it, and talked more about what they read than boys. The boys were more independent and original in choice.

Scheifler (70) has a paper on the tastes of boys and girls in games, based on a questionnaire given to 5,000 children. He divided plays into four classes, imitation plays (dolls, solders, etc.), plays of bodily movement and contests (ball, tag, etc.), plays of intellectual activity and contest (building, checkers, chees, etc.), and occupation plays (sewing, reading, collecting, etc.). His general result is that girls give a greater preference to imitation plays, and boys to plays of bodily movement and contest, while there is no sex difference in the other two groups of plays. However when he picked out a set of plays which he designates as constructive—such as drawing, building and chess—the boys predominate. Scheifler is much relieved to note that coeducation shows no tendency to make the plays of boys and girls alike. If it did he thinks it would be a sufficient reason for doing away with coeducations. "Freuen wir uns vielmehr der schonen Eigenart der Geschlechter und plefgen wir sie! Unser Volk braucht immer noch beides: Manner die da wagen und wagen, Frauen die im kleinsten Krreise unendlich Grosses wirken."

Melville (56) asked each member of the four high school classes to write down all the slang phrases he knew. He then selected 100 papers, evenly divided between the sexes, from each class. The boys were ahead of the girls in the number of expression by amounts increasing from 18.7 per cent. to 40.0 per cent. in the four classes.

(l) *Creative Ability in Art and Letters.* There have been several studies of children's drawings published. Cohn and Dieffenbacher (22) and Wagner (80) both followed the method of asking large groups of children to draw, under experimental conditions, illustrations for Han Sach's poem "Schlaraffenland." They both classified the drawings as Kerschensteiner had done, on the basis of representations of space, from the entire spacelessness of primitive drawings through linear and group arrangements to well-developed perspective. They agree that the primate spacelessness is more characteristic of girls' drawings than of boys', and that girls take more pains than boys with decorative details. Cohn and Dieffenbacher found that girls treated a greater number of themes than boys, while Wagner found the reverse. Wagner noticed more elaboration of details in the drawings of the boys, and found them superior in inventiveness, in the representations of humor, and of motion. On the whole Wagner considers the boys very superior. The girls in his group excelled only in details which had to do with feminine interests. Cohn and Dieffenbacher noticed that the drawings of the boys were

181

larger than those of the girls, and more characterized by heavy lines and strong colors, whereas the girls preferred delicate lines and soft colors. This difference in color preference had been previously noted in Kirkpatrick's monograph on "Studies in Development and Learning."

Muth (63) asked children from the first to the seventh years in school to decorate the outline of a plate and of a shield. She agrees with the two reports just quoted that girls prefer fine lines and a smaller more delicate type of drawing. She found that the sense of rhythm is earlier developed in girls and is stronger than in boys. The girls showed a better sense of proportion between the filled and the blank spaces of the surfaces. From the point of view of mere decorative effect, then, girls were superior, though she found the boys excelling in the expression of humor and in the originality of their drawings.

The generalization suggested by these pieces of work is that boys excel in perspective drawing and girls in decorative drawing.

Within the years with which I am dealing, I have found but one attempt to measure the relative merits of literary productions in the sexes. Cohn and Dieffenbacher (22) asked their group of children to write a theme on experiences at the local railroad stations. They found the themes of the girls superior in most of the measures which they applied. Their themes were longer, both in words and in statements, their sentences were longer, they used more figures of speech, and a greater number of unusual expressions. Their themes were richer in content, and better in literary style. Analyzed for content they found that the boys mentioned more objects, more definite numbers and spaces than the girls. The girls' themes were richer in feeling, and more subjective. The sexes differed in the kind of feeling expressed. With girls sentimental and comic moods predominated, and with the boys the loyal and ethical sentiments. Though it does not belong in my period, it seems worthwhile to mention the fact that Giese (33) arrives at more generalizations opposed to most of those just quoted! His monograph is an extended study of the free literary productions of boys and girls from the ages of five to twenty. The material he collected from all sorts of sources, chiefly from the public press. He criticizes Cohn and Dieffenbacher for passing judgment on a question of personal opinion like literary style, but does not seem to feel that his own work is open to the same criticism with reference to his selection of material, and his judgments of originality and value. He find that boys write more poetry than girls, and do it much better, that their compositions are longer, more philosophic, and of higher artistic quality. The monograph contains very detailed comparisons of a large number of factors, and is half devoted to a collection of literary productions representative of the various ages.

(m) *Suggestibility*. Two of the papers on the psychology of report (Aussage) contain measures of suggestibility. Breukink (15) in his group of adults found the women more suggestible than the men. They answered more of the suggestive questions both wrongly and correctly than the men did. Cohn and Dieffenbacher (22) in their group of school children found no sex difference in suggestibility, measured in the same way.

(n) *Variability*. Several of the experimental series to which we have referred have been formulated in terms of variability, but most of the groups have been too small to be significant unless there was wide agreement, which there has not been. The results dealing with the largest number of individuals, those of Goddard (35) on Binet-Simon tests and of Courtis (24) on tests in arithmetic fail to show any sex difference in variability. Ther have been two papers which sum up experimental evidence on the subject, one by L. S. Hollingworth (44) and one by Lipmann (see Bobertag, 13). Hollingworth sums up her review by saying, "If the evidence can be said to point in one direction rather than another, a greater female variability seems actually to be indicated in experiments so far made on the higher mental process." Unfortunately I have not seen Lipmann's original paper, but only the abstract of it in the report of the congress at which it was delivered. He says that he worked over all the available statistics on variability in the sexes, and found that in 53 per cent. of the series of measures males were more variable, in 37 per cent. females were more variable, and in 10 per cent. there was no difference. Thorndike (78) selected a set of measures of various traits which he thinks most reliable as a basis of estimating variability, and concludes that they indicate somewhat greater variability of the male. He is convinced that greater variability of the male must be the explanation of the greater preponderance of male geniuses. The amount of the sex difference in genius is most vividly brought out by comparing Cattell's former study of eminent men with that of Castle (21) on eminent women, and is of course not brought into question by sketches of the contributions to science mad by women, such as those by Mozans (60), interesting as they may be.

Hollingworth question the genuineness both of the greater number of male geniuses and of the greater number of meal deficient, facts which have usually been thought to be proofs of male variability. She points out (43) that most of the evidence for the greater number of male deficient rets on statistics from institutions for the feeble-minded, which she and others consider unreliable because it is easier for feeble-minded women to maintain themselves outside of institutions than for feeble-minded men, since the former may earn their way either as household drudges or as prostitutes. As evidence of the truth of this assumption she reports a series of 1,000 consecutive cases passing through the New York clearing house for mental defectives, in which she found the females much more numerous than the males in the older group, showing that they had been able to maintain themselves longer in society than the corresponding males. The Binet-Simon tests confirmed this by showing that of those individuals who tested at a given mental age, the women were older than the men. She concludes that if social pressure bore equally on the sexes, there would be as many females as males in institutions for the feeble-minded. The statistics from a social survey of the number of the feeble-minded outside of institutions, which gives more males than females, Hollingworth considers unreliable, though Thorndike apparently accepts them. With regard to genius (44) she makes the very pertinent suggestion that no one who has discussed the question has given sufficient weight to the fact that most women have devoted the greater portion of their time to occupations connected with bearing and rearing children, and in maintaining a home—occupations in which eminence is impossible though genius is not. No one can tell, she says, how much genius of a high order may have gone into these tasks where recognition in terms of fame is out of the question. She concludes that there is little ground for explaining the lesser scientific and artistic achievements of women on the ground of greater male variability. Finot (28, 29) makes much the same point in stating that in proportion to the number of women devoting themselves to scientific and artistic pursuits, the number of persons with eminence has compared favorably to the males.

II. GENERAL DISCUSSION

The general discussions of the psychology of sex, whether by psychologists or by sociologists show such a wide diversity of points of view that one feels that the truest thing to be said at present is that scientific evidence plays very little part in producing convictions. As Coolidge puts it: "In our present stage, the conclusions as to the permanence or significant of any feminine peculiarity at which any observer will arrive are in accordance usually with his anti- or pro-feminent bias." Hartley expresses the same idea. Among psychologists Burt and Moore (19), Stern (73), Heymans (39), Wreschner (87), and Thorndike (78) have expressed opinions with regard to the facts of the psychology of sex, based on the experimental evidence. The generalization at which Burt and Moore arrive is that sex differences are most marked in the simpler functions of sensation and motion and decrease as one rises to the higher levels of mental activity, until in the most complicated functions no difference is to be observed. Stern arrives at exactly the opposite generalization! The simpler and more easily measured functions show no significant difference of sex, he says, while we may be certain that as we penetrate further with experimental methods into the more complex mental functions, the significant differences will appear. Heymans, basing his opinion largely on the returns from the questionnaires which he and Wiersma sent out, though he considers experimental results also, derives a differential psychology of sex from two fundamental factors, first the greater emotionality of women, and second their greater activity, in the sense of readiness to act. The differences in intellectual capacity he explains in terms of interest and attention, which are ultimately determined by emotionality. Hermans's book is exceedingly readable, but not altogether convincing. His principle fails to work at a very vital point. The fact that women are in many respects poorer observers than men, he explains on the ground that their emotionality limits their interests, so that they observe well only that which has emotional value for them. When it comes to accounting for the better rank of women in academic work, he finds that while men put effort chiefly on that which interests them, women are industrious and conscientious in all tasks, whether they find them interesting or not. This contradiction he attempts to resolve on the ground that women are more readily spurred to action than men. Wreschner's book is in the nature of a popular lecture summarizing experimental studies of sex. He gives no references, and no indication of the strength of the evidence underlying his generalizations. The source of his material is easily recognized by anyone familiar with the field. As a matter of fact some of his statements rest on evidence so contradictory or so meagre that they are worth no more than a personal opinion. In his conclusions he agrees with Heymans in assigning to women a stronger emotional nature, and a smaller participation in abstract intellectual processes, but takes the opposite point of view with regard to activity, which he regards distinctly greater in men. Thorndike (78) regards the differences between the sexes of the type revealed by experimental psychology as too small, in view of the large variations within each sex, to be considered significant except with regard to the greater variability of the male. So far as central tendencies in various abilities are concerned, he assumes no difference of sex. He is inclined to agree with the others that women are more emotional than men, and thinks it probable that the chief difference of sex aside from variability is to be found in the fighting instinct of the male and the nursing instinct of the female, instincts which affect lines of conduct. One element in the success of men in scientific, artistic or social fields is their love of getting ahead of the other fellow, while women have less of a desire to win, and a more pronounced humanitarian tendency.

All of this group of men, in spite of their wide differences of opinion as to the nature of the psychological characteristics of sex, are convinced that they are inherent ant are not to be explained by environmental influences during the life of the individual. Burt and Moore base their conviction on the fact that the sex differences which they found in English children and adults were similar in kind and amount to those of my series of American university students. Differences which remain constant at different ages and in different countries must, they think, be inherent in sex itself. They do not seem to have considered whether or not there are factors in the social environment of sex which remain constant in all modern civilized countries. Stern believes that sex differences have been found in processes which are not influenced by social environment, such as spontaneous drawings. Wreschner holds that some of the traits most characteristic of women, notably emotionality, are of a nature to be repressed rather than fostered by the social environment of women. Heymens points out with much justice that much of the argumentation with regard to what social milieu would have on given traits is very inconclusive. It is no difficult matter to get up fairly plausible arguments to prove either that social conditions tend to foster emotionality in women (Finot) or that they tend to repress it. (Wreschner). Heymans thinks it quite as reasonable to suppose that differences in traits determined the differences in environment as vice-versa. Finally Wreschner inquires somewhat peevishly how in the world we are to know what is inherited and what socially acquired, and calls upon all good citizens to help along the course of evolution, whose direction he is confident he perceives, by cherishing our present valuable distinction of sex instead of subversively trying to overthrow them. However none of these men, except perhaps Stern, believes that the nature or amount of the psychological difference of sex is a sufficient ground for separate systems of education for the two.

There are a few points in the literature of experimental psychology which point to the importance of social influences. The sex difference in size whose hereditary origin has seldom been questioned, is decreasing with the change in the educational regime of girls. The Danish Anthropological Society (26) has found that within the last generation girls have made large gains in height and weight, while boys have not changed. It is interesting to notice, too, that in Germany, where the tradition of the mental inferiority of women is still strong, and the girls' schools are even yet inferior (Munsterberg, 62) experimental results are more likely than in other countries to show differences of sex, and to find them in the direction of male superiority. In the tests conducted by Cohn and Dieffenbacher in one of the few coeducations school of high school rank in Germany, they found the girls superior not only to the segregated girls, but tot the boys in the same school. They were a small group, and German psychologists explain their high rank on the ground that they were to a greater extent than the boys selected on a basis of ability. It is also significant that differences between the cultures and the uncultured in experimental results are usually far larger than those between the sexes (Breukink, 15).

When one turns to the books written more largely from the historical and sociological point of view, the trend of opinion is that mental differences of sex are of social origin. There are four scholarly and exceedingly interesting books of this type, Coolidge (23), Hartley (37), Finot (28, 29), and Muller–Lyer (61), coming respectively from the United States, England, France, and Germany. The last three all contain historical sketches of the position of women from primitive times to modern. Hartley and Finot also discuss the question of sex in animals, and its bearing on human problems. Coolidge's book is particularly interesting to American readers because it is written with immediate reference to the social position of women in the United States during the last few generations. They all lay stress on the view that social conditions account for most of the traits ordinarily considered feminine, and particularly for the limited accomplishment of women in art and science. Coolidge gives a vivid sketch of the way traditional domesticity limited and determined the intellectual life of women. The same point is effectively brought out from the German standpoint by Maurenbrecher (53).

REFERENCES

I.   AALL, A. Ein neues Gedachtinisgesetz? *Zsch. f. Psychol.*, 1913, 66, 1-51.

II.   AALL, A. Zur Psychologie der Wiederezahlung. *Zsch. f. angew. Psychol.*, 1913, 7, 185-210.

III.   ANDERSON, R. E. A Preliminary Study of the Reading Tastes of High School Pupils. *Ped. Sem.*, 1912, 19, 438-460.

IV.   ASH, I. E. The Correlates and Conditions of Mental Inertia. *Ped. Sem.*, 1912, 19, 425-437.

V.   BALDWIN, B. T. A Psycho-Educational Study of the Fourth and Fifth School Grades. *J. of Educ. Psychol.*, 1913, 4, 364-365

VI.   BALLARD, P. B. What London Children Like to Draw. *J. of Exp. Ped.*, 1912, 1, 186-197.

VII.   BALLARD P. B. Sinistrality and Speech. *J. of Exp. Ped.*, 1912, 8, 289-310.

VIII.   BANCHIERI, F. I sogni dei bambini di cinque anni. *Riv. di Psychol.*, 1912, 8, 325-330.

IX.   BEIK, A. K. Physiological Age and School Entrance. *Ped. Sem.*, 1913, 20, 277-321.

X.   BEVARD, K. H. Progress of the Repeaters of the Class of 1912 of the Public Schools of Washington, D. C. *Psychol. Clinic*, 1913, 7, 68-83.

XI.   BOBERTAG, O. Ueber Intelligenzprufungen (nach der Methode von Binet und Simon). *Zsch. f. angew. Psychol.*, 1911, 5, 105-203.

XII.   BOBERTAG, O. Ueber Intelligenzprufungen (nach der Methode von Binet und Simon). *Zsch. f. angew. Psychol.*, 1912, 6, 495-538.

XIII.   BOBERTAG, O. Dritter deutscher Kongress fur Jugendbildung und Jugendkunde zu Breslau von 4 bis 6 Oktober, 1913. *Zsch. f. angew. Psychol.*, 1913, 8, 345-353.

XIV.   BONSER, F. G. *The Reasoning Ability of Children of the Fourth, Fifth and Sixth School Grades.* New York: Teacher's College, 1910. Pp. 133.

XV.   BREUKINK, H. Ueber die Erziehbarkeit der Aussage. *Zsch. f. angew. Psychol.*, 1910, 3, 32-87.

XVI.   BROWN, J. C. An Investigation of the Value of Drill Work in the Fundamental Operations of Arithmetic. *J. of Educ. Psychol.*, 1912, 3, 485-492, 562-570.

XVII.   BURGERSTEIN, L. Coeducation and Hygiene with Special Reference to European Experience and Views. *Ped. Sem.*, 1910, 17, 1-15.

XVIII.   BURT, C. Experimental Tests of Higher Mental Processes and their Relations to Gneral Intelligence. *J. of Exp. Ped.*, 1911, 1, 93-112.

XIX. BURT, C. and MOORE, R. C. The Mental Differences between the Sexes. *J. of Exp. Ped.*, 1912, 1, 273-284, 355-388.

XX. CALFEE, M. College Freshmen and Four General Intelligence Tests. *J. of Educ. Psychol.*, 1913, 4, 223-231.

XXI. CASTLE, C. S. A Statistical Study of Eminent Women. *Arch. of Psychol.*, 1913, No. 27. Pp. vii + 90.

XXII. COHN, J. and DIEFFENBACHER J. *Untersuchungen uber Geschlechts-, Alters-, und Begabungs- Untershiede bri Schulern.* Leipzing: Barth, 1911. Pp. vi + 213.

XXIII. COOLIDGE, M. R. *Why Women are So.* New York: Holt, 1912. Pp. 371.

XXIV. COURTIS, S. A. Report on the Courtis Test in Arithmetic. *New York Committee on School Inquiry*, 1911, 1, 391-546.

XXV. CULLER, A. J. Interference and Adaptability. An Experimental Study of their Relation with Special Reference to Individual Differences. *Arch. of Psychol.*, 1912, No. 24. Pp. 80.

XXVI. DANISH ANTHROPOLOGICAL SOCIETY. Middelelser am Danmarks Antropologi. Reviewed in *Ped. Sem.* 1913, 20, 544.

XXVII. DOGLIA S. and BANCHIERI, F. I sogni dei bambini di tre anni. L'inizio dell' attivita onirica. *Cont. d. lab. psicol. d. univer. d. Roma*, 1910, x, 9.

XXVIII. FINOT, J. *Prejuge et problieme des sexes.* Paris: Alcan, 1912. Pp. 520.

XXIX. FINOT, J. *Problems of the Sexes.* (Trans.) New York: Putnam, 1913. Pp. xiv + 408.

XXX. FORSYTH, C. H. Correlation between Ages and Grades. *J. of Educ. Psychol.*, 1912, 3, 164.

XXXI. FOX, W. A. and THORNDIKE, E. L. Relations between the Different Abilities Involved in the Study of Arithmetic: Sex Differences in Arithmetical Ability. Colum. Univ. Cont. to Phil., Psychol. and Educ., 1911, 2, 32-40.

XXXII. FRANKEN, A. Aussageversuche nach der Methode der Entscheidungs- und Bestimmungsfrage bei Erwachsenen und Kindern. *Zsch. f. angew. Psychol.*, 1912, 6, 174-253.

189

XXXIII.   GIESE, F. *Das freie literarische Schaffen bei Kindern und Jugendlichen.* Leipzig:Barth, 1914. Pp. xiv + 220; iv + 242.

XXXIV.   GILBERTSON, A. N. A Swedish Study in Children's Ideals. *Ped. Sem.*, 1913, 20, 100-106.

XXXV.   GODDARD, H. H. Two Thousand Normal Children Measured by the Binet Measuring Scale of Intelligence. *Amer. J. of Psychol.*, 1911, 18, 232-259.

XXXVI.   HAGGERTY, M. E. and KEMPF, E. J. Suppression and Substitution as a Factor in Sex Differences. *Amer. J. of Psychol.*, 1913, 24, 414-425.

XXXVII.   HARTLEY, C. G. (Mrs. W. M. Gallichan). *The Truth about Women.* New York: Dodd, Mead & Co., 1913. Pp. xiv + 404.

XXXVIII.   HENTSCHEL, M. Zwei experimentelle Untersuchungen an Kindern aus dem Gebiete der Tonpsychologie. *Zsch. f. angew. Psychol.*, 1912, 7, 55-69; 211-222.

XXXIX.   HEYMANS, G. *Die Psychologie der Frauen.* Heidelberg: Winter, 1910. Pp. viii + 308.

XL.   HILL, D. S. Comparative Study of Children's Ideals. *Ped. Sem.*, 1911, 18, 219-231.

XLI.   HILL, D. S. *Exceptional Children in the Public Schools of New Orleans.* A Report of the Committee of the Public School Alliance. New Orleans: 1913. Pp. 36.

XLII.   HOLLINGWORTH, H. L. Experimental Studies in Judgment. *Arch. of Psychol.*, 1913, No. 29. Pp. vi+119.

XLIII.   HOLLINGWORTH, L. S. The Frequency of Amentia as Related to Sex. *Med. Record*, 1913.

XLIV.   HOLLINGWORTH, L. S. Variability as Related to Sex Differences in Achievement. *Amer. J. of Sociol.*, 1914, 19, 510-530.

XLV.   HUBER, E. Associationsversuche an Soldaten. *Zsch. f. Psychol.*, 1911, 59, 241-272.

XLVI.   JONES, G. E. Mental Differences between the Sexes. *Ped. Sem.*, 1913, 20, 401-404.

XLVII.   KLINKENBERG, L. M. Ableitung von Geschlechtsunterschieden aus Zensurenstatistiken. *Zsch. f. angew. Psychol.*, 1913, 8, 228-266.

XLVIII. KUPER, G. Group Differences in the Interests of Children. *J. of Phil., Psychol., etc.*, 1912, 9, 376-379.

XLIX.   LEM, M. H. Kinderaufsatze und Zuverlassigkeit der Zeugenaussagen. *Zsch. f. angew. Psychol.*, 1911, 4, 347-363.

L.   LIBBY, W., COWLES, H., etc. The Contents of Children's Minds. *Ped. Sem.*, 1910, 17, 242-272.

LI.   LOBSTEN, M. Ueber den Vorstellungstypus der Schulkinder. *Pad. Mag.*, 457H., 1911. Pp. iii + 67.

LII.   LURTON, F. E. Retardation in Fifty-five Western Towns. *J. of Educ. Psychol.*, 1912, 3, 326-330.

LIII.   MAURENBRECHER, H. *Das Allzuweibliche. Ein Buch von neuer Erziehung und Lebensgestaliun.* Munchen, 1912.

LIV.   MEAD, C. D. The Age of Walking and Talking in Relation to General Intelligence. *Ped. Sem.*, 1913, 20, 460-484.

LV.   MEIJERE, J. C. H. Zur Verebung des Geschlechtsmerkmale und secundarer Geschlechtsmerkmale. *Arch. f. Rassen und Gesell. Biol.*, 193, 10, 1-36.

LVI.   MELVILLE, A. H. An Investigation of the Function and Use of Slang. *Ped. Sem.*, 1912, 19, 93-100.

LVII.   MILES, W. R. A Comparison of Elementary and High School Grades. *Ped. Sem.*, 1910, 17, 429-450.

LVIII.   MONROE, W. S. Intelligence of 600 Young Children. *Psychol. Rev.*, 10, 74-75.

LIX.   MORGAN, T. H. *Heredity and Sex.* New York: Columbia University Press, 1913. Pp. 282.

LX.   MOZANS, H. J. *Women in Science.* New York: Appleton, 1913. Pp. xiii + 452.

LXI.   MULLER-LYER, F. *Phasen der Liebe. Eine Sociologie des Verhaltnisses der Geschlechler.* Munchen: Langen, 1913. Pp. xv + 254.

LXII.   MUNSTERBERG, H. The German Woman. *Atlantic Mo.*, 1912, 109, 457-467.

LXIII.   MUTH, G. Ueber Alters-, Geschlechts- und Individualunterschiede in der Zierkunst des Kindes. *Zsch. f. angew. Psychol.*, 1913, 8, 507-548.

LXIV.   MYERS, G. C. A Study in Incidental Memory. *Arch. of Psychol.*, 1913, No. 26. Pp. 108.

LXV.   OFFNER, M. *Mental Fatigue.* Baltimore: Warwick and York, 1911. Pp. viii + 133.

LXVI.   PHILLIPS, B. A. Retardation in the Elementary Schools of Philadelphia. *Psychol. Clinic*, 1912, 6, 79-90, 107-121.

LXVII.   PHILLIPS, F. M. Value of Daily Drill in Arithmetic. *J. of Educa. Psychol.*, 1913, 4, 61-70.

LXVIII.   PYLE, W. H. Standards of Mental Efficiency. *J. of Educ. Psychol.*, 1913, 4, 61-70.

LXIX.   PYLE, W. H. *The Examination of School Children; a Manula of Directions and Norms.* New York: Macmillan, 1913. Pp. 70.

LXX.   SCHIEFLER, H. Zur Psychologie der Geschlechter: Spielinteressen des Schulalters. *Zsch. f. angew. Pschol.*, 1913, 8, 124-144.

LXXI.   SCHRAMM, F. Zur Assuagetreue der Geschlechter. *Zsch. f. angew. Psychol.*, 1911, 5, 355-357.

LXXII.   STARCH, D. The Measurement of Handwriting. *J. of Educ. Psychol.*, 1913, 4, 445-464.

LXXIII.   STERN, W. Abstracts of Lectures on the Psychology of Testimony and on the Study of Individuality. *Amer. J. of Psychol.*, 1910, 21, 270-282.

LXXIV.   STOCKTON, M. I. some Preferences by Boys and Girls as Shown in their Choice of Words. *Psychol. Rev.*, 1911, 18, 347-373.

LXXV.   STRONG, A. C. Three Hundred Fifty White and Colored Children Measured by the Binet-Simon Measuring Scale of Intelligence. A Comparative Study. *Ped. Sem.*, 1913, 20, 485-515.

LXXVI.   STRONG, E. K. The Relative Merits of Advertisements. *Arch. of Psychol.*, 1911, No. 17. Pp. 81

LXXVII.   TANDLER, J. and GROSS, S. *Die biologishen Grundlagen der secundaren Geschlechtscharactere.* Berlin: Springer, 1913. Pp. iv + 169.

LXXVIII. THORNDIKE, E. L. *Educational Psychology.* Vol. III. New York: Teacher's College, Columbia University, 1914.

LXXIX.   VERTES, J. Das Wortgediientnis im Schulkindesalter. *Zsch. f. Psychol.*, 1913, 63, 19-128.

LXXX.   WAGNER, P. A. Das freie Zeichen von Volkshulkindern. *Zsch. f. angew. Psychol.*, 1913, 8, 1-70.

LXXXI.   WELLS, F. L. Some Properties of the Free Association Time. *Psychol. Rev.*, 1911, 18, 1-23.

LXXXII.   WELLS, F. L. The Relation of Practice to Individual Differences. *Amer. J. of Psychol.*, 1912, 23, 75-100.

LXXXIII. WELLS, F. L. Practise and the Work-Curve. *Amer. J. of Psychol.*, 1913, 24, 35-51.

LXXXIV.   WIERSMA, E. D. Intelligenzprufungen nach Binet und Simon, und ein Versuch zur Auffindung neuer Tests. *Zsch. f. angew. Psychol.*, 1913, 8, 267-275.

LXXXV.   WINCH, W. H. A Motor Factor in Perception and Memory. *J. of Exp. Ped.*, 1912, 1, 261-273.

LXXXVI.   WOODWORTH, R. S. and WELLS, F. L. Association Tests. *Psychol. Monog.*, 1911, No. 57. Pp. 85.

LXXXVII. WRESCHNER, A. *Vergleichende Psycholgie der Geschlechter.* Zurich: Art. Inst. Orell. Fussli, 1912. Pp. 40.

LXXXVIII. YOAKUM, C. S. and CALFEE, M. An Analysis of the Mirror Drawing Experiment. *J. of Educ. Psychol.*, 1913, 4, 282-292.

Hollingworth, L.S. (1916). Sex differences in mental traits.
Psychological Bulletin, 13(10), 377-384.

SEX DIFFERENCES IN MENTAL TRAITS

By LETA S. HOLLINGWORTH
Teachers College, Columbia University

Since the very complete and painstaking review of the literature of sex differences which appeared in the BULLETIN in October, 1914 (11), there have been few studies undertaken with the chief aim of investigating sex differences in mental traits. Such results as have been published in the last two years are derived chiefly as incidental matter from studies prosecuted with some other main problem in view. In this field, as in other scientific fields, little has come from abroad. The few articles and monographs which have appeared in Europe under titles which would imply that they contain data on sex differences have not been accessible to the present reviewer, and it is doubtful if they are at all accessible in this country.

Researches undertaken for the purpose of obtained developmental norms have yielded interesting data on sex differences. In the standardization of their Point Scale for measuring intelligence, Yerkes and Bridges (14) report that in their English-speaking groups girls attain higher scores than boys between the ages of five and seven; that they then tend to fall below the averages for the boys, with minor variations up to the age of eleven, when they again for a year or two surpass the boys, only to drop below once more from fourteen onward. The authors interpret this crossing and recrossing of the curves of the sexes to be a revelation of actual and reliable sex differences. As a result of their research they are "fully convinced that the accurate determination of norms for the sexes is eminently desirable," and the "suspect that at certain ages serious injustice will be done to individuals by evaluating their scores in the light of norms which do not take account of sex differences."

Terman (9) in his experiments with 1,000 unselected children, in revising the Binet-Simon Intelligence Scale, finds a small but fairly constant superiority of the girls up to the age of thirteen years. At fourteen years the curve for the girls drops below that for the boys. The apparent superiority of boys at the age of fourteen years is, however, fully accounted for by the more frequent elimination of fourteen-year-old girls from the grades by promotion to the high school. "The superiority of girls over

195

boys is so slight that for practical purposes it would seem negligible." Terman offers "no support to the opinion expressed by Yerkes and Bridges that 'at certain ages serious injustice will be done individuals by evaluating their scores in the light of norms which do not account of sex differences." Apart from the very slight superiority of girls, Terman finds the distribution of intelligence in the two sexes to be the same. The supposed greater variability of boys is not found. "Girls do not group themselves around the median more closely than do boys."

Terman suggests that the fact that so few women have attained eminence "may be due to wholly extraneous factors," the most important of which are (1) that the occupations in which it is possible to achieve eminence are for the most part only now beginning to open their doors to women, homemaking, the traditional occupation of women, being a field in which eminence is impossible; (2) that even of the small number of women who embark upon a professional career, a majority marry and devote a large amount of their time and energy to perpetuating the species; (3) that both the training given to girls and the atmosphere in which they grow up are unfavorable to the inculcation of the professional point of view. The author also notes the possibility that the affective traits of women may be such as to favor the development of sentiment at the expense of intellectual ability.

Trabue (10) in standardizing his Completion Test Language Scales find that on the whole boys make a somewhat lower median score than girls in the same grade, although the difference is small, and the amount of overlapping is enormous. His figures for 1,590 boys and 883 girls show that according to the quartiles there is no sex difference in variability.

Woolley and Fisher (12) report in full, in monograph form, their mental and physical measurements of working children in Cincinnati. The children were tested at fourteen years when they came to the work-certificate office to obtain certificates, and again, one year later. The physical tests applied were of height, weight, visual acuity, auditory acuity, vital capacity, steadiness of hand, strength of hand, rapidity of movement, and accuracy of movement. The mental tests included cancellation, memory, substitution, completion of sentences, association by opposites, and the puzzle-box test. Except for height at fifteen years, in which the two sexes are about the same, the girls excel the boys in height, weight, steadiness, and card-sorting, while the boys excel in strength, rapidity of movement and vital capacity. Boys excel in performances where strength is the chief factor, and girls in those where coordination and a fine control of muscles is more prominent. In the mental tests the only large sex difference in the entire series is that of the great superiority of the boys in the opening of the puzzle box. The authors feel that this test is unfairly selected on the ground of sex, as boys are more encouraged to take an active interest in mechanical construction, and accordingly understand more about how many things are made, and what the simple mechanical devices are. This would give the boys an unfair advantage on the ground of training, just as tying a bow-knot (in which Terman found girls superior to boys) would give an unfair advantage to girls.

In the preparation of a scale for the measurement of fourteen- and fifteen-year-old adolescents, Woolley (13) reports with respect to variability, that "if variability is measured by the difference between the five and ninety-five percentiles, the differences between the two sexes are small and not entirely consistent. In the physical tests the boys are a trifle more variable at fourteen, and decidedly so at fifteen. In the mental tests the boys are a little more variable at fourteen, while there is a somewhat greater difference in favor of the girls at fifteen." One fact with regard to variability holds for all series. The girls show a wider variation below the median than above it. The research covers 750 fourteen-year-olds and 680 of the same children at fifteen years of age, all being school children who were dropping out of school to go to work.

E. K. Strong, Jr. (8), publishes the results of an experiment with fragments of advertisements. Strong first exposed the advertisements to the subjects (forty women students, and group of forty men composed of college students, instructors and professors) at the rate of one per second. When fragments of the original advertisements were studied by these subjects, the women remembered 51 per cent. more details than did the men. The investigator then allowed the subjects to inspect another series at their leisure, giving unlimited time to look over the material. Under these conditions the women remembered 53 per cent. more details than did the men. Strong concluded that a genuine sex difference is disclosed in this experiment, but does not attempt to determine whether the difference is due to inherent capacities or to differences in training. He ascribes the more pronounced emotional response of women to advertisements, which he noted in a previous study, to their superior ability to note detail.

Among the investigations which have been undertaken for the explicit purpose of studying sex differences is Boring's experiment on capacity to report on moving pictures. Boring (1) experimented with both children and adults of both sexes, in order to make comparisons of the reliability of testimony as conditioned by sex and age.

197

Forty-four subjects were used: thirteen women, the majority of them being undergraduates in Cornell University; eleven men, the majority of whom were graduate students of psychology or professors of psychology; twelve boys and eight girls, taken from a single class in the Ithaca public schools, and having an average age of 12.3 years.

A scene from a photo-play was presented. The subjects weren't told what the purpose of the experiment was, but those who were students or professors of psychology suspected from the conditions and instructions that the test was to be one of ability to report. The traits scored were (1) range of report, (2) spontaneity of report, (3) range of knowledge, (4) accuracy of report, (5) assurance, (6) reliability of assurance, (7) warranted assurance, (8) assured accuracy, (9) tendency to oath, (10) warranted tendency to oath, (11) unwarranted tendency to oath, (12) reliability to oath.

The author concludes from the results of his experiment that "There is evidence that the boys exceed the girls in range of report, in tendency to oath, and also in unwarranted tendency to oath, and that the girls exceed the boys in reliability of oath. The significance of none of these coefficients is very high, although the last is undoubtedly reliable. With men and women the differences are more marked. The greatest difference occurs in the unwarranted tendency to oath, in which the women exceed the men. The men exceed the women in range of report, range of knowledge, assurance, warranted assurance, assured accuracy, and reliability of oath."

"It appears, then, that there is little difference apparent, with the material used, between boys and girls, whereas there is quite a marked superiority of the men over the women with respect to six (perhaps seven) coefficients. This conclusion accords with the general psychological principle that that even those mental sex differences which are large in adults are relatively slight in childhood." The author notes the fact that there is a source of error in the circumstance that the group of women was otherwise constituted than was the group of men. He nevertheless accepts the difference which he finds between the men and the women as a sex difference, although it coincides with what would be expected *a priori* from differences in age, training and preliminary knowledge of the experiment, quite apart from sex. In the group of children, where none of these factors was present, no reliable sex differences were found, except that the girls showed much greater caution in taking oath than did boys.

Gates (3) reports tests on a large number of school children of both sexes, conducted with the purpose of determining variations in diurnal efficiency. He finds no sex difference in the variations of diurnal efficiency; the records of both sexes may be combined in platting the course of the daily rhythm. The correlations of the various tests with each other also failed to reveal any sex difference. The average scores of boys and girls when compared revealed the following sex differences: "(1) In addition and multiplication the girls appear to be somewhat superior, although such is not invariable the case. (2) In the drawing test the girls appear to follow the method of emphasizing accuracy rather than speed, and the boys speed rather than accuracy. That one sex is actually capable of excelling the other in either speed or accuracy cannot be said with certainty...With respect to accuracy, there is a small amount of evidence favoring the superiority of boys. (3) In the completion test the girls show a distinct superiority. (4) The girls are decidedly more efficient in cancellation...(5) The girls excel without exception in money for auditory and visual digits, and in recognition of nonsense syllables. (6) Excluding the tests for speed and accuracy of movement, in which results, as far as ability is concerned, are uncertain, out of forty-two comparisons (six classes in seven tests) the girls excel in thirty-eight, and the boys in four."

Gates (4) also reports tests on 197 students of elementary psychology, for memory of visual and auditory digits, memory of verbal sense material, recognition of geometrical forms, and learning in a substitution test. The separate correlations for the sexes are very similar. The results of the memory tests are "in harmony with the generally accepted belief that women excel in this kind of work." The men excel slightly in the substitution test, but the difference is not great.

L. S. Hollingworth (5) presents a series of tests on twenty-five subjects to determine whether any relation can be established between the mental and motor efficiency of women and the catamenial period. Twenty-three women were subjected to the tests, and two men were tested at the same time as controls. The traits tests were speed and accuracy of perception, controlled association, speed of voluntary movement, steadiness, rate of learning and muscular fatiguability. The results of the experiment are negative. No influence of menstruation can upon the processes tested can be demonstrated from the data thus collected.

Pitting (7) has made a study of the choices of occupation, the scholarship, etc., of high-school graduates in five north central states. Fewer females than males undertake courses of advanced training. Variety of training or employment is less among females than among males. Various differences in occupations selected are indicated. The most scholarly of both sexes go on to take advanced training.

Jastrow (6) has added to the general discussion of sex differences in his chapter on the psychology of group traits. He had made a systematic attempt to cite sources of authority or data. Many of the traditional views about sex differences, which were advanced before experimental data were sought, are rehearsed. The author points out that "men and women are organically different," from which he derives the conclusion that a contrasted psychology is involved. Pathology is appealed to as furnishing valuable clues to innate sex differences. For instance, "Among the typically masculine insanities is general paralysis. Its early stages parallel the symptoms of alcohol intoxication: tremor of speech and movement; coarseness of expression; uncertainty of sensory action; and free indulgence of expansive thought. It develops quickly to the later stages with paralytic symptoms, illusions of grandeur, loss of control, and a generally disordered excessive functioning—throughout a picture of exaggerated masculine psychology." The author seems here to imply that the greater frequency of general paralysis in men is a clue to the existence of some innate sex difference in neural functioning. In such instances the appeal to pathology fails, as the etiological factor in general paralysis of the insane is not psychological but organic. It occurs more frequently among men because syphilis occurs more frequently among them.

Brown (2) and his co-workers have carried out a series of careful experiments to investigate individual and sex differences in suggestibility. As the experiments were numerous and the technique detailed, no brief summary can be successfully presented. Those who wish to consult the data in detail must be referred to the original monograph. Brown concludes that "a general review of the entire series of twenty-six experiments reveals a very distinct difference between the sexes. In thirteen of the experiments there is a clear difference between the sexes, and in only one of these experiments are the men more suggestible. There are only four experiments in which no sex difference can be made out...The difference between the sexes is more distinct in some of the groups of experiments than in other groups. There can be little doubt that women are more suggestible in tests which involve an imagined sensation, a series of progressive changes, distortion of memory, and estimation of magnitude. The tests with illusion do not give clear differences between the sexes, and the tests with aesthetic judgments give contradictory or indecisive results."

Two considerations have especially impressed the reviewer in going over these recent contributions to the literature of sex differences. The first has to do with method. Investigators seem to have acquired the habit of dividing their subjects automatically into two groups on the basis of sex. Thereupon they proceed to describe all differences found between the two groups as sex differences. As a matter of fact, differences thus found should logically be treated only as group differences, unless the author is able to show that the group of males differs more from the group of females than from other groups of males similarly selected. In general, the investigators here reviewed have not covered this technical point.

The second consideration has to do with the results bearing on the question of the comparative variability of the sexes. Terman, Trabue, and Woolley present variability figures on hundreds of boys and girls with the uniform result that neither sex is found to be more variable than the other. This is in accord with the result derived from the researches of Courtis and Goddard, previous reviewed in the BULLETIN. More extensive and reliable data have been made available on this point in the last five years than in all time preceding.

REFERENCES

I.   BORING, E. G. Capacity to Report upon Moving Pictures, as Conditioned by Sex and Age. *J. of Crim. Law & Criminol.*, 1916.

II.   BROWN, W. Individual and Sex Differences in Suggestibility. *Univ. of Cal. Pub. in Psychol.*, 1916, 2, 291-430.

III.   GATES, A. I. Variation in Efficiency During the Day, Together with Practice Effects, Sex Differences and Correlations. *Univ. of Cal. Pub. in Psychol.*, 1916, 2, 1-156.

IV.   GATES, A. I. Correlations and Sex Differences in Memory and Substitution, *Univ. of Cal. Pub. in Psychol.*, 1916, 1, 345-350.

V.   HOLLINGWOTH, L. S. *Functional Periodicity*. New York: Teachers College, 1914. Pp. 101.

VI.   JASTROW, J. *Character and Temperament*. New York: Appleton, 1915. Pp. xviii + 596.

VII.   PITTINGER, B. F. The Distribution of High School Graduates in Five North Central States. *Sch. and Soc.*, 1916, 3.

VIII.   STRONG, E. K., Jr. An Interesting Sex Difference. *Ped. Sem.*, 1915, 22, 521-528.

IX.   TERMAN, L. M. *The Measurement of Intelligence*. Boston: Houghton, Mifflin, 1916. Pp. 362.

X.   TRABUE, M. R. *Completion Test Language Scales*. New York: Teachers College, 1916.

XI.   WOOLLEY, H. T. The Psychology of Sex. *Psychol. Bull.*, 1914, 11, 353-379.

XII.   WOOLLEY, H. T. & FISHER, C. R. Mental and Physical Measurements of Working Children. *Psychol. Monog.*, 1914, 18, (No. 77). Pp. 247.

XIII.   WOOLLEY, H. T. A New Scale of Mental and Physical Measurements for Adolescents. *J. of Educ. Psychol.*, 1915, 6, 521-550.

XIV.   YERKES, R. M., BRIDGES, J. W., & HARDWICK, R. S. *A Point Scale for Measuring Mental Ability.* Baltimore: Warwick & York, 1915. Pp. viii + 218.

Hollingworth, L.S. (1918). Comparison of the sexes in mental traits.
Psychological Bulletin, 15(12), 427-432.

COMPARISON OF THE SEXES IN MENTAL TRAITS

By LETA S. HOLLINGWORTH
Teachers College, Columbia University

This review intends to cover work published during the year 1919, and also reports which were published in 1918 too late for inclusion in the review of this topic for that year.

Pressey (4) carefully studied 2,544 school children in three Indiana cities, who were tested by a group scale of intelligence, with the purpose of comparing the sexes in (1) central tendency in either general intelligence or special abilities, and (2) variability in either general intelligence or special abilities. The children ranged in chronological age from 8 through 16 years. The investigator found that girls averaged higher than boys on total score, though their excellence varied somewhat from test to test. On three of the ten tests the boys had a higher average score; the girls excelled on the remaining seven tests. The distributions showed greater variability among the boys in every test, and in total score. The sex difference in variability was far from constant in the various tests, however. Three tests showed little difference. The boys varied more from their mode in the direction of inferiority than in the direction of superiority.

Frasier (1) studied the grade location of all the 13-year-olds found in 20 cities, well scattered over the United States. As a result of this study the investigator states: "It is safe to conclude from the study of 62,219 thirteen-year-old boys and girls in 20 cities, that the greater variability claimed for the boys is not present." Both boys and girls were found at both extremes of the distribution; the numbers at extremes were approximately the same; and the range was the same for both sexes.

Terman (7) has given further data on the frequency of extreme degrees of intelligence, as related to sex. In a systematic search for superior children, conducted in the schools of Alameda and elsewhere, there was found a small proportion of children with I.Q. of more than 110. Of those testing between 110 and 135, there were 19 boys and 30 girls. Two groups of children are reported, having I.Q. of 140 and over. Of the first group of 45 such children, 32 were boys and 13 were girls. The highest of this group were a boy testing at 184 I.Q., and two boys testing at 174 I.Q. Of the second group of 21 such children, 11 were boys and 10 were girls. The highest of this group were a girl testing at 174 I.Q., and a girl testing at 167 I.Q. Terman stressed the waste of mental ability which comes about through vocational maladjustment, and says, "The waste is probably enormous in the case of women, because of the limited number of vocational opportunities open to them."

Whipple (8) in his experimental study of the education of gifted children has also added to the data on the incidence of extremely high intelligence among school children. Of the superior children selected for his experimental class, the majority were girls. These children were not, however, originally selected by objective tests, and it is not clear just how the sexes were finally distributed on the basis of objective measurement. The highest I.Q. found by Whipple was 167, and the child in whom it was found was a girl.

Specht (5) has contributed a distribution of very superior children, by sex and by I.Q. Her data were gathered from a boys' school, the girls being selected with difficulty from neighboring schools, and being permitted to attend the boys' special class. Thus the fact that more boys than girls appear in Specht's distribution may merely reflect these conditions. The maximum extreme of intelligence reported in this groups was in the case of a girl with I.Q. 164.

Madison and Sylvester (2) report that among the high-school pupils tested by them with the army Alpha tests, the boys made a very slightly higher median score, grade for grade, than did the girls, although the single highest score made by any pupil was made by a girl. The investigators attribute the differences in medians to the fact that the tests were standardized primarily for males, but they note that it is interesting to find it possible to standardize on one sex a test that will be in any degree fair to the other.

Porteus (3) declares that in standardizing his tests, he found "marked differences in sex performances in the tests. Boys, on the average, are in advance of girls up to and including age 11 1/2. The girls then make a remarkable spurt in development during the next 12 months, and pass the boys." It is at times somewhat difficult to follow Porteus in his presentation, since he often designates as a "spurt" an increment of growth no greater than might be expected as a continuation of the general trend of the curve, allowing for fluctuation due to chance factors.

Starch (6) in his chapter on sex differences, emphasizes the distinction between the popular view and the scientific view; concludes from a survey of the available scientific data that "so far as the native abilities involved in school work are concerned, boys and girls might as well pursue the same courses from the first day of school to the last"; and, in commenting upon the frequently alleged variability of the male, remarks that "the theory seems plausible, but has been proposed rather in advance of a convincingly wide range of experimental data."

The year's work yields nothing consistent as a result of the comparison of the sexes in mental traits. In this respect it resembles the work of other years. Pressey finds that girls excel boys in mental tests at all ages, from 8 to 16 years, inclusive; Porteus finds that boys excel girls at nearly all ages. Pressey finds that boys are more variable than girls; Frasier finds that there are no sex differences in variability. In group after group of superior children, the highest intelligence is found now in a boy, now in a girl. Perhaps the logical conclusion to be reached on the basis of these findings is that the custom of perpetuating this review is no longer profitable, and may well be abandoned.

REFERENCES

Fraiser, G. W. A Comparative Study of the Variability of Boys and Girls. *J. of Appl. Psychol.*, 1919.

Madison, I. N., & Sylvester, R. H. High School Students' Intelligence Ratings According to the Army Alpha Test. *School & Soc.*, 1919.

Porteus, S. D. *Porteus Tests: The Vineland Revision*, Vineland, N. J., The Training School, 1919.

Pressey, L. W. Sex Differences Shown by 2,544 School Children on a Group Scale of Intelligence, with Special Reference to Variability. *J. of Appl. Psychol.*, 1918.

Specht, L. A Terman Class in P. S. 64, Manhattan. *School & Soc.*, 1919.

Specht, D. *Educational Psychology.* New York: Macmillian, 1919.

Terman, L. M. *The Intelligence of School Children.* Boston: Houghton Mifflin Co., 1919.

Whipple, G. M. *Classes for Gifted Children.* Bloomington, IL: Publ. Sch. Publ. Co., 1919.

Gates, A.I. (1917). Experiments on the relative efficiency of men and women in memory and reasoning. *Psychological Review, 24*(2), 139-146.

EXPERIMENTS ON THE RELATIVE EFFICIENCY OF MEN AND WOMEN IN MEMORY AND REASONING[1]

By ARTHUR I. GATES

The majority of psychologists and educators who have expressed themselves on the subject are of the opinion that women, as a rule, are considerably more efficient than men in memory work and less efficient in applying the facts learned, in self-expression, and in reasoning power. For example one writer says:[2] "Girls excel in learning and memorization accepting studies on suggestion or authority, but are often quite at sea when set to make tasks or experiments that give individuality and a chance for self-expression, which is one of the best things in boyhood."

Opinions similar to these seem to prevail generally among psychologists, educators, and laymen. Many, moreover, are of the opinion that women, in addition to having quicker and more tenacious memories, are as a rule more diligent and painstaking in their work; the boy may often be satisfied with a fair knowledge of the general principles underlying a lesson, while the girl seeks a more detailed and exact knowledge. If such is the fact it should be taken into account in any attempt to determine the sex-differences in memory, for obviously the differences in the time spent on the work might easily account for the differences in the reproduction of the ideas.

The experiments to be described presently were performed first in 1913 and were repeated in 1914 and 1915, using as subjects a class in elementary psychology consisting of from 158-275 students of both sexes of the sophomore, junior, and senior years in the University of California.

The data were obtained from the answers to three sets of questions. Each set of two questions comprised the regular weekly examinations of the class. The first set called for a somewhat detailed reproduction of facts presented in the lectures of the week preceding. The second set called for the application of facts or principles given

---

[1] From the Psychological Laboratory of the University of California.
[2] Hall, G. S., "Youth: its Education, Regimen, and Hygiene." New York, 1912, p. 287.

in the lectures, the purpose being to call into action a mental process as closely as possible identical with that involved in reasoning. All the questions were framed by Professor Stratton, who was in charge of the classes, and who endeavored to make the tests as nearly as possible adequate to the purpose of the experiment. The papers in all cases were graded on a basis of ten, but the averages below, for the sake of clearness, are made on the basis of one hundred. All papers were corrected by the regular 'readers,' who were in no case aware that the results were to be used for experimental purposes. It happened, moreover, that each of the nine sets of papers was graded by a different 'reader."

The following table shows the results in the case of memory questions.

TABLE I
MEMORY

	1913		1914		1915	
	No. of Individuals	Grade	No. of Individuals	Grade	No. of Individuals	Grade
Women	95	77	162	89.2	154	86.4
Men	59	73	102	85.0	98	81.0
Dif. In favor of women		4.0%		4.2%		5.4%

The women show a slight superiority in memory work, amounting on the average to 4.5 percent. While the percentile difference is rather small, its reliability is indicated by the fact that it appears in all cases, although different questions were given at different times to three entirely different groups of individuals.

Table II. shows the average grades obtained by men and women to questions that involved reasoning.

The evidence indicates a slight superiority of the men in this sort of work. The average difference is approximately 2 percent, a difference which is so small as to have but little significance were it not for the fact that it is repeated by three separate groups.

TABLE II
REASON

	1913		1914		1915	
	No. of Individuals	Grade	No. of Individuals	Grade	No. of Individuals	Grade
Women	90	77.5	153	83.3	154	88.4
Men	58	79.5	103	86.4	99	89.2
Dif. in favor of men		2.0%		5.1%		0.8%

Table III. shows the results of tests in which the subjects were given free choice between a memory and a reason question. The two questions, constituting the regular weekly examination as before, were presented and the students were permitted to take their choice.

TABLE III
ONE MEMORY AND ONE REASON QUESTION

1913

	Memory Question		Grade	Reason Question		Grade
	No. of Individuals	Percent of Individuals of That Sex		No. of Individuals	Percent of Individuals of That Sex	
Women	60	72.3	85	23	27.7	86
Men	19	28.8	82	47	71.2	87
Diff.		43.5	3		43.5	1

1914

	Memory Question		Grade	Reason Question		Grade
	No. of Individuals	Percent of Individuals of That Sex		No. of Individuals	Percent of Individuals of That Sex	
Women	129	84.8	70.4	23	15.2	77
Men	80	78.4	64.5	22	21.6	80
Diff.		6.2	5.9		6.4	3

209

1915

	Memory Question		Grade	Reason Question		Grade
	No. of Individuals	Percent of Individuals of That Sex		No. of Individuals	Percent of Individuals of That Sex	
Women	144	91.8	88.4	13	8.2	87.2
Men	85	74.2	87.0	16	15.8	89.8
Diff.		17.6	1.4		7.6	2.6

Although both sexes show a distinct preference for the memory question, the preference is much greater in the case of women. The men show more willingness than do the women to take the reason questions, although the actual number of either sex that take these questions is small. In 1913 and 1915 twice as great a ratio of men, and in 1914 a ratio one third greater of men than of women chose the reason question. The grades received in the memory tests confirm the earlier finding that the women excel in this kind of work. The women excel in every case, although in two (1913 and 1915) the differences in their favor are very small. The grades received on the reason questions also confirm the earlier finding that the men excel slightly in this type of work. Although the superiority of the men is small it appears in every case.

Our general conclusions from the experiment thus far are as follows:

I. The women excel the men in memory work.

II. The men excel the women, but to a less degree, in reason work.

III. Both sexes prefer memory work but more men show a willingness to do reason work in lieu of memory work.

To let the experiment remain as it stands and to accept without further question the conclusions just enumerated would be hazardous and would certainly not take into account all of the factors which have an influence here. There is at least one possibility which if proven to be a reality would force us to modify the conclusions at which we have just arrived. It is possible that the apparent superiority of the women in reproduction from memory is due merely to a greater amount of study and not to an innate superiority of memory.

To take into account this possibility the following test was employed. The news item given below was read to the class at the beginning of the lecture hour, the students being informed, however, of the purpose of the test. The item follows:

THREE HOUSES BURNED[3]

Boston, September 5. A serious fire last night destroyed three houses in the center of the city. Seventeen families are without a home. The loss exceeds fifty thousand dollars. In rescuing a child, one of the firemen was badly burned about the hands and arms.

The students were first requested to write down all the facts they could recall from the article. Following the free account, they were asked to answer the following questions:

IV. In what city did the fire occur?

V. What was the date of the item?

VI. When did the fire break out?

VII. How many houses were destroyed?

VIII. In what part of the city were these houses?

IX. How many families were left homeless?

X. What was the total loss (in dollars)?

XI. Who was burned?

XII. On what part of parts of the body was this individual burned?

XIII. What was this individual doing when the burns were received?

The data used were obtained from the answers to the ten definite questions, for it was found that the additions or alterations of these answers from the free accounts were so slight as to be negligible. The papers were graded on a basis of ten, one unit being allowed for the correct answer to each question. Table IV. gives the average results.

---

[3] See Whipple, G. M., 'Manual of Physical and Mental Tests,' Baltimore, 1910, p. 504.

TABLE IV

	Percentage Reported	Percentage Correct	Percentage Positive Errors	Ratio of Pos. Errors to Amt. Reported	Ratio of Pos. Errors to Pos. Errors Plus Amt. Not Reported
			1913		
Women	97.4	84.4	13.0	.133	.833
Men	90.0	80.0	10.0	.100	.500
			1914		
Women	98.4	86.4	12.0	.121	.888
Men	94.2	83.1	11.0	.116	.650
			1915		
Women	94.1	82.5	11.6	.123	.662
Men	88.0	76.4	10.6	.120	.443
			Average of above		
Women	96.6	84.4	12.2	.125	.782
Men	90.7	79.9	10.5	.112	.519
Difference	5.9	4.6	1.7	.013	.263

The women in every case report a greater amount of the content of the item, as well as a greater amount of it correctly. On the average the women report 96.6 percent of the item and 84.4 percent of it correctly while the men report by 90.7 percent with 79.8 percent correct. The men, however, make fewer mistakes. The actual number of errors made by the women is greater in every case, although the difference between the sexes is small. The ratios of the number of errors to the total amount reported show even smaller differences because of the fact that the women in all cases report a larger amount. But the ratios of the amount of positive errors to the total amount of positive errors plus the amount not reported—i.e., to the field in which suggestion and kindred forces could operate because the ideas were not correctly remembered—were much larger for the women. That is to say, the women, much more than the men, were likely to make erroneous statements rather than mere omissions. The ratio is, on the average, about one third larger for the women.

The general conclusion from this tests is that the women in immediate memory tests can correctly reproduce more of the detail of a given group of facts but at the same time make more mistakes.

A question, however, may be raised with regard to the application of the results gained by this method to the determination of the relative ability shown by men and women in the tests first considered, because the present method tests immediate memory, or immediate reproduction, rather than delayed memory which is the function operative in the examinations.

Accordingly, the same students were requested, one week or five weeks after the immediate-memory test, to write, without previous warning, all that they could remember of the news items given above. The same set of ten questions as before was used. Table V. gives the results.

In delayed as well as in immediate memory the women have a greater range of report, a greater number of details are reported correctly, and more positive errors are made. The amount by which the sexes differ is about the same in both types of memory.

The experiments with the news item justify the following conclusions:

TABLE V
DELAYED MEMORY
1913. After 5 weeks

I.   The women excel the men in tests of immediate or delayed memory, at least in so far as the amount of material correctly reproduced is concerned.

II.   The women, however, make more positive errors in reporting.

The results obtained by other investigators are for the most part in harmony with the present findings. A summary of such experiments will be found in Whipple[4] who concludes: "Sex differences in this test [memory for ideas], as in the rote memory test, are in favor of girls."[5]

---

[4] Wipple, G. M., 'Manual of Mental and Physical Tests,' Part II., 17-43, 149-223.

[5] *Op. cit.*, p. 213.

213

	Percentage Reported	Percentage Correct	Percentage Positive Errors	Ratio of Positive Errors to Amount Reported	Ratio of Positive Errors to Positive Errors Plus
Women	82.0	64.0	18.0	.219	.500
Men	72.0	57.0	15.0	.208	.349
1914 After 5 Weeks					
Women	89.0	68.0	21.0	.236	.655
Men	79.0	60.0	19.0	.240	.475
1915 After 1 Week					
Women	94.4	80.7	13.7	.145	.650
Men	89.8	75.8	12.0	.137	.495
Average Of Above					
Women	88.5	70.9	17.9	.200	.602
Men	80.3	64.3	15.3	.195	.440
Diff.	8.2	6.6	2.6	.005	.162

A final consideration is the possibility that the women employed in these experiments constitute a more select group than the men. It is possible that these women are on the whole more capable, or their previous training has better adapted them to the particular subject of psychology. There is no obvious reason why this should be the case, but in order to throw some light upon it the average grade in the course has been computed for each sex.

TABLE VI

	1913	1914	1915
The women received an average grade of	77.0	75.5	74.0
The men received an average grade of	75.5	75.0	72.0

The women have slightly the higher grade. The mass of experimental evidence from other investigations, however, indicates that in groups of men and women of equal endowment and training, the women usually excel in memory work. We have found that in the three groups just considered, the women excel in memory. It seems that the small amount by which the women excel the men in the grades received in the course may be accounted for by the great predominance of memory work in the weekly and final examinations on which the grades are based. The women who apparently excel in memory work should in a long series of tests of that nature, come out with a somewhat better average.

The three main conclusions that the investigation seems to justify are as follows:

I.   The women excel the men noticeably in either immediate or delayed memory work.

II.   The men excel the women, but to a less degree, in reason work.

III. Both sexes prefer memory work, but a greater relative number of men show a willingness to do reason work in lieu of memory work.

Results obtained by other investigators and the supplementary tests for possible sources of error have brought forth no evidence contradictory to the conclusions we have reached.

Grier, N.M. (1918). Comparative mentality of Jews and Gentiles. *The Pedagogical Seminary, 25*(4), 432-433.

COMPARATIVE MENTALITY OF JEWS AND GENTILES

N. M. GRIER, *Academy of Science, St. Louis, Mo.*

Military records show that as a people the Jews have long been noted for their deficient vital capacity. The burden of evidence as presented by Smedley, DeBusk, and as corroborated by Goddard have shown that mental ability in school children (school standing) may be positive correlated with vital capacity.

A common impression seems to prevail at times that, as a people, the Jews have a greater mental ability than their less enterprising Gentile brethren. The "smartest" pupil of the public school classes was usually of Jewish descent, and it is undeniable true the some of the most brilliant scientific men and scholars of the 19th and 20th centuries have had a similar heritage. One phase of this supposed mental superiority has been exploded by Fishberg in his book on the Jews which points out that the greatest percentage of successful business men is found among the Gentiles, but that a greater percentage of business men in proportion to number of people in the race is found among the Jews.

The writer has been able to obtain records of the vital capacity of 112 Jewish boys and 54 Jewish girls of the high school age. These records show the following when compared with equal numbers of students of Gentile origin. The superiority of the latter in vital capacity as already indicated is manifest. When grouped by ages, and the average scholarship computed from their standing in the high school, a noticeable superiority in school standing as shown by the curriculum tests was found to be with the Gentiles. This was observed to come most strongly at the earlier ages, slowly decreasing upwards, but at the age of 16, Jewish boys were slightly superior, which may be explained by the fact that large numbers of them leave school before this age and the survivors are thus selected individuals.

On the other hand, it seems that Jewish girls are mentally superior in this respect to Gentile girls at most ages compared, although the latter show higher scholarship at the age of 14. Evidence here is less easily taken due to the fact that even larger numbers of girls than boys seem to leave school past the first half of the teens.

The same general results, however, are obtained when larger numbers of the more abundant Gentiles are compared.

Data obtained from tests conducted after the range of information plan on the biological subjects of the high school, when grouped as indicated previously, show that for 85 boys and 44 girls, each of both types of people, the error of marking is highest in Jewish boys and lowest in Jewish girls when compared with the Gentiles. As the error or marking may be fairly considered as some indication of discriminatory power, the results presented in the preceding paragraph receive some confirmation. In this case, they are more independent of the marking of teachers, as the student grades himself. Any such factor as racial prejudice thus seems to be eliminated.

The Jews with whom these tests were conducted were the first generation of immigrants, and in the opinion of many are best representative. Of recent years, the matter of conservation in education has been receiving greater attention, and the tendency is to give instruction more fitted to the peculiar individual. Aside from the humorous aspects of the proposition, if the preceding observations be more fully substantiated, it seems that special attention could be justifiably given to students of Jewish extraction. The writer at times has also noted large percentages of defective hearing and vision among children of this particular social stratum. The evidence for mental superiority in Jewish girls may be said by some to indicate greater application on the part of the latter, but it is perhaps worthy of the remark, that, following the conservation principle as fully as possible, something should be done to encourage larger numbers of them to complete a secondary education.

The writer offers the above tendencies observed, rather than conclusions taken. He is indebted to Miss L. Persow, a fellow worker, for aid in this connection.

Garth, T.R. (1921). The results of some tests on full and mixed blood Indians. *Journal of Applied Psychology*, 5(4), 359-372.

THE RESULTS OF SOME TESTS ON FULL AND MIXED BLOOD INDIANS[1]

By THOMAS R. GARTH, University of Texas

The objective of Racial Psychology of an experimental character should be first to find norms and the measures of variabilities around these norms. These should stand as inventories of the races measured. But if we follow out the latter conception the complete distributions of the measures would be a truer representation of the facts. And having obtained these, our next intention would be to make comparisons between the races. Even though our method may be avowedly scientific, we may well take caution in the making of these comparisons because of the ever present bias due to race prejudice which may cause us to hasten to conclusions and thus endanger the so-called inferior races with the stigma of being rated low. For this reason there ought to be a canon in the study of *race* psychology similar to the famous Canon of Lloyd Morgan in his studies of animal behavior. While Morgan's basal principle reads: "In no case may we interpret an action as the outcome of the exercise of a higher psychical faculty" (of lower animals), "if it can be interpreted as the outcome of the exercise of one which stands lower in the psychological scale;" the canon for race psychology might read after this fashion (with due apologies to the British scientist): In no case may we interpret an action as the outcome of the exercise of an inferior psychical faculty, if it can be interpreted as the outcome of the exercise of one which stands higher in the psychological scale, but is hindered by lack of training.

There is still a third objective to the study of racial psychology of which little has been said and of which insufficient use has been consciously made. Mental measurement has taught us to seek out the subnormal child so that we may give him such opportunity as he may need to bring him to his full development. Measures of the inferior races have indicated some superior individuals in the racial groups who even take a position beside those above the median of the superior race with which we are comparing them. The third objective then of racial psychology should be to discover

---

[1] Paper read before American Psychological Association, Chicago, December 30, 1920.

these superior individuals who find themselves contending with unfavorable environmental and traditional conditions. It is not in the province of racial psychology to indicate what should be done for these "superiors," but only to find these individuals.

While the problem involved in the experiment which is to be described and interpreted is to find out how Mixed and Full Blood Indians differ in the results of their performances of nine psychological tests, it has all the objectives mentioned above embodied in it, though it arrives at them in a preliminary fashion.

The subjects included three hundred and eighty-four Indians of the United States Indian School at Chilocco, Oklahoma, of whom 198 were males, 77 being mixed blood and 121 full blood Indians, and 186 females, 78 being mixed and 108 full bloods. Nearly all of them were Plains and Forest Indians. Their ages ranged from 9 to 26 years and their educational attainment ranged from the fourth to the tenth grade. To these Indian students were given four association tests: Opposites, genus-species, part-whole, and free (continuous) association; three memory tests: concrete and abstract rote memory and logical memory; and two word building tests; *apirle* and *acobmt*.

These tests were given in the spring of 1920. The technique was the same as that used by Pyle and his associates in giving all of these tests to Whites and Negroes, and some of them to Chinese (School and Society, Vol. I, p. 357 and Vol. II, p. 264). Other tests were given but the results are not presented in this paper.

While it will be observed from the above description that we have here groups of different ages, education, and sex, as well as different blood, the subjects were classified with reference only to sex, racial blood, and age. A further breaking up of the original group of subjects into educational grade groups would make the sub-groups too small, so that this classification has been deferred until larger numbers of Indian children can be secure for testing with the same material.

The first draft of the data is presented in the accompanying tables, the data for the males being given in Table I and that for the females in Table II. In both tables, as we have said, the data for the Mixed Bloods and Full Bloods are kept separate and these large groups are again subdivided into age groups running from 9 years to adult age, which means here from 19 to 26 years. The number of cases for each age group is designated also. In the Mixed Blood groups for both sexes the average degree of Indian Blood for an age group is indicated, and for all age groups we have the average school grade attainment. The subjects were just finishing the designated school grades, for the tests were given in March or toward the end of the school year. The tables give the averages, the A. D., P. E., and range for all age group divisions for every measurement undertaken. In addition is shown the overlapping in each age group from the 14th year up, which indicates the per cent of Mixed Bloods attaining and exceeding the median score of the Full Bloods.

The norms for Mixed and Full Blood Indians shown here are of necessity only tentative because of the size of the groups. It is likely that radical changes will occur in them when more racial material of a similar kind can be obtained. However, within the limits of the data at hand, we may say what follows. In our search for differences which these data show between Mixed and Full Bloods of the Indian race, we shall consider these facts:

I. The average of each age groups for Mixed Bloods and Full Bloods;

II. The instances where 60% or more of the Mixed Bloods attained the median of the Full Blood scores in each age group; and

III. A comparison of range of the Mixed Bloods and of the Full Bloods.

IV. However, inferences drawn from these findings must be modified by the differences in education attainment and social status between the Mixed and Full Bloods.

If we take for purposes of comparison the average performance of each group of mixed and full blood individuals for each test we find that the Mixed Bloods excel the Full Bloods in most of the cases. In the case of the comparison of the results for the males, the Full Blood fifteen year and adult groups excel in free association; their fourteen and eighteen year groups excel in concrete memory; their seventeen year group in abstract memory; their fifteen, eighteen year and adult groups in both word-building tests; and their seventeen year group in the second word-building tests. That is, there are twelve instances in which the average of these full blood Indians excel out of fifty-four possible instances, or 22% of the time. The case of the females is not even so good as this, for there are only four instances in which the Full Bloods excel the Mixed Bloods, *i.e.*, the adult group in genus-species, the fourteen year and adult group in concrete memory, and the adult group in abstract memory. This makes four out of a possible fifty-four, or 7% of the instances. Then the evidence from comparison of averages favors the Mixed Bloods.

A fairer test would be to find the overlapping, as for instance, to what extent the Mixed Bloods excel or attain the median of the Full Bloods. We find that for each test 60% and better of the Mixed Bloods attain and exceed the median of the Full Bloods for each age group in all tests except in the following instances: males, fifteen year olds in opposites, eighteen year olds and adults in genus-species, eighteen year olds and adults in part-whole, likewise, and fifteen, eighteen year olds and adults in both word-building tests; females, adult group in genus-species, fourteen year olds in free association, and adults in abstract memory, seventeen year olds and adults in part-whole association and also in the first word-building test, and sixteen year olds in the second word-building test. To sum this up the Mixed Bloods have this 60% and better of their respective groups attaining and exceeding the median of the Full Blood in 39 out of a possible 54, or 72% of the time for the males, and 46 out of 54 times, or 84.4% of the time for the females. This likewise favors the Mixed Bloods.

Attention should be called to the fact that in making the above comparisons certain age groups of the Full Bloods stand out prominently in several of the tests, particularly the fifteen year, eighteen year, and adult groups of males, and the adult females. There are evidently more superior individuals in these age groups than in the other age groups of the Full Bloods. This naturally brings us to a consideration of the range in the various age groups for purposes of comparison. Upon making such an investigation we find for the males that the upper range of the Mixed Bloods is greater than that of the Full Bloods 51.8% of the time, using the age groups here as bases for comparison as before, or 28 out of 54 times. For the rest of the time the latter excelled the former in going beyond their upper range, except twice, when their upper ranges were equal. In other words, for every excellent performance for any Mixed Blood individual, nearly half the time there was a full-blood Indian to match his performance or to excel it. It is not so for the females of this blood group, for when their upper range is compared with that of the other blood group of their sex it is seen that 40 times out of 54 the Mixed Blood upper range is greater than that of the Full Bloods i.e., 74% of the time. In only nine instances was the upper range of the latter female group greater than that of the former and in five instances it was equal to it.

As to the Full Blood lower range, it was below that of the Mixed Bloods 34 out of 54 times—62.9% of the time for the males, and it was about the same, 35 times out of 54—64.8% for the females, and as good or better for both sexes during the rest of the time. The presence of the superior performers among Full Bloods in the 14, 18 year, and adult groups for the males is again made evident by this examination of the range, and it is somewhat so for the female adults.

Before undertaking to draw conclusions from the above comparisons, two additional factors should be considered, *i.e.*, social status and education. The data at hand offer little information with reference to social status. We can say that the males, from the fourteenth year up, were on the average 54% Indian blood, and the females slightly more, but both are practically the same, and while we know little of the social status it is safe to draw the inference that since they were nearly half white, all of them being mixtures of whites and Indians, the influence of the white parent would necessarily improve the social status from the white standpoint and this would be above that of the individual of full blood parentage more or less biased by primitive traditions. And as to education, the average attainment for the Mixed Blood males is 7.4 grades, ranging from 5th to 10th grade and for the females was 7.3 grades, ranging from 4th to 10th; whereas for the Full Blood males the average school attainment is 6.2 grades ranges from 4th to 10th grades, and for the females 5.8 grades, ranging from 4th to 9th.

The relative lack of social pressure to go to school is evident in the Full Blood group which, to be sure, is the result of primitive apathy or lack of enthusiasm for the white man's education. Nevertheless, this should not be regarded as peculiarly an Indian trait, though it assuredly militates here against better performance in the psychological tests for the Full Blood Indian.

From the above experiment then we conclude that in a comparison of Mixed and Full Blood Indians as to their ability in the performance of certain tests, the Mixed Bloods tend to excel the Full Bloods on a score of averages, measure of per cent of the former to attain the median of the latter and as to upper range of scores, but many Full Blood individuals attain and excel the performance of Mixed Blood individuals. Furthermore the scores of the Mixed Bloods is favored by their superior social status and educational opportunity. However, the writer doubts if an equality of school attainment would remove the indicated differences, not as measured, but in their trend.

FROM THE PSYCHOLOGICAL LABORATORY OF THE UNIVERSITY OF TEXAS

THE RESULTS OF SOME TESTS ON FULL AND MIXED BLOOD INDIANS

The problem is to find out how Mixed and Full Blood Indians differ in the results of their performance on nine psychological tests.

TABLE I

Males:

Age-Years	9	10	11	12	13	14	15	16	17	18	Adult
Mixed Bloods:											
No. of Cases	1	0	3	2	5	7	11	13	9	12	14
*Av. De. I. B.	75	...	.50	.38	.75	.52	.61	.57	.47	.59	47
Av. Years Ed.	4	0	47	4.0	5.2	5.1	6.0	7.7	6.6	7.9	7.9
A.D.	...	...	...	...	...	1.5	.7	1.1	.8	1.3	.9
P. E.	...	...	...	...	...	1.2	.5	.9	.6	1.0	.7
Range	4	...	4-5	4-4	5-6	5-6	5-8	5-10	5-9	5-9	5-10
Full Bloods:											
No. of Cases	...	...	...	4	5	10	10	24	17	22	29
Ave. Years Ed	...	...	...	5.0	4.6	4.8	5.4	5.6	5.9	6.5	7.6
A.D.	...	...	...	...	...	1.0	1.1	1.7	1.3	.9	1.9
P. E.	...	...	...	...	...	.8	.9	1.4	1.0	.7	1.4
Range	...	...	...	4-7	4-5	4-6	4-8	4-8	4-9	5-9	4-10
Opposites' Test:											
+M.B. Ave. Score	10	...	7.3	7.5	11.2	9.6	9.2	12.0	12.9	11.0	11.4
A.D.	...	...	.8	.5	2.3	2.7	3.6	4.6	2.8	3.8	3.4
P.E.	...	...	...	...	...	2.1	2.9	3.6	2.2	3.0	2.7
Range	...	...	6-8	7-8	9-17	4-15	0-16	1-20	7-19	2-18	5-15
F.B. Av. Score	...	...	...	8.0	8.8	8.7	9.0	9.3	6.9	8.7	9.3
A.D.	...	...	...	3.5	1.5	1.8	2.6	3.2	3.0	2.3	3.7
P.E.	...	...	...	...	...	1.4	2.1	2.5	2.3	1.8	2.9
Range	...	...	...	3-15	5-11	2-17	4-14	3-15	3-12	3-17	1-19
++%M.B. at Med. Of F.B.	...	...	...	...	...	62.5	55.5	69.2	100	72.8	76.9
Genus-Species' Test											
M.B. Av. Score	12	...	6	.6	7.6	8.4	9.9	11.7	10.4	10.1	10.0

224

A.D.	...	...	.5	2.2	2.1	1.8	3.7	3.2	3.5	3.3	3.3
P.E.	...	...	...	...	...	1.4	2.9	2.5	2.8	2.8	2.7
Range	...	...	4-8	2-10	3-10	5-10	3-16	4-20	4-19	4-17	5-19
F.B. Av. Score	...	...	...	6.8	6.2	7.4	7.4	7.7	9.9	9.0	9.5
A.D.	...	...	...	2.2	2.2	4.0	2.2	3.2	2.7	2.9	4.0
P.E.	...	...	...	...	3.1	1.8	2.5	2.1	2.3	2.3	3.2
Range	...	...	...	5-11	3-9	1-19	4-13	1-15	4-13	2-16	3-16
Percent of M.B.'s Att. Med. Of F.B.'s	...	...	...	...	...	85.7	63.6	83.7	62.5	50	57.1

Part-Whole Test:

M.B. Av. Score	12	...	7.5	6.0	7.8	9.2	10.8	11.8	10.9	11.9	10.2
A.D.	...	...	?	?	?	2.2	4.5	3.0	2.3	5.2	5.2
P.E.	...	...	...	...	..	1.7	3.8	2.5	1.9	4.1	4.3
Range	...	...	5-9	6	5-11	4-13	0-19	5-18	5-17	3-19	1-20
F.B. Av. Score	...	...	...	7.7	7.0	8.2	9.6	8.9	9.0	9.0	9.4
A.D.	...	...	...	?	?	2.2	2.1	4.5	3.6	3.6	4.4
P.E.	...	...	...	...	...	1.9	1.7	3.7	2.9	2.7	3.4
Range	...	...	...	1-19	3-9	4-12	0-13	0-20	0-14	0-20	0-19
Percent of M.B.'s Att. Med. Of F.B.'s	...	...	...	..	...	80	55.6	75.0	60	60	57

Free Association Test:

M.B. Av. Score	37	...	49.3	56	50	46.7	44.8	50.3	46	50.4	44.3
A.D.	...	...	...	7	6.4	7.7	9.9	10.9	5.2	8.8	9.6
P.E.	...	...	...	...	...	6.2	8.1	8.7	4.1	7.1	7.7
Range	...	...	42-55	49-63	42-60	32-58	8-72	29-66	23-59	33-70	16-78

*Average degree of Indian Blood. F.B. indicates Full Bloods
+M.B. indicates Mixed Bloods.   ++Percent of Mixed Bloods attaining medium of
Full Bloods

FROM THE PSYCHOLOGICAL LABORATORY OF THE UNIVERSITY OF TEXAS—Con.

THE RESULTS OF SOME TESTS ON FULL AND MIXED BLOOD INDIANS

Males:

Age-Years	9	10	11	12	13	14	15	16	17	18	Adult
F.B. Av. Score	...	...	...	49.8	51.6	42.0	45.9	42.5	39.3	44.4	44.3
A.D.	...	...	...	8.8	5.3	9.4	12.5	10.5	10.9	8.0	11.5
P.E.	...	...	...	..	...	7.6	9.8	8.5	8.7	6.1	8.9
Range	...	...	...	35-67	42-58	27-58	27-72	11-67	13-70	5-75	10-84
Percent of M.B.'s Att. Med. Of F.B.'s	...	...	...	...	...	71	54.4	62	78	75	54.5

Rote Memory Test-Concrete:

	9	10	11	12	13	14	15	16	17	18	Adult
M.B. Av. Score	44	...	38.2	35.5	39.8	41.4	42.6	41.2	40.5	40.5	43.9
A.D.	...	...	...	...	...	3.5	5.8	5.6	5.6	3.5	4.2
P.E.	...	...	...	...	...	2.8	4.7	4.2	4.5	2.7	3.5
Range	...	...	33-45	33-38	33-44	36-51	27-55	30-52	31-46	34-47	33-59
F.B. Av. Score	...	...	...	35	33.8	37.4	41.8	39.9	38.8	40.8	39.3
A.D.	...	...	...	...	...	2.8	2.7	3.6	7.2	4.	1.4
P.E.	...	...	...	...	...	2.2	2.4	2.8	5.8	3.5	1.2
Range	...	...	...	23-42	24-39	33-42	36-47	31-49	26-49	28-56	32-53
Percent of M.B.'s Att. Med. Of F.B.'s	...	...	...	...	...	62	70	67	88	54	92

Rote Memory Test-Abstract:

	9	10	11	12	13	14	15	16	17	18	Adult
M.B. Av. Score	36	...	34.5	26.0	33.0	32.8	33.4	37.7	30.9	38.8	37.2
A.D.	...	...	...	...	...	4.9	3.2	7.6	5.1	3.9	5.4
P.E.	...	...	...	...	...	3.8	2.7	6.3	3.8	3.1	4.3

Range	...	...	31-37	24-28	24-49	15-39	21-43	19-49	22-42	24-46	26-48
F.B. Av. Score	...	...	...	29.5	27.6	26.1	33.1	30.4	31.1	33.8	33.6
A.D.	...	...	...	...	...	7.1	5.5	4.9	7.9	7.4	5.2
P.E.	...	...	...	...	...	6.1	4.7	3.8	6.3	6.2	4.3
Range	...	...	...	22-37	25-29	17-43	19-45	18-44	6-43	17-52	21-44
Percent of M.B.'s Att. Med. Of F.B.'s	...	...	...	...	...	87	70	75	50	85	69

Logical Memory Test:

M.B. Av. Score	36	...	21.3	35.0	25.0	28.9	21.5	30.3	34.9	24.5	26.2
A.D.	...	...	5.8	7.0	10.4	7.2	11.6	8.6	10.1	4.6	8.7
P.E.	...	...	...	...	...	5.8	9.4	6.8	9.9	3.6	6.9
Range	...	...	9-25	28-42	15-43	9-39	0-47	11-43	0-50	9-31	12-43
F.B. Av. Score	...	...	...	24.6	14.5	20.4	19.9	21.9	21.2	22.0	22.6
A.D.	...	...	...	7.9	8.0	13.1	14.3	12.2	10.1	10.7	10.0
P.E.	...	...	...	...	...	10.3	11.4	9.8	7.7	8.6	8.2
Range	...	...	...	15-35	0-22	0-35	8-34	4-37	0-44	0-51	0-45
Percent of M.B.'s Att. Med. Of F.B.'s	...	...	...	...	...	86.0	58.0	82.0	75.0	80.0	53.0

Word Building AEIRLP Test:

M.B. Av. Score	9	...	17	11.0	14.8	14.1	13.0	13.4	13.9	11.5	11.3
A.D.	...	...	...	...	...	4.1	4.0	4.4	3.9	4.5	4.5
P.E.	...	...	...	...	...	3.3	3.4	3.5	3.1	3.5	3.4
Range	...	...	16-20	10-12	9-17	6-20	4-20	3-20	9-21	0-18	0-21
F.B. Av. Score	...	...	...	14.8	11.4	12.4	13.5	11.9	11.3	12.1	12.5
A.D.	...	...	...	...	...	4.9	3.0	3.3	3.1	3.2	4.9
P.E.	...	...	...	...	...	3.8	2.4	2.6	2.4	2.5	3.9
Range	...	...	...	11-18	5-18	3-22	9-18	2-18	5-18	4-21	0-22
Percent of M.B.'s Att. Med. Of F.B.'s	...	...	...	...	...	75	37	66.7	66.7	45.5	55.5

Word Building AEOBMT Test:

M.B. Av. Score	15	...	13.3	11.0	15.0	13.2	13.0	14.4	12.0	11.6	12.2
A.D.	...	...	...	...	...	2.7	3.2	3.8	2.4	5.1	4.1
P.E.	...	...	...	...	...	2.2	2.5	3.1	2.1	4.1	3.3
Range	...	...	10-16	11-11	10-21	8-18	5-19	8-19	8-17	1-18	2-20
F.B. Av. Score	...	...	...	12.5	9.0	11.3	13.6	12.5	12.3	13.8	13.8
A.D.	...	...	...	...	...	3.4	3.6	3.8	3.4	2.0	3.7
P.E.	...	...	...	...	...	2.8	2.7	3.2	2.6	1.7	2.9
Range	...	...	...	5-20	5-8	5-17	7-19	3-20	5-19	7-18	5-23
Percent of M.B.'s Att. Med. Of F.B.'s	...	...	...	...	...	50	45.5	72.7	60	50	62

FROM THE PSYCHOLOGICAL LABORATORY OF UNIVERSITY OF TEXAS—Con.

THE RESULTS OF SOME TESTS ON FULL AND MIXED BLOOD INDIANS

TABLE II

Females:

Age-Years	9	10	11	12	13	14	15	16	17	18	Adult
Mixed Bloods:											
No. of Cases	0	0	2	1	3	15	9	17	15	11	7
Av. De. I. B.	...	...	.50	.50	.62	.56	.50	.57	.57	.57	.53
Av. Years Ed.	...	...	4.0	6.0	6.0	5.9	7.0	7.1	7.9	8.3	8.9
A.D.	...	...	...	...	...	1.1	1.8	1.2	1.5	1.7	1.4
P. E.	...	...	...	...	...	.9	1.4	.9	1.2	1.4	1.1
Range	...	...	4-4	6	5-7	4-8	4-10	4-9	5-10	6-10	4-10
Full Bloods:											
No. of Cases	...	1	1	3	5	18	15	15	27	16	7

Ave. Years Ed	...	4.0	5.0	4.0	5.6	5.2	5.3	5.4	6.4	5.2	7.5
A.D.	...	...	...	...	...	1.0	.8	1.5	1.0	1.3	1.5
P. E.	...	...	...	...	...	.8	.6	1.2	.8	1.0	1.3
Range	...	...	5	4-4	5-6	4-7	4-7	4-9	4-9	4-9	6-9
Opposites' Test:											
M.B. Ave. Score	...	...	15	20	13	11.1	14.2	13.4	14.4	15.2	13.5
A.D.	...	...	...	...	...	2.2	3.5	3.7	4.6	2.4	3.2
P.E.	...	...	...	...	...	2.7	2.6	3.0	2.9	3.1	5.1
Range	...	...	13-17	20	11-16	2-19	0-19	2-20	2-20	11-19	8-19
F.B. Av. Score	...	...	6	10	10.4	7.9	9.7	8.7	10.7	7.4	10.9
A.D.	...	...	...	...	...	3.0	3.2	3.8	3.6	3.9	6.2
P.E.	...	...	...	...	...	2.7	2.6	3.0	2.9	3.1	5.1
Range	...	...	6	9-11	5-14	1-14	4-17	0-16	0-17	0-18	1-18
Mixed Blood Att. Med. Of F.B.	...	...	...	...	...	68.8	100	88.2	71.4	100	75
Genus-Species' Test											
M.B. Av. Score	...	...	16.5	16.0	12.8	11.0	12.4	13.2	13.2	14.0	12.4
A.D.	...	...	...	...	3.4	4.4	2.7	4.7	4.1	4.2	3.2
P.E.	...	...	...	...	...	3.5	2.2	3.6	3.4	3.6	2.7
Range	...	...	9-15	12	9-16	4-20	6-17	2-20	3-19	8-20	4-19
F.B. Av. Score	...	...	6.0	8.5	10.6	8.0	9.8	7.8	10.8	8.3	13.6
A.D.	...	...	...	...	2.3	2.4	3.3	3.5	4.0	3.1	5.6
P.E.	...	...	...	...	...	1.9	2.6	2.8	3.4	2.4	4.7
Range	...	...	6	4-13	8-14	0-15	2-16	1-15	3-20	2-20	11-20
Percent of M.B.'s Att. Med. Of F.B.'s	...	...	...	...	...	73.8	80	88.2	66.7	100	29
Part-Whole Test:											
M.B. Av. Score	...	...	10.5	12.0	9.0	7.8	9.2	9.4	9.5	10.7	9.8
A.D.	...	...	...	...	...	4.1	4.4	2.1	3.1	3.4	3.6
P.E.	...	...	...	...	...	3.4	3.5	1.6	2.4	2.7	3.0

	9	10	11	12	13	14	15	16	17	18	Adult
Range	...	...	8-13	9-15	7-12	1-16	3-17	3-16	0-16	4-17	5-14
F.B. Av. Score	...	...	6.0	7.3	6.4	6.3	6.5	6.1	7.9	4.2	7.0
A.D.	...	...	...	...	...	2.5	2.8	3.7	3.2	3.4	3.8
P.E.	...	...	...	...	...	2.0	2.1	3.1	2.6	2.8	3.1
Range	...	...	6	3-10	1-10	1-11	3-15	0-12	1-14	0-12	2-12
Percent of M.B.'s Att. Med. Of F.B.'s	...	...	...	...	...	62.5	67	88.2	54	90	50

Free Association Test:

	9	10	11	12	13	14	15	16	17	18	Adult
M.B. Av. Score	...	...	38	55	43	45.8	48.9	53	52.7	55.5	56.6
A.D.	...	...	...	...	7.3	7.8	11.9	10.1	10.6	9.9	12.8
P.E.	...	...	...	...	...	6.1	8.5	8.0	8.3	7.4	10.2
Range	...	...	36-36	32-53	26-67	16-67	16-67	16-66	17-70	43-68	31-71

FROM THE PSYCHOLOGICAL LABORATORY OF THE UNIVERSITY OF TEXAS—Con.

THE RESULTS OF SOME TESTS ON FULL AND MIXED BLOOD INDIANS

Females:

Age-Years	9	10	11	12	13	14	15	16	17	18	Adult
F.B. Av. Score	...	...	48	54	36.8	43	46.9	43.2	42.5	39.2	54.5
A.D.	...	...	...	...	7.0	9.2	9.6	9.9	4.9	10.4	7.3
P.E.	...	...	...	...	...	7.1	7.5	7.8	3.8	8.5	5.8
Range	...	0	48	45-62	22-46	23-58	11-67	16-68	25-65	17-62	44-71
Percent of M.B.'s Att. Med. Of F.B.'s	...	...	...	...	...	46.7	67	93.8	73.3	91	71.4

Rote Memory Test-Concrete:

	9	10	11	12	13	14	15	16	17	18	Adult
M.B. Av. Score	...	...	39	44	45	37.5	44.8	42.3	41.4	45.1	46.3
A.D.	...	...	...	0	7.0	6.4	3.4	4.4	5.3	4.3	3.6

P.E. ...	...	...	...	...	5.2	2.8	3.9	4.2	3.5	2.7
Range ...	...	29-49	44	31-54	20-50	37-48	27-49	28-52	38-52	40-50
F.B. Av. Score ...	42	38	39	40.8	40.4	39.7	37.7	38.7	36.9	46.4
A.D. ...	...	...	2	4.2	5.7	3.9	6.4	5.1	5.8	5.2
P.E. ...	...	...	...	...	4.6	3.1	5.2	4.1	4.6	4.2
Range ...	42	38	37-41	37-50	28-58	33-47	31-58	22-48	26-51	40-51
Percent of M.B.'s Att. Med. Of F.B.'s ...	...	...	...	78	60	88	93	73	82	71

Rote Memory Test-Abstract:

M.B. Av. Score ...	...	33	29	39.5	34.8	41	38.6	38.3	40.3	40.5
A.D. ...	...	...	...	2.8	7.0	4.4	3.1	5.2	6.1	6.3
P.E. ...	...	...	...	...	5.6	3.5	2.5	4.2	4.9	4.9
Range ...	...	28-38	29	32-46	19-49	32-46	31-47	26-47	30-52	25-54
F.B. Av. Score ...	32	18	31.4	36.4	28.9	33.5	30.9	32.3	28.9	41.9
A.D. ...	...	...	...	7.3	6.3	4.7	6.9	7.5	7.5	5.2
P.E. ...	...	...	...	...	5.1	3.8	5.9	6.0	6.2	4.3
Range ...	...	18	23-40	26-46	15-43	25-51	11-45	10-47	9-47	37-50
Percent of M.B.'s Att. Med. Of F.B.'s ...	...	...	...	...	66	100	93	67	100	29

Logical Memory Test:

M.B. Av. Score ...	...	24	55	35.5	30.5	34.4	29.6	30.9	30.3	33.33
A.D. ...	...	...	...	...	11.6	4.7	7.2	5.4	8.0	13.2
P.E. ...	...	...	...	...	9.2	3.8	5.8	4.6	6.3	10.6
Range ...	...	21-50	55	26-44	19-47	18-42	12-46	24-44	21-41	13-49
F.B. Av. Score ...	...	11	31.5	26.3	24.0	24.2	21.9	23.9	16.9	27
A.D. ...	...	...	...	...	9.5	5.4	9.0	8.7	9.1	10.3
P.E. ...	...	...	...	...	7.6	4.2	7.2	6.8	7.3	7.7
Range ...	...	11	23-40	15-36	6-46	9-34	2-39	3-41	3-34	9-40
Percent of M.B.'s Att. Med. Of F.B.'s ...	...	...	...	...	72	90	81	79	93	67

Word Building AEIRLP Test:

M.B. Av. Score	...	...	7	11	12.5	11.7	15.8	15.2	13.7	16.4	13.9
A.D.	...	...	...	...	...	3.9	3.4	4.6	4.3	3.3	4.5
P.E.	...	...	...	...	...	3.2	2.8	3.7	3.5	2.7	3.8
Range	...	...	3-11	11	1-20	3-20	9-22	8-22	1-21	8-20	6-19
F.B. Av. Score	...	...	12	14.5	13.2	10.0	12.6	12.4	8.8	10.1	13.4
A.D.	...	...	...	...	...	3.5	4.6	5.0	2.5	5.3	2.6
P.E.	...	...	...	...	...	2.8	3.7	4.1	2.2	4.8	2.1
Range	...	...	12	10-19	10-16	1-20	2-20	1-20	0-22	0-18	7-16
Percent of M.B.'s Att. Med. Of F.B.'s	...	...	...	...	...	60	66.7	75	46.1	83.3	42.9

Word Building AEOBMT Test:

M.B. Av. Score	...	...	11.0	15.0	12-5	11.6	14.4	14.2	13.8	17.0	13.0
A.D.	...	...	...	...	...	3.9	4.0	3.2	5.0	3.0	3.2
P.E.	...	...	...	...	...	3.2	3.3	2.7	4.3	2.5	2.4
Range	...	...	11-11	15	3-19	2-18	4-20	4-20	1.21	3.22	2.16
F.B. Av. Score	...	1.0	1.0	15.5	12.8	11.4	11.8	13.1	12.4	12.7	12.7
A.D.	...	...	...	...	...	3.4	3.7	2.6	3.2	4.4	4.5
P.E.	...	...	...	...	...	2.8	3.2	2.1	2.6	3.5	3.4
Range	...	...	11	15-16	10-16	4-17	0-18	2-14	1-19	5-21	2-20
Percent of M.B.'s Att. Med. Of F.B.'s	...	...	...	...	...	46.7	70	56.2	66.7	9-	85.7

232

TABLE III

In this table the data of Tables I and II are combined into totals for both sexes and all ages, but the divisions of Mixed and Full Blood remains.

	Age		Educational Attainment		Opposites Test-Score	
	M.B.*	F.B.*	M.B.	F.B.	M.B.	F.B.
No. Cases	158	226	158	226	157	214
Average	16.4 yr.	16.1 yr.	6.9 yr.	5.9 yr.	12.2	3.5
A.D.	1.1	2.4	1.6	1.1	3.4	2.7
P.E.	.9	2.0	1.3	.9	2.9	2.3
Median	15.7	16.1	6.4	5.3	12.2	8.5
Range	9-23	10-26	4-10	4-10	0-20	0-19
% Reaching Med. Of F.B.	43%		67%		78%	

*M.B., Mixed Bloods. F.B., Full Bloods.

	Genus Species Test-Score		Part-Whole Test-Score		Free Ass'n Test-Score		Logical Memory Test-Score	
	M.B.	F.B.	M.B.	F.B.	M.B.	F.B.	M.B.	F.B.
No. Cases	166	223	162	209	151	227	164	214
Average	10.7	8.9	10.0	7.3	48.5	43.9	29.3	21.9
A.D.	3.5	3.4	3.8	3.8	5.0	10.7	9.2	9.6
P.E.	2.9	2.9	3.2	3.2	4.2	8.5	7.8	8.2
Median	10.5	8.1	9.5	6.9	49.6	44.5	29.9	22.1
Range	2-20	0-20	0-20	0-20	8-78	1-74	0-50	0-51
% Reaching Med. Of F.B.	67%		78%		64%		68%	

	Rote Memory Concrete-Test Score		Rote Memory Abstract-Test Score		Word-Building Test-aeirlp Score		Word-Building Test-aeobmt Score	
	M.B.	F.B.	M.B.	F.B.	M.B.	F.B.	M.B.	F.B.
No. Cases	155	224	155	224	153	223	157	224
Average	39.9	39.4	36.6	31.8	13.5	11.6	13.1	12.6
A.D.	2.7	5.7	5.4	2.9	4.2	3.7	3.9	.9
P.E.	2.3	4.8	4.6	2.5	3.6	3.1	3.3	.8
Median	42.1	38.5	35.5	31.5	13.2	12.3	13.4	13.5
Range	20-59	22-58	15-54	6-52	0-22	0-22	1-22	0-23
% Reaching Med. Of F.B.	79%		75%		63%		54%	

234

Goldberg, J.A. (1922). Incidence of insanity among Jews. *Mental Hygiene, 6*, 598-603.

INCIDENCE OF INSANITY AMONG JEWS*

Jacob A Goldberg, PhD
Free Synagogue, New York

For years it has been maintained by the psychiatrical world that the Jewish race contributed more cases of insanity than any other race.[1] Of late years, however, some investigators in this field have begun to doubt this traditional view; they have found that it was not sufficiently demonstrated that the Jew differed in his liability to insanity from the Gentile, and some have gone so far as to assert that the converse is true.[2] This conclusion was also reached a few years ago by the United States Department of Commerce which stated in a report: "On the contrary, facts from which deductions can be made point rather to a comparatively smaller amount of insanity among Jews than among people of several other races."[3] Studies of the incidence of insanity among Jews have been made in a number of European countries where these people have lived for many centuries. Lombroso found that the seemingly larger percentage of insanity among Jews was not so much a matter of race as of intellectual work, for among the Semitic races in general (Arabs, Bedouins) insanity is very rare. The results of a more recent study of the problem as it exists in Germany were published in 1909 by Sichel, whose deductions were based on careful investigation of the records of the Frankfort Hospital for the insane. He found that although there were relatively more Jewish inmates than the corresponding percentage of the Jewish population in Frankfort, this could be demonstrated only in reference to certain groups of mental disorders; the other types revealed a smaller percentage of Jews than of non-Jews.[4] Studies by A. Pilez in Vienna and C. F. Beadles in London seem to indicated a higher percentage of insanity among Jews than among non-Jews.[5] In this country Spitzka, in 1880, came to the conclusion, after a careful study of the problem, that on the whole the various forms of insanity occur in nearly the same proportions in the Anglo-Saxon, Teutonic, Celtic, and Hebrew races.[6] In considering the figures for Europe, it should be remembered that in a number of the larger European countries, as late as the nineteenth and in some even in the present century, Jews have been harassed and forced to endure unusual stresses and strains and even the torture of violent death at the hands of their persecutors. For these reasons it would hardly be advisable, for purposes of scientific knowledge and accuracy, to consider statistics gathered in such lands. The largest number of Jews within modern times congregated in a limited area are to be found in New York State and City; for this reason the admissions to the psychopathic wards of Bellevue Hospital, New York City, have been made the basis of the statistical study of the problem considered here.

INSANITY IN RURAL AND URBAN DISTRICTS

The total number of first admissions to the civil state hospitals in New York for 1917 was as follows: males 3,604; females 3,272; total 6,877. Of these, 398 males and 402 females, a total of 800, were Jewish, or 11.0 per cent males and 12.3 per cent females, with a general average of 11.6 per cent.[7] The total state population in 1917 was 9,917,438,[8] the total Jewish population approximately 1,600,000,[9] or 16.0 per cent of the general population. In 1918 the figures were about the same – total number of first admissions, 6,797; total number of Jewish patients, first admissions, 832.[10] The figures indicate a much lower percentage among Jews in the state than in the remaining general population. It should be observed also that very close to 100 per cent of the Jews in the state live in New York City, only a small proportion living in the other cities in the state, with very few in the rural districts.

During the year 1910, the urban population of the United States contributed 102.8 admissions and the rural but 41.4 admissions per 100,000 of the population to the institutions for the insane and feebleminded.[11] An important factor having a bearing upon this question is the difference between the two portions of the population in age distribution; only 27.2 per cent of the urban population and as many as 36.3 per cent or the rural population fall in the group under fifteen years of age, a group contributing but a small fraction of the admission to institutions for the insane.[12] The marked difference between urban and rural commitments, especially in New York State, is still further emphasized by the fact that the rate of first admissions per 100,000 population is much higher in the counties of the state in which cities are located than in those in which there are few, if any, cities of considerable size. Thus the rate per 100,000 population for New York County in 1918 was 105.9, whereas it was only 29.9 in Warren County, 30.7 in Schoharie County, etc.[13] As aforementioned, the Jewish first admissions to the civil state hospitals in 1917 and 1918 averaged about 11.6 per cent of the total first admissions, while they formed approximately 16.0 per cent of the general population of the state, indicating a rather low rate of first admissions to institutions for the insane.

JEWISH INSANE IN NEW YORK CITY

Another definite and perhaps somewhat more exact way to arrive at the ratio of the occurrence of insanity among Jews to their proportion in the general population is to consider the admissions to the psychopathic wards of Bellevue Hospital, New York City, for there the population is practically all urban, the admissions are all from the city proper (nearly altogether from the Boroughs of Manhattan and the Bronx), and the Jewish population is centered in the city.

The number of admissions to the psychopathic wards, male and female, of Bellevue State Hospital from September 1, 1917 to August 31, 1918 totaled 6,678, of which 1,127, or 16.4 per cent, were Jews. For the following year, beginning September 1, 1918 and ending August 31, 1919, the total number of admissions to the psychopathic wards of Bellevue Hospital was 8,255, of which 1,133, or 13.7 per cent, were Jews. During the second year, as has been noted, the total number of admissions was considerably larger than the year previous. This can be accounted for by stated that directly after the signing of the Armistice on November 11, 1918, the number of cases of alcoholism and alcoholic psychoses admitted to the psychopathic wards increased considerably; also, during this year a number of soldiers who had become insane while in service in various camps in the United States were sent to Bellevue Hospital, psychopathic division, and later transferred to their relatives in the city. The incidence of alcoholism and alcoholic psychoses among Jews has been considerably less than in almost any other element of the general population of New York, and for this reason, using the Bellevue Hospital figures, the percentage of insanity among Jews was 13.7 per cent for 1918-1919, whereas it had reached 26.4 per cent the year previous. The total population of New York City in 1917 was approximately 5,800,000,[14] the total Jewish population was about 1,500,000, or 25.8 per cent of the general population, with admission rates to the psychopathic wards of Bellevue Hospital of 16.4 per cent one year and 13.7 per cent the following year.

To Bellevue Hospital are brought the insane or alleged insane from the boroughs of Manhattan and the Bronx only. Kings County Hospital in Brooklyn receives such patients from the boroughs of Kings and Queens; Richmond Borough, with a Jewish population of only 5,000, sends its insane directly to Manhattan State Hospital after examination by two local physicians. A consideration of the total admissions to the psychopathic wards of both Bellevue and Kings County Hospitals for two years, thus including practically the entire city, will give a still better and more accurate index of the occurrence of insanity among the Jews of New York. The total number of admissions to Kings County Hospital psychopathic words, from September 1, 1917 to August 31, 1918, was 2,326, of which 392, or 16.9 per cent, were Jews. For the following year, September 1, 1918 to August 31, 1919, the total admissions were 2,550, of which 429, or 16.8 per cent, were Jews, there being in both years a markedly lower rate of admissions than the percentage of the total population. For the entire city (exclusive of Richmond, which is practically negligible) the following table indicates the admissions and percentages:

Total Admissions to the Psychopathic Wards, New York City

	Bellevue Hospital		Kings County Hospital		Total Admissions	Total Number	Jews per cent
End of Fiscal Year	Total	Jews	Total	Jews			
August 31, 1918...	6,878	1,127	2,326	392	9,204	1,519	16.5
August 31, 1919...	8,255	1,133	2,550	429	10,805	1,562	14.5

In view of what has been said regarding the unusually large total admissions to Bellevue Hospital for the year 1918-1919, it might be advisable to make sufficient allowance for the increase over the preceding year by setting the total admissions at about what they were in 1917-1918. In any event, the percentage of Jewish admission for the entire city would not average over 16.5 per cent, which is considerably less than 25.8 per cent, the proportion of Jews in the general population of New York City.

---

*   Excerpt from *Social Aspects of the Treatment of the Insane*. New York: Longmans, Green, and Company, 1921. 247 p.

1. Brill, A.A. and Karpas, M.J. *Insanity among Jews. Medical Record*, Vol. 86, pp. 576-579, October 3, 1914.
2. *Ibid*, p. 219
3. Sichel, Max. *Die Geistestorungen bei dun Juden.* Leipzig, 1909. pp. 13-31
4. Jewish Encyclopedia, article *Insanity*, Vol. 6, p. 606.
5. Spitzka, Edward C. *Race and Insanity. Journal of Nervous and Mental Disease*, Vol 7, pp. 613-30, October, 1880.
6. State Hospital Commission, Twenty-Ninth Annual Report, 1916-1917. p. 426.
7. State Hospital Commission, Thirtieth Annual Report, 1917-1918, p. 57.
8. *Jewish Communal register, New York City*, 1917, p. 89. Alexander M. Dushkin, in *A Survey of Jewish Religious Education in New York City* (Dissertation, Teacher's College, Columbia University, 1918), places the Jewish population for New York City in 1917 at 1,500,000. Henry Chalmers, in *Jews in New York City (American Journal of Statisticals*, 1914-1915, pp. 68-75), placed the Jewish population at 1,330,000 in 1913. *The American Jewish Year Book*, 1919-1920 (p. 605) estimates the Jewish population in New York State in 1918 as 1,603,923.
9. State Hospital Commission, Thirtieth Annual Report, 1917-1918, p. 405.
10. *Insane and Feebleminded in Institutions.* Washington: Bureau of Census, 1914, p. 27
11. De Fursac, R. and Rosanoff, A. *Manual of Psychiatry.* New York: John Wiley and Sons, 1916. p. 15
12. State Hospital Commission, Thirtieth Annual Report, 1917-1918, p. 438.
13. State Hospital Commission, Twenty-Ninth Annual Report, 1916-1917. p. 426.
14. State Hospital Commission, Thirtieth Annual Report, 1917-1918. p. 57.

15. *Jewish Communal Register, New York City,* 1917, p. 89. Alexander M. Dushkin, in *A Survey of Jewish Religious Education in New York City* (Dissertation, Teacher's College, Columbia University, 1918), places the Jewish population for New York City in 1917 at 1,500,000.
16. The Department of Health, New York City, estimated the total population on July 1, 1917, at 5,737,498. *Weekly Bulletin,* July 7, 1917. p. 223.

Brierley, S.S. (1923). A note on sex differences, from the psycho-analytic point of view. *British Journal of Medical Psychology, 3*(4), 288-308.

A NOTE ON SEX DIFFERENCES, FROM THE PSYCHO-ANALYTIC POINT OF VIEW

By S. S. BRIERLEY

I. Introductory.

The psychological problem of sex differences shares with other psychological inquiries, in contrast to the problems of the physical sciences, the essential difficulty that the very facts under discussion, the particular trends and mechanisms at issue, may themselves colour our observations and influence our judgments. These inherent difficulties would seem to be unusually great with this problem, for a study of both popular and quasi-scientific literature on the subject gives one the impression that there is nowhere a greater confusion between what is and what 'ought' to be the truth, what is and what we should like to be the truth. To the psycho-analyst, this is scarcely surprising; for it is clear that the question of sex differences must be peculiarly liable to affective judgments, since from its nature it lies so close to the major elements in the unconscious life of both men and women. Indeed, a study of the unconscious factors in opinion and belief on the matter would indirectly be, in large measure, a psycho-analytic study of the sex differences themselves. One knows that no one is exempt from these influences; but one has, nevertheless, to press forward with at least the intention of objectivity, and with the hope that awareness of the nature of some of the pitfalls in one's path may somewhat lessen the risk of falling into them.

The total differences between the sexes in the human species may be divided, for the purpose of this discussion, into three groups (a) the primary anatomical differences, (b) the secondary sex characters, and (c) the psychological differences. These three groups are by no means independent of each other, but the relation between them is highly complex and to some extent variable. I refer to the primary distinction between male and female as 'anatomical' for a good psychological reason. The strict definition of maleness and femaleness is in physiological terms, a female being any individual organism producing egg-cells or ova which, after uniting with cells of different character derived from a male, give rise to new organisms. Normally, however,

241

this egg- or sperm-producing power is accompanied by the appropriate external genitalia; and these constitute for the ordinary mind the gross physical distinction between male and female, awareness of which is the fundamental and primitive content of specific sex consciousness, reverberating profoundly, as psycho-analysis has shown, throughout the mental life as a whole.

The second group of differences, those known as the secondary sex characters, covering differences in the skeleton, musculature, rate of growth, skin, hair, voice, gait, and the other obvious or more subtle physiological sex characteristics, are now, as is well known, attributed to the internal secretions of the essential reproductive organs, acting in conjunction with the secretions of the other ductless glands. They are, in fact, an expression of the total and highly complex metabolisms of the male and female. Here, however, as both common and more exact observations show, we do not find the sharp distinction between male and female which normally occurs in regard to primary maleness and femaleness. As might, perhaps, be expected from the number of variables which enter into the determination of these characters, we find, within the range of normality, an indefinitely graded series passing over from the typical male to the typical female, the great majority of actual men and women lying somewhere in between the completely feminine female and masculine male. This, again, is a fact of considerable psychological importance. It is so directly, since our third group of sex differences, the mental, are in their turn determined, at least to some extent, by the action of the endocrine secretions, and would for many purposes be included in the secondary sex characters. This is generally held to be true of emotional and temperamental characteristics, at least. And the serial gradation of actual men and women between the typical male and female, so easily to be observed in the more obvious differences of outward structure, affords a strong presumption that there will be no sharp line of difference in the case of the subtler emotional and temperamental characteristics, but that every degree of difference will be found. A study of the experimental evidence suggests that the gradation is even smoother in the latter than in the former respects. In any case, it is clear that any thorough study of the problem involves not merely the identification of the sex groups, for purposes of comparison, with the mean difference found rather than with the extreme case, but also a reference to the actual curve of distribution, to the degree of scatter of the differences.

This fact of the gradation of the secondary sex characters, including the emotional and temperamental, and the contrast of this gradation with the sharp primary distinction of maleness and femaleness, is also of importance indirectly, for it will have to be kept in mind at a later stage of the discussion, when the question of predisposing factors in the 'castration-complex' has to be raised. We may content ourselves at this point with suggesting that some of the psychological differences actually to be observed between grown men and women must be, not so much secondary sex characters, as tertiary, the offspring of the self-consciousness of sex, of the intense primitive awareness of the primary sex distinction. We are here in contact with the problem which most students of sex differences have kept in mind, viz. how far the observable differences are innate and how far acquired, being in the latter case the result of suggestion, custom and tradition, and psycho-analysts may add, an expression of the 'castration-complex.' To take an example, how far the generally acknowledged imitativeness of women, their readiness to follow a plan laid down for them, their comparative lack of initiative and originality, are innate, or due to the effect of a tradition of sexual modesty and submissiveness. This is an obscure issue, and one which experimental methods have so far been unable to decide. Neither is the psycho-analytic method yet able to give a full answer. It does, however, throw some valuable new light upon the problem; and that, mainly because this question of sex differences is essentially a genetic problem, and must in the end be approached from the standpoint of a genetic psychology. In this respect there is a striking parallel between the history of this study and that of criminology. Not so very long ago, criminology was a mere accumulation of facts about adult criminals. It was what one might call a fortuitous concourse of atomic facts; and it was this condition which made the Lombrosian theory possible, the theory being an attempt to substitute a speculative evolutionary dynamics for a concrete individual history. The science did not begin to move until it shifted its attention from the adult to the child, and the individual genesis of the criminal was studied. So with our present problem; a static enumeration of mental differences between the adult man and woman has only limited scientific value. What is needed is a genetic study of the individual boy and girl. And the psycho-analytic method is essentially genetic. The time would thus seem ripe for a brief review of the new facts as to sex differences which psycho-analysis has been able to bring together in the pursuit of its individual studies.

There is a further reason for looking to psycho-analysis for important contributions to this problem. It is becoming increasingly clear to students of sex differences that those differences are greatest in the region of emotional and temperamental characteristics, and that the factor of interest is the key to such intellectual differences as are found in practical life. The experimental studies of sex

243

differences[1] in the cognitive processes, while scantier than one could wish, and sometimes based upon too few or too unrepresentative cases, are on the whole convergent in tendency. That tendency is to minimise the extent and significance of sex differences. There appears to be little or no difference in the mean level of general intelligence and the higher mental functions; where any has been shown, it has been negligible in comparison with the extent of individual variations. Differences with regard to specific mental functions, particularly those on the lower mental levels, appear to be somewhat greater in degree and general significance; but even here the range of individual variation is too wide to allow the sex group difference any great weight. (The band of individual variability itself appears to be the most striking sex group difference found, being, on all counts and with regard to most measurable qualities, greater in the male than in the female.)

It is, however, in those tests in which the detailed nature of the task to be performed is prescribed by the conditions of the experiment, those designed to measure quantitative differences in one or two determined qualitative processes, as for instance tests of controlled association, memory and reasoning, that the sex differences turn out to be minimal. Where the task given is less rigidly fixed by the conditions of the experiment, and subjective factors have free play, as in experiments on free association, positive and significant sex differences appear, in the form of divergent 'interests.' And interest is the bridge between the cognitive processes and the emotional and temperamental aspects of the personality. Following on this hint, and led by the recent general development of the psychology of emotion and instinct, the student of sex differences has seen the focus of attention shift from the intellectual processes to the conative and affective. It is in this field however that the psycho-analytic method is an indispensable instrument of research, and we must therefore turn to it for any specific contributions it has to offer to the problem of sex differences. It is not hoped to do more in this brief note than to state the nature of the problem from the psycho-analytic point of view, and to hint at possible specific lines of inquiry.

----

[1] See, for instance: (1) Thorndike, *Educational Psychology, III* (Columbia University, 1914). (2) Burt and Moore, 'The Mental Differences between the Sexes' (*J. Exp. Psychology*, 1911). (3) Burt, *Mental and Scholastic Tests* (King and Son, 1921). (4) Burt, 'The Development of Reasoning in School Children' (*J. Exp. Psychology*, v). (5) Jastrow, in *Psychological Review, III*. (6) Thompson, *The Mental Traits of Sex* (University of Chicago Press, 1903). (7). *Report on Differentiation of Curriculum between the Sexes* (H.M. Stationery Office, 1923).

II. Analysis of genetic problem.

An analysis, from the genetic point of view, of the problem of sex differences leads to the following necessary lines of inquiry: (a) What are the primitive and specific differences between male and female in the nature of the sex impulse itself? (b) Are there any differences as regards the relations of the sex impulse to the ego trends? (c) Are there any psychological mechanisms characteristic of male and female? (d) What differences are there in the external relations of the male and female child, and in the problems of adjustment set for each by these external relations? (e) Finally, what are the relations between all the foregoing factors and the observable differences in the general mental life of adult men and women? It is important to distinguish these aspects of the problem, although it is hardly practicable to keep them quite separated in the discussion, since they are so closely interwoven in the facts.

(a) With regard to the nature of the sex impulse, it is clear that we must take into account not only the normal sex reactions of the adult, but infantile forms of sexuality also, since we are making a genetic study. The classic writers on the subject of sex differences, and all pre-psycho-analytic students have dealt only with the mature sex impulse. Speaking of this first, there can be no doubt as to a specific difference between male and female in the nature of the impulse, as regards the essential sex act and the fore-pleasures preparatory to it. The male impulse is from the nature of the case relatively active, the female relatively passive; and this complementary activity and passivity are in part an expression of the sadistic-masochistic components of the impulse, and in part of the greater freedom of the object-libido in the male, and the greater narcissism of the female. This distinction as to activity and passivity is not, of course, an absolute one, and it refers to the form or aim of the impulse, rather than to its inner character, since the libido, as Freud points out[2], is in one sense always active. It is, however, a sufficiently deep distinction to justify us in speaking of the male sex impulse as predominantly active, and of the female as predominantly passive, as far as the act of coitus and the immediate preparatory stages are concerned. These are not the whole of the sex reactions of the adult; but as soon as we leave them for the region of what we may usefully call the courting phase (using this term not in the narrow sense of a specific social custom, but in the biological sense, as covering all the phenomena of the preliminary stages of sex attraction), we find ourselves already very far from pure impulse, and at the point where the question of innate and 'acquired'

---

[2] Freud, *Three Contributions to the Theory of Sex*, p. 79

differences arises. We already have here what we described as tertiary sex differences, which are not so much the direct spontaneous expression of the essential metabolisms of male and female, as the interplay of these with the self-consciousness of sex. Moreover, we are not here dealing with the sexual trends alone, but with complex psychical formations in which the ego-ideal is a considerable determining element. The whole round is so complex and obscure that I shall not attempt to cover it, but will content myself with a brief reference to some of the factors entering into female modesty, as illustrative of the difficulty of disentangling inherent differences between male and female from conscious and unconscious sophistications.

We cannot doubt that there is an organic element in female modesty, that in so far as it is what we may call a relative sex inertia, a passive waiting for stimulation by the active approach of the male, it is a secondary sex character, and is intimately bound up with the profound cycle of the reproductive processes in the female, contrasted with the biological freedom of the male. And even where modesty passes over the actual coyness, into a withdrawal at the first signs of pursuit by the male, it may still be regarded as a simple secondary sex character, because of its obvious biological values, serving to heighten the excitement and efficiency of the male in the sexual act. These aspects of modesty in the human female are shared with infra-human creatures and we must regard them as direct expressions of innate sex differences.

This organic core of sexual inertia and reticence is liable, however, in the human female, to undergo various degrees of reinforcement and exaggeration, until, as we know, it may even reach to an entire unawareness of sexual desire and an entire ignorance of the facts of intercourse and reproduction, in otherwise highly informed women. But, apart from such pathological exaggeration, a more normal modesty and reticence still appears, on psycho-analytic evidence, to be in part an expression of what we have called the self-consciousness of sex, acting through the familiar 'castration-complex.' The shame of having no penis, of bearing only the wound which is itself a sign of having been despoiled of the phallus, and of enduring the menstrual flow, which is in turn for unconscious fantasy a confirmation of the wound theory of the female genitalia, this shame is a powerful element in female modesty. It receives further reinforcement from the disgust arising from the proximity of the excretory apertures to the sexual centre, a disgust attaching itself also to the menstrual flow, which commonly tends to be thought of as an excretion. This disgust is, of course, itself a reaction barrier to primitive excretory and 'perverse' interests, the strength of which reaction is the outcome of human self-awareness. Since, however, the excretory processes occur in the same relation to the organs of sexual pleasure in men, this cannot be the differentiating element in female modesty, save that there is the additional source of disgust in the menstrual flow in women. The main differentiating factor would undoubtedly appear to be the castration shame. And in the castration shame the ego trends, or at least the libidinous components of the ego, are inextricably interwoven with the more strictly sexual elements. The pride of possession and the pride of power on the male side, envy and chagrin at the supposed loss of these on the female side, are unmistakably egoistic trends, and indeed, from one point of view, the castration-complex might well be said to be an expression of the instinct of self-preservation. The prototypes of castration, the loss of faeces and deprivation of the nipple, undoubtedly have both libidinous and egoistic values, and the genitalia themselves must lie at the very heart of the bodily and social self. I shall presently raise more fully the question of the relation of the sex impulse in male and female to the ego trends, and at the moment am only concerned to point out the egoistic elements n female modesty, which will have some bearing on that further discussion.

Turning now to infantile sexuality, it would not appear that the normal differences in reaction between male and female are here so marked. In the pregenital phases, oral and anal conditions would appear to be the same in boy and girl. The one important difference is with regard to urination. The differences in structure must from the beginning carry with them corresponding differences in organic sensation, characteristic of each type of urinary experience; and we have ample evidence of the great personal significance assumed by the process of urination as soon as visual attention and comparison can be directed to it. Urination, in its characteristic form in the two sexes, is of importance not only because of its direct libidinous value, and its direct organic contribution to the primitive ego, but also because of its role in infantile fantasies of love and power. Moreover, it introduces a difference in the earliest phase of genital sexuality, since the genital zone and the urethral coincide in the male, whilst in the female they are relatively distinct. Apart from the urethral elements, however, the earliest phase of genital sexuality would seem to be little differentiated as between boy and girl, since the main genital centre in the girl child is the clitoris, the homologue of the penis, rather than the vagina, its complement. The girl child under four or five years of age is not noticeably less positive, active, sadistic and exhibitionistic than her brother, and knows little of the modesty and passivity of the normal adult woman. She is, in fact, characterised by what we may call the clitoral attitude. There are, of course, individual variations here as elsewhere; but there is no marked group difference in the

247

nature and direction of the sexual impulse in the earliest years. There is, indeed, no very great divergence as regards activity and passivity before the onset of adolescence, but the first hint of difference occurs during the first great period of object-love, from two to seven years. This would appear to be in part organically conditioned, since recent physiological research has shown that there is a period of activity of the interstitial glands of the reproductive organs during these years, which is later followed by a phase of quiescence, until the time of full ripening in adolescence. This organic stimulus must bring with it the first predisposition to the characteristic sex attitude of male and female; and probably also conditions the psychological tensions of interest in the problems of sexual relations and the facts of birth, which we know is characteristic of the period. Then comes the first action of what we have called the self-consciousness of sex, and the pride of possession and power in the male child is set over against the envy and sense of less in the female. The evolution of the female modesty appears to begin here, a process which is not complete until the chief centre of sexual excitability has passed over from the clitoris to the vagina, carrying with it the appropriate change in mental attitude.

The normal passivity and reticence of the adult woman is thus seen as a goal to be reached by normal development, rather than as a condition inevitably given in the primary fact of femaleness. Indeed, we know that it is a condition which a not inconsiderable portion of women fail to reach, who remain in the clitoral attitude of the girl child, and are anesthetic to vaginal stimulation. Yet although characteristic femininity is not irrevocably given in the female constitution, but is rather the end result of a long process of development involving the interplay of many complex factors, we cannot doubt that there is an organic predisposition to it, a tendency to the organisation of those factors under the dominance of the primary condition of femaleness.

If this account of the history of differentiation in the nature and direction of the sexual impulse is sound, it would almost appear as if that differentiation were chiefly on the female side, as if in the course of development the female had to turn aside at various points from the more or less straight line normally kept by the male, from infancy to maturity. There is certainly a good deal of evidence that the sexual history of the female is in some respects more complex than that of the male; and this, I think, will be still more clear with regard to the relation of the sexual impulse to the ego trends, which we may now take up.

(b) We may put the problem in this way—how far are the activity and passivity of the sexual impulse in male and female necessarily characteristic of the mental life as a whole, in each? Does the deep and pervasive physiological and psychological differentiation of sex go down to the very roots of the go? Is the female go essentially different from the male? Is it penetrated with the passivity characteristic of the female sex impulse? This is a view which common observation would make foolish, and one which, so far as I am aware, has not been explicitly held by any serious writer, although there have been many whose mode of statement of sex differences has verged, perhaps, unintentionally, towards this. I might instance Mr. Walter Heape, and to a less degree Professors Thomson and Geddes, and even Havelock Ellis. Thomson and Geddes, as is well known, hold that in a profound biological sense, maleness is activity, and femaleness is passivity. Starting from the striking difference in the size and motility and physiological characteristics of the sperm and the ovum, interpreted in the light of the evolution of sex from unicellular organisms onwards, they base their theory of the essential nature of sex on a primary and fundamental differentiation, towards katabolism in the male and anabolism in the female. It would be of great interest in our present connection to attempt to bring this widely accepted view into relation with Freud's recent reflections on the katabolic death instincts. It would lead us to the conception of the male as the representative of the individual, of the soma, which die; and of the female as representative of the life of the race, of the immortal germ plasm. It is tempting to develop this, but to do so would lead us off the main path of this note, which is to unravel the concrete psychological problem of the detailed development of male and female—or, rather, to suggest the directions in which this may be possible. It is clear that the generalisation just suggested, or even the emphasis which Thomson and Geddes place on male activity and female passivity, can only have any truth so long as it is stated in the form of an abstract tendency; it becomes ludicrous if pressed too far, and is methodologically unsound if it is allowed to obscure the contradictory elements, and to draw us from the detailed study of the concrete facts. It is, I think, certain that the full psychological truth is much richer and more complex than has yet been made clear, owing to the preoccupation of those who have theorised about the problem of sex differences with this generalisation as to the activity of the male and the passivity of the female. We have, in our final statement, to account for the anomalies of development, and to find room for the fact to which we have already referred, the fact of the range and smooth gradation of sex differences is actually observed, which we are quite unable to do if we over-simplify our problem from the start by the lure of this great generalisation.

249

I would suggest that the real psychological situation is something as follows: The ego trends, whether in male or female, are inherently and always, in themselves, positive, active and katabolic. In the male, however, they harmonise in nature and direction with the sex impulse; whereas in the female they are in essential and perpetual conflict with the latter. (I am, of course, here speaking of conflict, not in the general sense in which the sex impulses as such are in conflict with the ego trends as such; but in a special sense relating only to the character of activity and passivity of the sex trends in male and female.) It is not that the female ego is inherently and from the first permeated by sex characteristic, nor indeed that the male ego is so; but rather that the essential characteristics of the ego are in the one case reinforced, in the other strongly modified and limited. And, as we have already seen in our discussion of female modesty, this reinforcement in the one case and limitation in the other is partly a physiological process, due to the direct action of the endocrine secretions, at various periods of normal development, on the general somatic and nervous tissues; and partly also a psychological process, moving in the paths familiar to us as psycho-analysts. Hence the possibility of the anomalies which occur, of the masculinoid woman and the feminoid man, and of all the more normal range of individual differences to which we have already referred. If the feminine ego were inherently and from the start feminine, there clearly could not be any conflict between the demands of the individual life and biological destiny, in the female. There would be no need for an 'ideal' of femininity or modesty, no question of what are desirable qualities in a woman, or suitable occupations and recreations for her. And there could certainly be no such thing as a 'castration-complex,' in which, as I have suggested, the ego trends play such an important part. In every case, the woman would accept herself and her destiny without knowing that there was anything to accept. As indeed, the larger proportion of women actually do; but the anomalies and exception have shown that this is by no mean a simple inherent state, but is, as we have put it, the end-result of a long and complicated process of development. And it is the details of this development which we have as psychologists to inquire into.

On this view, then, briefly, the male and female infant are alike in the general character of the ego trends, and at first hardly differentiated in their sexuality. The little girl is almost as positive, active, sadistic and exhibitionistic as her brother, inevitably showing in her earliest love situations the clitoral attitude, as we have called it, rather than the reticence and modesty of her older sister. But presently, towards the end of the first period of object-love, a hint of the divergence of the sexual and egoistic trends is seen in the girl child and of their convergence in the male, a phenomenon repeated more dramatically and on a much large scale, with the onset of adolescence. And throughout the period of development there is a complex interplay, on both physiological and psychological levels, of the egoistic and sexual components of the personality.

The basic biological facts have often been stated, that the reproductive functions of the female set very definite limits to the development of her individuality, keeping her closer to type than the male, in whom, as we have seen, there is a greater range of individual variability. On the psychological side, it means that in the woman the reproductive functions and the qualities of femininity itself have to be taken up into the ego-ideal, so as to transform the initial power elements of the go trends, in harmony with the character of the sex impulse and biological destiny. It is clear that the problem of reconciliation of the ego and sexual trends is more complicated for the female than it is for the male. Male sex activity becomes, indeed, the prototype for all activity, for the ego trends themselves. The penis is the organ of power and of knowledge; and in the fantasy of male and female alike, the first actual power experiences, the possession and expulsion of the faeces, are later equated to the male organ. Castration fantasies are not, of course, peculiar to the female mind; the essential difference is that the female ego has in reality to become reconciled to what is expressed on the unconscious level as castration. There has to be a reconciliation to the loss of the penis, to the limiting of the direct expression of the power tendencies, to the transformation of the ego functions. And, as we know, this transformation is brought about, not only by the incorporation of femininity into the ego ideal during the formative period, but, at a much deeper level, by the unconscious mind, the birth of a child; and to bear a child, especially a man child, is to recover the penis. This is the egoistic element in the self-forgetfulness of mother-love. Or, for other women, the possession of a lover, or of many lovers, is the possession of a penis; and power becomes the power to attract and hold the desire of a man.

Castration elements must thus be present in the unconscious mind of all women, although they are not necessarily pathogenic, nor so marked as to deserve the name 'castration-complex.' They undoubtedly play a large part in the genesis of that state of total repression of sex interest and sex knowledge in highly educated women, where there is present a strongly marked ego development with a complete repudiation of even the existence of sexual facts.

251

This would raise for us the question of what are the predisposing conditions to the development of a castration-complex, in women. (I confine myself here to women, because I am inclined to think that the genesis of the complex in men is related much more to the Oedipus situation, than it is to the question of sex differences— although there are of course important common elements.) I would suggest that the predisposing conditions fall into four groups. (1) Circumstantial; which I mention first, not because I think them the most or the least important, but because there is so little to say about them. We do not yet know what they may be, although we cannot doubt that they are operative. In discussing the external relations of the child presently, we shall come near to this issue. (2) The fact, to which I am inclined to attach a good deal of importance, that the awareness of the primary sex distinction comes to the child well before there is any marked development of the appropriate sex characters. To put it simply, the little girl discovers that she is short of what her brother possesses (for, of course, to the child and the primitive, it is a matter of the mere presence or absence of a single positive organ, as there can be no knowledge of the real complementary organs and processes of the female), long before the characteristically feminine emotions and impulses, conditioned by the endocrine secretions, have come into play to any extent, and long before the development of the breasts, the equivalent of the penis in unconscious fantasy. (3) The fact that the secondary sex characters, including the emotional and temperamental, natively present every degree of difference from individual to individual. It will clearly be less easy for a girl child who is near the middle region of differences as regards type of energy, and instinctive and emotional endowment, to accept the supposed loss of the phallus, and effect the normal feminine transformation of the ego. The castration fantasy will in such a case tend to be pathogenic, for the conflict will be greater. Where there is from the beginning a more typically feminine organic and emotional setting, the psychological problem will be less acute. (4) We may consider also initial differences in anal and urethral eroctism, which are unmistakeable elements in the complex, and are, as we have already noted, closely connected with the power aspects of the ego trends. Wherever we found strongly marked anal defiance and obstinacy in the girl child, we should, I think, expect to see hints of a castration-complex; and, conversely, wherever we found a well-developed castration-complex, we should expect to find strong anal interest and dislike of interference in connection with the process of evacuation. (The most marked case I have observed of the castration-complex in a girl child, A., showed this very clearly. From the period of infancy onwards there was always a refusal to evacuate at the required time and place, the process being postponed as long as possible with every show of defiance and obstinacy, traits which were excessively developed in every direction. She was an unusually questioning, 'naughty' and unhappy child. In her second and third years, she developed the habit of drinking her bath water, and was on one occasion found drinking the water in which tadpoles had been kept. When about four and half years of age, she persuaded her brother (eighteen months her senior) to cut off her hair, remarking "Now I am a boy." And was presently discovered in the act of swallowing some large object with great difficulty, an object which turned out to be her brother's whistle; her comment was "I didn't like the noise, so I hid it in myself.")

(c) We may now turn to our third question, that of whether there are any psychological mechanisms peculiar to or more characteristic of either male or female, a question which will occupy us only a few moments. It is, I think, probable that there is only one specific sex difference here, viz. that women show a greater tendency to reaction-formation than do men. We might take as examples, the greater frequency in women of over-devotion, over-conscientiousness, over-cleanliness and prudishness. But when we have called these reaction-formations, we cannot leave the matter. Further analysis is required before anything very significant can be said. It is clear that two of our examples, viz. over-cleanliness and prudishness, are related to the processes we discussed in our last section, and two, viz. over-devotion and over-conscientiousness, to the problem we are to take up next, that of the external relations of the boy and girl. Over-cleanliness is probably the simplest case of reaction-formation; it is a strong disgust barrier erected against strong interests in the excretory processes; and, as one might expect, includes a marked masochistic element. The situation is more complicated in the case of prudishness, which is not a simple reaction barrier to a simple primitive tendency. It includes a pure reaction element, against the active sex curiosity and exhibitionism of the clitoral phase in the girl child; but it is more than this. As we have seen, it is in part the outcome of the castration-complex, a repudiation of the female role, and of the limits which this imposes upon the direct expression of the power elements in the ego trends. By denying sex, the childish interest in sex, and the fact of femaleness, are at one and the same time repudiated.

In addition to this specific fact of the greater frequency of reaction-formations in women, it is also clear that the total degree of repression appears to be greater, and more widely diffused, over the sexual life.

(d) We may now consider differences in the external relations of boy and girl, and in the problems of adjustment which these relations dictate. We may leave on one

253

side the relations with brothers and sisters, since the situation varies so greatly with the number and relative ages of these; and content ourselves with a brief survey of the phases through which the boy and the girl travel in their relations with parents and parent surrogates.

The first phase, covering the intra-uterine and suckling periods is, of course, exactly similar for boy and girl. Both are sheltered in the mother's womb, both suffer the first great trauma of birth, both find nourishment and pleasure at the mother's breast, and have to endure the loss of the nipple at the time of weaning. Thus, for both, there is a stage when child and mother are one; and for both, the mother first means shelter, warmth and tenderness. And in each case the first interferences and discipline come from the mother, interferences with anal and urethral powers and pleasures; the mother is thus the first and most intimately personal authority, for both boy and girl. She is also, however, for both, the first object of love. When, in the child's second year of life, the growing ascendancy of the exteroceptors and the power of active exploration of the world establish more active relations with the persons around him, there develops the gradual awareness of them as persons, and the movement of the libido outwards. The mother, with whom the child has had physical union, and who has served his most intimate personal needs, then forms the natural bridge between the phase of complete auto-erotism and that of developed object-love; she, as the first source of pleasure, is the first natural focus for the outward-flowing libido, whether in boy or girl. The child's first attitude to the mother is thus ambivalent; she is the first love, and the first hostile force, the emphasis on one or other of these aspects varying with the child and the characteristics of the mother. Behind the intimate figure of the mother is that of the father, more remote, more powerful, vaguer, and larger, coming and going more mysteriously and independently. And presently, with the gradual widening of experience and growth of intellectual power, he becomes linked with the great power symbols of the child's world, with the policeman, the soldier, the tram-conductor and engine-driver. He thus early becomes the more impressive figure of authority and power, an image which must be made immensely vivid and compelling where the young child is allowed to be witness of the marital embraces of the parents, as is most usually the case. This, again, must be true for both boy and girl.

During this same period, however, the sexual preferences of the parents, whether they find conscious or unconscious expression, begin to act upon the young child. The father is more easily indulgent and demonstrative with the girl child, the mother with the boy; the father is more ready to find fault with and to check the waywardness of his son, the mother to restrict and correct her daughter. This differentiated reaction of the parents must be the earliest stimulus to the differentiation of the sex object in the child; but very presently it is reinforced by the organic stimulus of the first functioning of the interstitial glands of the reproductive organs, bringing the earliest hint of secondary sex characters, and of differentiation in the sexual impulse, as we have already noted. And thus the sex preferences of the child himself are established. From this point there is an important difference between boy and girl, in external relations. We may follow out the boy's development first.

For him, the first infantile love-object, the mother, who drew his budding affection in the transitional period between complete auto-erotism and differentiated object-love, remains as the true and normal centre of his sex interest, and the prototype of all normal love-objects for him. The early discipline situations with the mother, her interference with excretory pleasures, are then sexualised, the faeces and the urine becoming love-gifts to her. And the father becomes the sexual rival, sexual hostility fusing with and heightening the ego-assertiveness of the boy child against power and authority. A normal condition of tension in relation to authority is thus set up in the boy, which is a constant stimulus to individual development. Thus, we have the same convergence of the sexual and egoistic trends with regard to the normal relations of the male child to his parents as we found to be the case with the internal nature of the sex impulse.

This, then, is the normal situation. Normality, however, is not a fixed and static condition or relation; it is a moving equilibrium, a broad balance of many complex tensions. And the normality we are considering may be disturbed in either of two directions. The normal Oedipus situation may be, as it were, either under- or over-stated; and we may usefully give brief attention to the resulting distortions of the boy's development, for comparison with that of the girl. Where, in the first instance, the mother is of a more dominating type than the father, or the father is withdrawn because of death, illegitimacy of the child or other circumstances, the mother remains the centre of authority, and the initial and infantile ambivalence to the mother is perpetuated. She becomes the love-object, but rather than the undifferentiated love-object of the transitional phase than the normal heterosexual love-object; and the infantile hostility of response to her interference with oral, urethral and anal pleasures remains untransformed, and intensified.

The original nuclei of the castration-complex, the compulsory loss of faeces and withdrawal of the nipple are reanimated, and the male castration-complex develops, castration in this case by the mother. The initial and of course inevitable assumption that the mother has a penis like the boy's own is retained and reinforced in fantasy; and since the external object is undifferentiated, the internal impulse remains so; the boy, "tied to his mother's apron strings,' fails to develop normal masculinity of sex impulse or disciplined and effective ego assertiveness. He retains the submissiveness proper to the infantile phase, an outcome of the first narcissistic identification, along with the infantile hostility. The ground is thus prepared for later impotence, the pathogenic element being the fantasy of castration by the mother. Here, the normal Oedipus situation has never been developed, the divergence from normality taking place at a level below this.

When, however, normal development is carried further, to the point of the Oedipus situation, difficulties may arise from a too stern and unyielding attitude of authority, or too great unconscious hostility on the part of the father. This may lead to the fantasy of castration by the father, with the resultant identification with the mother, and homosexual tendencies. The pathogenic element here is mainly the incest tendencies, with the guilt attaching to these, and the fantasy of castration as a punishment; but the resulting regressive movement of the libido may here again reanimate the more primitive anal and oral nuclei of the castration fantasy, connected with the mother; there is then a markedly ambivalent attitude to both parents. The identification with the woman, although it may take origin at the level of the Oedipus situation, is regressive, a return to the earlier undifferentiated state, in which the equation of the penis and the breast and the fantasies of giving birth based on the process of defaecation are normal to the small boy. A small boy of four years gave a clear instance of the naïve identification of the penis and the nipple, on an occasion when a large dog approached and sniffed at the genital region, remarking, "Oh, he wants to suck." For the boy, as well as for the girl, the possibility of neurosis is bound up with the existence of the relatively undifferentiated infantile phase of the sexual impulse and of the emotional relations, coupled with the peculiarly human fact of the self-consciousness of sex.

Turning now to the development of the external relations of the girl; with her, after the period of transition from auto-erotism, when differentiated object-love appears, the object-libido has to change its object as well as its mode, the mother being displaced by the father, who is already the major focus of authority, and now becomes also the normal centre of sexual interest. For the girl, thus, authority is an authority that calls out sexual passivity rather than ego-assertiveness. Submission to authority in the person of the father and his surrogates is sexualised, and hence there is little stimulus to defiance and adventurous challenge. The normal castration element in femininity has reference primarily to the father, who takes the penis only to give the child, subdues only in order to love. The conception of the deflowering of the woman as a castration, fantasies of rape, and of the death-symbolism of coitus are linked with this aspect of sexual development in the woman. This is the normal movement of the libido in the girl child; and it is reinforced by the primary narcissistic identification with the mother, which normally persists in the girl child, whereas it has to be broken down for normal development in the case of the boy. The girl child is allowed, in the language of fantasy, to remain in the mother's womb; and this narcissistic identification with the mother adds its quote to the transformation of the power trends into harmony with the sexual and reproductive functions of the female.

We may consider for a moment some of the deviations which may arise in the girl owing to a disturbance of normality in the relation of the parents to each other and to the child. As in the case of the boy, so with the girl, where the mother is the dominating parent, ruling by power rather than by love, the castration fantasy is referred to her, the oral and anal disciplines of the earliest phase consequently retaining an emotional over-valuation. Hostility to the mother is then very strongly developed, the sadistic component of the sexual impulse rather than the masochistic becomes accentuated, and the power elements in the ego trends remain untransformed and intractable. A marked identification with the male is apparent, with a persistence of the clitoral attitude. As with the boy similarly situated, the normal differentiation of the sex impulse on the one side and of the sex object on the other fails to occur. In the later analysis of such cases, masculine and feminine symbols appear to be interchangeable and almost fluid. In the case of B., a young woman with a castration-complex so heavy that she is unable to pursue any interest or occupation for more than a short time, this is very clear. In early childhood there had been great difficulty with the control of urination, and the mother had commonly stood over the child with a stick, to make her observe the time and place. In her present fantasies the 'Hound of Heaven' is unmistakeably a mother symbol, and there is a frequent image of B.'s sister "riding on a bull, and a hound pulling her off." Where, in these cases, the normal Oedipus situation does develop the resulting sexual hostility to the mother may then reawaken the over-development resentment regarding interferences with anal and urethral pleasures, so that the two fuse into an almost inescapable hatred of the mother.

257

I may perhaps, at this joint, be allowed to guard myself against the misunderstanding that I am attempting to explain the castration-complex and homosexuality, in terms of the external stimulus of the personality of the parents, only. I am very much aware that the problem is by no means so simple, and that the obscure organic factors and innate psychological predispositions to which I have made no reference here are probably more important. I am not, of course, attempting to give an account of the genesis of the castration-complex and homosexuality, but only to ask what relations can be found between these problems and the question of sex differences. Moreover, the organic determinants and psychological predispositions are not here relevant, since they appear to be individual rather than sex group differences. I should, however, like to suggest very tentatively, that there is a sex difference as regards the genesis of the castration-complex, viz. that in women it springs primarily from the anal and urethral levels, and is mainly a function of the ego trends, being connected with the incest trends only secondarily; whereas in the male, it is more intimately connected with the incest tendencies, and with genital auto-erotism. If this distinction holds good in any measure, it is, of course, entirely a matter of emphasis and degree and of the immediate point of origin, since all these elements are common to both sexes and to all individuals.

A further word may be added to the relation between the inner and outer factors. It is clear that in some cases the weight is thrown on the inner conditions, and in others, on the outer. There is no doubt, for instance, that an over-dominant and interfering mother does produce a tendency to the castration-complex, with its ambivalence and failure of differentiation, in both boy and girl. I have had occasion to quote the case of a woman as an example of this, and have known a very similar case in a man. Yet it is equally clear that where the anal interest in a girl, for instance, are natively very strong, a mild and gentle mother may be felt as hostile and interfering to an exaggerated extent. This was strikingly true in the case of A., whose mother was mild to the point of weakness. The matter of defaecation, however, was, I should judge, the point in which she was most tenacious of discipline and persistent in attempts to control the child—doubtless for reasons both conscious and unconscious. And in a child in whom the anal-sadistic tendencies were so strongly developed, this particular recurrent conflict would inevitably count for more than any ease of discipline elsewhere.

III. Summary and Conclusion

It may now be possible to draw together some of the threads of our discussion; this can, however, only be done in the most tentative and partial manner, for I have not hoped to do more in this note than to suggest how relevant and important to the problem of sex differences psycho-analytic material is.

It is clear that the observable mental differences between men and women are the result of a highly complex interplay of three groups of factors, viz. (a) the organic differences springing directly from the primary fact of maleness and femaleness, (b) the accompanying innate psychological characteristics, which vary in degree and ensemble from one individual to another, and (c) the awareness of the fact of sex; this latter functioning not merely through the subtle operation of tradition and social pressure, but also, as it has been left for psycho-analysis to show, through the acute awareness, in the mind of the little child of the possession or non-possession of the phallus.

In the case of certain of the mental differences of sex, it is possible to trace a direct relation with psycho-analytic facts, or, at least, to show how some of these differences hang together.

That group of temperamental differences which includes the greater social submissiveness of women, their relative lack of initiative and greater willingness to follow a convention, or to work along lines laid down for them by others, these are clearly connected with a group of physiological and psychological conditions which include (1) the fundamental organic conditions of the reproductive functions in the female, involving the lesser range of variability and closer approximation to type; (2) the specific nature of the sex impulse in the female, with its passive and masochistic colouring; (3) the fact that the sex impulse and the ego trends diverge in the female, while converging in the male; and (4) the fact that the father is normally at one and the same time the object of the first sex impulse, and the major, more impersonal focus of authority. It would thus appear that the characteristics in question are, at least to a considerable degree, an inevitable accompaniment of normal feminine development; but it is equally clear that they are considerably heightened by an over-development of the fantasy of castration by the father; and that, if social conditions are such as to call for greater freedom of initiative and greater independence on the part of women, the point of educational attack must be the early period when that fantasy is developed.

It is likely that the supposed greater gregariousness of women is a function of the same conditions. There is little evidence that women seek each others' society more than men, either in primitive or civilised communities, and it would seem unnecessary

259

to postulate the presence or absence of a specific instinct of gregariousness to account for the greater individualism of the male, since the physiological and psychological conditions referred to are already ample.

The much greater frequency of juvenile and adult delinquency among males is but another and more strongly marked expression of the same group of conditions, and particularly connected with the relation of the sexual and egoistic components of the personality, and the distinctive functioning of the Oedipus complex in the boy and girl respectively.

The fact that, on the whole, women show a lesser degree of scientific curiosity is undoubtedly to be correlated with the greater degree of repression typically occurring, as a general condition; and with the castration-complex as a specific determinant.

In concluding, we may give a moment's attention to practical considerations, particularly as regards the educational bearing of sex differences. It is hardly possible for the psycho-analyst to subscribe to the view taken by some psychologists that because intellectual differences between the sexes, as tested by laboratory experiments, are practically negligible in degree, educationists need take no account of sex differences as such, but need only insist on ample individual opportunity irrespective of sex. We must agree with this latter; but the problem does not, on the findings of the psycho-analytic method, cease there. We should rather agree with those who hold that the emotional and temperamental differences between the sexes, and the long-run effect of these upon the mental life as a whole are of considerable educational and social importance. The educational problem for both boy and girl is that of reaching the goal of normal sexuality in a balanced relation with the individualised ego; but the emphasis is different in each case.

A word needs to be said as to what is meant by normality of development, since we have used this concept here, and in speaking of the reconciliation of the ego trends with the female sexual impulse and biological functions. It is clear that our conception of normality must itself be governed by the 'reality principle' and have reference to the actual social and economic conditions of the world in which we live. The population problem is perhaps more relevant to the question of what is the desirable balance of individuality and biological function in women, than any male infantile fantasy of the all-perfect mother. Nor, it must be further said, is the castration-fear of the male, when it impels him to deny intellectual power and personal independence to the woman, any more trustworthy guide than that of the woman herself, when it drives her to the refusal of her feminine functions. External conditions in an industrial and highly individualistic civilisation demand the most delicate adjustment; and we might well have added to our enumeration of the predisposing factors to the castration-complex in the woman, the changing and conflicting demands of modern life. Like any other neurosis, it is largely a function of the discrepancy between the demand of our top-heavy civilisation, and our native resources; and relief does not come by way of turning from the reality of those demands to a woman-imago.

We may perhaps end on a note of paradox, and say that, from the psycho-analytic point of view, neurosis occurs because sex differences are so deep—and yet is only possible because they are not deep enough.

Garth. T.R. (1923). A comparison of the intelligence of Mexican and mixed and full blood Indian children. *Psychological Review,* *30*(5), 388-401.

A COMPARISON OF THE INTELLIGENCE OF MEXICAN AND MIXED AND FULL BLOOD INDIAN CHILDREN[1]

By THOMAS R. GARTH
University of Denver

Of many principles of genetics we must be ever mindful in investigations of race psychology, but in the present experimental problem we would test out: First, the principle that like begets like, so that its mental product—here intelligence—tends to be different from the product of other origins;[2] Second, the principle that isolation of groups brings about differences in intelligence; Third, the principle that mixture of different lines brings about differences in intelligence as measured;[3] Fourth, the principle, which is an anthropological one, that nomadic peoples, because of the rigorous play of the law of natural selection, are more intelligent than sedentary peoples. Finally, we wish to arrange the blood groups which we are considering, *i.e.* Mexicans, mixed-blood Indians (composed of individuals having white and Indian ancestry, the latter being descendants of the Plains and Southeaster Indians in this case), full-blood Plains and Southeastern Indians (descendants of tribes of nomadic habits), full-blood Navajo and Apache tribes (likewise of nomadic ancestry but of habits somewhat different from that of the foregoing group), and full-blood Pueblo tribes (having ancestry with sedentary habits) in a series on an accepted scale for the measurement of intelligence in use in testing white children, *i.e.* the National Intelligence Test—Scale A.

In all experimental studies of this sort it is the obligation of the experimenter to endeavor to measure the behavior or such somatic tendencies producing mind as may be alone due to tendencies peculiar to racial germ cells and not to environmental

---

[1] Paper read before the American Psychological Association at Cambridge, Mass., December 29, 1922. A preliminary report of this experiment appeared in *Science*, 635-636.

[2] E. L. Thorndike, 'Educational Psychology,' Vol. 3, p. 250.

[3] E. L. Thorndike, *ibid.*, p. 264.

influences alone. If he was not able after strenuous effort to control all other factors so that the result may be said to be a measure of behavior due to the influence of germ plasm, no desire on his part to make a clean-cut statement should induce him to hasten to draw conclusion relative to race differences.

THE SUBJECTS OF THE EXPERIMENT

We have for study behavior due to the influence of germ plasm on somatic behavior of three full-blood Indian groups, two of them of nomadic ancestry; that is, first, a group of Plains and Southeastern Indians; second, a group of Navajo and Apache Indians; and we have one of sedentary ancestry; that is, third, a group of Pueblo Indians. A fourth group is of mixed-blood Indians representing a mixture of germ plasm of whites and Plains and Southeastern Indians. Group five is composed of Mexicans, representing the typical 'Mexican' whose ancestry is largely of Spanish blood and of various—probably all—nomadic tribes of Mexico.

We were obliged to take the statements of the Indian subjects as to degree of Indian blood, as *full* or *mixed*, since there were at hand no means for us to determine this by anthropometric measures. Such figures are taken at their face value by the United State Government in the absence of better determination of amount of blood.

When the tests were given to the Mexican children, the experimenter likewise took at its face value the classification of the white teachers of the several schools who said that they knew the subjects to be Mexicans. As it was, most of the subjects themselves claimed to be Mexicans, though four said they were of Italian and Mexican parentage, four of Irish and Mexican, two of French and Mexican, two of Danish and Mexican, and one of English and Mexican parentage. In all these cases but one, the mothers were said to be Mexicans. We should say, however, that the term Mexican as used here is rather hard to define. At least we believe that it signifies the mixture of Spanish with Mexican Indian (of nomadic habits) germ plasm, with the few exceptions mentioned. To be sure this means that we are taking the reports at their face value and they appear to be correct.

264

THE TEST AND ITS ADMINISTRATION[4]

The tests used in the experiment were the National Intelligence Tests, Scale A, and they were administered by the writer himself, except in two instances where he observed two of his students give them to two groups of Mexicans.

The tests of the Indians were given in the United States Indian Schools at Chilocco, Oklahoma, and at Albuquerque, New Mexico, and were likewise administered by the writer personally.[5]

HANDLING THE DATA

We have handled the data looking to the solution of the following problems:

1. Do the frequencies for the measures of the groups arrange themselves with multimodality, or are the measures continuous on the scale?

2. Are there differences in central tendencies between the several groups as indicated by overlapping?

3. Are the differences consistent for all subgroups of the blood group as measured by the central tendencies?

4. Are these tendencies to differ consistent when the performances of the upper and lower ranges are compared in all subgroups of the blood groups?

5. Which blood groups differ most?

6. Are the differences to be regarded as race differences?

―――――――――

[4] Acknowledgment is here made to Superintendent Jeremiah Rhodes and his assistant, Mr. W. J. Knox, for the courtesy extended the experimenter in allowing him to give the tests in the San Antonio (Texas) Schools, as well as to the various principals and their teachers who rendered especial assistance. Likewise the writer acknowledges the help of Miss Georgia Colvin, A.B., and Miss Irma Gesche, A.B., who acted as attendants in the administration of these tests at San Antonio. These tests to the Mexicans were given in the spring of 1922.

[5] The expedition to the Indian Schools in which these tests were given was financed by the Grants Committee of the American Association for the Advancement of Science, and occurred in the spring of 1921. The writer acknowledges the courtesies shown by Superintendent C. M. Blair, of the Chilocco U.S. Indian School, and Superintendent Reuben Perry, of the Albuquerque U.S. Indian School, in affording him the privilege of giving the tests to the students in their schools. In the latter school Mr. Fred Lobdell assisted in planning the testing program.

265

THE QUESTION OF MULTIPLE TYPES

The question will be answered by examining the distribution surfaces for the blood groups. Because many of the blood groups are small we have been compelled to combine the age and sex groups, so that we have of Mexicans 307 cases; mixed-blood Indians 126; Plains and Southeastern full-blood Indians 176; Pueblo full-blood Indians 249; Navajo and Apache full-blood 85. Whether or not our data when arranged in five frequency distributions indicates in single instances multimodality may be seen by an examination of the curves representing the distributions themselves, as shown in Fig. 1a. It will be seen here that the scores of each of the blood groups tend to cluster around single central tendencies, though the distribution surfaces are not absolutely symmetrical. The greatest disposition toward flattening is shown by the pure-blood groups—the Plains and Southeastern group and the Pueblo group. We may ignore the appearance of the Navajo and Apache group because of its small number, 85. But in the mixed-blood group, where we would expect to find bimodality, it does not appear. However, the Mexican group shows some indication of multimodality because of the two small subsidiary peaks. Even so they are only slight and but for the largeness of the groups and homogeneity as to age of the subjects (12-16 years), might be ignored. But we cannot think this multimodal tendency here indicated is necessarily due to diversity of germ cells, because if the curve here shown were broken into three smaller curves based on age, only one of these, the curve for the 12-13 year olds, shows the multimodality. The others represented are fairly symmetrical.

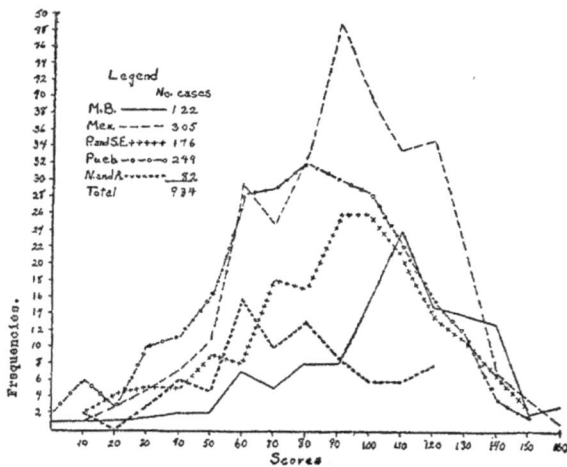

FIG. 1a

266

The answer, then, to the question as to the multimodality would seem to be a negative one; that is, each group whether mixed or full-blood tends to have a single central tendency.

GROUP DIFFERENCES AND SCORE SEQUENCES

The classification of the subgroups of the blood groups has been made on the basis of age. The ages run from 12 to 19 years. Because these numbers for a single age were too small it was necessary to combine the age subgroups, and even then some of the subgroups are all too small. Table I. gives the number of cases, average score, median, and percent of any age subgroups attaining the median score of the Plains and Southeastern respective age subgroups.

It will be seen that always the central tendencies of the mixed-blood scores are highest; that on the same base of determining, the Mexicans invariably come second; the Plains and Southeastern full-bloods come fourth, except in the last, 18-19 years subgroups, when the Navajo and Apache scores are slightly superior. The central tendencies of scores for the last named group, the Navajo and Apache, but for the smallness of the groups, would indicate that they are the least intelligent, as indicated by these tests, of all the blood groups. See Table I.

TABLE I

THE RELATIVE INTELLIGENCE OF INDIANS AND NOMADIC AND SEDENTARY TRIBES AND MIXED BLOOD INDIANS

The scores are of the National Intelligence Tests, Scale A, Form I.

	No. Cases	Score Median	% attaining median of P.I & S.E.	Average Score	P.E.
12 and 13 years:					
Mixed Bloods	15	103	80%	83.6	12.6
Mexicans	145	85	60	81.7	19.2
Plains and S.E.	8	76	–	74.8	–
Pueblo	46	64	40	68.8	5.24
Navajo and Apache	12	52	10	57.8	13.2
14 and 15 years:					
Mixed Bloods	30	110	80	93.9	15.1
Mexicans	132	92	70	91.5	17.9
Plains and S.E.	55	85	–	85.2	20.5
Pueblo	82	80	44	79.4	18.6

Navajo and Apache	19	60	20	66.3	18.7
16 and 17 year olds:					
Mixed Bloods	41	104	71	96.9	14.4
Mexicans	28	91	54	92.3	15.3
Plains and S.E.	60	90	-	87.3	18.5
Pueblo	95	78	34	78	21.2
Navajo and Apache	30	77	23	76.2	19.1
18 and 19 year olds:					
Mixed Bloods	31	114	60	101.6	19.9
Mexicans	2	-	-	-	-
Plains and S.E.	53	88	-	81.4	19.8
Pueblo	26	71	30	70	22.7
Navajo and Apache	24	77	40	75.3	18.6

The tests for a difference as indicated by the overlapping, using the median scores of the Plains and Southeastern age subgroups as a base, indicate that these differences are real differences generally, except in the case of the Plains and Southeastern and Pueblo full-bloods where the differences only tend to be real in favor of the former. Moreover, the differences seem to grow less secure as the ages of the subgroups increase, in the case of all but the Pueblos, who lose somewhat by this comparison, for the older Pueblo Indians seem to be less intelligent, as thus indicated, than the younger ones when brought into comparison with Plains and Southeastern Indian intelligence as measured. On the other hand, the Navajos and Apaches gain. The facts are very well represented by the percentile charts which show graphically the above mentioned sequences. See Figs. 1*b*, 2, 3, 4.

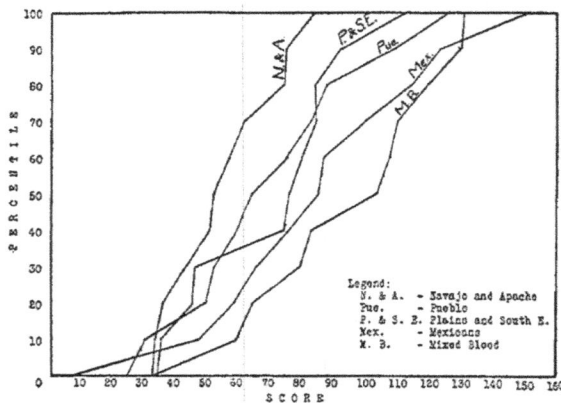

FIG. 1*b*.   Percentile chart for N. I. T., Scale A.   12 and 13 years.

268

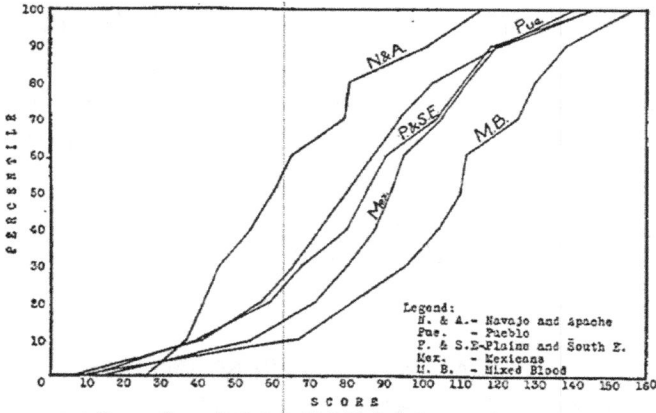

Fig. 2. Percentile chart for N. I. T., Scale A. 14 and 15 years.

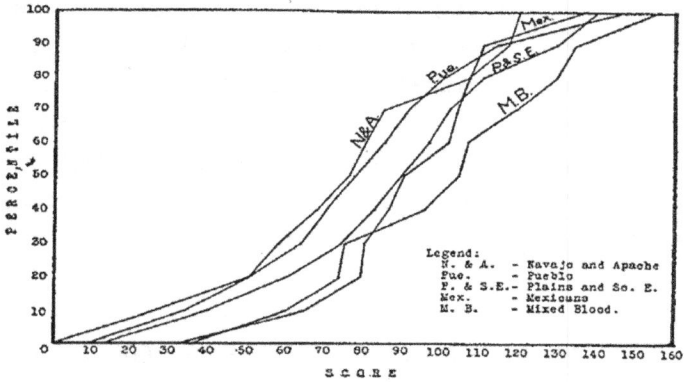

Fig. 3. Percentile chart for N. I. T., Scale A. 16 and 17 years.

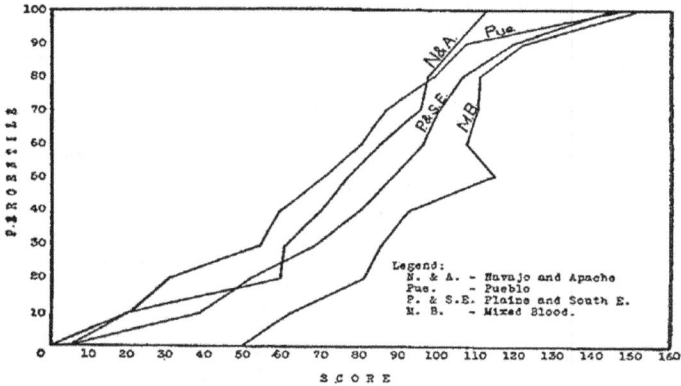

Fig. 4. Percentile chart for N. I. T., Scale A. 18 and 19 years.

269

If we take the overlapping of a subgroup on the Plains and Southeastern median as the index of a difference, the figures of the table show that these measures are just about as great when we compare Mexicans and Plains and Southeastern blood groups, as when we compare Plains and Southeastern and Pueblo subgroups. That is, there is not quite as much difference between Mexicans and nomadic Indians as there is between the latter and the sedentary Indians. In both cases the differences tend to be real. If the number of cases of the Navajo and Apache subgroups were larger we might hazard some similar conclusions. Here the measures of overlapping show them to stand below the Pueblo Indians.

UPPER AND LOWER PERCENTILES

An examination of the scores in the upper and lower percentiles, as represented in Table II. in the percentile graphs, indicates less of a difference than is found in a comparison of the interquartile ranges. This is what would be found presumably in the comparison of any groups measured by a similar device. It appears that the most intelligent individuals in the several groups are more alike than the representative or average individuals, and even so may this be said of the least intelligent ones. However, the sequence as indicated by comparing median and averages holds fairly well in these groups upon comparing upper and lower percentile scores.

TABLE II
SHOWING PERCENTILE SCORE FOR AGE GROUPS
NATIONAL INTELLIGENCE TEST
SCALE A

12 and 13 years

	No. Cases	Scores										
Navajo and Apache	12	32	33	36	43	51	52	57	62	74	75	84
Pueblo	46	24	30	44	52	59	64	75	83	88	109	126
Plains and S.E.	8	34	35	45	46	74	76	80	84	84	92	112
Mexicans	145	7	47	58	65	76	85	87	100	114	123	152
Mixed Bloods	15	32	58	64	79	83	103	107	110	119	129	131
Percentile		0	10	20	30	40	50	60	70	80	90	100

14 and 15 years

	No. Cases	Scores										
Navajo and Apache	19	26	37	42	46	54	60	65	79	81	102	116
Pueblo	82	6	42	57	66	73	80	88	94	103	121	141
Plains and S.E.	55	12	40	58	67	80	85	91	104	111	118	146
Mexicans	132	15	54	72	80	87	92	95	105	112	120	146
Mixed Bloods	30	10	67	82	96	104	110	112	126	130	138	156
Percentile		0	10	20	30	40	50	60	70	80	90	100

16 and 17 years

	No. Cases	Scores										
Navajo and Apache	30	9	34	51	58	68	77	81	86	107	117	120
Pueblo	95	0	26	51	64	71	78	86	92	101	114	147
Plains and S.E.	60	13	40	61	74	83	90	97	102	111	129	140
Mexicans	28	33	65	79	81	87	91	102	104	107	111	137
Mixed Bloods	41	36	60	74	76	96	104	107	119	129	134	156
Percentile		0	10	20	30	40	50	60	70	80	90	100

18 and 19 years

	No. Cases	Scores										
Navajo and Apache	24	4	21	59	61	70	77	86	95	97	109	112
Pueblo	26	0	21	31	54	59	71	61	87	98	107	147
Plains and S.E.	53	3	38	52	68	80	88	96	100	106	119	145
Mexicans	2	–	–	–	–	–	–	–	–	–	–	–
Mixed Bloods	31	49	63	82	86	93	114	107	110	111	122	151
Percentile		0	10	20	30	40	50	60	70	80	90	100

271

THE DIFFERENCES MEASURED

Table III. shows the median score of any blood subgroup expressed as a percent of the median score of the respective Plains and Southeastern subgroup. It will be seen that on the average the mixed-blood median score is 27 percent better than that of the Plains and Southeastern median scores; the Mexican 7 percent better, on the average; the Pueblo 14 percent poorer and the Navajo and Apache 23 percent poorer on the average.

TABLE III
MEDIAN INTELLIGENCE SCORES FOR SUBGROUPS EXPRESSED AS PERCENTAGE OF RESPECTIVE PLAINS AND SOUTHEASTERN MEDIANS

Subgroup Age	Mixed Blood %	Mexican %	Plains and Southeastern %	Pueblo %	Navajo and Apache %
12-13	135	112	100	84	68
14-15	129	108	100	94	70
16-17	115	101	100	86	85
18-19	128	-	100	81	87
Average %	127	107		86	77

SOCIAL STATUS AND EDUCATION

Any conclusions which may be here reached must be made in the light of the facts of nurture, or modification of native tendencies. School children in the United States Indian Schools were selected for the reason that it was desired to control the factors of education and training as far as possible.

TABLE IV
SHOWING AVERAGE AMOUNT OF SCHOOL ATTAINMENT

Subgroup	12–13 yrs.	14–15 yrs.	16–17 yrs.	18–19 yrs.	Average
Mixed Bloods	5.1 yrs.	6.0 yrs.	6.4 yrs.	6.8 yrs.	6.1 yrs.
Mexicans	5.3 "	5.9 "	6.3 "	0.0 "	5.9 "
Plains and S.E.	4.6 "	5.6 "	5.6 "	5.9 "	5.4"
Pueblos	4.8 "	5.7 "	6.4 "	6.3 "	5.8 "
Navajo and Apache	4.8 "	4.7 "	5.2 "	6.3 "	5.2"

Table IV. shows the amount of school education of each of the age subgroups. On the whole the blood group having the most school training is seen to be that of the mixed-blood; next or second, the Mexicans; third, the Pueblo Indians; fourth, the Plains and Southeastern group; and fifth, Navajo and Apache. As to social status we shall have to depend on expert opinion alone which is given merely as a general impression after much experience in working with Indian schools. We quote here a statement of Superintendent C. M. Blair, of the United State Indian School of Chilocco, Oklahoma.

He says: "1. I think there is no question but that the presence of a child in the home where one parent is white will influence the child to behave more as a white man behaves. It is simply a question of the influence of environment. In the full-blood home the atmosphere of the home is more backward and less influenced by the white civilization.

"2. The mixed-blood has more opportunities to learn English in the home because the English language is used to a greater extent than the Indian language. In the full-blood home, generally speaking, the Indian language is used to a considerable extent even though the parents may be well educated, just as in the home of the Swede of German the old mother-tongue is used to a considerable extent. Therefore, I would say that a mixed-blood has a better opportunity to learn the English language than a full-blood by reason of the difference in the home.

"3. There is no question but that the Oklahoma Indian has been more closely associated with white civilization than the Pueblo Indian, and is more familiar with white ways and the English language. His contact with the white has been of longer duration and more intimate.

"4. The Navajo and Apache are both farther removed, in my judgment, from the white influence than the Pueblo. The Pueblo lives along the Rio Grande valley in

273

New Mexico, which has attracted white people more strongly than the mesas and desert country which is the home of the Navajo and Apache. Therefore the large reservations on which we find the Navajos and Apaches have very little contact with the white and are consequently not so much influenced as to habits and language as the Pueblo. Also the Navajos and Apaches have stronger characters naturally than the Pueblos and do not assimilate the white civilization as readily. The Navajo, to my mind, is the finest Indian unspoiled in our life today. He has been working out his living for centuries, and for him, making a success of it.

"5. It is more legitimate to compare the Pueblo with the Mexican as a mixed-blood than with ordinary mixed-bloods of Oklahoma. The Pueblo speaks Spanish and his mode of living is very similar to that of the Mexican. However, the Pueblo is not very fond of the Mexican and there are many differences in characteristics."

In view of this statement which we believe gives the facts as to social status in a rather trustworthy way, we may say then—recognizing that the Mexican is a mixed-blood individual from a home in which Spanish is the language largely spoken—the social status of the mixed-blood is the most superior of all the blood-groups; second, come the Mexicans; third, the Plains and Southeastern Indians; fourth, the Pueblo; and fifth, the Navajo and Apache groups. It will be noted, however, that the Pueblo blood-groups have had more schooling than the Plains and Southeastern Indians and this seem to offset somewhat the latter's better social status.

There are two other studies of intelligence of Indians in the literature of racial psychology to date: one by E. C. Rowe, who gave Binet-Simon individual tests to 268 Indian children and found that 94.2 percent tested below age, 4.6 percent at age, and 1.2 percent above age, making no allowance in these figures for social status.[6] The other study is by Walter S. Hunter, who, assisted by Eloise Sommermier,[7] investigated the relative intelligence of Indians of different degrees of Indian blood and intelligence score. As in the case of Rowe's study and of the present study, it was impossible to secure figures measuring the social status. However, Hunter is of the opinion that

---

[6] E. C. Rowe, 'Five Hundred Forty-Seven White and Two Hundred Sixty-Eight Indian Children Tested by the Binet-Simon Tests,' *Ped. Sem.*, 1914, 21, 454-468.

[7] Walter S. Hunter assisted by Eloise Sommermier, 'The Relation of Degree of Indian Blood to Score on the Otis Intelligence Test,' *J. of Comp. Psychol.*, 1922, 2, 257-275.

"Inferior social status may well be the result of low intelligence rather than its partial cause."[8]

AGE-GRADE COMPARISON

In an experiment of this sort it would be desirable, in order to control all possible factors except the one to be measured, to make an age-grade comparison. We have not been able as yet to do this with any satisfaction as to conclusiveness of results.

SUMMARY

1. In the distribution surface we find unimodality to be the general rule even in the case of the mixed-blood groups. Finer measures might bring to light multimodality in these cases.

2. The measure of intelligence indicates the following sequence: first, mixed-bloods; second, Mexicans; third, Plains and Southeastern Indians; fourth, Pueblo Indians; fifth, Navajo and Apache Indians. The ratios are respectively: 127, 107, 100, 88, 77, using Plains and Southeastern Indians as the base.

3. Estimates of social status indicate the same sequence as the foregoing.

4. The average amount of education of the blood groups runs in the same sequence except that the Pueblo Indians have slightly more of this than the Plains and Southeastern Indians.

5. The mixed breeds excel the pure breeds in intelligence scores.

6. The scores of those individuals of nomadic tribes excel those of sedentary tribes.

7. If these groups may be taken as representative of their racial stocks, the results indicate differences between their racial stocks in intelligence as here measured.

8. Because of the fact that social status and education have not been controlled, we may not positively state that these data indicate innate racial differences in intelligence but one is inclined to believe that differences in opportunity and in mental attitude toward the white man's way of thinking and living are here made apparent. In some schools the latter is taken as indicative of degree of intelligence according as to whether the attitude is positive, indifferent, or actually negative.

---

[8] *Ibid.*, p. 274.

Goodenough, F.L. (1926). Racial differences in the intelligence of
school children. *Journal of Experimental Psychology, 9*(5), 388-397.

RACIAL DIFFERENCES IN THE INTELLIGENCE OF SCHOOL CHILDREN

By FLORENCE L. GOODENOUGH
Institute of Child Welfare, University of Minnesota

The widespread interest in tests of intelligence which has sprung up in this country during recent years has led to a number of studies of the comparative performance of various immigrant groups and their immediate descendants. No attempt will here be made to review these studies in detail; but the general nature of the results of them with respect to children of school age has been summarized in the accompanying list. For the greater part these studies are based upon American-born children; although it is probable that in some instances foreign-born children have also been included.

The figures presented are representative of the findings of a number of other investigators whose results have not been included. They also correspond rather closely to the scores made by the different nativity groups in the Army Intelligence Tests as reported by Brigham (3). It should be emphasized that figures such as these have reference only to the representatives of the various nationality groups who have immigrated to this country, and that selective immigration may be in large measure responsible for the results which have been obtained. That these immigrant groups and their immediate descendants markedly differ in their performances in the ordinary type of intelligence-test is a fact which appears to have been reasonably well established.

Two theories have been offered to account for these differences. The first ascribes the inferior showing made by the South Europeans and the negroes to such post-natal factors as inferior environment, poor physical condition and linguistic handicaps. The second point of view, while it recognizes that the factors named may to some degree affect the test-results, nevertheless holds that it is impossible to account for all the facts which have been observed upon any other hypothesis than that of innate differences among the groups under consideration.

INTELLECTUAL ABILITY OF AMERICAN SCHOOL CHILDREN BY RACIAL STOCK

Racial Stock	Reported by	Cases	Test used	Result
White American	Pintner and Keller (28)	249	Stanford-Binet	Mean IQ 95
White American	Sheldon (34)	100	"	104
White American	Dickson (9)	49	"	106
American Negro (Ohio)	Pintner and Keller (28)	71	"	88
American Negro (Tennessee)	Petereson (27)	All children 8-10 yrs. in several schools	Pressey	75
American Negro (Arkansas)	Jordan (18)	247	N.I.T.	14-yr. negroes equal to 10-yr. whites
American Negro (Northern)	Thorndike (40)	349	I.E.R.	Ca. 4 per cent. negroes passed median scores for whites of same grade
American Negro	Sunne (36)	Over 1,000	N.I.T. and Myers	Negro ave. 1-13 yrs. below whites (mental age)
English	Pintner and Keller (28)	24	Standford-Binet	Mean IQ 97
English	Brown (4)	90	"	101.8
Italian	Pintner and Keller (28)	313	"	84
Italian	Dickson (9)	25	"	84
Italian	Young (45)	Several hundred	Army Alpha and Beta	About 83
Italian	Brown (4)	51	Stanford-Binet	77.5
German	Pintner and Keller (28)	37	"	91
German	Brown (4)	67	"	102.3
Jewish	Pintner and Keller (28)	79	"	95
Jewish	Murdock (24)	Several hundred	Pressey	Jews. approx. equal to white Americans
Chinese (San Francisco)	Young (44)	109	Stanfrod-Binet	Median IQ 97

Chinese (Hawaiian)	Symonds (38)	513	Pintner non-language	Mean IQ 99
Spanish-Mexican	Sheldon (34)	100	Stanford-Binet and Cole-Vincent	89
Spanish-Mexican	Dickson (9)	37	Stanford-Binet	78
Portuguese	Young (45) (Quoting unpub'ed data by Roll)	119	Stanford-Binet	86
Portuguese	Dickson (9)	23	"	84
Norwegian	Brown (4)	34	"	101.8
Swedish	Brown (4)	187	"	101.9
Austrian	Brown (4)	28	"	99.5
French	Brown (4)	199	"	95.4
Finnish	Brown (4)	226	"	90
Slavish	Pintner and Keller (28)	130	"	85
Hungarian	Pintner and Keller (28)	99	"	89
Indian (Michigan)	Rowe (32)	268	Goddard-Binet	Only 5.8 per cent. of Indians tested at or above
Indian	Hunter (17)	711	Otis	Whites excel Inidans by 1.6 P.E. of latter. Correl'n bet. degree of white blood and score = .51 ± .017

It is unquestionably true that the home surroundings of certain racial groups, notably the Italians and negroes, are, as a rule, far less favorable than those of average American children. Not only is this true of the foreign-born Italians, but their American-born descendants frequently continue to live in the same neighborhoods and with little or no improvement in social or hygienic conditions. In this respect a notable difference may be observed between the Italian and the Jew. Both find a home in the slum on first coming to this country; but while the Italian remains there, the Jew soon moves to a better neighborhood.

"Social pressure" or "race prejudice" is often urged as a reason for the segregation of certain racial groups within the poorer neighborhoods. In this connection it should be remembered that while racial prejudice may bring about segregation, the character of the neighborhoods thus set off is primarily dependent upon the people living within them. It is doubtful whether even the Southern negro has more to contend with in the way of this prejudice than the Chinese or Japanese in California; yet the contrast between the typical Oriental neighborhood and the Italian or negro district is marked. Poverty there may be; but the squalor which is characteristic of the Italian and the negro sections is lacking.

It seems probable, upon the whole, that inferior environment is an effect at least as much as it is a course of inferior ability, as the latter is indicated by intelligence tests. The person of neighborhoods where the economic requirement is minimal; and, once there, he reacts toward his surroundings along the line of least resistance. His children inherit his mental characteristics.

The question of a possible handicap in language as a cause of low scores on intelligence tests is, however, more serious. Berry (2), Brown (4), Jordan (19), Darsie (46) and others have shown that children from foreign homes rank, on the average, somewhat lower in tests requiring the use of English than they rank on non-language scales. On the other hand, the use of a non-language scale does not result in equal ratings for the various nationality-groups. The Italian continues to rank low even on the non-verbal tests; while the average Japanese child who has had three or four years' training in American schools makes a good showing, despite the handicap of language, on such a test as the Stanford-Binet.

In this connection it is interesting to compare races with respect to the persistence of the use of the foreign language in the home. Jordan (19) has collected information on this head from his study of the school children of Minneapolis and St. Paul. His method of treating the data is unfortunately misleading, since he bases his figures upon the total number of parents of a given nationality, regardless of the length of time they have been in this country. He shows, for each of the eleven nationalities which he considers, the percentage of the total number of parents who have adopted English as the language of preferential use in the home; also the percentages who continue to use the foreign language after ten, twenty, and thirty years; residence in this county. It is not possible, from the data which he gives, to arrive at the really significant figures which would be either the average length of residence before English is adopted as the home language, or the percentage of those who have been in this country ten, twenty, or thirty years and still use the foreign language in the home.

When the ratio of the number of parents who have been in this country twenty years or longer and still use the foreign language in the home to the total who have either been in this country twenty or more years or (disregarding length of residence) have adopted English as the home language (Jordan, pp. 28-29, Tables 8-9) is calculated, results are obtained as shown in the following table. The median IQs for nine of these nationality-groups as reported by Brown (4) or Murdock (24) are given for comparison. Jordan's results do not include the IQs for his groups.

TABLE I
PERSISTENCE OF FOREIGN LANGUAGE COMPARED WITH INTELLIGENCE

Nationality	Foreign Language Ratio	Median IQ
German	20.1 to 100	102.3
Danish	31.6 " 100	.....
Roumanian Jew	39.7 " 100	98.0
Norwegian	49.2 " 100	103.8
Swedish	53.1 " 100	101.9
Bohemian	76.9 " 100	.....
Austrian	77.8 " 100	99.5
Russian Jew	79.7 " 100	98.0
Italian	86.4 " 100	77.5
Slovak	88.4 " 100	85.0
Finnish	97.4 " 100	90.0

The rank-order correlation between foreign language ratio and IQ, as given above, is - .754. This might be considered evidence that the use of a foreign language in the home is one of the chief factors in producing mental retardation as measured by intelligence tests. A more probable explanation is that those nationality-groups whose average intellectual ability is inferior do not readily learn the new language.

The results about to be presented are based upon results obtained from 2,457 public school children, practically all of whom were American-born but in whose

281

immediate ancestry a number of racial stocks are represented. Children of mixed parentage have not been included except in the case of the negroes, where no attempt has been made to differentiate between the mulatto and the pure negro, and the Indians, many of whom are "half-breeds." The test used was the Goodenough intelligence test for young children.[1] This test is based upon drawings of the human figure, and is completely independent of language. It would seem, therefore, that it should be entirely fair to the child of foreign parentage. The distribution of intelligence quotients earned on this test by children of different racial origin is shown in Table II, the data being collected from the following schools.

1. Three schools for colored children; one in Chattanooga, Tennessee, one in Mt. Pleasant, Tennessee, and one in Natchitoches, Louisiana.
2. Three schools for white children from the same cities.
3. Three schools from Fresno, California. The enrollment of these schools was largely foreign.
4. One school from Los Angeles, California. This school was made up almost entirely of Italian and Mexican children.
5. The Hoopa Valley Indian School, California.
6. Five kindergarteners from Santa Clara County, California.
7. One school from San Jose, California. The population was largely foreign, embracing a number of nationalities.
8. Grades one to four were included in the case of groups 1, 2, and 5. In the remaining cases only the first three grades were taken. All children enrolled in these grades for whom facts as to racial stock were available are included in these distributions.

Insofar as this scale can be considered a measure of intellectual development, the results are significant. Although the test is entirely independent of language, the South European and negro groups rank very much below the American children and those of North European stock. The rank-order of the various nationality-groups corresponds very closely to that found by means of other intelligence test. (See the list above.) The coefficient of variability is highest for the negroes and lowest for the Jewish children. The high variability of the negroes is probably due to the mulattoes.

---

[1] F. L. Goodenough, *The measurement of intelligence by drawings*, World Book Co., Yonkers, 1926; A new approach to the measurement of the intelligence of young children, *Ped. Sem. & J. Genet. Psychol.*, June, 1926.

The comparative homogeneity of the Jewish group may be due either to the effects of selective immigration (these are all California cases) or to the alleged ethnological "purity" of the Jewish race.

There is no reason for thinking these children to be other than fairly representative of their several racial groups as found in this country, except in the case of the American children. In order to be absolutely fair to the foreign groups, it was decided not to include any schools from superior residential districts in these distributions. The population of such schools is, as a rule, made up almost entirely of American children whose intelligence is, on the average, distinctly above that of the American children residing in foreign sections, who make up the bulk of the cases included under this group in Table II.

IQ	American	American	Italian	Spanish-Mexican	California Negroes	Southern Negroes	Hoopa Valley Indians	Jewish	Chinese	Japanese	Germans	Portuguese	English and Scotch	French and Swiss	Danish, Swedish and Norwegian	Assyrian, Slavonian, and Siberian
160	1		1	1												
150	2	0	0	1												
140	11	1	1	0	0	1		1	1	1	1				1	
130	22	1	3	4	0	1		4	1	4	1	1	1		1	1
120	44	2	15	12	3	8	2	5	4	1	5	0	0	2	3	0
110	75	13	27	27	5	19	1	14	2	7	1	0	4	2	8	5
100	103	20	58	45	4	52	8	11	7	8	6	2	2	1	5	5
90	116	32	100	73	10	84	20	12	4	10	7	4	3	3	5	7
80	69	29	115	93	17	104	22	5	4	8	4	3	2	3	6	3

IQ	American	American	Italian	Spanish–Mexican	California Negroes	Southern Negroes	Hoopa Valley Indians	Jewish	Chinese	Japanese	Germans	Portuguese	English and Scotch	French and Swiss	Danish, Swedish and Norwegian	Assyrian, Slavonian, and Siberian
70	44	16	98	65	17	125	15	3	2	2	3	0	2	2	1	4
60	11	9	34	35	10	155	10			1	1	1		0	1	3
50	2		4	9	2	51	1							1		1
40				3		11										
30						2										
Total Cases	500	123	456	367	69	613	79	55	25	42	29	11	14	14	31	29
Mdn	100.3	91.8	87.5	87.2	82.7	76.5	85.6	106.3	103.1	99.5	98.8	93.3	99.5	92.8	104.5	94.5
Mean	101.5	92.3	89.1	88.5	85.8	78.7	85.6	106.1	104.1	101.9	101.1	94.5	100.2	94.5	103.5	92.8
S.D.	18.3	15.6	16.0	17.5	18.7	17.5	14.1	16.2	18.0	18.0	19.3	16.5	16.8	19.6	17.8	18.8
Coeff of Var	18.0	16.9	18.0	19.8	21.8	22.2	16.5	15.3	17.2	17.7	19.1	17.5	16.8	20.7	17.2	20.3

SUMMARY

1. Children of different racial groups have been found to differ greatly in their performance on a primary group-test designed to measure intellectual capacity. Since the test used is entirely non-verbal, these differences cannot be explained on the basis of a linguistic handicap.

2. Although the test is completely independent of language, the rank-orders of the various racial groups correspond very closely to the results of other investigators using verbal tests.

284

REFERENCES

1. ARLITT, A. H. On the need for caution in establishing race norms, *J. Appl. Psychol.*, 1921, 3, 179-183.

2. BERRY, C. B. The classification by tests of intelligence of ten thousand first grade children, *J. Educ. Res.*, 1922, 6, 185-203.

3. BRIGHAM, C. A study of American intelligence, *Princeton Univ. Press*, 1923.

4. BROWN, G. Intelligence as related to nationality, *J. Educ. Res.*, 1922, 6, 324-327.

5. BRUNER, F. C. Racial differences, *Psychol. Bull.*, 1914, 11, 384-386.

6. COOLEY, C. H. Genius, fame, and the comparison of races, *Ann. Amer. Acad. Pol. & Soc. Sci.*, 1897, 9, 317-358.

7. DAVENPORT, C. B. Comparative social traits of various races, *School & Soc.*, 1921, 14, 344-348.

8. DERRICK, S. M. A comparative study of the intelligence of 75 white and 55 colored college students by the Stanford revision of the Binet-Simon scale, *J. Appl. Psychol.*, 1920, 4, 316-329.

9. DICKSON, V. E. *The relation of mental testing to school administration, with special reference to children entering school*, Master's Thesis, Stanford University.

10. FARIS, E. The mental capacity of savages, *Amer. J. Soc.*, 1918, 23, 603-619.

11. FERGUSON, G. The psychology of the negro, *Arch. of Psychol.*, 1916, no. 36, 138.

12. GARTH, T. R. The results of some tests on full and mixed blood indians, *J. Appl. Psychol.*, 1921, 3, 359-372.

13. GARTH, T. R. A comparison of mental abilities of mixed and full blood indians on a bases of education, *Psychol. Rev.*, 1922, 29, 221-236.

14. GARTH, T. R. White, Indian, and Negro work curves, *J. Appl. Psychol.*, 1921, 5, 14-25.

15. GARTH, T. R. Racial differences in mental fatigue, *J. Appl. Psychol.*, 1920, 4, 235-244.

16. HERRICK, D. S. A comparison of Brahman and Panchama children in South India with each other and with American children by means of the Goddard foam board, *J. Appl. Psychol.*, 1921, 3, 253-260.

285

17. HUNTER, W. S., & SOMMERMIER, E. The relation of the degree of Indian blood to score on the Otis intelligence test, *J. Comp. Psychol.*, 1922, 2, 257-277.

18. JORDAN, A. M. Notes on racial differences, *School & Soc.*, 1922, 16, 503-504.

19. JORDAN, R. H. *Nationality and school progress; a study in americanisation*, Pub. School Pub. Co., 1921.

20. MCDOUGALL, W. *Is America safe for democracy?* 1921.

21. MAYO, M. J. The mental capacity of the American negro, *Arch. of Psychol.*, 1913, no. 28.

22. MITCHELL, I., ROSANOFF, I. & A. A study of association in negro children, *Psychol. Rev.*, 1919, 26, 354-359.

23. MORSE, J. A comparative study of white and colored children by the Binet tests, *J. Educ. Psychol.*, 1913, 366-367.

24. MURDOCH, K. A study of race differences in New York City, *School & Soc.*, 1920, 11, 147-150.

25. MYERS, C. S. *International race problems*, (G. Spiller, ed.), 1911.

26. PERRING, L. F. A study of the comparative retardation of negro and white children in Philadelphia, *Psychol. Clinic*, 1915, 8, 87-93.

27. PETERSON, JOSEPH. The comparative abilities of white and negro children, *Comp. Psychol. Monog.*, 1923, 1, (no. 5).

28. PINTNER, R., & KELLER, R. Intelligence test of foreign children, *J. Educ. Psychol.*, 1922, 6, 214-222.

29. PYLE, W. H. A study of the mental and physical characteristics of the Chinese, *School & Soc.*, 1918, 8, 264-269.

30. PYLE, W. H. The mind of the negro child, *School & Soc.*, 1915, 1, 357-360.

31. REUTER, E. B. *The Mulatto in the United States*, Badger, 1918.

32. ROWE, E. C. Five hundred forty-seven whites and two hundred sixty-eight Indian children tested by the Binet-Simon scale, *Ped. Sem.*, 1914, 21, 454-468.

33. SCHWEGLER, R. A., & WINN, E. A comparative study of the intelligence of white and colored children, *J. Educ. Res.*, 1920, 2, 838-848.

34. SHELDON, W. H. The intelligence of Mexican children, *School & Soc.*, 1924, 19, 139-142.

286

35. SUNNE, D. A comparative study of white and negro children. *J. Appl. Psychol.*, 1917, 1, 71-83.

36. SUNNE, D. Comparison of white and negro children in verbal and non-verbal tests, *School & Soc.*, 1924, 19, 469-472.

37. STRONG, A. C. Three hundred fifty white and colored children measured by the Binet-Simon scale of intelligence; a comparative study, *Ped. Sem.*, 1913, 20, 485-515.

38. SYMONDS, P. M. The intelligence of Chinese in Hawaii, *School & Soc.*, 1924, 19, 442.

39. THOMAS, W. I. Race psychology, *Amer. J. Soc.*, 1912, 17, 725-775.

40. THORNDIKE, E. L. Intelligence test scores of colored pupils in high schools, *School & Soc.*, 1923, 18, 569.

41. WALCOTT, G. D. The intelligence of Chinese students, *School & Soc.*, 1920, 11, 474-480.

42. WOODS, F. A. The racial origin of successful Americans, *Pop. Sci. Mo.*, 1914, 84, 397-402.

43. WOODWORTH, R. S. Racial differences in mental traits, *Science*, 1910, 31, 171-186.

44. YOUNG, KWOK T. The intelligence of Chinese children in San Francisco and vicinity, *J. Appl. Psychol.*, 1921, 5, 267-274.

45. YOUNG, K. Mental differences in certain immigrant groups, *Univ. of Oregon Pub.* 1922, 1 (no. 11).

46. DARSIE, M. L. The mental capacity of American born Japanese children. *Comp. Psychol. Monog.*, 1925.

Lamb, E.O. (1930). Racial differences in bi-manual dexterity of Latin and American children. *Child Development*, *1*(3), 204-231.

RACIAL DIFFERENCES IN BI-MANUAL DEXTERITY OF LATIN AND AMERICAN CHILDREN

EMILY O. LAMB

In testing Latin and American children with the Stanford revision of the Binet-Simon tests over a period of ten years, the writer arrived at the conviction that Latin children are more dexterous with their hands than American children, so this investigation has been undertaken to prove or disprove that belief. Hollingworth and Poffenberger (5) in discussion form-board studies of different races, made by Woodward, (15), ask, "are there characteristics of mind peculiar to different races of men, which need to be considered from the point of view of efficiency?" There is "practically no attempt to separate the facts of inheritance from the effects of education, customs and general environmental conditions." "Experiments have been made on rather simple functions, such as sensory acuity, motor ability and simple judgments. Although the traits are simple, yet they are characteristics in which peoples are supposed, in the popular minds, to differ. The upshot of all the experimental tests seems to show that the racial differences in fundamental qualities, independent of training, are slight."

Woodward (15) considered the form-board test he used to be a fair test of intelligence, and depending very little on training. He found "between whites, Indians, Eskimos, Amus, Filipinos, and Singalese, the average differences were small and much overlapping occurred." But between these groups and the Ingorot and Nigroto from the Philippines and a few Pigmies from the Congo, the average differences were great and overlapping was small. Woodward says that the results would seem to indicate differences in intelligence, but as the fairness of the test is not beyond question, it may have been a more unfamiliar sort to these wild hunting folk than to the more settled groups.

Herrick's (4) studies of Brahman and Panchama children in South India, bring out interesting points on the question of physical maturity. At four years Brahman children exceeded American children in quickness of reaction, but at five years the American children have caught up, and from six years on the American children hold

289

the lead, being faster at every succeeding age studied. Herrick gives as one of the causes that in the tropics children mature earlier than in colder climates, so it is not surprising that four years old Indian children should be capable of faster performance than American four-year-olds.

Paschal and Sullivan (10) gave a series of standardized performance tests to Mexican children to attempt to determine racial differences in the mental and physical development of Mexican and American children. They found considerable overlapping in the top third of the distribution of most tests, but from the median downward the American children show increasing superiority, the difference being greater at nine years than at twelve. Less sex difference is found in Mexican children than in American children on performance tests.

Koch and Simmons (8) in an experimental study of American, Mexican, and Negro children, found that the city white children are younger, in grade for grade comparisons, than are the city Mexicans. That the city groups, whether American or Mexican, are younger for their grades than are their respective rural groups.

Murdock (9) studied 3 different racial groups in Hawaii, the Chinese, Japanese, and Korean, and found that the Chinese and Koreans were superior to the Japanese in tests involving language but in the Beta test the superiority of the Japanese is clearly shown.

Seashore (13) makes the statement in his "Psychology of Musical Talent"

"Thus we find among children those who are slow and sure, slow and erratic, quick and sure, quick and no one seriously expects these tendencies to be altered any more than he expects the leopard to change his spots. These permanent peculiarities we call 'the personal equation.' Raymert (12) carried out a study of a series of reactions of various muscle groups, to validate Seashore's claim, on the assumption that if the personal equation existed, it would manifest itself within recognizable limits. His conclusions were that 'a distinct personal equation for speed exists,'—with the reservation, however, that this personal equation is to some extent a different one for instantaneous motor performances than for motor performances of a continuous nature."

Other findings, which seem to indicate a "personal equation" are re-quoted by Ream (11). In an experiment on tapping rates, he states that,

"Every individual has his own motor set-up, one is geared slow, and another geared fast, the chief factor is probably a physiological openness of nerve paths which is inherited. The extended practice experiments of this study seemed to indicate that the test measures fundamental basic abilities since improvement was, on the whole, conspicuously lacking. The inference is that the motive neural set, undoubtedly an important condition of such basic ability, is inherited."

Among experiments employing but one hand at a time, is a very extensive and painstaking study by Wellman (14) on the Development of Motor Coordination in Young Children. Some of the results of her study of motor coordination are recorded as follows. There were no sex differences in the scores on either test. The scores at six years nearly doubled those made by the three-year-old children. Movements with the left hand were more difficult than movements with the right hand, and the differences with the two hands became greater as age increased. Children who made more accurate movements with the right hand, than others in the group, also made more accurate movements with the left hand.

As early as 1892 Bryan (1) invented a very complicated tracing-board which he used to considerable extent. Among the conclusions he reached was that the maximal rate of movement probably furnishes a test of the general condition of the central nervous system, of the nerve centers by which the muscles involved in the movement are controlled. He estimated that the rate of the child of six years was two thirds the rate of the youth of sixteen. Girls excel boys at thirteen years but are inferior at all other ages.

PROBLEM, TESTS, AND SELECTION OF SUBJECTS

During the teaching and supervising of art in schools in California some years ago, I found, especially in the low elementary grades, little difficulty in interesting both Italian and Mexican children in the subject of clay modeling and other hand work, such as basketry. Moreover Mexican children seemed unusually deft in handling clay and frequently turned out much more interesting results than did American children.

Later, in giving Binet tests to mixed groups, I found that the California Spanish, Mexican, and Italian children seldom failed on such tests as the tying of a bow, and the discrimination of weights, while the American children often failed to score a plus on those tests. Whether these differences are chance, environmental or real differences in ability is a problem upon which little conducive experimental work has been done.

The purpose of this investigation is to study the results of certain manual processes given to groups of American and Latin children with the hope that it may throw some light upon the question as to whether there are racial differences in bi-manual ability or whether it is a traditional attitude with some persons to expect Italian and Mexican children to be more gifted manually than American children.

Selection of tests

The tests in this study do not in any way represent a scale of performance tests, such as the Pintner-Paterson scale. Although the 11 tests used do not all require the actual use of both the right and left hand, the tests have been so arranged that the activity or passivity of the left hand was always observed and noted. The chief thought was to choose tests that would be simple and thus avoid discouraging young children, ranging from four years, nine months to seven years, nine months. Another consideration was to find tests that would contain somewhat familiar processes and would be attractive, and it was necessary to make a selection that would require only the simplest directions in order to be certain that the foreign children understood the requirements, moreover the desirability of arranging a group that could easily be completed in one hour or less to avoid fatigue and its consequent inertia and loss of interest was paramount.

As it seemed desirable to have some definite method of getting at the mental status of the subject, and as it would have consumed too much time to give each one a Binet test, two tests were finally decided upon. One was the Goodenough (3) test of "The Measurement of Intelligence by Drawings," the other was a set of picture puzzles based upon Rossolimo's "profile method," which according to Johnson (6), Rossolimo designated as a test in the "capacity to combine."

Age and race groups

The ages of five, six, and seven were chosen because it was desirable to select children who had been given little instruction in manual processes. Those ages could be easily obtained in the public schools. The average ages were as follows. Baltimore Americans, 6 years, 6.6 months; San Diego Americans, 5 years, 7.5 months, Sicilians, 7 years, 1.1 months; Mexicans, 6 years, 2.8 months.

Social status

The Italian children studied were all Sicilians, found in a city school of Baltimore which was entirely made up of Sicilians. The neighborhood was dirty and ill-kept. The school also was in harmony with the district, with its small, dusty, windswept yard but it had a corps of enthusiastic teachers; women who were studying

292

their distinct conditions and endeavoring to better them. The school nurse had gained the confidence of these suspicious and superstitious people, and was doing excellent work with mothers in inducing them to allow corrective and preventive work to be done. Nearly all the children were wearing various amulets around their necks, and one child was wearing the same dress for a year, without having it washed, because the grandmother had promised that she would, if her younger sister lived through a severe illness. The children looked undernourished, many with obvious physical defects. This group was by far the lowest type group studied, and could not compare even with the poorest of the Mexican or San Diego American group.

The determination of what constituted and American child was based upon the fact that the parents, and, as far as I was able to determine, the grandparents were born in America. A group of 52 American children in one of the most exclusive residential districts of Baltimore was tested. Their school was new, beautifully equipped with every modern convenience to do an advanced type of school work. The children in the kindergarten changed to tennis-shoes on coming in doors, and all were taught to tie their own shoe-strings, so their score on this bow-knot test was high. Because of the very different social status and environment of this group in comparison with the Sicilians and Mexicans, I have used another American group, whose school and home conditions were more nearly comparable for correlations with the foreign groups.

The other group of American children was selected from the same school that the Mexicans came from, and were children living in the same neighborhood as the Mexicans, and in comparable limitations of income and housing. The average age of this American group was 5 years, 7.5 months, while the average age of the Baltimore group was 6 years, 6.2 months. In none of these studies did I find any group living in the squalor and poor housing that I found the Sicilians living in. Not that such conditions for other nationalities possibly could not be found, but, living for the Mexicans, for instance, in Southern California does not offer the problem of over-crowded cities and lack of space and the closing of houses to fresh air in the winter, that such a city as Baltimore offers. However, Goodenough (2), in comparing the living conditions of Chinese and Japanese in California with Italians, states that social pressure of "race prejudice" is often urged as a reason for the segregation of certain racial groups within poorer neighborhoods, but that

"It should be remembered that while racial prejudice may bring about segregation, the character of the neighborhoods thus set off is primarily dependent upon the people living in them. It is doubtful whether even the southern Negro has more to contend with in the way of this prejudice than the Chinese or Japanese in California, yet the contrast between the typical Oriental neighborhood and the Italian (or Negro) district is marked. Poverty there may be, but the squalor which is characteristics of the Italian (and the Negro) sections is lacking."

The Mexican children were all the first generation born in the United States. The group of Mexicans represented in this study was tested in one of the San Diego Public Schools, located in a Mexican district, while a few were taken from kindergartens in Santa Barbara. In each class, however, the entire group of five, six, and seven year old children was examined. The San Diego school building was very much like the one in Baltimore where the Sicilians were housed, but it was augmented by many bungalows in the school yard. In these were held the lower primary and kindergarten classes. The yard was inadequate in size and equipment, but because of the mild climate, all the physical exercises were done out of doors, as well as many class recreations and activities.

The numbers in the groups tested are nearly equal Sicilians 55, Mexicans 53, San Diego Americans 50, and Baltimore Americas 52. The sexes are unequally divided, for it seemed a less selective method to take all the children of the three age-groups in the classes, than to take the same number of girls as boys. So the groups run Sicilian boys 24, girls 31; Mexican boys 18, girls 35, San Diego American boys 22, girls 28, Baltimore American boys 26, girls 26.

ORDER OF TESTS

Careful consideration was given to the order of presenting the tests, since the series took an hour to give, fatigue and loss of interest had to be avoided.

The following order was finally decided upon as it seemed to offer the maximum of variety in those to be performed while standing and those performed sitting.

Peg board	standing
Drawing of man	sitting
Tying of bow	sitting
Goddard formboard	standing
Nut and bolt	sitting
Buttoning of belt in back	standing
Peg board in colors	standing
Threading of needles	sitting

Motor coordination	sitting
Picture puzzles	sitting
Stringing buttons	sitting

DRAWING OF A MAN

For the Goodenough Drawing test the child was given a 9 by 12 inch sheet of drawing paper and a large soft pencil, the directions were as follows "On this paper I want you to make a picture of a man. Make the very best picture that you can. Take your time and work carefully."

TABLE I

IQ score in the test of the drawing of a man

	CA	MA	IQ
	Mexican		
	Boys		
1	5-3	6-3	119
2	5-4	6-6	122
3	5-4	5-0	99
4	5-4	5-6	103
5	5-7	4-9	85
6	5-11	8-3	140
7	6-0	6-9	102
8	6-0	7-3	121
9	6-1	7-9	127
10	6-1	6-9	111
11	6-5	6-3	97
12	6-6	5-8	92
13	6-7	5-9	88
14	6-7	10-0	147
15	6-8	6-9	101
16	7-0	7-0	100
17	7-0	9-6	135
18	7-1	7-6	105
	Girls		
1	4-9	6-0	126
2	4-10	6-0	126
3	5-0	6-0	120
4	5-0	5-9	115

5	5-0	6-3	105
6	5-0	6-0	120
7	5-0	6-3	125
8	5-2	6-0	116
9	5-3	6-9	128
10	5-3	5-9	109
11	5-4	6-9	126
12	5-5	7-3	134
13	5-7	5-3	94
14	5-8	7-0	123
15	5-8	7-6	133
16	5-9	7-3	125
17	5-9	5-3	91
18	5-11	6-0	114
19	5-11	6-0	101
20	5-11	7-6	127
21	5-11	6-9	114
22	5-11	5-0	85
23	6-0	6-6	108
24	6-0	6-6	108
25	6-1	7-3	119
26	6-2	5-3	85
27	6-4	10-9	170
28	6-7	7-3	111
29	6-7	7-3	105
30	6-7	6-0	92
31	6-9	9-6	140
32	6-11	5-3	76
33	7-0	6-6	93
34	7-5	6-6	87
35	7-6	7-0	93
Sicilian			
Boys			
1	4-10	6-0	123
2	5-5	7-0	128
3	5-9	6-6	112
4	6-1	8-9	143
5	6-5	5-0	73
6	6-5	5-3	82
7	6-5	6-3	97
8	6-5	7-9	120
9	6-7	5-0	76

10	6-7	6-3	95
11	6-7	6-9	102
12	6-7	5-6	84
13	6-7	7-3	110
14	6-7	5-9	87
15	6-10	7-6	110
16	7-0	5-9	82
17	7-0	5-9	82
18	7-1	5-6	78
19	7-1	5-3	74
20	7-2	7-3	101
21	7-2	9-0	125
22	7-3	6-6	89
23	7-3	8-6	116
24	7-3	6-6	90
	Girls		
1	4-6	5-0	111
2	5-3	5-6	105
3	5-7	7-0	125
4	5-8	7-0	123
5	5-9	5-9	100
6	5-9	6-6	113
7	5-9	7-9	135
8	5-9	6-0	104
9	5-10	6-0	103
10	5-10	6-3	107
11	5-10	5-9	98
12	6-3	6-9	107
13	6-3	7-6	120
14	6-4	6-6	102
15	6-4	7-0	110
16	6-5	10-0	155
17	6-7	6-0	89
18	6-7	6-6	99
19	6-9	5-3	78
20	6-10	6-9	98
21	7-0	7-0	100
22	7-0	7-3	104
23	6-7	6-0	92
24	6-8	5-9	86
25	7-0	6-0	95
26	7-1	6-9	95

297

27	7-1	5-6	78
28	7-3	6-6	89
29	7-4	9-0	122
30	7-4	7-6	102
31	6-8	6-3	94
San Diego American			
Boys			
1	4-11	6-3	126
2	5-0	5-0	100
3	5-2	4-6	87
4	5-4	5-4	100
5	5-4	5-3	98
6	5-4	5-9	107
7	5-4	5-0	93
8	5-4	5-9	107
9	5-7	5-3	94
10	5-8	4-9	84
11	5-9	4-9	83
12	5-11	6-6	110
13	5-10	6-6	103
14	6-0	6-9	102
15	6-1	6-9	111
16	6-5	5-9	90
17	6-7	7-0	106
18	6-7	6-6	99
19	6-9	6-6	96
20	6-9	7-0	103
21	6-10	4-9	70
22	7-1	6-6	93
Girls			
1	4-6	5-6	122
2	4-7	6-0	130
3	4-10	4-3	87
4	5-0	5-3	105
5	5-0	6-3	125
6	5-2	4-6	87
7	5-2	5-3	101
8	5-3	6-3	119
9	5-3	6-0	114
10	5-4	5-9	107
11	5-5	6-6	120
12	5-6	5-6	100

13	5-6	7-3	133
14	5-7	7-6	135
15	5-8	5-0	88
16	5-9	5-6	96
17	5-9	6-9	117
18	5-9	4-6	79
19	5-11	5-6	93
20	6-0	7-3	121
21	6-0	4-6	75
22	6-0	6-9	112
23	6-2	5-6	90
24	6-2	5-3	85
25	6-4	7-0	110
26	6-8	6-9	101
27	6-9	6-6	96
28	7-1	5-6	78
	Baltimore American		
	Boys		
1	5-5	3-9	69
2	5-5	5-9	106
3	5-7	5-6	98
4	5-7	7-0	125
5	5-7	8-0	143
6	5-9	6-6	112
7	5-9	6-9	117
8	5-11	7-9	131
9	6-0	7-3	125
10	6-2	6-0	97
11	6-3	7-0	112
12	6-3	6-3	100
13	6-4	6-0	95
14	6-5	5-9	89
15	6-8	6-0	90
16	6-9	4-0	60
17	6-9	6-6	96
18	6-9	6-6	96
19	6-9	5-6	81
20	6-9	6-9	100
21	6-10	6-3	91
22	6-11	6-9	97
23	7-1	5-6	78
24	7-3	6-0	83

25	7-3	8-0	110
26	7-5	6-9	91
	Girls		
1	5-1	5-3	102
2	5-3	7-9	147
3	5-4	6-0	113
4	5-5	5-3	97
5	5-7	7-0	125
6	5-7	6-0	108
7	5-8	8-0	135
8	5-10	6-6	111
9	5-11	10-6	176
10	6-0	6-3	104
11	6-0	7-9	128
12	6-0	6-0	100
13	6-3	6-6	104
14	6-7	6-9	102
15	6-8	6-0	90
16	6-9	6-0	89
17	6-9	6-0	89
18	6-10	7-0	103
19	7-0	6-6	93
20	7-1	6-6	92
21	7-2	8-3	142
22	7-4	6-6	88
23	7-7	7-6	98
24	7-8	9-0	117
25	7-9	11-0	142
26	7-2	8-3	115

Some of the children had to be encouraged to make a start but not a child refused to make the drawing. Many of the American children chatted all the time they were drawing, naming each part as they put it in. This chatting was not so voluble with the foreign children, although they commented on an item now and then.

Over 77 per cent of the total test of the Drawing of a Man by the 53 Mexican children gave a higher mental age than the chronological age of the child, 58 per cent of the Sicilians, 56 per cent of the San Diego Americans, and 60 per cent of the Baltimore American group.

The drawings made by the Sicilian group were unlike those of the other groups in that they contained much more anatomical detail. Very often a circle or elipse across

300

the middle of the trunk was "the belly." The navel was often represented. These drawings were, on the whole more dramatic than those of the other groups. The men would be running, or raking, or smoking, or even shooting. One man had a large pistol in his pocket. The fact that they were drawing "a man" was evidently seldom remembered by any of the children, for when they clothed him, he was just as liable to be wearing a dress as coat and pants. The incongruities seemed to be unrecognized by most of the children: the fact that the man was wearing nothing but a tie or hat with no other clothing received no consideration.

It is a notable fact that the difference in social status and type of environment of these groups is clearly shown by the comparison of the drawings of the Sicilian group, who came from very poor and ignorant homes, with the drawings of the American group studied in Baltimore. In the latter group more clothing is shown, and such things as golf-sticks and canes and umbrellas were depicted. One drawing is of a "Pilgrim." In not one is the stomach drawn or the navel. In the drawings of the Sicilian children fewer show clothing, and when the man carries something, it is usually a gun. One child, when he was finishing, put a vertical and horizontal line across the trunk, when asked what it was he said, "The cross of Jesus." Another child, after finishing the drawing of the man, drew a series of vertical lines in the space to one side. I asked what that was, and he said, "Macaroni for the man to eat."

One Mexican child drew a man with six fingers, a line out from each finger and a circle on the end, this was a "balloon man." Such comments as "he's running," "he's shooting a gun," would come from the foreign children but the American children often told a whole story about their drawings as they progressed. Only a few children, in any of the groups, drew profile, almost all were front view. In a few cases the children drew the man upside-down through-out the entire test, but in all cases, when they had finished they turned the drawing around to the correct position. Quite a number began with the legs instead of the head.

In over two hundred drawings only one could be said to show what Goodenough (3) terms "flight of ideas." The arms and hands were like feather dusters and were huge as compared with the size of the rest of the figure. The feet were like lily-pads with lines like the veins of the leaves, running out from where the legs form the feet. The head was mostly hair. This child was five years, four months old, and was considered a great problem in school. She showed little ability to give attention and was erratic and unable to follow directions. The mother was much troubled about her but the mother also showed a high degree of nervous tension, was very anxious and extremely talkative.

The only other drawing that was unusual was done by a boy of five years, five months. This consisted of an oblong with 2 circular scribble in the right half, joined to another small oblong. When asked what these were, he said, "Eyes, mouth, nose, big feets." The "big feet" were the sides of the smaller oblong. This drawing does not come into the class showing indications of psychopathy, however, but simply shows unusual immaturity. He was a tiny, very babyish child in looks and in speech and made a mental age by the drawing test of three years, nine months. Both these children were in the socially highest-type group.

Left hand

After the drawing of a man was completed with the right hand (only 3 preferred the left hand) then the picture of a man was drawn with the left hand. Many of the children did not hesitate, but put the pencil into the left hand and started drawing at once, but others said "I can't," one child said, "I'll make a funny man." For many of the children the change was so awkward that they had to make a great effort to do it. One child put his tongue in his cheek, several "chewed their tongues." There were a number of children who appeared to use the left hand as easily as the right. They showed fairly good motor-control; the lines were firm and the joining of lines good.

In most of the cases where the use of the left hand seemed so difficult, the right hand would go over to the left again and again to help, especially when it came to the drawing of the features and other details. Without seeming to realize it, the child frequently changed the pencil back to the right hand. For the most part, those who found the left hand drawing difficult would hold the pencil with fingers far back from the point, or would hold it with a fist-like grip and press down hard upon the paper.

There were children who appeared to be ambidextrous and who seemed to enjoy using the left hand. One of these children, when making the first drawing, would use the right hand to work on the right side and then would change the pencil to his left hand when drawing the details of the opposite side of the picture. In most cases, the use of the pencil for drawing with the left hand was difficult. The position of the hand in holding the pencil was awkward and the motor-control much poorer than when the right hand was used. The opposite was true for two of the children who were left-handed.

FIG. 1

FIG. 2

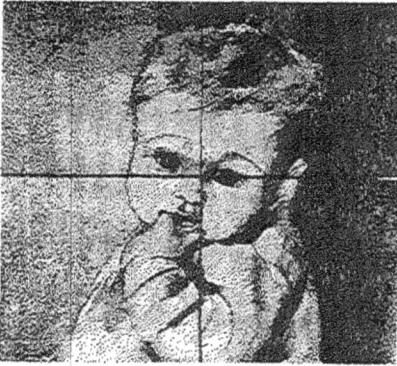

FIG. 3

FIG. 4

FIG. 5

FIG. 6

303

Fig. 7

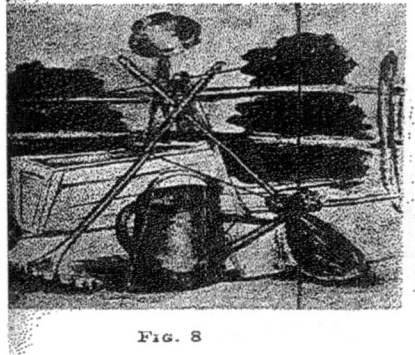

Fig. 8

Fig. 9

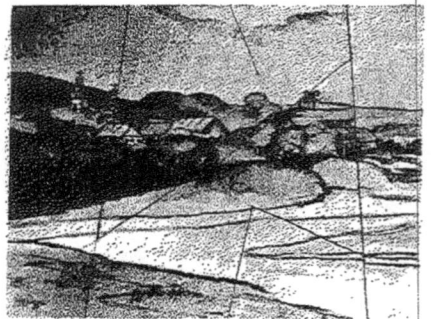

Fig. 10

PICTURE PUZZLES

The picture puzzle test was placed as the eleventh in the last of the performance tests, but since it was based upon the Rossolimo test that was designed to measure mental capacity the discussion of it is given here in order to compare it with the standardized test of Goodenough (3). This test has not been standardized, nor are there norms for the Rossolimo.

This test consists of a graded series of 10 pictures 6 by 6 inches done in water-color, mounted on fourply veneer, shellaced and cut. The subjects are similar to the Rossolimo series but substitutions have been made for the 5 familiar objects that seemed to the writer to be more attractive to young children than Rossolimo's, and the 5 geometric figures that are black on a white ground in the Rossolimo, have been changed to color. The circle is red, the square, orange, the oval, purple, the snake-like design, two tones of green, and the star, two tones of blue. As the Rossolimo series is copied in water-color and the white water-color paper soils so quickly the substitute set is protected by shellac. Otherwise one set of dissected pictures might not have lasted through the experiment. This process has somewhat changed the character of the color, yellowing the whites, and mellowing the brilliancy of the colors. It is just possible that had picture varnish been used there would have been a little less change in the color. The 10 pictures are cut in the same shapes as those of the Rossolimo series.

The five that have been changed as to subject are shown in the accompanying photographs. For the geometric figures see Johnson (7).

One reason for putting this series toward the end of the gamut of tests was the thought that the performance took a much longer time than any other single test and that it might be discouraging if given toward the beginning. Then, too, the child tests would be better acquainted with the examiner and more at ease, and so would be likely to make a better prolonged response. Experience with these 212 children makes me conclude that this was probably a wise decision.

TABLE 2
Scatter of failures in picture puzzle test

Puzzle Number	5 YEARS				6 YEARS				7 YEARS				TOTALS			
	Mexicans	Sicilians	San Diego	Baltimore	Mexicans	Sicilians	San Diego	Baltimore Americans	Mexicans	Sicilians	San Diego	Baltimore Americans	Mexicans	Sicilians	San Diego Americans	Baltimore Americans
	Number of children															
	21	11	28	14	25	25	19	23	7	19	3	15				
1	0	1	0	0	0	0	0	0	0	0	0	0	0	1	0	0
2	0	0	0	0	0	0	0	0	0	0	0	0	0	0	0	0
3	1	0	1	3	0	1	0	3	0	0	0	0	1	1	1	6
4	1	2	2	5	2	2	0	2	0	1	1	0	3	5	3	7
5	4	5	12	6	0	7	0	5	0	9	0	2	4	21	12	13

6	1	1	4	4	3	4	2	5	0	1	0	0	4	6	6	9
7	10	8	17	9	8	19	0	12	0	8	0	5	18	35	17	25
8	8	5	18	12	7	19	8	16	1	11	2	7	16	35	28	35
9	21	11	28	13	23	22	19	23	7	19	3	13	51	52	50	49
10	20	9	27	14	17	23	16	22	5	18	3	13	42	50	46	49
Total	66	42	109	66	60	97	35	88	13	67	9	40	139	206	163	194

Procedure

The pieces of the pictures were placed in the same order for presentation as that given by Johnson (6) but the instructions were slightly changed, and were as follows "This is a picture that has been cut into several pieces, see if you can put it together again to make a picture." The time record was kept with a stop-watch, 3 minutes being the limit of time allowed for each picture.

The method of procedure, was similar to Johnson's in stopping the test after 2 successive failures were made. In a few cases she allowed the child to try other pictures after 2 failures, but she states that in no case was the attempt successful.

With the series of pictures substituted in this experiment for those of the Rossolimo series, all the children were allowed to try all of the pictures, stopping the trial at the three-minute time-limit for each picture. The findings differed from Johnson's in that matter of successful scores after 2 successive failures, which leads to the question as to whether the series used in this study is as well graded as the Rossolimo series. With this possibility, or perhaps probability, in mind, the method of scoring was changed. Instead of considering the score to be the "number designating the place in the series of the final picture which is correctly solved," (after 2 successive failures), the aggregate of all the correctly solved pictures was used as the score. This lowers the score in some cases where the finals result showed much scattering.

TABLE 3
Distribution of picture puzzle scores

SCORE	5 YEARS				6 YEARS				7 YEARS			
	Mexicans	Sicilians	San Diego Americans	Baltimore Americans	Mexicans	Sicilians	San Diego Americans	Baltimore Americans	Mexicans	Sicilians	San Diego Americans	Baltimore Americans
0												
1												
2								1				
3	1			3								
4	2	3	4	2		4	1	2		1		
5	3	4	5	2		4		3		1		
6	2		10	4	1	10	3	7		5		4
7	9	3	9	3	6	5	3	3	1	7	2	2
8	11	3	4	3	6		7	6	2	3		5
9	1	1			4	1	2	1	3			
10					1							1
Total	29	14	32	17	18	24	16	23	6	17	2	12
Average	6.7	6.0	6.1	5.7	7.8	5.8	7.9	6.8	8.3	6.5	7.0	7.3

The scores given in table 2 show the extent of scattering. Although the burden of failures is found on puzzles 9 and 10, yet 1 also shows that quite a number of individuals succeeded with picture 10 who failed with 9. As picture 9 is one of the substitutions for the Rossolimo pictures, it may be that the one used in this study presents more difficulties than number 9 of the Rossolimo series.

In table 3 showing the distribution of scores, the Mexican group is far in advance of all the other groups in the number of high scores, the aggregate being 8 for score 9, and 1 for score 10. Neither the San Diego American group nor the Sicilian group had a score of 10; the Baltimore American group shows one such score.

It was notable throughout this test that during the first of the series, where the picture was relatively simple for most of the children the stimulus-pattern was the picture represented, but as the picture became more complicated, they began to work to fit shape rather than design.

In the case of the Mexican boy who had a score of 10, picture-design was his motive throughout. In puzzle 9, he said, "This is a house and it's near the water." In the star he systematically put the corner squares together, making the design match' then he put the four squares together, clearly showing that the picture pattern was what he was working for. One little girl who also worked for design throughout said, "The sky is at the bottom of the picture, too," referring to the reflection of the sunset in the water. Many of the children in doing the star-puzzle seemed to work for pattern, but were satisfied with a very irregular picture-pattern result. Some of the younger children showed the tendency that Johnson (6) reports. In putting the third picture together, they would put the pieces in a row and say "Baby;" or perhaps they got three pieces together correctly, then put the fourth in whatever way it happened to be on the table, and were satisfied with the result.

When the San Diego groups were examined it was near Easter, and many of the children at once said, "It's an Easter egg" when they correctly solved the puzzle with the oval pattern. The majority of the children named the pattern as soon as they had the pieces put together correctly. The red circle was usually called "a red apple." Twice the orange square was called a "handkerchief" by girls. Some of the children would get pieces together correctly, not recognize the fact and pull them apart again. This was especially true of the snake-like pattern. One little girl who failed on this test said, "That is a hard one, looks like a round snake." One child said of the oval, incorrectly assembled, "It's a water-bottle." One boy who had a score of 4, never did seem to get the real idea of assembling for a pattern. He shoved the pieces around with no apparent idea of what he was working for. This was a San Diego American boy. It was surprising at times how satisfied a child would be with a perfectly incongruous and irregular grouping. One unsuccessful little girl of the Baltimore American group said, "Gosh, I think this is fun!" There were some who, after the first one, used a "trial and error" method throughout the test. One of the Sicilian group made a score of 9, using this method.

PLAIN PEG BOARD

The first test given was a peg board. This board is of varnished maple, with pegs to match. The size is 12 by 12 inches with 36 half-inch holes, 6 on a side, equidistant, leaving a margin of 1 1/2 inches. The pegs are 3 inches long and 7/16 inches in diameter, with the edge of both ends beveled to prevent the peg from chipping and from being difficult to slip into the hole.

The pegs were in a shallow pan at the right of the board (at the left, if the child were left-handed). The table was low, so the child looked down upon the board as he stood in front of it.

The directions were: "Put your left hand (indicating it) on the lower corner of the board, and with the other hand put all these pegs in these holes just as fast as you can, picking up only one peg at a time. Ready, go!" The time was kept with a stop-watch.

Most of the children began to put in rows of pegs beginning at the right side, and either put the pegs in rows from front to back or from back to front, but some worked forward and back all the way across the board instead of starting each new row at the front. Few of them had the idea of starting at the left side and so avoid reaching over those pegs that were already placed. Almost every combination of method was employed; however, the most frequent was in rows from front to back or the reverse, with the exception of the San Diego groups. There were only 2 children who used a hit or miss manner.

The San Diego children, almost without exception, put in all the outer rows of pegs first, then filled in the center either in concentric squares or in rows across. This was the only group of children who used this method; a very few individuals had done so. In talking with the teachers of this group one kindergartener said that in their use of the peg board they generally told the children to put a fence all around the board first.

TABLE 4
Average time for peg-board

		BOYS		GIRLS	
		Minutes	*Seconds*	*Minutes*	*Seconds*
Mexicans					
	Plain	1	28	1	26
	Colored	1	28	1	30
Sicilian					
	Plain	1	23	1	25
	Colored	1	32	1	32
San Diego Americans					
	Plain	1	26	1	25
	Colored	1	35	1	32
Baltimore Americans					
	Plain	1	26	1	26
	Colored	1	30	1	28

The averages for all the groups were very close as is shown in table 4.

Both the best and the poorest records appear in the Baltimore group of American children, the best record being 59 seconds. This was made by a little girl of seven years, four months who made a record of ten years, three months on the Drawing of a Man and a score of nine on the Picture Puzzles. However, on the finer coordination, such as the threading of needles, she was very slow, taking 4 minutes and 30 seconds to thread the six needles. She was left-handed.

All the children who were left-handed were allowed to use that hand. The poorest record was made by a boy five years, five months who took 2 minutes 50 seconds for the test. His rating for the Drawing of a Man gave him a mental age of three years, nine months and his score in the Picture Puzzles was three. His procedure was unlike that of the other children in that several times he picked up a whole handful of pegs, and was sufficiently distractable to leave the board at one time to ask if we were going "to play a game with those," pointing to other apparatus. He was a tiny, undeveloped child, very babyish in his manner.

In the other 3 groups the highest as well as the lowest records are found in the Mexican group. There were 3 children in this group who took over 2 minutes for this test, the longest record being 2 minutes and 26 seconds. The shortest record was one minute.

There was one child who was so steady in putting the pegs in that her reactions were almost rhythmic. It was difficult, with some of the five year old children to give them an idea of speed. One child of four years, seven months, stopped to blow her nose, another started to tell me about her baby brother, and held a peg up until she was reminded to hurry. Some of the children were prone to pick up 2 pegs at a time until reminded not to do so. One child did this every time he thought I was not looking. In 2 cases the children had to be urged to "go on," as they appeared to think that after one row was in, the test was finished. One child even started to take the pegs out.

Left hand

All the children who were left-handed were allowed to use that hand instead of the right hand in these tests, in which case the apparatus was arranged with the same relation to the left side of the child as for the right side of those who were right-handed. There were 3 left-handed children, 2 Mexicans and 1 Baltimore American. One of the former appeared to be ambidextrous, especially when using a pencil. At first, when told to "put the left hand on the corner of the board," some of the children would press the left hand down hard until they became interested enough to forget and relax.

COLORED PEG BOARD

Although the Colored Peg Board test is number seven in the list of tests as given, the results of that test will be given here in order to compare them with the results obtained with the Plain Peg Board.

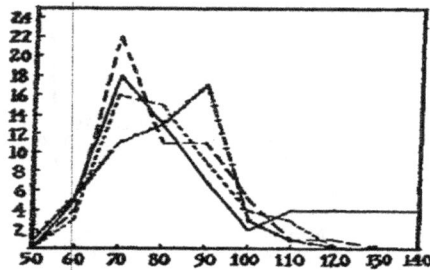

FIG 1 RELATIVE TIME SCORES PLAIN
PEG BOARD
———————— Mexican, ————————Italian, — —
— — S D American; —●——●— Baltimore
American

This board is constructed like the other peg board with the exception that it is painted in three stripes of color, one blue, one deep yellow, and one green. Each stripe covers twelve peg-holes, and the twelve pegs belonging in these holes are painted the same color as the stripe.

The directions were:

"Here is another peg board, just like the first one, but in 3 colors, with pegs to match the blue pegs go into the blue stripe, (illustrate by putting in a blue peg); the yellow in the yellow stripe (illustrate), and the green pegs in the green stripe (illustrate). Put your left hand on the corner of the board and pick up only one peg at a time. Let me see how fast you can put these pegs in the holes where they belong. Ready, go!"

Most of the children greeted the second peg board test with seeming pleasure, and some would have started to put the pegs in before the directions were completed if they had been permitted.

The board was so placed with reference to the child that the blue stripe came to the right, the orange in the center, and the green to the left. The stripes ran at right

311

angles to the front edge of the table. The pan of pegs was placed at the right of the board unless the child were left-handed, then both pan and board were reversed.

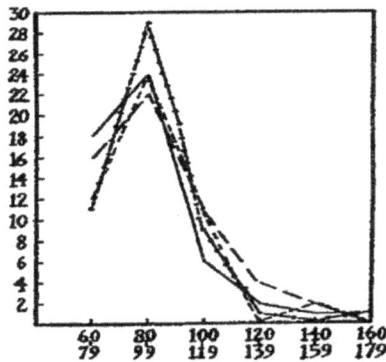

FIG 2 RELATIVE TIME SCORES COLORED PEG BOARD

———— Mexican, ———— Italian; — —
— — S D American; —•—•— Baltimore American

The pegs were thoroughly mixed in the pan so the colors had to be picked out. This may have been a reason why the test took a longer time than the plain peg board, for in the latter test the children who made the best time did not look back at the pan of pegs each time, but picked up a peg without looking. In the case of the colors, the peg had be selected each time, and, when it came to the last two or three of a color, the child would perhaps have to hunt for them. The pan is which the pegs were kept was large enough for all the pegs to be flat without covering each other if they had been placed in order, but this was not the procedure.

In over two hundred children tested, not a single child appeared to be color-blind, at least as far as these 3 colors (blue, yellow, green) were concerned. If by chance a child put a peg in the wrong stripe he either changed it immediately or when he found a peg left over of the color he was filling. One child discovered that she had put a blue peg in the green space and said "Do you know why I got the blue one in there? Because my eyes are bad."

The majority of the children selected one color and filled all openings there first, then took another color. But in this, as in the plain peg board test, every variety of procedure was used. One child put one row of each color in first; then filled in the second rows in the same order. Some began with the blue and put in rows front to back and back to front uniformly all the way across, ending with the green pegs. Only one

312

child put into the appropriate stripe whatever peg he happened to pick up without looking. About half of the children filled in the green stripe first, though some of them filled the blue second and yellow last.

There were still quite a number who found it difficult to refrain from picking up more than one peg at a time. The control of the left hand, as far as its reaching over to help the right hand was concerned, was much improved in this test, though it showed much the same activity or relaxation that it showed in the first peg board test.

The average time in performing this Colored Peg Board test was slightly higher than the time for the Plain Peg Board test. Table 4 shows these differences.

With some children the left hand would leave the corner of the board and be dramatically held out to the side with the fingers spread. Never was that particular manner of holding the left hand observed with the American children. This may have been chance but it seemed worth noting. In a number of cases of both Americans and foreign children the left hand left the board to grasp the dress tightly, or, in 2 cases to be held against the stomach or with the fingers spread apart. Sometimes the left hand was taken from the corner of the board and the edge of the table grasped. Some of the children held the index finger only on the corner of the board. In several cases the child started to take a handful of pegs in the left hand to feed the right hand. In many cases, more especially among the American children, the left hand would either be held in relaxed position in the corner of the board or the child would drop it by his side. It was notable that the more tense positions were shown when the child appeared conscious of trying to go fast.

TYING A BOW-KNOT

In the Stanford Revision of the Binet-Simon tests, Terman places the tying of a bow in the seventh year, but in this study it was used for all three ages represented. The procedure differed in 2 points from that given by Terman: first, the term "bow-knot," was changed to "bow" as the word *knot* confused the foreign children. The second point of difference was that the bow-knot was not tied around my finger, as with very young children where there is any shyness to be overcome, it has been my experience that one gets better results if the personal element is entirely eliminated, so a stick was substituted with the model on the same stick.

There is also a time element in the procedure of tying around the finger, the child may feel more hurried than when tying around a stick. The directions were "See, here is a bow, I want you to take this string and make the same kind of a bow on this

313

stick." The criticism made by Terman that the stick often fell out of the string was not true of the test in this study. The stick was large enough (8 inches long and 1 inch wide) so the child kept it down on the table while he worked.

Table 5 shows the distribution. Of seven-year-old Mexicans none failed, of the 19 seven-year-old Sicilians 4 failed, of the 15 seven-year-old Baltimore Americans 3 failed. The Mexicans show the lowest percentage of failures.

Considering the fact that the Baltimore American children were taught to tie their shoe-strings when they entered the kindergarten and the other 3 groups were not, it seems that the Baltimore Americans showed a high percentage of failures. There were several types of failure in this test, some had no idea at all about any procedure to accomplish the task, others made the first loop, put the other string around it but when it came to pulling through the second loop they put it through the first loop instead of the wrapped around string. Others laid out 2 loops, 1 for each string-end, then picked up the loops and tied in a knot. This made a two-loop bow that would not pull loose easily but was not like the model.

TABLE 5
Distribution of failures in tying a bow-knot

	5 YEARS				6 YEARS				7 YEARS				TOTALS			
	Mexicans	Sicilians	San	Baltimore	Mexicans	Sicilians	San Diego	Baltimore	Mexicans	Sicilians	San Diego	Baltimore	Mexicans	Sicilians	San Diego	Baltimore
Number of boys	4	3	10	7	12	11	10	13	3	10	2	6	18	24	22	26
Number of girls	17	8	18	7	14	14	9	10	4	9		9	35	31	28	26
Boys— failures	2	2	8	2	0	8	4	2	0	2	2	1	2	12	14	5
Girls— failures	8	3	7	1	1	4	1	5	0	2	0	2	9	9	8	8
Totals	10	5	15	3	1	12	5	7	0	4	2	3	11	21	22	13
Percentage of failures	47	45	53	21	40	48	26	30	0	21	66	20	20	38	44	25

314

When the children failed and were asked, "Don't you tie your own shoe-strings?" the child's invariable reply was "My mother does it." Johnson (6) states that "It was observed that the Italian children who failed almost universally in tying a bow-knot, wore button shoes and upon inquiry it was ascertained that these children rarely wore shoes with laces." In observing the groups used for this study, some of the failures were made by children wearing button shoes but by no means was this universally true.

In comparing the percentage of failures in each group with the San Diego American group, (this is the group used in the correlations), the group making the least number of failures is the trained Baltimore American group. The Mexican percentages are lower for the six and seven-year-olds than the San Diego Americans, but higher in the six-year-old group but the aggregate of percentages is much lower for the Mexicans. The same data are found in the comparison of the Sicilian group with the San Diego American group, as for the Mexican and San Diego American. In comparing the Mexican and Sicilian groups, the five-year-olds of the Mexican group show a slightly higher percentage of failures, but the six-year-old group is lower and the seven-year-old group of Mexicans has no failures at all while the Sicilian group has .21 percent of failures.

In the test of the tying of a bow the Mexican group rates higher than any but the Baltimore American group.

SEGUIN-GODDARD FORM-BOARD

The fourth test was the Seguin-Goddard Form-Board, which is too well known to require a description here; suffice it to say the standard form-board procedure was used. The procedure with these young children was to place the 3 piles of forms to the right of the board and not at the back, because the latter presented some difficulties in reaching for the small children. The directions were: "See how fast you can put these blocks back in the holes where they belong. Ready, go!" The time was kept with a stop-watch. There were 3 trials on this test, the shortest time of the three was taken as the score.

The average time and median for each group was as follows.

The above average scores show that in this test the Mexican group made the shortest time of any of the groups, the longest time being scored by the Sicilian group.

315

Goddard form-board

	AVERAGE TIME	MEDIAN
	Seconds	
Mexicans		
Boys	29	~ 28
Girls	29	
Sicilians		
Boys	42	~ 41
Girls	48	
San Diego Americans		
Boys	31	~ 31
Girls	36	
Baltimore Americans		
Boys	40	~ 40
Girls	45	

There was no difficulty in securing cooperation on 3 trials, for the children were sent to me "to play games," and they took this repetition as part of the game. At the end of the first trial I said: "We do this 3 times to see if we can do it faster each time." In some cases the shortest time was made on the first trial, but in many of the cases on the second trial. At times it would see, in observing the performance in this test, as if they last trial was going to prove much shorter, then perhaps the child would fumble in putting in the star or cross, or would hesitate over the placing of some form that had gone in with no hesitation in the other 2 trials, and instead of making a shorter time, he would take longer for this trial than for either of the other two. There was one performance that occurred in a number of cases, the child would put the blocks in place in the first trial with practically no hesitation nor "hovering," but on the second trial would begin to hesitate and hold the block hoveringly above the board before finding its place. Sometimes this response was even more pronounced in the third trial than in the second. Yet all the time such a child had the appearance of greater interest even than in the first trial.

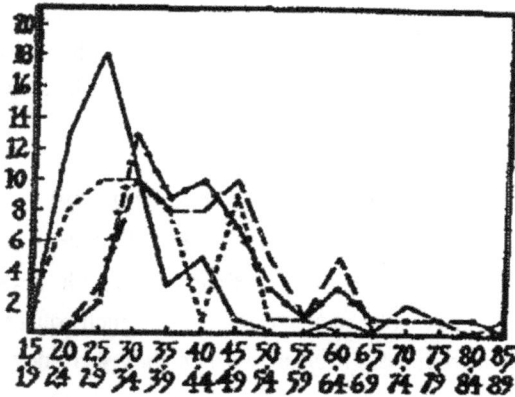

FIG 3 RELATIVE TIME SCORES   GODDARD
FORM BOARD

——————— Mexican, ———·——— Italian, ——·—
— — S D American; ——•——•—— Baltimore
American

Sometimes a child would drop a block on the board, or lay it to one side on the board, if he did not at once recognize the place for it. Then it would be placed when he recognized its proper place or would be left there to be put in place after all the others were in. Many of the children attempted to put the forms into the wrong places. Most of these mistakes occurred in forms of similar shapes, for example, the ellipse in the circle, or the diamond in the hexagonal space or vice-versa. There were some who had tried to fit into the openings shapes that were dissimilar, such as the triangle in the circle and square in the diamond. A few started out with a trial and error method, giving no attention to the shapes but merely trying the blocks in the different openings until they found the right one. This method was not employed after the first trial in any of these cases.

The first performance was often very different from the other performances and offered a much more interesting study, as to the time element as well as the form perception and quality of attention shown.

Left hand

In this test the children were given no instruction concerning the use of the right or left hand, so in some cases the child used the left hand as much as the right hand, after the blocks were picked up by the right hand. In only 2 cases was it noted that the child reached to pick up the blocks with the left hand. The left hand was sometimes used to hold a block for which the proper place was not immediately recognized, and when the place for it was recognized this block would be put in with the left hand.

SCREWING NUTS ON BOLTS

The fifth test was screwing nuts on 6 bolts. The bolts were 4 1/2 inches long and 1/2 inch in diameter with square head and square nut. They were threaded at one end 1 1/2 inches on the shaft. The nuts were 1/2 of an inch square and 1/2 of an inch thick and had been cleaned and slightly oiled when they were new, so the nuts would run on freely. The bolts were laid in a row, the head end toward the child, the nuts were in a row, one at the thread end of each bolt.

The directions were "I want to see how fast you can put all these nuts on these bolts, running the nuts on as far as they will go, like this." I took up a bolt and, holding it in my left hand, started the nut and then ran it on as fast as possible with the fingers of my right hand, put it down quickly and started to pick up another without actually doing it. The children seemed anxious to do this test and, unless restrained would have started to carry out the directions before I put the bold back. As soon as bolt and nut were in place, I said, "All right, ready, go!" starting the stop-watch as soon as bolt and nut were in the hands of the child.

There was one feature in this test affecting the amount of time the test took that was true in nearly every case. If a right-handed child kept the bolt in his right hand and put the nut on with his left hand, almost without exception, the time for completing the task was longer, in some cases very much longer than when the nut was in the right hand and bolt in the left. In the first method the child was apt to experience great difficulty in getting the nut started, for he would screw it the wrong way and sometimes drop it off three and four times; sometimes it would drop to the floor. Some children would suddenly realize what the difficulty was and shift the bolt to the other hand. If they did not do this they were obliged to screw the nut toward them instead of away from them. Some children tried to run the bolt on against the palm of the left hand, but for the most part they laboriously turned the nut on little by little. Some of the children shifted the position of nut and bolt in the hands several times during the test.

A number of the children would hold the bolt upright on the table, balance the nut on top, then run it on with the right hand. The children employed a surprising number of different methods of procedure in performing this task. Some were very particular, in putting the assembled bold and nut down, to lay it straight on the table and line the next ones up with it. Those who were quickest in the test were the ones who held the bolt in the left hand and ran the nut on either with the palm or fingers of the right hand, or very often with only the first finger of the right hand. Twice one child changed the direction of the turning of the nut and nearly screwed off 2 nuts before he realized the fact. Then, in changing from a method of slowly turning the nut on, the children would try to run it on in the palm of the hand and would turn the nut off instead of on. Some of the children chattered all the time until urged to hurry. A number of children who had difficulty getting the nut started would change the nut for another. One boy said "Gosh, this one sticks, I guess it isn't the right one." It was observable that most of the children who had any difficulty in getting the nut started would show a reaction of the mouth, either it would be open, or the tongue would come out, or be twisted. Whenever there was difficulty starting, the children almost universally tried to force the nut on, some pushing as hard as possible with the nut quite crooked on the end of the bolt.

Very few of the children retained the idea of the necessity for speed, once in a while a child would appear to try to "go as fast as he could," but in only 2 cases was this attitude maintained throughout the performance. The comments of the boys on seeing the bolts were; "My father has some bolts like those." "We got some of these in our machine." "I can do that." "Gee! That's easy!" "I have these in my tricycle." The comments of the girls were of quite a different character, "None of the kids can do things as fast as me." "Hard to do, ain't they?" "Come on here, you old nut!"

The shortest time-score for this test was 44 seconds, made be a San Diego American girl; the longest time was taken by a Sicilian child who took 5 minutes 40 seconds for the test.

The average time for the test is as follows:

319

	AVERAGE TIME	MEDIAN
	Seconds	
Mexicans		
Boys	107	~ 112
Girls	141	
Sicilians		
Boys	118	~ 125
Girls	191	
San Diego Americans		
Boys	119	~ 130
Girls	149	
Baltimore Americans		
Boys	166	~ 120
Girls	157	

The only group in which the girls' average was lower than that of the boys was the San Diego American group. In this test the average for the Mexican boys was lower than the boys of any other group and the average of the Mexican girls lower than the girls of any other group.

BUTTONING A BELT IN THE BACK

This was the sixth test and offered a very interesting set of reactions for study. The belt was 2 inches wide and 34 1/2 inches long, made of plain blue calico, with a button 5/8 of an inch in diameter sewed on one end with strong linen thread in such a way as to leave a shank of 1/8 of an inch. A buttonhole was on the other end of the belt, 13/18 of an inch long, through which the button passed with ease. When a child was given this test the belt was adjusted to his waist size by taking a plait in the middle and pinning with a safety pin.

The directions were: "Hold this belt out in front of you like this (illustrating the button end in the left hand and buttonhole in the right), and when I say 'Ready, go!' I want you to put it around you and button it in the back as quickly as possible," (illustrating the action of putting it around the waist without buttoning). The belt was handed to the child with the button end in the left hand and buttonhole in the right, and the directions given.

Although, before starting the tests, the children had the explanation given them that nearly all the tests were timed "with this watch to see how fast you can do them," and in spite of the fact that this method of direction had been given for previous tests, 3 of the children, in taking this test, started to run across the room at the word "Go!" However, all the others followed the directions. If a boy had on a heavy sweater it was taken off; if a little girl's dress were full and loose, a plait was pinned over in the front so that it would not get in the way.

Three trials were given and the shortest time-record for the three taken as the score.

The average time for each group was as follows.

	AVERAGE TIME	MEDIAN
	Seconds	
Mexicans		
Boys	6	
Girls	9	~ 5
Sicilians		
Boys	7	
Girls	7	~ 7
Baltimore Americans		
Boys	8	
Girls	7	~ 7.5
San Diego Americans		
Boys	11	
Girls	8	~ 7

The Mexican boys show the shortest time record, but in the aggregate of records for both boys and girls the Sicilians are the lowest and San Diego Americans, the highest.

Some of the children buttoned the belt easily in 2 seconds, but others took a long time. One Mexican child took a minute on one trial.

The action of the hands in this test was very interesting. The child who had the shortest time records put his first finger through the buttonhole and the button in thumb and finger of the left hand when he held the belt out in front. The time scores for the 3 attempts were many times very wide apart. Sometimes the poorest score would be the last attempt. Very often the shortest score was the first or middle score. When a child was having difficulty in getting the belt buttoned, he would often open his mouth, run out his tongue or shut his mouth tight and twist his leg or foot around, nearly losing his balance. Some grunted and said, "Gee, this is hard."

The Baltimore American group and the Mexican group had the longest and shortest time-scores. The shortest time was 2 seconds.

THREADING NEEDLES

The only tests in this series of eleven, requiring fairly fine motor coordinations were the threading of needles and the drawing of lines within a certain path without touching the sides of the path.

Certainly both of these tests offer very interesting study material for steadiness of hand which might form a basis, in the writer's estimation, for the study of the neural condition of the child, his general body-vigor, perhaps of his temperamental reactions also.

The 6 needles used in this test were the long-eyed needles used for wool embroidery and were number 1, the thread was linen, number 25. The threads were cut about 8 inches long and were waxed at both ends, they were re-waxed for each child and a new set of threads was cut each day, so each set was used by only 4 or 5 children.

The needles were stuck in a small cushion, and the thread laid in a row on the table in front of the child. The directions were: "Here are 6 needles and 6 threads, the threads are waxed at both ends, so they will go into the needles easily. If you spoil one end of the thread you can turn it around and use the other end. I want to see how quickly you can thread all these needles with these threads, like this." (I illustrated by threading a needle and dropping it on the table, then picked up another needle but did not thread it). Replacing the needles and thread, I said, "Ready, go!" A stop-watch recorded the time. The length of time taken by the children in this test depended largely on the steadiness of hands, but one other element affecting the time-score was whether the needle was held in the left hand and the thread in the right or the reverse. When the needle was held in the right hand the scores show that the performance took a longer time in most instances. The left hand showed a greater amount of unsteadiness, and would sometimes give little jerks. The only exception to this observed condition was when the thread was held stationary in the left hand while the needle was put on it. This method took a shorter time than when the child tried to put the thread through the eye of the needle with the left hand. When the needle was held in the left and the thread put through with the right, in most instances the time-record was shorter. Some of the children had very unsteady hands, sometimes a continuous tremor was noticeable and sometimes the hands would jerk. This was a test in which the left hand certainly showed poorer motor coordination than the right.

In some cases the child would fail to see that the center part of the long eye had a wider opening than the top or bottom, and would make many futile attempts to put the thread through where the opening was too small. The time was also prolonged when the child would split or bend one end of the threat and had to turn the thread around and use the other end.

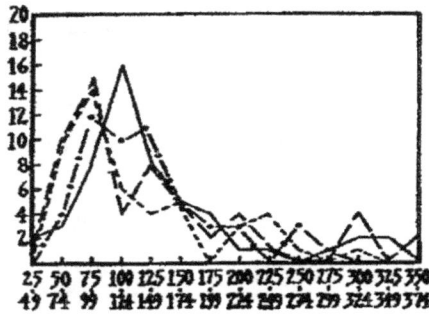

FIG 4 RELATIVE TIME SCORES THREAD-
ING NEEDLES

———— Mexican, ——— Italian; ———
—— S D. American; —●——●— Baltimore
American

The shortest time taken for this test was 29 seconds, found in the San Diego American group. In this group is also found the longest time-record, 450 seconds.

The medians for this test appear rather high. In the averages the San Diego American group makes the best record.

	AVERAGE TIME	MEDIAN
	Seconds	
San Diego Americans		
Boys	118	
Girls	144	~ 100
Sicilians		
Boys	118	
Girls	155	~ 110
Mexicans		
Boys	138	
Girls	139	~ 114
Baltimore Americans		
Boys	145	
Girls	125	~ 125

MOTOR COORDINATION

Another coordination test was given using the blanks of the Hopkins series of coordination tests. Since they are not numbered, a blank is inserted in this test to show the size of the design. The instructions were "I want you to draw a line in the middle of this path as fast as you can go from this point to this point. Take your pencil this way and keep your arm up from the paper." (I illustrated the method by holding my pencil vertically and drawing an imaginary line in the path all the way across). After this method of instruction no other difficulties were encountered except in the position of holding the pencil, in order to keep the hand up from the table. This position was well maintained if the child were watched and reminded to hold his hand up in case he forgot.

When the child's hand was in position, the signal was given. "Ready, go!" The time was kept with a stop-watch.

Some of the children went slowly in order to keep in the middle of the path, others, perhaps keeping the time element in mind, went fast. Some drew the line lightly and showed very poor coordination, others who hands appeared just as unsteady bore down heavily on the pencil giving a very steady, firm looking result. There were some who dashed along the path letting the line strike the sides again and again. When this happened in the first response, and it appeared that he had not really understood the importance of the instructions, "in the middle of the path," was repeated.

JOHNSON COORDINATION TEST

The time varied from a record of 6 seconds for a line, up to 21 or 22 seconds.

The score was the sum of all the contacts with the sides of the path found in the 4 designs on the blank. The contacts recorded were from 0 to 37, and the averages were as follows:

	AVERAGE TIME	MEDIAN
	Seconds	
Baltimore Americans		
Boys	6	
Girls	8	~ 6
Mexicans		
Boys	9	
Girls	6	~ 7
San Diego Americans		
Boys	9	
Girls	9	~ 8
Baltimore Americans		
Boys	11	
Girls	9	~ 9

Left hand

It was very noticeable that when the children were making a great effort to draw a steady line in the path, the left hand would press down heavily on the paper. Sometimes when the tension was great, in trying to draw the line quickly, the child would hold his left hand in a fist on the paper.

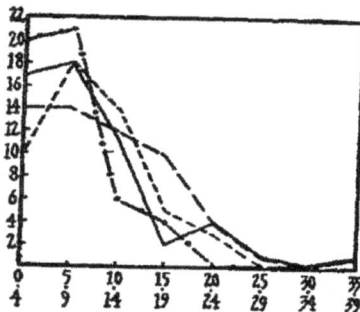

FIG 5 RELATIVE NUMBER OF CONTACTS. MOTOR COÖRDINATION

———————Mexican, ——— Italian, — —
— — S D American, —•—•— Baltimore American

325

STRING BUTTONS

The last test given in this series was the stringing of 36 wooden button-molds on a round shoestring. The button-molds were circular, flat on one side and convex on the other, with a hold in the center 1/8 inch in diameter, so the button slipped easily on the string. The string had a knot at one end and a tin tip at the other.

The buttons were placed in a shallow pan. The child was given the tip-end of the string and the directions were "See how fast you can string all these buttons on this string picking up only one at a time. Ready, go!"

The children who had been in the kindergarten were very familiar with this performance and that fact doubtless had some effect upon the scores obtained. Many seemed to take the attitude of settling back and taking it easy. A number of the children chattered about home, brothers and sisters and other things until reminded to hurry. There were many others, however, who kept up the spirit of playing a game until the end, and these children made the best time-scores.

The children used many different methods of accomplishing this task. Some of the children took the string in the right hand and put the buttons on with the left hand, and others reversed this process. Some kept the bunch of string buttons on the table and drew the string through each time as if sewing with a very long thread.

There were those who let the bunch of string buttons lie on the floor, and as they strung the single buttons on would let those buttons drop to the floor without giving them any further attention; others would shove each button all the way down the string until it reached those already strung.

Sometimes the entire time would be lengthened by the fact that the string was held in the right hand and the bunch of buttons strung dropped to the floor on the opposite side, so the button had to be shoved down the string each time. Only a few of the children let the buttons fall wherever they chanced to, without giving them further thought. There was one method that lengthened what otherwise would have been a short-time score. The arrangement of string and bunch of buttons would be good, the child would let the buttons drop down the string giving them no more attention, once they were on the string, but every few seconds he would hold up the bunch of strung buttons for one to admire, with the remark, "See what a lot I have strung," or "It looks like a big worm." It was noticeable throughout the 3 nationalities that most of the children put the string through the button from the flat side, few of the children had a hit or miss arrangement on this particular point. Three children strung first from the convex side then from the flat side giving an entirely different appearance to the finished product. One of these children would remove a button and string it from the reverse side if he chanced to put one on wrong. These children's records were among the long-time ones.

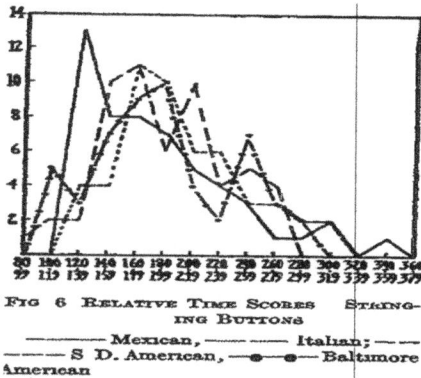

FIG. 6 RELATIVE TIME SCORES STRING-
ING BUTTONS
————— Mexican, ————— Italian; — —
———— S. D. American, —●—●— Baltimore
American

There were a goodly number of children who retained the idea of its being a timed test throughout, and who started out with the string in the left hand, the knotted end on the floor to the left, and who put the buttons on the string rapidly with the right hand letting them drop wherever they happened to. These were the children who made the shortest time-records.

The shortest time was made by a Sicilian child, 98 seconds; the longest time-record by a Sicilian child also, 386 seconds.

The averages are as follows:

	AVERAGE TIME	MEDIAN
	Seconds	
Mexicans		
Boys	190	~ 169
Girls	184	
Baltimore Americans		
Boys	191	~ 185
Girls	188	
Sicilians		
Boys	195	~ 187
Girls	191	
San Diego Americans		
Boys	206	~ 197
Girls	199	

327

The above averages show that the Mexican children made a slightly better record than the children of the other groups.

SUMMARY

A comparative study of racial differences in manual dexterity has been made for Sicilian, Mexican, and native American children, the criterion of race being the birthplace of their parents. There were 2 groups of American children, one from the Atlantic coast and of favored social status, the other from the Pacific coast and of approximately the same economic level as the Mexicans.

There were 212 children between the ages of four and seven tested, almost evenly distributed among the race groups. The sex differences within the groups were not so well equated.

Two forms of tests were given for obtaining an approximation of the mental level of the children in relation to standards for children of these ages. The scores for the Goodenough Drawing Test gave intelligence quotients that ranged from 70-170; these quotients were above the norm or 100 for 77 per cent of the Mexicans; 60 per cent of the Eastern Americans; 58 per cent of the Sicilians, 56 per cent of the Western Americans. For the Picture Puzzle series there are no norms. The scores compare favorably with the similar Rossolimo series and show that the group as a whole do as well as a larger group of American children. The Mexicans showed superiority in this test.

There were 8 performances in which manual dexterity played an important part. The Mexicans ranked highest in four of these tests and tied for superiority in another test. Their average rank on the series was 17, Baltimore Americans 23; Sicilians and San Diego Americans 28 each. For these groups the Mexicans are clearly superior in the quickness and accuracy of manipulation such as the tests involved. The conclusion cannot be drawn for Latin races and not for races in general. It does appear that certain racial groups or stocks develop early skill in manipulation greater than that of the average of American children. A control of the environments from the first months might throw light on the origin of such differences.

REFERENCES

(1) BRYAN, W. L. – On the development of voluntary motor ability. Am. J. of Psychol., 1892, 5, 123-204.

(2) GOODENOUGH, F. Racial differences in the intelligence of school children. Jour. of Exp. Psychol., 1926, 9, No. 5.

(3) GOODENOUGH, F. A new approach to the intelligence of young children. Jour. Genet. Psychol., June, 1926.

(4) HERRICK, D. S. A comparison of Brahman and Panchama children in south India, with each other and with American children by means of the Goddard Form-board. Jour. Appl. Psychol., 1921, 5, 253-260.

(5) HOLLINGWORTH, H. L. AND POFFENBERGER, A. T. Applied psychology, Chap II. New York, D. Appleton, 1917.

(6) JOHNSON, B. J. The mental growth of children. New York, E. P. Dutton and Co., 1925, 157.

(7) JOHNSON, B. J. AND SCHRIEFER, L. Comparison of mental age scores obtained by performance test and the Stanford revision. Jour. Educ. Psychol., 1922, 13, 408-417.

(8) KOCH, H. L. AND SIMMONS, R. A study of the test performance of American, Mexican and Negro Children. Psychol. Monog., 1926.

(9) MURDOCK, K. A study of mental differences due to race. Proc. of the An. Meeting of the Am. Psychol. Ass., 1923.

(10) PASCHAL, F. C., AND SULLIVAN, L. R. Racial influences in the physical and mental development of Mexican children. Comp. Psychol. Monog., 1925, 3, No. 14, 1-77.

(11) REAM, M. J. The tapping test, a measure of motility. Univ. of Iowa Stud. in Psychol., 1922, 31, No. 8, 292-320.

(12) REYMERT, M. L. The personal equation in motor capacities. Scand. Sci., Rev., 1923, 2.

(13) SEASHORE, C. E. The psychology of musical talent. Boston, Silver, Burdette and Co., 1919.

(14) WELLMAN, BETH. The development of motor coordination in young children. University of Iowa Studies, 1926, 3, No. 4.

(15) WOODWORTH, R. S. Racial differences in mental tests, Science, 1910.

Conclusions

By making it this far through the book, we offer you our congratulations! You have managed to trek into some of the darker aspects in the history of psychology (although by no means the absolute darkest). We hope that you are not discouraged by what you have seen. Indeed, it is only by examining the mistakes and successes of our past that we progress in life as well as in science. Well-respected journals published what we see in retrospect to be poorly conducted research, influenced by prevailing social opinions rather than sound design and interpretation; ignoring those scientists who fought against such stereotypes through careful observation and experimentation. Each of us in the field of psychology should bear both the shame and the pride of what our field can do to advance ignorance or advance knowledge.

Examining these writings, which are anywhere from 80 to 120 years old, also raises some interesting questions. How much of what is published today, and viewed as strong science, will be examined 100 years from now and found sorely wanting? How can we, as researchers, as students, as consumers of knowledge best evaluate information presented to us? It is our hope that this book instills caution in the reader when presented with findings that purport to be scientific. Do not accept them as accurate and true automatically, or just because they confirm already held beliefs. Instead, use the tools you have honed by reading and critically examining the reprints here, using the guidelines herein.

There are also some strong themes that come across in the reprints, which although misguided and debunked, are still commonly repeated today. For example, several make reference to "modern civilization" putting a stop to evolutionary processes in developed countries. The "noble savage" stereotype of those not living in "civilized" societies, and thus being more in tune with nature is also frequently seen. Another especially strong underlying assumption in many of the articles is that group differences are to be attributed to innate biological causes, rather than environmentally and culturally influenced. More recent research has shown that all three of these ideas are misguided, and yet they are still promulgated in both the popular media and lay conversations.

Finally, it is our hope that this book will also inspire budding young scientists to conduct research into both the differences and the similarities between groups,

331

whether human or non-human, in a methodologically sound fashion. We only gain a more accurate picture of our world and its inhabitants by building it piece by piece, incrementally improving our understanding. As Isaac Newton wrote in a letter to Robert Hooke, "If I have seen further, it is by standing on the shoulders of giants."

Supplemental Resources

The remainder of this book consists of three sections which will likely be of interest to our readers. First is a list of further suggested readings. These books and articles are all broadly concerned with the issue of racial and sex differences. Some present pro-difference stances and ideals that are at odds with the information presented in this book, while others present supporting evidence against the reality of racial or sex differences in ability. All should be easily acquired through your local university library or an interlibrary loan service.

Next we present a collection of notable quotes in the history of scientific sexism and racism, the majority of which will undoubtedly offend our readers (as well they should). We have selected the quotes from various sources, with a number coming from Thomas F. Gossett's book (1997) *Race: The History of an Idea in America*. We would like to note that the number of potentially offensive quotes we have found would have filled numerous volumes, so we restricted ourselves to some of particularly outrageous (from a modern point of view) ones. Particularly interesting is a series of newspaper articles that ran in the Dearborn Independent from May 22 to October 2, 1920. The issues presented in these articles were considered important enough to be published as a monograph under the title *The International Jew: The World's Foremost Problem* (1920).

After that you will find a list of websites that you can use to learn more about scientific sexism and racism. Also included are pages on related topics, such as famous Americans' writings on race and sex and two debates on these controversial topics.

Finally, the full text of a 1913 eugenics law from Wisconsin restricting marriage is reprinted, to show the type of impact that the articles in this book had in the real world. Sadly, this is merely the tip of the iceberg when it comes to eugenics-informed laws that were enacted in the United States. The majority of the states enacted such laws, many of which stayed on the books for decades and resulted in thousands of men and women being forcibly sterilized. To see if your state was one, please visit professor and sociologist Lutz Kaelber's excellent website "Eugenic Sterilizations in the U.S." available online at:

http://www.uvm.edu/~lkaelber/eugenics/

Suggested Further Readings

Banton, M. (1998). *Racial Theories* (2nd ed.). Cambridge, United Kingdom: Cambridge University Press.

Barkan, E. (1992). *The Retreat of Scientific Racism. Changing Concepts of Race in Britain and the United States between the World Wars.* Cambridge, United Kingdom: Cambridge University Press.

Jencks, C. and Phillips, M. (Eds.) (1998). *The Black-White Test Score Gap.* Washington, District of Columbia.: Brookings Institution Press.

Daniel, R.P. (1932). Basic considerations for valid interpretations of experimental studies pertaining to racial differences. *The Journal of Educational Psychology, 23*, 15-27

Dennis, R. M. (1995). Social Darwinism, scientific racism, and the metaphysics of race. *Journal of Negro Education, 64*, 243-252.

Devlin, B., Daniels, M. and Roeder, K. (1997) The Heritability of IQ. *Nature, 388*, 468-71.

Farber, P. (2003). Race-mixing and science in the United States. *Endeavour, 27*, 166-170.

Gossett, T.F. (1997). *Race: The History of an idea in America* (2nd ed). Oxford, United Kingdom: Oxford University Press.

Gould, S.J. (1996). *The Mismeasure of Man, revised and expanded.* New York, New York: W.W. Norton.

Hannaford, I. (1996). *Race: The History of an Idea in the West.* Baltimore, Maryland: Johns Hopkins University Press.

Herrnstein, R.J., & Murray, C. (1994). *The Bell Curve: Intelligence and Class Structure in American Life.* New York: Free Press

Lewis, B. (1990). *Race and Slavery in the Middle East.* Oxford: Oxford University Press.

Loehlin, J.C., Lindzey, G., & Sphuler, J.N. (1975). *Race Differences in Intelligence.* San Francisco, California: W.H. Freeman and Company.

Richards, G. (1997). *'Race,' Racism and Psychology: Towards a Reflexive History.* New York, New York: Routledge.

Rushton, J. P. (2000). *Race, evolution, and behavior: A life-history perspective* (3rd Edition). Port Huron, Michigan: Charles Darwin Research Institute.

Sarich, V., & Miele, F. (2004). *Race: The Reality of Human Differences*. Westview Press: Boulder, Colorado.

Snowden, F.M., Jr. (1983). *Before Color Prejudice: The Ancient View of Blacks*. Cambridge, Massachusetts: Harvard University Press.

Wilson, A.S. (Ed.). (2004). *Defining Difference: Race and Racism in the History of Psychology*. Washington, District of Columbia: American Psychological Association.

Notable Quotations on Scientific Sexism and Racism

These numbers fell upon poor women like a sledgehammer, and they were accompanied by sarcasms more ferocious than the most misogynist imprecations of certain church fathers. The theologians had asked if women had a soul. Several centuries later, some scientists were ready to refuse them a human intelligence.

- Léonce Manouvriere (1903, p. 406), statistician, on the impact of statistics in measuring sex differences

The scale, properly speaking, does not permit the measure of the intelligence, because intellectual qualities are not superposable, and therefore cannot be measured as linear surfaces are measured.

- Alfred Binet (1916, p. 40), on the limits of his measure, originally designed to help identify those schoolchildren in need of special education services

The Negro is primarily affectionate, immensely emotional, then sensual and under stimulation passionate. There is love of ostentation, and capacity for melodious articulation; there is undeveloped artistic power and taste – Negroes make good artisans, handicraftsmen – and there is instability of character incident to lack of self-control, especially in connection with sexual relation; and there is lack of orientation, or recognition of position and condition of self and environment, evidenced by a peculiar bumptiousness, so called, that is particularly noticeable. One would naturally expect some such character for the Negro, because the whole posterior part of the brain is large, and the whole anterior portion is small.

- Robert Bennett Bean (1906, p. 408), Virginia physician, on the conclusion of his scientific study of white and black brains

In the most intelligent races...there are a large number of women whose brains are closer in size to those of gorillas than to the most developed male brains. This inferiority is so obvious that no one can doubt it for a moment; only its degree is worth discussion.

- Gustave LeBon (1879, p. 60), student of Paul Broca

A group with black skin, woolly hair and a prognathous face has never been able to raise itself spontaneously to civilization.

- Paul Broca (1866, pp. 295-296)

But we must not forget that women are, on the average, a little less intelligent than men, a difference which we should not exaggerate but which is, nonetheless, real.

- Paul Broca (1861, p. 153)

Woman's body and soul is phyletically older and more primitive, while man is more modern, variable, and less conservative. Women are always inclined to preserve old customs and ways of thinking. Women prefer passive methods; to give themselves up to the power of elemental forces, as gravity, when they throw themselves from heights or take poison, in which methods of suicide they surpass men.

- G. Stanley Hall (1904, p. 194), on why higher rates of suicide are observed in women

Now the fact is, that workmen may have a 10 year intelligence while you have a 20. To demand for him such a home as you enjoy is as absurd as it would be to insist that every laborer should receive a graduate fellowship. How can there be such a thing as social equality with this wide range of mental capacity?

- H.H. Goddard (1919, p. 237), speaking to a group of Princeton undergraduates on the inherent right of the "intelligent"

Not all criminals are feeble-minded, but all feeble-minded persons are at least potential criminals. That every feeble-minded women is a potential prostitute would hardly be disputed by anyone. Moral judgment...is a function of intelligence.

- Lewis Terman (1916, p. 11), on why criminals and the "feeble-minded" should be both confined to institutions and prevented from procreating

Their dullness seems to be racial, or at least inherent in the family stocks from which they came.... Children of this group should be segregated in special classes and given instruction which is concrete and practical.... There is no possibility at present of convincing society that they should not be allowed to reproduce, although from a eugenic point of view they constitute a grave problem because of unusually prolific breeding.

- Lewis Terman (1916, pp. 91-92), after giving intelligence tests to a group of children living in an orphanage

The author presents not theories or opinions but facts.

- R.M. Yerkes, in his forward to Brigham's A Study of American Intelligence (1923)

The able Jew is popularly recognized not because of his ability, but because he is able and a Jew.

- C.C. Brigham (1923, p. 190), psychology professor at Princeton University and student of R. M. Yerkes

The decline of American intelligence will be more rapid than the decline of the intelligence of European national groups, owing to the presence here of the Negro.

- C.C. Brigham (1923, p. 209)

In short, by custodial state, we have in mind a high-tech and more lavish version of the Indian reservation for some

substantial minority of the nation's population, while the
rest of America tries to go about its business.

- Richard J. Herrnstein & Charles Murray (1994, p. 526), on what should be done to those with low intelligence and of low social rank

This work must not be misinterpreted into an attack upon
the Hebrew race.

- Arthur T. Abernethy (1910, p. 7), in his introduction to The Jew A Negro: Being A Study Of The Jewish Ancestry From An Impartial Standpoint...

Like the Negroes, the Jews have no country; like the
Negroes, their whole history shows they were never
capable of self-government without direct assistance from
God; like the Negroes, they have lived, and when in
temporary ascendancy have manifested their control by
austerity and criminal brutality everywhere.

- Arthur T. Abernethy (1910, p. 107)

The Jews, like the Negroes, are pathetically devoid of
regard for the truth.

- Arthur T. Abernethy (1910, p. 109)

Other characteristics essentially Jewish and Negro are
the cunning and susceptibility to bribery; and their
peculiar formation of the pigmentations of the hair, eyes,
and lips. Another is the peculiarity in the formation of the
Jewish finger nails as compared with those of the Negro
which they exactly resemble, being unlike those of other
races.

- Arthur T. Abernethy (1910, p. 109)

The Jews, like the Negroes, who this mania [sexual drive]
often drives to crimes against womanhood, are equally
abnormally full-blooded; but what the unfortunate Negro
may accomplish only by brute force and crime, the Jew

340

who is richer, artfully effects by the gentler process of blandishment, ingenuity and gold.
- *Arthur T. Abernethy (1910, p. 110)*

Their bad qualities are many, and the blacker they are the uglier their faces and the more pointed their teeth. They are of little use and may cause harm and are dominated by their evil disposition and destructiveness...Dancing and rhythm are instinctive and ingrained in them. Since their utterance is uncouth, they are compensated with song and dance...They can endure hard work...but there is no pleasure to be got from them, because of the smell of their armpits and the coarseness of their bodies.
- *Ibn Butlan (1373/1954 as cited in Lewis, 1990, p. 92)*

[Indians are] naturally lazy and vicious, melancholic, cowardly, and in general a lying, shiftless people. Their marriages are not a sacrament but a sacrilege. They are idolatrous, libidinous and commit sodomy. Their chief desire is to eat, drink, worship heathen idols, and commit bestial obscenities. What could one expect from a people whose skulls are so thick and hard the Spanish had to take care in fighting not to strike on the head lest their swords be blunted.
- *Gonzalo Fernandez de Oviedo (1851 as cited in Gossett, 1997, p. 12).*

[Indians have] a germ in their minds which only wants cultivation. They astonish you with strokes of the most sublime oratory; such as prove their reason and sentiment strong. But never yet could I find a black had uttered a thought above the level of plain narration; never saw even an elementary trait of painting or sculpture.
- *Thomas Jefferson (1803, as cited in Gossett, 1997, p. 43)*

Very many approved when I suggested that the best remedy for whatever was amiss would be if every

341

Irishman should kill a Negro and be hanged for it. Those who dissented most commonly on that ground that, if there were no Irish and no Negroes, they would not be able to get any domestic servants.

- Edward A. Freeman II (1883, as cited in Gossett, 1997, p. 110)

...an idle and thriftless race of savages cannot be permitted to guard the treasure vaults of the nation which hold our gold and silver, but that they shall always be open, to the end that the prospector and minor may enter in and by enriching himself enrich the nation and bless the world by the results of his toil.

- James B. Belford (1880, as cited in Gossett, 1997, p. 236)

Oh, Harvard's run by millionaires,
And Yale is run by booze,
Cornell is run by farmer's sons
Columbia's run by Jews

- Columbia University campus song (circa 1921, as cited in Gossett, 1997, p. 372)

The principle has been propounded and urged by certain broad-minded and sympathetic persons that there should be no racial discrimination in any American legislation. Nothing could be more unsound, unscientific, or dangerous. Racial discrimination is inherent in biological fact and in human nature. It is unsafe and fallacious to deny in legislation forces which exist in fact.

Henry Fairchild (1926, as cited in Gossett, 1997, p. 387)

The valiant, bespectacled psychos are we
Prepared to assign every man his degree
And the place he's best fitted for in the armee
By psychologee, psychologee.
Bill Kaiser will shake in this throne 'cross the sea
When he feels the earthquake of our efficiency
Pencils up! Forward march! to the great victory

Of psychologee in the Army.

- *Anonymous poem "The March of the Psychos" from the army post newspaper Camplife Chickamauga (1918, as reprinted in Brown, 1992)*

References

Abernethy, A.T. (1910). *The Jew A Negro: Being A Study Of The Jewish Ancestry From An Impartial Standpoint....* Moravian Falls, N.C.: Dixie Publishing Company.

Anonymous. (1920). *The International Jew: The World's foremost problem.* Dearborn, MI: The Dearborn Publishing Company.

Bean, R.B. (1906). Some racial peculiarities of the Negro brain. *American Journal of Anatomy, 5,* 353-432.

Binet, A. (1916). *The Development of Intelligence in Children (The Binet-Simon scale).* Baltimore: Williams and Wilkins.

Brigham, C.C. (1923). *A Study of American Intelligence.* Princeton, NJ: Princeton University Press.

Broca, P. (1866). Anthropologie. In A. Dechambre (ed.), *Dictionnaire encyclopédique des sciences médicales,* pp. 276-300. Paris: Masson.

Broca, P. (1861). Sur le volume et la forme du cerveau suivant les individus et suivant les races. *Bulletin Société d'Anthropologie Paris, 2,* 139-207, 301-321, 441-446.

Brown, J. (1992). *The Definition of a Profession: The Authority of Metaphor in the History of Intelligence Testing, 1890–1930.* Princeton, NJ: Princeton University Press.

Darwin, C. (1839/1996). *The Voyage of the Beagle or Journal of Researches into the Geology and Natural History of the Various Contries Visited by H.M.S. Beagle under the Command of Captain Fitzroy, R.N. from 1832 to 1836.* New York, NY: Plume Books.

Goddard, H.H. (1919). *Psychology of the Normal and Subnormal.* New York, NY: Dodd, Mead, and Company.

Gossett, T.F. (1997). *Race: The History of an idea in America* (2nd ed). Oxford: Oxford University Press.

Hall, G.S. (1904). *Adolescence. Its psychology and its relations to physiology, anthropology, sociology, sex, crime, religion, and education (2 volumes).* New York, NY: Appleton and Company.

Herrnstein, R.J., & Murray, C. (1994). *The Bell Curve*. New York, NY: Free Press.

LeBon, G. (1879). Recherches anatomiques et mathématiques sur les lois des variations du volume du cerveau et sur leurs relations avec l'intelligence. *Revue d'Anthropologie, 2*, 27-104.

Lewis, B. (1990). *Race and Slavery in the Middle East*. Oxford: Oxford University Press.

Manouvrier, L. (1903). Conclusions générales sur l'anthropologie des sexes et applications socials. *Revue de l'Ecole d'Anthropologie, 13*, 405-423.

Terman, L.M. (1916). *The Measurement of Intelligence*. Boston: Houghton Mifflin.

Websites Related to Psychology,
Race, and Sex

- "Debunking Intelligence Experts: Walter Lippmann Speaks Out." Available at http://historymatters.gmu.edu/d/5172
- "In Defense of IQ Testing: Lewis M. Terman Replies to Critics." Available at http://historymatters.gmu.edu/d/4960/
- "A History of Women in Psychology." Available at http://psychology.okstate.edu/museum/women/cover2.html
- "The Charles Henry Turner Website." Available at http://psychology.okstate.edu/museum/turner/turnermain.html
- A gateway to various anti-Semitic websites. Available at http://forum.nationstates.net/viewtopic.php?t=76574&f=20
- "Stuff Black People Don't Like" (an anti-African American website). Available at http://stuffblackpeopledontlike.blogspot.com/
- Jim Crow Museum of Racist Memorbilia. Available at http://www.ferris.edu/jimcrow/antiblack.htm
- Misogony: The Sites (a collection of anti-female websites from the Southern Poverty Law Center). Available at http://www.splcenter.org/get-informed/intelligence-report/browse-all-issues/2012/spring/misogyny-the-sites
- "Domestic American Extremist Websites" (a list of various extremist websites complied by California State University – San Bernardino). Available at http://hatemonitor.csusb.edu/extremist_websites.htm
- "Extremists Online" (This page provides a directory of links to the official and unoffical web sites of groups advocating the use of violence in promoting political, religious, or social causes.). Available at http://www.bombsecurity.com/extremists.html
- "Eyes on the Prize" (a famous documentary about the civil rights movement in the United States). Available at http://freedocumentaries.org/int.php?filmID=370

345

- "A Class Divided" (award winning PBS Frontline documentary on Jane Elliot's famous "light eyes vs. dark eyes" experiment that demonstrated how easily it was to cause discrimination among people) Available at http://www.pbs.org/wgbh/pages/frontline/shows/divided/etc/view.html
- "Prof. Philippe Rushton - Latest Research on Race" (Professor and psychologist Rushton was, until his death in 2012, one of the most prominent supporters of the hypothesis that there were biological differences in the intelligences of various races). Available at http://youtu.be/t1mgrTGeDPM -
- "Rushton Refuted: David Suzuki vs. J. Philippe Rushton" (In this debate from 1989, Rushton and Suzuki review their positions on Race and Intelligence and debate the credibility of the theory that there are mental differences between races). Available at http://youtu.be/GA0XLxG2o2E

CHAPTER 738, LAWS OF 1913
AN ACT

To create section 2339m of the statutes, relating to marriage and venereal diseases.
The people of the State of Wisconsin, represented in Senate and Assembly, do enact as follows:—

Section 1.—There is added to the statutes a new section to read: Section 2339m.—I. All male persons making application for license to marry shall at any time within fifteen days prior to such application, be examined as to the existence or non-existence in such person of any venereal disease, and it shall be unlawful for the county clerk of any county to issue a license to marry to any person who fails to present and file with such county clerk a certificate setting forth that such person is free from acquired venereal diseases so nearly as can be determined by physical examination and by the application of the recognised clinical and laboratory tests of scientific search. Such certificate shall be made by a license physician, shall be filed with the application for license to marry, and shall read as follows, to wit:

I, _____ (name of physician), being a legally license physician, do certify that I have this _____ day of _____ , 19___ , carefully and thoroughly examined _____ (name of person), having applied the recognised clinical and laboratory tests of scientific search and find him to be free from all venereal diseases so nearly as can be determined.

(Signature of physician.)

2. Such examiners shall be physician duly license to practice in this State, shall be persons of good moral character and of scientific attainments, and at least thirty years of age. The fee for such examination, to be paid by the applicant for examination before the certificate shall be granted, shall not exceed three dollars. The county physician of any county shall, upon request, make the necessary examination and issue such certificate, if the same can properly be issued, without charge to the applicant, if said applicant be indigent.

3. Whenever there is a dispute or disagreement regarding the findings of any medical examiner, laboratory tests shall be made in the State laboratory of hygiene from

347

material submitted by such examiner, and the findings of the said laboratory shall be accepted as evidence of the presence or absence in the person examined of any venereal disease.

4. In any case wherein the certificate of health required by subsection 1 of this section shall be refused and the applicant shall make and file with the county clerk of the proper county an affidavit setting forth the fact that such applicant has not had a fair and impartial examination and that he is entitled to such certificate of health, it shall be the duty of such county clerk to certify such proceedings, at once, to the county court of such county without formality or expense to such applicant. Such application shall be heard by a judge of said court, at the earliest time practicable, without a jury in court or in chambers, during the term or in vacation as the case may be. Notice of the time and place of such hearing shall be given to such applicant by mail. A certified copy of an order of such judge upon his findings in such matter determining that such applicant is entitled to such certificate of health presented and filed with such county clerk, shall have the same force and effect as such certificate and such county clerk shall thereupon issue a license to marry, to such applicant.

5. Any person a resident of this State, who with intent to evade the provisions of this Act shall go into another State and there have a marriage solemnized and who within one year from date of such marriage shall return and reside in this state, shall upon information or knowledge to the district attorney of any county be required by him to file with the county clerk of any county in which such person may be then a resident, a certificate of examination from such physician as set forth in this section. Any person violating the provisions of this subsection shall be punished by imprisonment in the county jail not less than thirty days nor more than one year.

6. Any county clerk who shall unlawfully issue a license to marry to any person who fails to present and file the certificate provided by subsection 1 of this section, or any party or parities having knowledge of any matter relating or pertaining to the examination of any applicant for license to marry, who shall disclose the same, or any portion thereof, except as may be required by law, shall upon proof thereof be guilty of a felony, and shall be punished by imprisonment in the State prison not less than one year nor more than five years.

7. Any physician who shall knowingly and willfully make any false statement in the certificate provided for in subsection 1 of this section shall be guilty of perjury and upon conviction shall be punished as for perjury, and a conviction under this subsection shall revoke the license of such physician to practice in this State.

Section 2.—All Acts or parts of Acts inconsistent with the provisions of this Act are repealed.

Section 3.—This Act shall take effect on and after January 1ˢᵗ, 1914.

This Act originated in the Senate.

Approved by the Governor, August 1ˢᵗ, 1913.

Charles I. Abramson, Ph.D. is Regents Professor of Psychology and holds the Dr. Lawrence L. Boger Endowed Professorship in the School of International Studies at Oklahoma State University. He is the author of over 200 articles and book chapters and has edited or authored a number of books including *A Primer of Invertebrate Learning: The Behavioral Perspective*; *Russian Contributions to Invertebrate Behavior*; *A Scanning Electron Microscopy Atlas of the Africanized Honey Bee (Apis mellifera L.): Photographs for the General Public*; *Selected Papers and Biography of Charles Henry Turner (1867-1923), Pioneer of Comparative Animal Behavior Studies*; *Zoo-scope: Animal behavior Activities for the National Zoo of Slovenia*; and the children's book *Betty the Boozing Bee*. Dr. Abramson has been recognized both in the United States and in Brazil for his teaching and for his studies in the comparative analysis of behavior. In addition to developing many hands-on inquiry based teaching activities, his laboratory is one of the few in the United States to study a wide range of animal behavior from ants to elephants to humans. He currently is on the editorial board of eight journals and is the founding editor of the new journal *Innovative Teaching*.

Caleb W. Lack, Ph.D. is an Associate Professor of Psychology at the University of Central Oklahoma. He is the author of over 40 articles and book chapters, as well as three prior books: *Tornadoes, Children, and Posttraumatic Stress*; *Anxiety Disorders: An Introduction*; and *Mood Disorders: An Introduction*. He received his doctorate in clinical psychology from Oklahoma State University and has won numerous awards for his innovative teaching and research, including an honorary degree from the Escuela de Psicologicá at the Universidad Dr. José Mataís Delgado in El Salvador. Outside of the realm of clinical psychology, he also teaches undergraduate and graduate courses on critical thinking, science, and pseudoscience. These recently culminated in the edited, online text *Science, Pseudoscience, & Critical Thinking* as well as the documentary series *Pseudoscience in Oklahoma*. He also writes the "Great Plains Skeptic" column on the Skeptic Ink Network and presents frequently on how to think critically about paranormal and supernatural claims. You can learn more by visiting his website at www.caleblack.com.

351